THE JOHN HARVARD LIBRARY

The American Party Battle

ELECTION CAMPAIGN PAMPHLETS
1828–1876

Volume 1, 1828–1854

EDITED AND WITH AN INTRODUCTION BY

JOEL H. SILBEY

HARVARD UNIVERSITY PRESS
Cambridge, Massachusetts
London, England
1999

Printed in the United States of America

Library of Congress Cataloging-in-Publication Data

The American party battle : election campaign pamphlets, 1828–1876 /
edited and with an introduction by Joel H. Silbey.
2 v. cm. — (The John Harvard library)
Contents: v. 1. 1828–1854 — v. 2. 1854–1876.
ISBN 0-674-02642-X (vol. 1 : alk. paper).
ISBN 0-674-02645-4 (vol. 1 : pbk. : alk. paper).
ISBN 0-674-02643-8 (vol. 2 : alk. paper).
ISBN 0-674-02646-2 (vol. 2 : pbk. : alk. paper).
1. Political parties—United States—History—19th century.
2. Campaign literature—United States—History—19th century.
3. United States—Politics and government—19th century.
I. Silbey, Joel H. II. Series.
JK2260.A54 1999
324.7′0973′09034—dc21
98-50174

To my colleagues in the
Cornell University History Department

There is no other way to carry out in practice the theory of our Republican Government but openly and clearly to declare principles and measures and for men and parties to divide upon them as they are for them or against them.

PRESTON KING, *1855*

Contents

Preface

> The time is *at hand* when your responsible votes are to be cast. Let no elector presume that *his* vote is too insignificant to be needed. Let no one fail to do *his* duty.
>
> "Address to the Voters of the Ninth Congressional District of Massachusetts," 1860

Between the 1820s and the 1850s two major political parties took firm control of the American political landscape. Divisive political conflict at the national level raged in the 1820s, particularly in the aftermath of the controversial presidential election of 1824, and moved into high gear over the next two decades. The sense of outrage felt by those defeated in the "corrupt bargain" of 1824 and what followed when John Quincy Adams became president clarified what was at stake in American national politics to a degree not realized in the preceding decade. The issues raised in the mid-1820s were thereafter codified, regularized, and routinized by nationwide political parties. First Jacksonians and National Republicans, then Democrats and Whigs came together to confront one another in unceasing "mortal combat."[1]

The Jacksonians and their opponents developed far-reaching institutional structures to organize this highly adversarial political nation and to mobilize its voters by defining, with great vigor, what was at issue in the many elections that took place annually, year in and year out—sometimes several in a twelve-month period. As other parties subsequently appeared, as the Republicans

1. On the election of 1824, see James F. Hopkins, "Election of 1824," in Arthur M. Schlesinger and Fred L. Israel, eds., *History of American Presidential Elections* (New York, 1971), vol. 1, pp. 349–412; on the emergence of political parties, see Richard P. McCormick, *The Second American Party System: Party Formation in the Jacksonian Era* (Chapel Hill, 1966). Party names varied during the first decade or so of party formation. At first calling themselves Republicans, the supporters (or "friends") of Andrew Jackson evolved into the Democratic-Republican and ultimately the Democratic Party. The National Republicans were joined by other enemies of Jackson to become the Whig (sometimes the Democratic-Whig) Party by the late 1830s.

replaced the Whigs in the 1850s, and as partisan warfare took on new elements and direction, these structures of partisan conflict remained, functioned as they were designed to do, and grew even more powerful.[2]

At the center of their electioneering activities, each party put forward a set of claims about themselves and about their opponents, which they pressed with great intensity in robust polemical discourse.[3] Party leaders and candidates for office presented these claims to the electorate through speeches on the stump and in legislative halls, in newspaper editorials, in each party's central periodical (the *Democratic Review* and the *Whig Almanac*), and, in particular, in a wide range of printed pamphlets, issued in the thousands by local, state and national party organizations in each campaign season. These pamphlets were a major part of a panoply of campaign documents, from single-page broadsheets and handbills to elaborately compiled textbooks and campaign biographies, that the parties put out each year, and were at the center of the parties' mobilizing efforts.

Although nineteenth-century partisan election pamphlets varied in source, length, and type, they were alike in purpose and structure. This vast rhetorical output was designed to be a call to arms that would stoke the fires of political conflict, agitate the voters, and awaken party supporters to their duty by reminding them why they were Democrats, National Republicans, Whigs, Antimasons, Know Nothings, Republicans, and the rest. American party leaders had to canvass a very large geographic expanse of local communities and often localism in thought and outlook as well. The people had to be mobilized and brought together for successful nationwide political activity. Pamphlets accomplished that as efficiently as nineteenth-century technology allowed.[4]

The art of political advocacy, communication, and mobilization through pamphleteering was an old and well-established tradition in American public life.[5] It had never disappeared after its heyday during the Revolution, reviving

2. Joel H. Silbey, *The American Political Nation, 1838–1861* (Stanford, 1991).

3. See Andrew Robertson, *The Language of Democracy: Political Rhetoric in the United States and Britain, 1790–1900* (Ithaca, N.Y., 1995); Kenneth Cmiel, *Democratic Eloquence: The Fight over Popular Speech in Nineteenth-Century America* (New York, 1990); Daniel T. Rodgers, *Contested Truths: Keywords in American Politics since Independence* (New York, 1987); Daniel Walker Howe, *The Political Culture of the American Whigs* (Chicago, 1979).

4. Elections took place in most months of the year, except the summertime, and in most years; and voter turnout was on the rise as the party system settled in and matured. Good overviews of the emerging political environment include William Gienapp, "'Politics Seems to Enter Into Everything': Political Culture in the North, 1840–1860," in Stephen Maizlish and John J. Kushma, eds., *Essays on American Antebellum Politics, 1840–1860* (College Station, Tex., 1982), pp. 15–69; and Silbey, *American Political Nation.*

5. See, for example, Bernard Bailyn, ed., *Pamphlets of the American Revolution, 1750–1776* (Cambridge, 1965).

somewhat in the Federalist-Republican era and continuing thereafter, even as political confrontation cooled. In the 1820s, reliance on political pamphleteering was reinvigorated as newly emergent partisan leaders sought ways to meet the needs of a growing electorate and the increasingly contentious political system. After that decade, no party let an election go by without issuing a wide range of these publications.

Occasionally, one or another pamphlet would be nonpartisan, focusing on single issues or on larger themes but without arguing on behalf of a specific party. But these were unusual in the political climate from the 1820s onward. The great bulk of the pamphlets were partisan in origin and fully engaged in partisan conflict. They varied in length from four pages or so at the minimum, to the twelve, sixteen, and thirty-plus pages of most of them, to the scores of pages in the individual Democratic and Whig *Almanacs* that each of the major parties began to publish in the 1840s. Some were reprints of stump or legislative speeches already given, or letters from major candidates accepting the nomination of a party convention. Others were full-range summary statements of a party's stance in general, or about one or another specific issue.

The pamphlets were among the major tools of America's political activists in these years. To many, they were *the* major element of party warfare. As the beleagured Northern Democrats put it during the Civil War, "When a party in power violates the Constitution and disregards state-rights, plain men read pamphlets."[6] In them, party leaders found material they could use in their electioneering efforts at the popular level. Pamphlets provided compilations of useful information about where a party and its opponents stood, including extensive quotations from party members and from their opponents that could be used to demonstrate, with great force, a particular, or a general, point; they reprinted the ubiquitous formal addresses issued by state party conventions to the voters, as well as speeches by party leaders in Congress, in state legislatures, and at meetings and rallies of the faithful.

Many of the pamphlets were the work of a single writer; others were prepared by party-appointed drafting committees.[7] We know who wrote some of them, but most of the authors were anonymous newspaper editors and party leaders. The key point about them was that they were designed not to express the position of a particular writer, but to represent forcefully a collective out-

6. This statement appeared on the title pages of the pamphlets issued in the series "Papers from the Society for the Diffusion of Useful Political Knowledge."

7. One meeting in 1827 appointed "a general committee of correspondence" charged with the task "to prepare a suitable argumentative address on the subject of the presidential election." "To the Citizens of Washington County" (Washington, Pa., 1827), p. 1.

look. Pamphlets differed from party platforms in that they were much more than a list of desires and proposals; they were a worked-out argument that spelled out the problems the people faced, positions that were being taken, and the outcomes to be desired (and to be avoided), all presented at length, with great force.

"Please Read and Circulate"

Party sponsors aggressively promoted the pamphlets. "Please read and circulate" was a frequent request on their title page. In 1827, John Quincy Adams's supporters in Louisiana resolved that 2,000 copies of their convention proceedings be published in pamphlet form in English, another 2,000 in French. Adams's Virginia supporters that same year ordered 30,000 copies of their convention proceedings and address to be "circulated" along with other material that would "sustain the facts and principles set forth in the address of this convention." Their opponents were no less busy. "Democratic editors," the title page of one pamphlet suggested, "are requested to copy, and advertise in behalf of the Cause, the Terms [the cost] given below; and Clubs and Committees are invited to order for Distribution."[8]

When James K. Polk ran for president in 1844, he expressed his interest in this material and his awareness of its role in a particularly direct way. *"Majr. Heiss* writes me," he noted in a letter to a political associate,

> that the Pamphlet Edition of the "Vindication of E. Polk &c." will be out this week, a part of them on wednesday evening. I wish you to send 100 of the first that are struck to *Edwin Polk Esqr* [at] Bolivar, through the mail. Send them in such a way that he will only have newspaper postage to pay.
>
> Send one copy, of the first that are out to each Democratic member of Congress. When all are out send 25. copies to each Democratic member of Congress.
>
> Send 10 copies to each Democratic Elector in the Union, as far as their names can be ascertained from the newspapers.
>
> Send one copy, to each Democratic newspaper in the Union.
>
> Request *Mr. Southall* to send one copy of each one of the list of persons in this State which he has.

8. "Proceedings of the Delegates of the Friends of the Administration of John Quincy Adams Assembled in Convention in Baton Rouge" (New Orleans, 1827), p. 28; "The Virginia Address" (Richmond, 1828), p. 8; "Plain Facts and Considerations Addressed to the People of the United States . . ." (Boston, 1856).

> Send one copy to each Democratic Speaker in this State.
> Send to any others in any part of the Union whom you may think of . . .[9]

Party leaders throughout the country responded to such calls to action. Raising money to pay for printing and distribution, and securing the pamphlets from state and national party committees, party activists then circulated them as widely as they could to editors and other local enthusiasts.[10] By the 1840s, national committees of each party, such as the Whig Congressional Executive Committee, had taken charge of the national campaigns and were organizing this material and sending it out in systematic and sustained ways. As they arrived in a locality, the pamphlets were read at party rallies, reprinted in local newspapers, and passed around among candidates and the politically committed in a widening arc from state capitals to county seats to far-flung hamlets. Their contents became the basis of even more stump speeches, partisan editorials, and single-page fliers and posters dramatizing what was at stake in these fervent contests.[11]

A particular style and framework of argument were always present in the pamphlets. They were extremely repetitious, reflecting their origins in a set of core beliefs held within each party, beliefs that did not change much despite the passage of time and the rise of new issues and impulses. There was little difference between pamphlets and other sources of party ideology, newspaper editorials and stump speeches, except in tone and occasional emphasis. The pamphlets' tone was, more often than not, apocalyptic. They always conveyed a sense of impending threat, even doom. Great interests were always at stake, or "the present crisis" was always "without precedent" in the nation's history. Each such political crisis—that is, upcoming election—was one that "menaces our dearest interests."[12]

At the same time, most of the pamphlets never had the literary or intellectual qualities of earlier such publications of the pre-partisan era. They were not written by Jeffersonian political intellectuals and did not reflect the subtleties of the earlier group of writers, well-educated elites conversing with one another about the nature of power and proper governance. They did not deal

9. James K. Polk to Robert Armstrong, September 16, 1844, in Wayne Cutler, ed., *The Correspondence of James K. Polk* (Knoxville, 1993), vol. 8, pp 69–70.

10. Horace Greeley's important 1843 essay, "The Grounds of Difference between the Contending Parties," originally published in the *Whig Almanac,* was offered at $10 per thousand copies, $1.25 per hundred, and 20 cents per dozen, with "no copyright. Any are at liberty to reprint unaltered."

11. See Silbey, *American Political Nation,* chap. 3 and passim.

12. "Proceedings of the Friends of John Quincy Adams," p. 7; "Address and Proceedings of the State Independent Free Territory Convention of the People of Ohio, Held at Columbus, June 20 and 21, 1848" (Cincinnati, 1848), p. 7.

extensively, directly, or in a sophisticated way with large and abstract themes of the nature of political sovereignty and systems of government. Nor did the writers often describe a complex political world.

Rather, the pamphlets were most often cast in tones of ordinary political discourse as it had evolved in the fifty years since the Revolution. An age increasingly characterized by a raucous egalitarianism had its own kind of rhetoric and argument during its election campaigns, a polemical style reflecting the rough and tumble of the new politics.[13] They were written with specific purposes in mind by active politicians and partisan newspapermen, who were skilled in their ability to appeal to an increasingly broad-based electorate no longer outnumbered by the nation's upper classes. The writers' clear aim was to awaken and bring the voters forth to the polls in ways useful to the engaged contestants.

To do this, while the pamphleteers shouted at each other, at the same time they used all of their shrewdness, knowledge, and experience to make their shouting meaningful to their intended audience. They defined the nature of the American party battle and powerfully characterized it by offering firm explanations of the virtues of one party's approaches and the disasters inherent in those of the other side. Their discourse was usually framed in military style: armies of sworn enemies confronted each other in full battle array. Belief, commitment, and discipline were all.

What further distinguishes these pamphlets is not so much that they contain a range of previously undiscovered insights about where the parties stood on the issues of the day (there are few surprises in them for the scholar well versed in nineteenth-century party warfare); rather, the pamphlets generally confirm much of what is understood about the party conflict of the time. Historians have marked well the grounds of difference between the parties, although emphases, contested points, and often sharp differences among scholars do exist. The pamphlets contain most of the themes that scholars have identified as the core of the era's political discourse. But they served a number of practical functions as well, as Polk's letter indicates.

The pamphlets constructed a picture of the world that their authors believed was politically effective in rousing partisans to the cause. Political leaders had to find ways to touch voters, interact with them, involve them, and call them to their duty. The way they structured the pamphlets answered that need. They brought together the range of arguments each party offered and revealed much about the worldview of the contestants as they wanted the electorate to understand them.

13. See the volumes by Robertson, Cmiel, Rodgers, and Howe cited in note 3.

"To Indulge in General Abusive Declamation"

The pamphlets were forceful, reflecting their purpose to mobilize a wide array of potential voters—farmers, tradesmen, and skilled and unskilled workers who lived in the rural communities that dominated the American landscape as well as in its few urban centers. The partisan activitists who wrote them pulled no punches. They believed in the impact of sharply focused and strongly worded propaganda to affect voters. Whetever else was on their minds, the authors of these pamphlets linked their message to a general audience, the increasing number of those eligible to vote. They tried to touch the texture of personal experience.

The pamphlets contained extravagant overstatement, heated defamation, polarizing excess, and threatening and divisive imagery. Their tone was unremittingly negative, harsh, and hostile, filled with fearful images. Their authors conjured monsters: the avaricious bank, the uncontrolled despot, and later the aggressive slavocracy and the rampaging abolitionist. They personalized their attacks with aggressive incantations against the wickedness of their opponents, dire warnings about the looming degradation and collapse of the Republic if the other party won, and not a little mud-slinging, particularly against individual leaders. "It has been the fate of every man running for office in this country," a Democratic writer lamented late in the era, "to be abused and misrepresented by those opposed to him in politics." Their opponents agreed. "Slander," a National Republican pamphleteer ruefully noted in 1832, "is undoubtedly one of the crying sins of this nation. Next to intemperance in the use of liquor, it may be looked upon as our chief national vice."[14]

Occasionally there were disclaimers, disingenuous or not. "There is no intention," a Whig writer declared in 1840, "to indulge in general abusive declamation, or in indiscriminate declamatory praise. Those are but empty sounds, noisy and boisterous; but communicating no knowledge, and signifying nothing." Sometimes they did not so indulge—but rarely. The writer of the above quotation managed to remind his audience that so far as President Martin Van Buren was concerned, "the interest and the welfare of the country are the last things in his thoughts."[15]

Most often, each writer cast matters in terms of the other side's antirepublican degeneracy in contrast to their own party's commitment to the Republic's bright future. Each party made it clear that "we contend for our Consti-

14. "The Record of Horatio Seymour" (n.p., 1868), p. 1; "The Conduct of the Administration" (Boston, 1832), p. 13.

15. [Richard Hildreth], "The Contrast: or William Henry Harrison versus Martin Van Buren" (Boston, 1840), pp. 6, 55.

tution and our country," while the other side did not.[16] And they were usually anguished about the state of affairs they confronted given the other side's baseness. To be sure, the pamphlet writers never quite reached the same degree of pithy negativism contained in such handbills as the single-page coffin flier used against Andrew Jackson in 1828, which asserted that Old Hickory was a murderer.[17] Usually the pamphlets were more restrained. Still, they delivered their share of color, bite, and bile. As the author of the *Democratic Textbook* of 1848 wrote, the Whig opponents were animated by "a degree of desperation and recklessness unprecedented in our political history" due to their policies and behavior, which have "rendered their cause and their party appelation odious and repulsive." Modern readers may become glassy-eyed from the constant vituperation, whatever echoes of more recent times they also hear.[18]

Whatever the level of their invective and the excessive and inflated nature of the portraits they painted, the pamphlets also contained another, more substantive dimension. They reveal the consensual elements always present in a nation's political discourse. Both parties structured their appeals within the same general framework of shared values. As they squared off, each claimed repeatedly (and unsurprisingly) that it was working "to promote political objects" that each considered "vital to the prosperity of the country and the proper administration of the government."[19] On such platitudes it was easy to agree. But the parties then proceeded to sharpen the differences between them as they sought to achieve these good ends. Beyond that limited consensus, the rest of what they offered in their election discourse was unabashedly divisive.

Within broad consensual notions of republican freedom, personal liberty, and individual achievement, the pamphlet writers thought in contrasts and worked very hard to offer serious, polarizing differences in expression, outlook, and specific policy options to the electorate. The pamphlets underscored how divided the parties were in their public advocacy. Their normal

16. "Speech of Mr. Bartlett at a Meeting of Citizens Opposed to the Re-election of Andrew Jackson, Holden at Portsmouth, N.H., October 15, 1832" (Portsmouth, 1832), p. 14.

17. There is a reproduction of the coffin handbill in Stefan Lorant, *The Presidency: A Pictorial History of Presidential Elections* (New York, 1951), p. 105.

18. "The Democratic Textbook, Being a Compendium of the Principles of the Democratic Party" (New York, 1848), p. 3; Cato, "A Defense of the National Administration in an Address to the People of New Hampshire," (Concord, 1828), p. 18; "Address to the Voters of the Ninth Congressional District," *op. cit.*, p. 1.

19. "Speech of the Hon. John A. Dix, of New York, at the Mass Meeting . . . Newburgh . . . 26th of July, 1852" (n.p., n.d.), p. 1.

mode of thought and expression was confrontational. Each party's own vision, however, as expressed in the pamphlets, was remarkably coherent and consistent. Although each constantly struggled with its own factional differences, some of which were quite serious, such struggles rarely appeared in the campaign pamphlets, unless the other side saw some advantage in highlighting them to demonstrate some evil, deceptive, partisan trait and/or illegitimate activity on the part of their opponents.[20]

Some later observers have been struck by the ideological limits of what was offered in partisan discourse, that is, an alleged consensual nature of the arguments, a lack of real differences between the parties, and a sense that the discourse disguised the fact that party leaders were more electorally than ideologically driven. In their view, party leaders would say anything to win, were willing to (and did) deceive a gullible electorate, and avoided tough issues that would not pay off for them.[21] I do not share these skeptical, even cynical, beliefs.

There was less of such deceptive or consensual practices than some scholars have claimed and more policy divisiveness then is often accepted. What lay behind the parties' polarized expressions was more than electorally driven hyperbole and automatic commitment to a Manichaean perspective. The presenters of these arguments realized that they could not just say anything; they had to touch voters' concerns, fears, and hopes directly and clearly in their electioneering. The fact that their opponents were always vigorously watching their every claim prevented deviation: party spokesmen had to be consistent in their arguments or be denounced as fraudulent and deceptive by their opponents.

More to the point, despite their origins in, and their persistent tone of, narrowly partisan discourse, the pamphlets contained at their core an ideological presentation of some power, part of which was specific to a particular issue or set of policies, and part to more reflective and long-range considerations. Their advocacy proved to be a laboratory for the exploration of a range of critical issues and notions important to the nation, from the proprieties of democratic politics and the role of government in a free republican society to the nature—the accomplishments and deficiencies—of that society. Some of

20. This internal unity can also be seen in the way party representatives cohered when they voted on policy matters in the state legislatures and in Congress in these years. See Thomas B. Alexander, *Sectional Stress and Party Strength: A Study of Roll-Call Voting in the United States House of Representatives, 1836–1860* (Nashville, 1967); Joel H. Silbey, *The Shrine of Party: Congressional Voting Behavior, 1841–1852* (Pittsburgh, 1967); Herbert Ershkowitz and William Shade, "Consensus or Conflict? Political Behavior in the State Legislatures during the Jacksonian Era," *Journal of American History* 58 (December 1971): 591–621.

21. See, for example, Edward Pessen, "We Are All Jeffersonians, We Are All Jacksonians: Or a Pox on Stultifying Periodizations," *Journal of the Early Republic* 1 (Spring 1981): 1–26.

the arguments looked forward; others longingly recalled a lost arcadia in the past. Some raised questions about the role and legitimacy of parties; others vigorously defended the critical need for parties in a sprawling democratic republic.

To suggest that ideas of substance formed the mainstream of organized political discourse in the electoral and policy-making arenas is not to deny the existence of other, less laudable impulses. But the writers of these pamphlets began with the notion that there were real and very important differences within the nation and that it was the duty of the parties to clarify and present these differences without evasion, obfuscation, or humbug. They did so. As Daniel Walker Howe suggests, the party battles organized by these and similar materials "accustomed people to ferocious, *issue oriented,* political polarization."[22]

I have been reading the vast amount of nineteenth-century pamphlet literature for a very long time, trying to understand and interpret it and to consider the pamphlets' place in that century's political world. I am convinced that they are as important, and as worth publishing, despite their "narrowly" partisan origins, as pamphlets from other great periods of American history. First and foremost, though not everything in the nation's politics was electoral, a great deal was. Elections were the dominant element of the American party battle in the nineteenth century. They were the culmination of a process of defining, understanding, and resolving what was at stake in American political life.

The pamphlets were central to that process. They helped organize the world of campaigns and elections, bringing together party leaders and potential voters. The interests of the latter could be perceived, and their commitment reinforced, only so long as they could be effectively described and articulated. And they were. The pamphlet writers' rhetoric was purposive. They defined and characterized what was at issue and elaborated, supplemented, deepened, and expanded the reach of other campaign material, texturing and echoing, sharpening and codifying, with particular force, the partisan truths that were expressed in platforms, newspaper editorials, and stump speeches, all in the hope and expectation that they would thus connect to the voters in substantial and critical ways.

At the same time, the pamphlets revealed much beyond the immediacy of electoral campaigning. The clouds of rhetoric were not empty of content.

22. Daniel Walker Howe, "British Historians and the Second American Party System," *Reviews in American History* 13 (September 1985): 372–373. Italics added.

They always expressed many larger truths about the nation's notions about itself, its present, and its future. Their authors articulated, within an electoral context, the shape and nature of America's major ideological concerns—about liberty, about the proper role of government, and about the connections between the two—concerns that underlay and structured the partisan warfare taking place. In short, what emerges from these documents are the contours of a particular set of arguments and a particular pattern of American political discourse characteristic of a period that was itself unique. In the campaign pamphlets, the language and ideologies of an age come alive as voters prepared to make their way to the polls on the many election days in nineteenth-century America. They provide the opportunity for a fresh look at material that contains both ideological substance and electoral focus.

A Note on the Texts

Not all of the pamphlets issued in the half century after the 1820s have survived. Many that have are, unfortunately, in advanced stages of decay. That condition only underscores the usefulness of bringing them out of their comparative obscurity.

These pamphlets were not overadorned. Most were plainly presented, sometimes with a cover, often not. The texts are presented here as they were originally printed, with the wording, spelling, and punctuation—as well as typographical errors—intact.

Taken together, the pamphlets included here form an impressive record of the discourse of American political battles in a critical era, from the development of the two-party system in the 1820s and 1830s and its maturation through the early 1840s, to the rise of new issues, challenges, and parties in the late 1840s and 1850s, to their settling down in the fires of Civil War and Reconstruction. They reveal the dominant clusters of ideas, beliefs, and attitudes; they show how political leaders organized and represented these ideas to the voters and how each of the parties cohered. They reflect the variety of sources from which they came as well as the underlying pattern of beliefs held by the combatants. They give the flavor of the electoral confrontation of their time.

Acknowledgments

For sharing the conviction that this material deserves publication, I am grateful to Aida Donald and her colleagues at the Harvard University Press, who welcomed these volumes into the John Harvard Library. Aida's commitment and encouragement were exemplary. Donna Bouvier's guidance of the manuscript through the publication process was done with understanding, grace, and expertise.

Several historians of nineteenth-century American politics have helped me understand the American party battle in the period covered in these pages. Without implicating any of them in the particulars of my interpretation, I want to express my gratitude to Lee Benson, Allan G. Bogue, Ronald Formisano, William Gienapp, Michael Holt, Daniel Walker Howe, and William Shade, all of whose fine scholarship has been cogent, informative, and singularly important to me as I deciphered the play of nineteenth-century partisan confrontation.

The staffs of the Library of Congress, the New York Public Library, and the Cornell University Library were most forthcoming as I perused their collections, helping me find and reproduce material that was often difficult to locate. They too deserve my appreciation and gratitude. In particular, both Julie Copenhagen and the interlibrary loan staff she heads at Cornell's Olin Library and the staff of the Rare Books and Manuscripts Department in the Kroch Library at Cornell were relentless in their commitment to locating many hard-to-find pamphlets.

As always, my family, Rosemary, Victoria, and David, and a number of good friends, led by Glenn Altschuler and Alain Seznec, have energized and cosseted me in many important ways. I very much appreciate the warmth and constancy of their support. I dedicate this book to my colleagues in Cornell's History Department, who for more than thirty years have, by their example and in their actions, created a flourishing intellectual atmosphere that I have greatly benefited from and deeply cherish.

THE AMERICAN PARTY BATTLE

Introduction: Defining the Soul of the Nation

The bases of nineteenth-century America's partisan confrontation—the ideological and policy differences between the contending parties—always reflected specific concerns of the time. In each of the thirteen presidential elections between 1828 and 1876, and in the many off-year elections for Congress, state governorships, and other offices in that era, different issues appeared, were taken up, and were argued about, with one or another or a combination of them dominating the political arena at a particular moment. There was no shortage of such issues in any given election, and the advocates of the two major parties touched on a great many, from banking, the tariff, internal improvements, land policy, and other aspects of the nation's political economy, to foreign affairs, immigration, religion, social reform, and sectional differences, to the momentous and transforming issues raised by the Civil War and Reconstruction. The debates over these matters were constant and pointed. In their electoral discourse, the parties clearly identified themselves with contrasting positions about all of these issues without stint, as they also did in their behavior when holding office.[1] Their policy divisions formed the basic construct of American politics.[2]

The Great Themes: Continuity and Change

At the same time, American political discourse had another characteristic as well. Whatever the particular policy matter discussed, there were overall con-

1. "The Contrast" is the title of at least two Whig pamphlets: [Richard Hildreth], "The Contrast: or William Henry Harrison versus Martin Van Buren" (Boston, 1840); and "The Contrast: The Whig and Democratic Platforms—the Whig and Democratic Candidates for the Presidency" (n.p., 1852).

2. There are a number of excellent studies of the various party ideologies throughout these years. For the

tinuities in the nature of the arguments offered in this great partisan debate that moved beyond the individual issue or immediate context to stretch over the whole period. The arguments offered to the electorate were always framed within a set of boundaries that encompassed similar concerns affecting the American people across an entire half century, from the 1820s through the 1870s. Pamphlet writers were always adept at crystallizing current policy issues and immediate concerns while remaining cognizant of more constant, longer-run themes in the nation's political culture. They effectively integrated, and surrounded, immediate concerns with larger arguments about the nation's future, the ever-present threats and dangers to it and to the people's liberties, Americans' expectations, hopes, fears, and prejudices, and the future course of American freedom.

These general concerns remained always at hand and were powerfully displayed in every election campaign as the clear framework of American political discourse. This was not surprising given the continuities of American political life. Battles that had begun earlier over the extent of the government's power were reborn in the 1820s, if in a quite different context. The appearance of potent issues stimulated by the Adams and Jackson presidencies and the emergence of national political parties, as well as a series of later wrenching changes on the political landscape, not the least of which was the Civil War, did not materially transform the nature of the general subjects that American political discourse focused on, nor the different perspectives that each party brought to them, whatever the important contextual differences in the specific policies being contested.

Visions of a more secure and better society achieved through political action were always the core of the pamphlet writers' arguments. They expressed first an abiding and intense concern about the weaknesses, and susceptibility to overthrow, of the American nation—about the security and well-being of a republic that was always endangered, particularly in the face of the illegitimate antecedents, goals, leadership, and behavior of most of those on the other side from the writer. In the 1820s and later, stark negative characterizations of both the opposition and the general situation abounded, including expressions of the fear of an ill-intentioned and malevolent leadership and the subsequent decline and degeneracy of the society. These remained potent organizing themes for political discourse.[3]

---

early years, see Daniel Walker Howe, *The Political Culture of the American Whigs* (Chicago, 1979); John Ashworth, *"Agrarians" and "Aristocrats": Party Political Ideology in the United States, 1837–1846* (London, 1983); Lawrence F. Kohl, *The Politics of Individualism: Parties and the American Character in the Jacksonian Era* (New York, 1989).

3. For background on the abiding concerns about the future of the republic that resonated throughout

The second organizing theme grew out of the panoply of specific issues rooted in the political economy and the social matrix of the nation. These issues, articulated usually by the Democrats (to which their opponents had to respond), raised basic questions and provoked sharp disagreements about the limits of the authority, power, and reach of the national government in America's free society. Did the national government have a responsibility to promote "development"? Did its power reach as far as the most demanding wished that it did? If not, where were its limits? These questions echoed from the first days under the new constitutional authority and had continued to be debated since.[4]

The third theme concerned the meaning, and continuing improvement, of the American experience—what was the nature of liberty in the nation, what were its possibilities and limits, and who among the partisan contestants was most willing, and best prepared, to preserve and/or extend it in the face of threatening or restrictive tendencies present on the political landscape. Who was included in the American republic? Who could participate in its decision making? What did liberty mean on this continent? Did the nation's commitment to liberty extend to its expansion to groups not usually considered full-fledged members of civil society? Should political authority be used to monitor who was an American and who was not? If so, and under what circumstances? Should such authority determine who could enter the nation and who could not? Could it be used to confront social evils and weaknesses in the society, all in the name of improvement, stability, and general welfare?

In both the electoral battles fought and the descriptions offered in the pamphlets, these basic themes were never rigidly separated from one another. Rather, the pamphlet writers tended to mix them together. Most arguments put forward by party publicists raised a number of different subjects and brought together a great deal of information that quickly and inevitably became intertwined, so that problems of political economy, for example, were rarely discussed outside of expressions of concern for the liberty of the people.

The central thrust of the discourse also varied over time among the three general themes. Emphasis on the dangers to the Republic, for example, dominated the early years of party warfare and reappeared later, during the Civil

---

this period, one should begin with Robert Shalhope, *The Roots of Democracy: American Thought and Culture, 1760–1800* (Boston, 1990); and Steven Watts, *The Republic Reborn: War and the Making of Liberal America* (Baltimore, 1987).

4. On the early background of these battles, see (among the most recent of many such studies) Stanley Elkins and Eric McKitrick, *The Age of Federalism* (New York, 1993); and J. Roger Sharp, *American Politics in the Early Republic: The New Nation in Crisis* (New Haven, 1993). On the renewed outbreak of ideological conflict, Harry L. Watson, *Liberty and Power, The Politics of Jacksonian America* (New York, 1990), is a good introduction.

War years, while disagreements over the power of government grew central in the 1830s and remained so thereafter, at the heart of the battle to define what was at stake in the evolution of the American nation. Questions about the extent of liberty in America were always present and became politically salient at a number of moments, particularly in the 1850s and thereafter. But even in these cases the themes were always intertwined and could never be rigorously separated from one another. Each theme, as it was presented, contained elements of the others. Separately and together they structured American political discourse into sharply honed and clearly articulated partisan channels. By incorporating these themes in their partisan debates, each party's pamphlet writers made it clear that the United States was, as yet, far from being a settled country, secure in its destiny and on its way irrepressibly to ever-growing freedom, prosperity and power. Rather, the pamphleteers agreed, a great deal remained to be done. There was much to be protected and preserved, and there were many things to be resisted as well if the nation was to maintain itself and realize its full potential.

"THE RUINS OF REPUBLICS"

American politicians' sense of the present's roots in the past was constantly manifested in their discourse. At the outset of the party battle in the years when Andrew Jackson came onto the scene, and frequently thereafter, values and battles from another era remained alive to the participants and shaped the substance and style of their argument. Each party structured its appeals around the traditional concerns of America's political culture and what could be learned, or should not be forgotten, from the nation's history. There were always lessons, party publicists argued, in the careful reading of the historical record. "May the people of Louisiana," that state's pro-Adams convention warned in 1827, "never permit its past to be effaced from their memory."[5] As a result, partisan discussions from the 1820s onward began as the politics of memory and never completely lost that dimension, with linkages to past events and to critical ideological marking points constantly being made and used for the illumination of current issues.

In particular, certain elements of eighteenth-century republican ideology helped shape particular aspects of the two-party battle in the subsequent political era. The system of partisan discourse in the late 1820s centered on the fragility and survivability of republican liberty in a world that was hostile and

5. "Address of the Delegates of the Friends of the Administration of John Quincy Adams . . . to the People of Louisiana" (New Orleans, 1827), p. 23.

dangerous because of the constant presence of destabilizing political intentions and practices on the American landscape, including potent antirepublican subversion and the purported inadequacies or malevolence of some of the nation's leadership. Republics were always in danger of backsliding due to their own internal controversies and divisions, or of being overwhelmed by their many external enemies. The danger was very real to those who sought to define where they stood a decade after the War of 1812. Once the American Republic had glowed with promise in its "earliest and purest times." But something had gone wrong. The present looked dark. The future contained a strong possibility of apocalypse; the very survival of the Republic was at stake.[6]

Partisans on both sides of the emerging political divide picked up this traditional theme as a major component of their campaign discourse. Fear of monarchy, aristocracy, fraudulent and malevolent leadership, and political improprieties, all traditional banes of republics, formed an important part of their calculus. As Harry Watson has written, "though Whigs, Democrats, and Anti-Masons all pointed to different sources of menace, all were clearly troubled for the future of free government and all drew on traditional republican rhetoric to express themselves." This is consonant with Bernard Bailyn's and others' picture of both the later eighteenth-century worldview of American political activists and their followers, and the potency of this theme well after the Revolution. Some of the dark themes present in the notion of republicanism still had the power to be America's universal ideological solvent in the 1820s.[7]

While both major parties used the gloomy history of republics as the basis of their outlook, each drew on the nation's historical record selectively and differently from each other as they assessed their current condition. The Democrats' historical analysis focused on the Federalist-Republican conflict during the first generation of American national politics. While the Jacksonians were particularly outraged by what had been going on since the presidential election of 1824, they were not surprised at the destructive tendencies present on the political landscape given who their opponents were. There may have been many differences between the political wars of the 1790s and those that emerged in the 1820s, but the Democrats did not see them. They were still in

6. "The Virginia Address" (Richmond, 1828), p. 3.

7. Watson, *Liberty and Power*, p. 153; Bernard Bailyn, *Pamphlets of the American Revolution, 1750–1776* (Cambridge, 1965); Milton M. Klein et al., eds., *The Republican Synthesis Revisited: Essays in Honor of George Nathan Billias* (Worcester, 1992); Joel H. Silbey, *The American Political Nation, 1838–1893* (Stanford, 1991).

a battle with antirepublican "monarchists" who would twist the nation away from its heritage of republicanism and freedom.

The battle for America, Democrats argued, had erupted at the time of the ratification of the Constitution. Two "distinct parties" developed then and had continued into the present. Both of these parties "advocate and endeavor to carry into effect, measures diametrically opposite." Their differences were "nearly as old as the government itself," according to New York Jacksonian John Adams Dix. The people of the United States now "stand in the same attitude" toward each other "as the democrats of 1798 and 1800 did to the federalists of that day." Tennessee Democrats agreed. "The great fundamental principles of government which directed the People of the UNITED STATES into two distinct parties in 1799–1800, essentially divide and separate the two great parties at this day." The "principles at issue were the same" now as then. The differences between them were "not obliterated" by the passage of time.[8]

The Democrats saw themselves as "the disciples of Jefferson and Jackson," whose task it was "to preserve in their purity, those great republican principles, which from the earliest period of our government, it has been the great object of the democratic party to sustain." In contrast, their opponents had a dark history that they should never be allowed to hide or disavow. Democrats saw John Quincy Adams and his National Republican (soon to be Whig) supporters as the inheritors of the Federalist lust for an antirepublican centralized power sure to crush American liberties. The Whig "is the same party which, under the name of 'Federalist,' was encountered by Jefferson in the early days of the Republic . . . Scarcely a principle or a practice can be named in which ancient Federalism and modern Whiggery are not entirely parallel."[9]

All the essential elements of the case against the Federalists—their monarchial tendencies, their love of central power, and their disdain for popular liberty—appeared in Democratic discourse from the outset of this renewed party battle and gave it much of its particular bite. Their opponents' "*names* [may] have changed, but the[ir] principle is the same—an unhallowed thirst for power arrayed against popular rights." In the 1820s, for example, there was much focus on the pedigree of John Quincy Adams (as well as on his many personal inadequacies). Adams was a closet federalist as well as being a sup-

8. "The History of the Federalist and Democratic Parties in the United States, by a Citizen of Wayne County, Indiana" (Richmond, Ind., 1837), p. iii; "An Address Delivered by John Adams Dix before the Democracy of Herkimer County [New York] on the 4th of July, 1840" (n.p., 1840), p. 8; "Speech of Hon. John Adams Dix, of New York . . . 26th July, 1852" (n.p., n.d.), p. 1; "Voice of the Southwest: Proceedings of the Democratic State Convention of Tennessee . . . 1840" (Nashville, 1840), p. 9.

9. "Proceedings of the Democratic-Republican Convention of the State of Indiana" (Indianapolis, 1836), p. 2; "Address to the Democratic Republican Electors of the State of New York . . . 1840" (Albany, 1840), p. 13.

porter of "Aristocracy" and of "consolidationism" (concentrating power in the national government) against democracy. He and his National Republican, later Whig, supporters were "dangerous to the institutions of the country." Adams had always "inflexibly maintained . . . his monarchial principles," while "the party we oppose has again and again changed its name, but its designs are the same . . . What else is Whigism [sic] than the degenerate offspring of Federalism?" Will Americans support this member of a "degraded nobility" for president, "or will you make a republican, a farmer, and a hero, a self-made man . . . your president?" The answer was clear. In Adams's hands, the fragile republic could only, and would, fail.[10]

The Democrats added to this indictment frequent mention of the most compelling test of the Federalists' behavior and evidence of their intentions: their activities during the War of 1812, which culminated in the convening of the anti-American and antirepublican Hartford Convention. Adams and his supporters remained now in a "treaty of alliance" with the survivors of that infamous assemblage. Whiggery today, Jacksonians emphasized, was "identical with War Federalism . . . reeking with their pollution." When contrasted with Andrew Jackson's behavior then and his position now, only one question was relevant. "Will you support monarchists?" his supporters asked rhetorically. "Will you ratify the treaty of alliance which has been formed with the Hartford Convention?" Or "will you stand by those who stood by their country in its utmost peril?"[11]

But there was more to be said. The National Republicans, and then the Whigs, had added a new element to their behavior since Federalist days. Honesty in political affairs, Jacksonians insisted, was absolutely necessary for the survival of the Republic. Earlier republics had died as a result of the corrupt and dishonest behavior of their political class. Ignoring that lesson, the Whigs constantly engaged in such destructive practices. They tried to hide what they were and used "the stratagems of party" to distort and confuse what they and their opponents stood for. Their cabals were everywhere, deceiving the people in order to attain their goals. "In political warfare," Democrats claimed, "our opponents have taught us to expect misrepresentation."

10. "Proceedings of the Democratic-Republican Convention of . . . Indiana" p 6; Samuel D. Ingham, "An Exposition of the Political Character and Principles of John Quincy Adams" (Washington, 1827), pp. 3, 9; "Address of the Democratic Republican Young Men's General Committee of the City of New York . . ." (New York, 1840), pp. 4, 13; "Address of the Committee Appointed by the Democratic State Convention Which Met at Nashville . . . 1843" (Nashville, 1843), p. 8; "Address of the Jackson Central Committee to the People of Kentucky" (Frankfort, 1828), p. 11.

11. *Albany Rough Hewer* (a Democratic campaign newspaper), August 13, 1840, p. 204; "Address of the Democratic Republican Association of the Seventh Ward to Their Democratic Brethren" (New York, 1838), p. 7; "Address of the Jackson Central Committee to . . . Kentucky," p. 11.

They never retain the same name, so that "they are enabled for a time, to obscure and conceal their principles, and, thereby, to deceive many honest minded Republicans."[12]

The Whigs behaved this way because they were really not a true political party as were the Democrats, who were united in outlook and policy commitments and therefore able to compete honestly for the people's vote in a forthright, open manner. The Whigs, in contrast, were "the fragments of an ill-digested combination, united only in an unscrupulous opposition to the party in power, and faithless to each other; with no common bond of fellowship, but like a mercenary soldiery, ready to contend for him who will pay best." Their policy was particularly damaging because it was "fraught with portentious evil." Such a combination made the Whigs extremely dangerous to the American people. They were "anti-republican; . . . [their] object being to defeat the wishes of the majority . . . probably to open the door to bribery and corruption."[13]

The National Republicans of the late 1820s and their Whig successors in the next decade disdained the Democratic version of world history and the lessons the Jacksonians drew from it. "We have neither taste nor skill," one of them wrote, "for groping among the mouldering relics of dead controversies. To us, it matters very little whether a man were on the right or wrong side of a question which was put at rest twenty years ago." In fact, "the mere names of parties which have sprung up and passed away before our day, are to us nothing." There had been "no Federal party nor Federal candidate [in 1824] . . . The assertion was therefore grossly false: in the mouths of those who made it [the charge] was not merely false but BASE and MEAN."[14]

Whig explanations of what they saw as the potential for republican decline had little to do with the past battles and unhappy moments that the Democrats emphasized. Rather, the Whigs focused on the problem of civil order in the present, especially the necessity for effective civil leadership in a republic. Every anti-Democratic pamphlet seemed to include what one writer referred to as the "contrast between [candidates of] preeminent ability and illustrious public service on the one hand, and bare mediocrity and comparative obscu-

12. "Proceedings of the Democratic Legislative Convention Held in Boston, March 1840" (Boston, 1840), pp. 3, 5; "Address of James K. Polk to the People of Tennessee" (Nashville, 1841), p. 12; "To the People of Pennsylvania" (n.p., 1848), p. 1.

13. "Republican Legislative Address and Resolutions" (Albany, 1836), pp. 2, 6.

14. *New York Log Cabin,* (a Whig campaign newspaper), October 17, 1840; "The Northern Man with Southern Principles, and the Southern Man with American Principles . . ." (Washington, 1840), p. 32; "Proceedings of a State Convention of Whig Young Men of Connecticut" (Hartford, 1840), p. 4; "The Conduct of the Administration" (Boston, 1832), p. 12.

rity [that is, the Democratic leader] on the other." The focus was on the personal. The Whigs engaged in individual vilification of a type familiar to later generations. Both parties saw Andrew Jackson as a transformative figure, the Democrats happily, the Whigs with horror. Adams's supporters in 1828 and thereafter worried incessantly about Jackson's past, his profession, and his resulting capabilities.[15]

While the disparagement of the other party's candidates was a constant motif of the early days of the renewed partisan warfare (and would continue unremittingly thereafter), it was never confined to simple character assassination. Rather, it focused on who the candidates were and what they stood for, what they represented, what their quality was in terms of the Republic's needs and dangers. For example, a powerful early theme of those in the anti-Jackson camp was the danger of an unbridled militarism intruding into civic affairs, a phenomenon that they believed had led to the fall of all earlier republics. "Ours is a contest between civil authority and military power," a writer calling himself Cato warned New Hampshire's National Republicans in 1828, "a contest between the constitution and the sword." Furthermore, "the besetting danger of Republics, is the proneness in our natures to pay a blind and indiscriminate homage to martial renown." History was strewn "with the ruins of republics destroyed by the ambition of military chiefs exercising civil authority . . . Rome had her Caesar, England her Cromwell, France her Napoleon, Mexico her Iturbide. Let us be wiser than these nations, or at least profit by their lessons, and suffer not ourselves to be dazzled by the lustre of military glory." Therefore, Louisiana's National Republicans concluded, "if you prize the free institutions of your country, we entreat you not to founder them upon the rock w[h]ere every republic heretofore, has split." A military despotism "will overawe the exercise of our privileges, and make them subservient to the will of a tyrant."[16]

Jackson himself made this danger even worse than the historical record suggested. To his enemies, he was "altogether unfit for the Presidency, . . . his election would be eminently dangerous." His "public conduct has been at war with all our republican feelings and principles." His "whole life has evinced an arbitrary temper, not congenial to our institutions, and justifying fears of disastrous consequences, should the sword be entrusted to his hands." Jackson's "temper is impetuous, insubordinate and cruel." His is a "violent spirit" whose "disposition is ungovernable and vindicative." In short, "talents

15. "The Contrast" (1852), p. 3.

16. Cato, "A Defense of the National Administration in an Address to the People of New Hampshire" (Concord, 1828), p. 17; "To the Citizens of Washington County" (Washington, Pa., 1827), p. 31; "Address of the Delegates . . . to the People of Louisiana," p. 21.

merely military, even of the highest order, do not qualify a man for the office of President." Are we, they asked in conclusion, "already so degenerated, as to look, without horror, upon the possibility, of giving ourselves a master, and submitting our necks to the yoke?"[17]

This characterization was confirmed after 1828 by Jackson's record in office, which revealed all of his arbitrariness and lust for power, the usual characteristics of the undisciplined and dangerous military chieftain. To the National Republicans and the leaders of the emerging Whig party, Old Hickory's election had been a national disaster, it had "proved . . . to be, a *curse to the country*," distinguished by the president's "rude, arbitrary, and often absolutely unconstitutional" behavior. "If repeated for another term, [it] will in all probability be . . . [the] country's ruin." They focused a great deal of attention on Jackson's use of the veto to thwart what in their eyes was the people's will. As a result of his actions, the executive power in the United States had become "stronger than that of George the Third." The country has moved in seventy years "from despotism to despotism." In consequence, the American people had "now reached that fearful crisis in our history, when a few months will decide whether the constitution and with it the Union of the states is to stand or fall." What was at stake, in Henry Clay's words, was nothing less than "the free institutions inherited from our ancestors."[18]

Nor did Jackson's chosen successor as president, Martin Van Buren, calm the fears of his political opponents. No military man, the longtime political organizer and behind-the-scenes operator had always greatly offended the National Republican and Whig sense of what constituted appropriate leadership for the nation. His first term in the presidency demonstrated the larger danger that he and the other Jacksonians embodied. Under Van Buren, "the first American Nero," who ignored the national disasters he had fomented and concentrated instead on expanding his personal power through the growing Democratic party organizational network and his call to enlarge the American army, the country was now "but one remove from a practical monarchy!" If the people reelected him to the presidency in 1840, the Whigs argued that the country's "liberties are at an end."[19]

The Democrats slashed back, reminding their opponents as well as their own supporters that "it is often more important to examine the principles of

17. "Virginia Address," p. 4; "Address of the Great State Convention of Friends of the Administration Assembled at the Capitol in Concord, June 12, 1828," (Concord, N.H., 1828), p. 12; Cato, "Defense," pp. 14, 15; "Address of the Delegates . . . to the People of Louisiana," pp. 7–8.

18. "Conduct of the Administration," pp. 27, 50, 86; William Henry Seward to Robert C. Winthrop *et al.*, July 29, 1840, William Henry Seward Papers, New York Historical Society, New York, N.Y.; Clay quoted in Maurice Baxter, *Henry Clay and the American System* (Lexington, Ky., 1995), p. 97.

19. "To the Whigs and Conservatives of the United States," (Washington, D.C., 1840), pp. 1–2.

that party" that has nominated someone than the alleged personal deficiencies "of the individual they propose for office." And here clearly it was the Democrats' opponents who were found wanting, and who were the real threatening and destructive element in the nation, no matter who their candidate was. "When time has dispelled the illusions of faction, their conduct will appear in its true light and the only epitaph recorded on their tombs will be, Here lie the men who were born under the only free government upon earth, but who lived and died opposing it." The Democratic principles, in contrast, were clearly different, recognizing the triumph of freedom in America and aimed toward the preservation of the republic and its liberties.[20]

At the same time, Democrats also attacked the Whigs on the question of the appropriateness of particular candidates. In 1840, in 1848, and especially in 1852, when the Whigs themselves nominated generals as their presidential candidate, their opponents had a field day. "Why has the whig party forgotten," the young Stephen A. Douglas asked a Virginia Democratic rally during the campaign against General Winfield Scott, "with an oblivion so complete all that it once said about military politicians?" Remember, he went on, "we have yet to see a professional soldier succeed as a statesman" (Jackson, in Democratic eyes, was not a professional, but a volunteer, soldier). The answer was clear. The Whigs simply thought that they could win by doing so. Unfortunately, whether they would win or not, the American republic could only be the loser in consequence of the Whigs' hypocritical actions.[21]

The Democrats, National Republicans, and Whigs laid down this discourse of danger and decline forcefully and repetitiously from the 1820s onward. At the same time, the voice of the first of the third parties to appear on the national scene added its perspective to the debate. The members of the Antimasonic party had a story to tell as well, a story in which they rejected the two-party hegemony of the Democrats and National Republicans–Whigs in American politics. But their story was similar to that of the two major parties. They rejected neither the rhetorical style nor the substantive structure of their enemies as they focused on the looming threats to the republic and the country's extreme danger in the face of its many enemies.[22]

Antimasons shared with their political enemies deep fears for the American

20. William R. King *et. al.,* "Address to the Democratic Republican Party of Alabama" (n. p. [1840]), pp. 3–4.

21. "Speech of Hon. Stephen A. Douglas, of Illinois, Delivered in Richmond, Virginia, July 9, 1852" (Richmond, 1852), pp. 6–7.

22. On the Antimasons see William Vaughn, *The Antimasonic Party in the United States, 1826–1843* (Lexington, Ky., 1983); Paul Goodman, *Toward a Christian Republic: Antimasonry and the Great Transition in New England 1826–1836* (New York, 1988).

republic from internal threats, although they had their own twist on what those threats were. Organized Masonry provoked an uproar among some Americans in the 1820s, an uproar powerful enough that its opponents became highly politicized and electorally potent in a number of places. Masons belonged to a secret society, and, it was charged, they ignored the conventional social commitments of the communities in which they lived. Worst of all, adherents of the masonic movement were said to have committed a heinous crime—the kidnapping and murder of William Morgan, a Mason who had publicly discussed their secret rituals—and allowed to escape punishment for it. Masonry, therefore, with its denial of law and order and its refusal to submit itself to the open marketplace of ideas and public opinion, was surely a threat to the Republic. "Freemasonry is now extensively believed by Americans to be an institution," an Antimasonic party pamphlet writer summed up, "fraught with danger to their liberties." Its practices are "subversive of individual rights and public justice." Masonry *"tends to subvert Republicanism by introducing a privileged class among us, thereby giving birth to aristocracy."* Finally, Masonry was antireligious; its rites and ceremonies were "of the most revolting character, bordering on blasphemy." The American republic was indeed in danger from its power and reach.[23]

It may be argued that there was much that was obvious and conventional in such dire assertions about the political consequences of the other side's winning office. To be sure, there is some truth to that charge. But the extent and specific focus of the arguments, and the relating of them to specific people and events, suggest that there was a particular kind of reality in the discourse as well. The amount of time and energy that went into elaborating the argument about national dangers, for example, suggests something of the seriousness with which the pamphlet writers believed their audience viewed the problems of the Republic. The themes of the country's fragility and danger, so frequently reiterated in standard political discourse, framed a set of concerns that those shaping political confrontation believed were important to the American people. They were also a way of winning votes, if the electorate could be made to understand not what was at stake in politics—they already knew that—but where each party stood and what each would do, or was capable of doing, when in office. In cultural terms, such emphasis suggests a great deal about the nature of American perspectives in this period; in political terms, it reflects a continuity of concern that offered opportunities to

23. "Proceedings of the Antimasonic Republican Convention of the State of Maine . . . 1834" (Hallowell, Me., 1834), pp. 11, 13, 21.

frame politics in a singular way. The pamphlet writers followed through on those opportunities with talent and gusto.

"THE HAND OF GOVERNMENT"

Persistent fears about the daunting threats that the nation faced helped organize much of the American party battle at its outset in the late 1820s and for some time thereafter, coloring the conflict and directing it into well-marked channels. But the traditional theme of the fragility of the Republic was always supplemented by other, related matters of comparable importance. As their competition and arguments matured, Democrats and Whigs moved away from their early focus on the Republic's fragile condition to what seems to be, at first glance, the commonplace discourse of conflict between different economic interests in society and debate about the best means to deal with the widespread changes and development that were taking place in the United States.

In the midst of vast transformations of American society after 1815, fueled by the so-called market revolution and the opening of new resource areas in the west, American politicians had to deal with major questions arising from the nation's vast and rapid economic growth, including the boundaries of such growth, its needs, and its management.[24] Issues concerning banking and land policy, the nature of the tariff, and the extent of government-financed internal improvements—road and railroad construction, river clearing, harbor deepening—filled the pages of the electoral pamphlets from the early 1830s onward. Some of these matters were discussed extensively; others drew less attention. But from the beginning they all raised the same significant issue: Did the United States need a purposeful national government in this area? If so, what was its appropriate (and necessary) size and the reach of its power, and what would be its effect on other values and commitments of the society? The political parties, unsurprisingly, stood in very different corners on these questions; and, as they did on all matters, they made their points vigorously and vociferously.

The National Republicans and their Whig successors were expansive and optimistic about the national government, and they were not bashful to admit their commitment to a vigorous national authority in their election pamphlets. Their conception of the union, its needs, and its prospects was closely

24. On the market revolution, see Charles Grier Sellers, Jr., *The Market Revolution, Jacksonian America, 1815–1846* (New York, 1991).

tied to the positive role that they believed the government should play in national affairs. They argued that vigorous government authority was the necessary agent for the promotion, even the guarantee, of the nation's economic development. After all, suggested President John Quincy Adams's Ohio supporters in 1827, "the hand of government never touches us, but to promote the general good." A decade later, Whigs argued "that the first object of the Government should be to take care of the people." They believed that government activism opened up opportunities for every American; its opposite did not. The Whigs, as a party, "advocate no such anti-republican principle as that which declares that 'the people must take care of themselves and the government [must] take care of itself.'"[25]

Expansive credit, protection for American goods, and the financing of an infrastructure adequate for American economic growth were the mainstays of the Whig political economy—and, in their view, were necessary to meet the needs of the nation. They could not understand their opponents' failure to grasp what the Whigs contended were basic economics. The Bank of the United States was "in a manner, indispensable." To destroy it would be to cause the American people unnecessary suffering and the nation as a whole significant economic retrogression. "Banks are the life and soul of credit and of commerce, and through these means it may be confidently asserted, [they] have done more to improve the social condition of man than all other human agencies. They have everywhere been the friend of the artisan, the mechanic and the laborer. They have everywhere been identified with the spirit of liberty and regarded with jealousy by arbitrary power."[26]

To the Whigs, therefore, President Andrew Jackson was "arresting the progress of DOMESTIC INDUSTRY and INTERNAL IMPROVEMENT" through his and his supporters' opposition to the national bank, government-funded construction of transportation projects, and a protective tariff. In particular, the tariff was "the question which directs itself most strongly to the attention of the people." It was "emphatically their measure, for it is the bread and sustenance of life to the toiling millions." Government ought "to protect and cherish the Industry of the Country to the fullest extent as a matter of legitimate and necessary concern . . ." In the Whig view, "Enlightened Protection" was "emphatically the hope and stay of the toiling millions over the whole face of the earth."[27]

25. "Proceedings and Address of the Convention of Delegates . . . to Nominate . . . John Quincy Adams . . ." (Columbus, Ohio, 1827), p. 7; "Address of the Hon. Willis Green, of Kentucky, before the Alexandria (D.C.) Clay Club," (n.p., 1844), p. 6.

26. "Conduct of the Administration," p. 54; "Proceedings of the Whigs of Chester County [Pa.] Favorable to a Distinct Organization of the Whig Party" (West Chester, 1838), p. 54.

27. "Conduct of the Administration," p. 53; "Address of . . . Green," p. 7; Horace Greeley, "The

Jackson's opponents similarly found favor—and necessity—in the government-financed construction of canals, roads, and other transportation schemes, funds for which were raised through public land sales. Whigs regarded such projects "as calculated and intended to give employment to Labor, secure a market to produce, and contribute generally and vastly to the physical improvement of the country, and its advancement in Arts, Civilization and Morality." In contrast, the Whigs delighted in pointing out, the Democrats remained "hostile to any action of the Government designed to promote affirmatively the welfare of the People." Failing to see the absolute necessity of these things, the Democrats appealed instead—and destructively—"to the worst passions of the uninformed part of the people."[28]

To the Whig pamphlet writers' regret, conditions remained the same after Jackson, the economic primitive, left office. In the late 1830s and into the 1840s, Democrats, with their "agrarian, infidel Principles," continued to demonstrate their failure to grasp the necessaries of the new economic order that promised so much to the American people. They were "Locofocos; no other name suit[ed] them." There was "nothing good or conservative about them"; they were "the worst of destructives." The new president, Van Buren, the Whigs warned the American people, "made it the great business of his administration to obstruct your prosperity, strip you of your wealth, and overthrow your most useful institutions." Under his administration, no new appropriations were made, even for existing and necessary construction projects. "The workmen have been dismissed, and the unfinished works have been left to go to ruin." Later, in the midst of the depression that his policies had brought on, Van Buren "mocked at the sufferings he had created, and tauntingly told them [the American people] 'that they looked to Government for too much.'" The Democratic president's object clearly was "to prepare you for deeper humiliations and a worse vassalage; to wrest from you your liberties, and subject you to an iron and relentless tyranny."[29]

In the 1840s, under President James K. Polk, "Young Hickory," matters became worse. The Democrats continued to demonstrate that they remained the "BRITISH FREE TRADE PARTY—the uncompromising enemies of American labor—the friends of the British manufacturers—the foes of the AMERICAN mechanic and farmer." If Polk and his Democratic cohorts re-

Grounds of Difference between the Contending Parties," and Greeley, "The Protection of Industry," both in *Whig Almanac and United States Register for 1843* (New York, 1843), pp. 11, 16; "To the People of Michigan" ([Detroit], 1844), pp. 1, 8.

28. "Grounds of Difference," p. 17; "Conduct of the Administration," p. 75.

29. "Proceedings of the Democratic Whig National Convention . . . Harrisburg, 1839," (Harrisburg, 1839), p. 35; "Address of . . . Green," p. 4; Concivis, *Letters to the People of the United States* (New York, 1840), letter 13, p. 96; [Hildreth], "The Contrast," p. 36; "To the Whigs and Conservatives," p. 1.

pealed the Whig protective tariff of 1842 in favor of lower rates and free trade (as they did in 1846), "we shall again be reduced to a state of dependency on Europe, and her mechanics and laborers will take the bread from the very mouths of our mechanics and laborers." Whigs contended, in contrast, "that it is the duty of the Government to foster and cherish American labor and American enterprise, in preference to the labor and enterprise of Europe." It had always been "plain that the protective tariff was a great benefit to all the laboring men, both the farmers and the mechanics." If one votes Democratic, therefore, "you will sign the death warrant of domestic industry, and condemn yourselves, your children, and your country to the direst evils."[30]

The Democrats, in their forceful disagreement to all of this, raised a familiar cry about the condition and problems of their society. The party battle, their pamphleteers argued into the 1830s and beyond, remained rooted in a basic, overwhelming situation, the ongoing threats to the liberty of Americans from too much government power. "From the beginning of time, a perpetual war has been waged by *privilege* on *popular rights.*" The Democrats were for limited government because "history clearly shows the tendency of all power to exceed its proper limits." They firmly believed that there was only one way to preserve—and ultimately extend—individual freedom. A large, or "splendid" government was always "built on the ruins of popular rights." It is better, therefore, "to concede rather too little [power] to it than to[o] much."[31]

Such advocacy underscored the Democrats' unstated belief, in contrast to the Whigs' outlook, that they lived in what a later generation would call a zero-sum universe: that the rights of the people decayed as the power of government increased. Liberty and power were opposites. Government expansion fostered undemocratic privilege: a national bank or a protective tariff created unacceptable hierarchies of power on the backs of popular rights because while these institutions enhanced the power and prosperity of some, they always did so at a major cost to the rest of society. "The only use of government," Democrats believed, "is *to keep, off evil.* We do not want its assistance in seeking after good."[32]

Unfortunately, the Whigs were incapable of understanding, or were indifferent to, the threat to the people's liberties from too much government

30. "To the People of Michigan," pp. 1, 8; "Address of . . . Green," p. 11; [Hildreth], "The Contrast," p. 37.

31. King, "Address to the Democratic Republican Party of Alabama," p. 3; "History of Federalist and Democratic Parties" p. 19; "Proceedings and Address of the Massachusetts Democratic State Convention, Held at Worcester, September 1838" (n. p. [1838]), p. 7.

32. Howe, *Political Culture of American Whigs,* p. 139; "Address of the Central Hickory Club to the Republican Citizens of the United States" (Washington, D.C., 1832), p. 7.

power. They were centralizers to their bones despite the dangers from a powerful national government. They readily accepted—and indeed wanted—an "aristocracy" in America. They "would clothe the general government with large and dangerous powers, hostile to the independence of the states and the liberties of the people." Whigs would always favor the "centralized consolidation" of power. The reason for that was clear enough given their Federalist antecedents. Like the Federalists before them, they will never understand that "a simple and frugal government will achieve more for a people, than gorgeous splendor and consolidated wealth."[33]

This theme emerged in particular, in the Democrats' view, in the long battle over the power of the Bank of the United States, a battle that dominated partisan discourse in the early 1830s and whose echoes reverberated for more than a decade thereafter. Democrats demonized the bank and its president, Nicholas Biddle, in the harshest terms possible and linked the Whigs to that demonology. They argued that their opponents were "heated to madness by their zeal for the bank." Extensive credit availability was the mainstay of Whig political economy, even if such prompted—as it did in Democratic eyes—the "extravagant speculations, the visionary projects, and the enormous over-trading of the times." Whigs always "ardently desire" to regulate money and credit as a means of promoting the interests of the privileged in the society. "This is simply the principle of monarchy, carried directly into the banking system, and indirectly into the national government."[34]

The bank question was "between the Aristocracy on the one hand, and the Friends of Equal Rights and Free Institutions on the other." Whigs were engaged in "the great work of subverting the Government of the people, and of substituting in its stead the Government of [the] Bank," of raising "a great moneyed power, hostile in its very nature to free principles, and far beyond the reach of the popular will." The presence of banks "defiles the Temple of Liberty." Its nefarious presence had become "a question for the industrious producing classes—mechanics and sturdy agriculturalists of the country—how far they will degrade the pursuits of labor, giving to the manufacturer of paper money an ascendency, which shall make labor still more tributary to the exactions of the paper system."[35]

33. "Papers for the People" (New York, 1852), p. 47; "Address to the Democratic Republican Convention of the State of Georgia" (Milledgeville, Ga., 1840), p. 12.

34. "Proceedings . . . of the Massachusetts Democratic State Convention, 1838" p. 6; Samuel Young, "Oration Delivered at the Democratic Republican Celebration . . . July Fourth, 1840" (New York, 1840), p. 21.

35. "Address of the Republican Members of Congress from the State of New York to Their Constituents" (Albany, 1834), pp. 3, 5, 16; Robert Rantoul, "An Oration Delivered before the Democratic Citizens of the County of Worcester . . . 1837" (Worcester, Mass., 1837), p. 71.

Because of the Whigs' advocacy of the bank, Americans were forced to engage in a "war of PUBLIC VIRTUE against BANK CORRUPTION." Only the Democrats could lead the forces of right because they clearly saw the bank as extravagant, overly powerful, corrupt and corrupting in its activities, dangerous to the nation, and unnecessary for its prosperity. "If we sum up in one grand total all the woes to which paper money, banking, and the over-extended system of credit growing out of it, have given birth, we shall pronounce it to be the most tremendous of the plagues which the Almighty in his wrath has suffered to afflict degenerate men." Something had to be done. It was the Democrats' role to restore "the government of the country to its primitive simplicity."[36]

Instead of a national bank, Democrats ultimately came together to promote an independent treasury to hold the federal government's receipts—an institution created during the Van Buren administration in the late 1830s and subsequently anchored by the Polk administration in 1846. This "dissolve[d]" the government's "unnatural and impolitic connections with the private pursuits of its citizens." And, the Democrats argued, since the country's leaders no longer deposited government money in private banks, they had at last "separate[d] the business from the politics of the country," an action vitally necessary and constitutionally proper.[37]

A high protective tariff, which the Whigs always sought, was, Democratic publicists insisted, also very dangerous to the American people's liberties. Tariffs that limited the free exchange of goods always benefited the few at the expense of the many. To the Democrats, such legislation was "one of the heir-looms of monarchy." They regretted that "in the United States; where all other liberal principles have gained such vigorous growth, protective oppression has been clung to with greater tenacity than even in Great Britain." In contrast, under the Democrats, "a just and equal revenue tariff has been established, yielding more revenue than could be raised under the prohibitory system of the Whig party."[38]

Finally, the Democrats sharply disagreed with the Whigs about federal financing and construction of internal improvement projects. Despite the many demands for federal aid in building transportation projects throughout the country (including many in Democratic constituencies), the Democrats

36. "Address of the Central Hickory Club," p. 22; Rantoul, "Oration, p. 68; *Democratic Review* 40 (December 1857): 517.

37. "Proceedings and Address of the Democratic State Convention at Worcester, Mass., June 17, 1840" (Boston, 1840), p. 6.

38. "The Democratic Textbook, Being a Compendium of the Principles of the Democratic Party" (New York, 1848), pp. 49, 51; [Edmund Burke], "Taylor Whigery Exposed," (n. p., 1848), p. 4.

maintained their position on the national government's having a negligible role in the political economy. They connected internal improvement policies with other aspects of the Whigs' reach for power, while expressing their own disdain for many of the proposals. "We are not yet so infatuated with the blessings of the credit system," one Democratic pamphleteer wrote, "as to build canals in untrodden forests, or throw railroads over unfrequented mountains at the expense of an irretrievable debt to ourselves and our posterity."[39]

The Democrats always claimed to be "in favor of a steady and judicious progress" despite their strong opposition to government intervention in the economic realm. And despite what one historian has called their "rusty ideas," the Democrats seemed to accept, however grudgingly, the presence and continued development of the emerging market-driven economy even as they challenged any government monitoring or full-scale promotion of its activities, as demanded by the Whigs. The latter, however, remained skeptical; they—and some historians since—perceived in the Democrats' electoral rhetoric much evidence that the Jacksonians did not readily accept the economic revolution then well under way in the United States or the policy and attitudinal imperatives that followed from such a dynamic society.[40]

In the Democrats' repeated underlining of their commitment to a set of diffuse populist principles and prejudices—a fear of bankers and banking, a powerful, if romantic, commitment to the producing classes, and a belief in equality of the people—Whigs found economic naïfs incapable of understanding their society and its needs and unfit to rule it as a consequence. Whig pamphlet writers sneered at such notions as the Democrats' independent treasury scheme as one particular example of their enemy's silliness. "From commerce and credit," Daniel Webster argued, "it returns [the nation] to hoarding and hiding."[41]

All of which was true enough. Traces of an anti-industrial, anti-urban cast of mind were present in the Democratic pamphlets, as were other elements of a precapitalist faith. But such "republican" commitments had been greatly stretched since their heyday a half century before, and the Democrats' arguments about economic development now took on a much more ambiguous tone in their pamphlet presentations, often because those presentations fo-

39. "Address of the Democratic Republican Young Men's . . . Committee of . . . New York," p. 8.

40. Ibid.; Rowland Berthoff, "Independence and Attachment, Virtue and Interest: From Republican Citizen to Free Enterpriser, 1787–1837," in Richard L. Bushman et. al., eds., *Uprooted Americans: Essays to Honor Oscar Handlin* (Boston, 1979), p. 109; Sellers, *Market Revolution,* passim.

41. Quoted in Melvyn Dubofsky, "Daniel Webster and the Whig Theory of Economic Growth, 1828–1848," *New England Quarterly* 42 (December 1969): 568.

cused on the larger theme of liberty as well as on economic development. Charges that the Democrats were precapitalist or anti-capitalist were, and are, exaggerated. Whatever the Whigs believed, there were some Democrats who were market capitalists and who expressed themselves as such, whatever their differences with their opponents.

In the 1840s, as the grounds of difference between the contending parties firmly settled in, the lines concerning the nation's political economy were clearly drawn in the speeches of two prominent party leaders. Senator William R. King of Alabama told his state's Democrats in 1840, "In short, we believe that the election of General Harrison would be the triumph of northern Federalism, bankism, and abolitionism; . . . that it would be followed by a strong Federal Government, a high tariff, a mammoth Federal bank, a system of internal improvements by the Federal Government, and by all the concommitants of Federal usurpation, which are subversive to the rights of the states and the liberties of the people."[42] King spoke only to one state's party members, but the substance and style of his oratory strongly echoed similar presentations made throughout the Union by his party colleagues. His was the voice of Jacksonian Democracy as it always presented itself to its supporters.

The Whig William Henry Seward saw things differently. "The party which is now administering the federal government," he complained to a Whig audience in upstate New York in 1848 during the Polk administration, "is a party of inaction in regard to education, industry, internal improvement, melioration and emancipation. It is their creed that the powers of government for beneficent action are very limited." To Whigs such as Seward, this was unacceptable, dangerously restrictive, and ultimately destructive of American prosperity and progress. Vigorous, positive government, from "the beneficent operation of the tariff" to "the improvement of our interior communications by land and by water," was clearly required for the nation's present salvation and future prosperity and happiness.[43]

"THE WELFARE OF THE WHOLE PEOPLE"

The ubiquitous concern that Americans had for the preservation of their republican freedom was expressed in debates over issues besides that of the

42. King, "To the Democratic Republican Party of Alabama," p. 6.

43. "To the Orleans County [New York] Whig Meeting" [August 21, 1848] and "To the Whigs of Michigan" [June 12, 1844], both in George E. Baker, ed., *The Works of William H. Seward* (Boston, 1884), vol. 3, pp. 399, 410.

power of the national government. The Democrats' constant fears for the people's liberties ultimately raised questions about the nature and extent of those liberties, and what guarantees and protection they needed. Those questions, in turn, came up repeatedly as a focus of party confrontation. The United States, most recognized, was a nation of striking social, economic, and geographic diversity, with many problems and tensions arising from that fact. Social disharmony based on class tensions, different religious perspectives, and prejudice against certain ethnic groups was a major part of the American social scene from the 1830s onward and spilled over into political discourse.

Each party disagreed about what was needed to be done and, once again, what the role of the national government should be in determining the boundaries of inclusion in America, the nature and extent of the nation's liberties, and the necessity for—and method of—reforming and improving society. For example, should the boundaries of American political freedom be expanded to include those who were on the margins of society, most of whom were denied the vote and the rights of citizens, such as wage earners who were unable to meet suffrage requirements, African-Americans, and women? Did the concern for liberty and its protection inevitably lead to the necessity for specific actions by the national government? The intrusion of nativism, conflict over slavery, and other issues of reforming the republic became part and parcel of this general concern over national meaning and popular liberty.[44]

Democrats, Whigs, and the minor parties of the 1830s and 1840s continually battered each other over these questions. Much of their discourse began with the use of class rhetoric to establish their positions. There were repeated attempts in the pamphlets to array the poor against the privileged and to construct a sense of outrage, resentment, and frustration about how things stood in American society. This was followed by exchanges over the role of others—slaves, women, and immigrants—and their relationship to the society and its politics. These arguments were persistent, bitter, and extremely divisive; in the 1850s they would grow powerful enough to permanently destabilize the existing political system.

Writers of the early pamphlets made much of their society's differences, churning up agitation about corrupting hierarchies and the inequalities that still existed in the United States. Both parties knew how to use the rhetoric of class tensions for their own purposes. The Democrats quickly claimed the

44. A useful introduction to these issues is Ronald G. Wolters, *American Reformers, 1815–1860* (New York, 1978).

egalitarian mantle, injecting a great deal of class resentment into their arguments. They repeatedly and heatedly asserted that too much special privilege still existed in the nation, and that their political enemies were to blame for such inequities. In contrast to themselves, their opponents were monarchists, aristocrats, and/or representatives of cabals of illegitimate interests determined to do in the American people in order to promote their own elitist aims. "From the beginning of time," New York's John Adams Dix told an audience of Democrats in 1840, "a perpetual war has been waged by privilege on Popular rights." Furthermore, "our political opponents have publicly avowed their adhesion to the maxims of aristocracy." They "set up the city against the country, the rich against the poor, the interests of stockjobbers and speculators and bankrupt debtors against the welfare of the whole people." If anyone is for Harrison [in 1840] he will "PLACE IN POWER THE MONARCHISTS WHO SUPPORT HIM." In contrast, Democrats were committed to protect "the rights of the many against the encroachments of the privileged few."[45]

The Whigs also became adept in their use of the rhetoric of egalitarian populism and ultimately developed their own appeal to the same democratic spirit that their opponents did. At first they had worried about "the excess or abuse of liberty" and about the Democrats' arousal of "the worst passions of the least informed portion of the people," both of which would only lead to anarchy or despotism. Jackson's endeavors "to stir up the poor against the rich" were dangerous, they thought, to the nation's social harmony, a harmony that benefited all. "The capitalist," the Whigs argued, "is useful to the mechanic, and the mechanic makes himself useful to the capitalist, each reciprocally aiding the other upon the true principles of the social system."[46]

Beyond that, Whigs often condemned the Democrats' egalitarian posturing in contrast to what they argued was their own true egalitarian commitment, especially about matters specifically related to the political economy. Their policies were not class biased, as the Democrats claimed. Rather, it was Whig policies that best aided the working classes in American society. The Whigs claimed, for example, that mechanics were hurt by low tariffs. "Read this table, mechanics and working men!" one of their pamphlets suggested; "artisans and laborers, reflect on it."[47] It seemed to prove the Whigs' contention that their policies were best for the workingman.

Such repeated expressions of class-based division by both national parties

45. "An Address Delivered by Dix," p. 8; King, "Address to the Democratic Republican Party of Alabama," pp. 1, 3; "Proceedings of the Democratic Legislative Convention Held in Boston, 1840," pp. 3, 8; "Whigery Is Federalism" (n.p., 1840), p. 23.

46. "Conduct of the Administration," pp. 60, 75.

47. "The Sub-Treasury: A Tract for the Times" (Washington, D.C., 1844), p. 13.

may have grown out of real inequities in the American economy. At the same time, there was a consensual quality in all of this rhetoric. Both sides wore the mantle of *all* of the people in their presentations. One does not find sharp class-reinforcing notions in them. Much of what was said was generalized and fuzzy; only rarely can be found coherent analyses of, or claims about, hard-edged class divisions. The tendency was to stick with one's party principles and claim that they were beneficial to all classes in society, that one's party was not particularist but had the good of everyone in American society at heart—while the other party was the prisoner of some group or misled in its policies by some basic misconception detrimental to the good of every American.[48]

Where the parties differed in social matters lay beyond class polarization and more on the question of the boundaries of inclusion. Who constituted the nation and how was "nation" defined? Who should participate in the American republic? How flexible should inclusiveness be? These questions involved matters of definition and personal behavior, including specific religious and ethnic qualities. To no one's surprise, Democrats and Whigs found much to disagree about in this area and did so with the same intensity and confrontationalism as they displayed in their debates on the other issues that defined the American party battle.[49]

The Democrats were always quick to condemn the nativism and religious bigotry that was frequently heard in the early 1840s as "contrary to the spirit of the Constitution, and repugnant to the principles of the democratic party." But they were not surprised that such attitudes dominated their opponents' outlook and belief system. "The hatred of the whigs toward our foreign-born population, comes by natural generation. They are the legitimate offspring of the party that enacted the alien and sedition laws. During the last ten years they have occasionally dabbled in the dirty waters of Nativism, and supported tickets nominated by the church-burning faction." In contrast, Democrats believed that "America has been selected out from all the world, by the God of Liberty, to be the asylum of the oppressed of every nation, and his chosen land of freedom."[50]

The Whig argument on these matters was never too far from what the

48. Martin J. Burke, *The Conundrum of Class: Public Discourse on the Social Order in America* (Chicago, 1995), usefully discusses these matters. "It is interesting to note," he suggests, "that in a political culture where a great deal of energy was expended in campaigning against social groupings—be they Freemasons, immigrants, Catholics, or slaveholders,—no party ran against the 'working classes,' or identified themselves with the interests of the 'nonproducers'" (p. 127).

49. See Robert Kelley, *The Cultural Pattern in American Politics: The First Century* (New York, 1979); and Michael Holt, *The Political Crisis of the 1850s* (New York, 1978).

50. "Proceedings and Address of the Democratic State Convention of the State of Ohio . . . 1844" (Columbus, 1844), pp. 8, 23; "Papers for the People," p. 158.

Democrats accused them of advocating. Some of their spokesmen made it clear that they feared that "our beloved country" was in danger of "becoming the seat of Papal thraldom." Some Whigs believed that the "despotism" of the Catholic Church was on the march, sending hundreds of thousands of its believers to the United States where they would help destroy the country. Of course, the Democrats were to blame because they accepted that outrage to the republic. To support that party was "to aid Romanism in disguise." Were any "Romanists," they asked, "not a modern Democrat?" In fact, "every catholic on the continent . . . [is] a modern Democrat."[51]

Such arguments were not unusual; they reflected what appears to be a genuine partisan divergence of view about the matter of societal inclusion. As Daniel Walker Howe has written, "the Whigs proposed a society that would be economically diverse but culturally uniform; the Democrats preferred the economic uniformity of a society of small farmers and artisans but were more tolerant of cultural and moral diversity."[52] Both parties were quick to establish the differences between them and reiterated them incessantly in their electoral discourse.

There was a major ambiguity in all of this. As has been noted, the Democrats' ideas of freedom were articulated broadly. The party was hostile to privilege and government-imposed restraint. But their egalitarian claims were also exclusive. While their defense of liberty was broad, it was always centered only on white, male liberty. They made no room for equality for African-Americans, Indians, and women. Quite the contrary: they argued *against* the inclusion of nonwhite racial groups as part of the American nation, and vehemently refused to limit slavery where it existed. All of this made the Democrats often stridently racist in their rhetoric.[53]

The Whigs, though hardly racial egalitarians, were much less ready to limit social inclusion in the nation only to whites, or to condone the existence of slavery. In the first half of the nineteenth century, the continued presence of African slavery in the nation troubled some Americans. Many of those who were so troubled were northern Whigs. Some of them took an antislavery stance early on, and, while most of them did not press their position very hard, they did hold to a different standard from that of their partisan opponents. "Slavery," Whig leader William Henry Seward told an upstate New

51. William G. Brownlow, *A Political Register . . .* (Jonesborough, Tenn., 1844), pp. 77, 78, 110, 111, 113.

52. Howe, *Political Culture of American Whigs,* p. 20.

53. See, for example, Michael Rogin, *Fathers and Children: Andrew Jackson and the Subjugation of the American Indian* (New York, 1975); and David Roediger, *The Wages of Whiteness: Race and the Making of the Working Class* (London, 1991).

York audience in 1844, "is the bane of our social condition . . . True democracy," he continued, "is equality and liberty. The democracy of the Texas party is aristocracy for the white race, and bondage for the black." But what did that mean in policy terms? As Howe suggests, some Whigs were willing to challenge slavery (or at least its extension), as Seward clearly was, and were even willing to help blacks directly as they encountered them. But the Whigs wished to do this "without having to acknowledge their equality."[54]

Some Whigs went further in their commitment, and here they were joined by some of the alternative parties' voices. The Liberty party, which contested two presidential elections in the early 1840s, appealed to the moral qualities of the American people, calling for the extension of the nation's liberty to people not then usually accepted as part of the society. This party expressed great concern about the virtue of the Republic and about its falling off into degradation. This was reminiscent of the rhetoric of the major parties—albeit with a very different cause. The Declaration of Independence was being ignored, the Constitution shunted aside, by the old parties. "The alarming influence of the Slave-power" in its "corrupt and corrupting" actions had led to a degraded state within the nation. The Liberty party therefore sought to "rescue . . . the grandest country on the globe, from the dominion of a slaveholding aristocracy." Only they, the Liberty activists, were capable of doing so: "We believe, both of the large parties have bowed down ignominiously, to slaveholders, and have thereby made the North into conquered, tax-paying provinces of slavery."[55]

As the Liberty party's presence indicated, political tensions were rising out of sectional sensitivities over slavery. These tensions were part of American political life in the 1820s and 1830s as the new party system developed, though they were not yet dominant. In addition to the Liberty party assault, southern spokesmen weighed in on the other side. The defenders of slavery were always quick to oppose any pressure articulated or exerted against their way of life. Beyond these sectional activists, many of the pamphlets issued by the main parties articulated various positions on the issue of slavery and helped to intensify the nation's sectional divide. Even before the appearance of the Liberty party, political parties used sectional sensitivity in an attempt to gain partisan advantage. As early as the 1820s, in National Republican campaign

54. William Henry Seward, "Speech at a Whig Mass Meeting, Yates County, October 29, 1844," in Baker, *Works of Seward,* vol. 3, pp. 269, 272; Howe, *Political Culture of American Whigs,* p. 20.

55. "Address of the Liberty Party of Pennsylvania" (Philadelphia, 1844), p. 9; "The Creed of the Liberty Party Abolitionists; or, Their Position Defined in the Summer of 1844, as Understood by Alvan Stewart" (Utica, N. Y., [1844]), pp. 7, 8.

pamphlets, the Jacksonians and Van Buren in particular were sometimes presented as being under the control of Southerners and acting on their behalf in such matters as their opposition to a higher tariff.

These attacks did not stop with the retirement of the southern slaveholder, Jackson, from the presidency. In the presidential races of 1836 and 1840, Van Buren and his supporters had to deal with such Whig pamphlets as "The Northern Man with Southern Principles," which made the argument that was to follow the candidate throughout his career. As a "northern man with southern principles," Van Buren, in order to be elected president, "threw himself on the platform of profound subserviency to the South, bowing and cringing to the slave power for a long course of years."[56]

Conversely, another of Van Buren's many opponents argued in 1836 that because Van Buren was from New York, he would not be as attentive to southern interests as Jackson had been, or as a Whig candidate from the South (Hugh Lawson White of Tennessee) would be. That same year the Democrats, in response to such southern Whig representations about the danger of electing a northern president, issued a pamphlet for southern consumption. "Opinions of Martin Van Buren . . . upon the Powers and Duties of Congress in Reference to the Abolition of Slavery" established the New Yorker's conservative bona fides on questions that bothered some Southerners: it asserted that Van Buren was against any federal interference with slavery as it existed and allowed him to challenge the partisan obfuscations being engineered by such Whig allegations.[57]

Democrats did not remain on the defensive. They responded to the sectional assaults of their opponents in kind. Senator William R. King's 1840 "ADDRESS TO THE ALABAMA DEMOCRATS" was particularly revealing. King claimed that a Whig victory "would bring into power a political party whose ascendency would be fatal to the rights and institutions of the South," since it would be followed by the expansion of the power of the federal government, high tariffs, a bank and all of the other "concomitants of Federal usurpation, which are subversive to the rights of the States and the liberties of the people."[58]

What is compelling here is that whatever the sectional anger manifested in these, its first appearences in the Whig-Democratic dialogue, it was well con-

56. "The Northern Man with Southern Principles, and the Southern Man with American Principles . . ." (Washington, D.C., 1840); "The Charles F. Adams Platform; or, a Looking Glass for the Worthies of the Buffalo Convention" (Washington, D.C., 1848), p. 1.

57. The pamphlet was published in Washington, D.C., by the great Democratic editorial team Blair and Rives. On the election of 1836, see Joel H. Silbey, "Election of 1836," in Arthur M. Schlesinger, Jr., and Fred L. Israel, eds., *History of American Presidential Elections* (New York, 1971), vol. 1, pp. 577–641.

58. King, "Address to the Democratic Republican Party of Alabama," p. 6.

tained by the existing partisan system. There was something ritualistic about the way the matter came up in party discourse, usually as a litany of complaints, a litany that became very familiar through frequent repetition, that assailed the other party for its misbehavior on the issue or its lack of understanding of what was going on. In its early stages, sectional expression was often vague, usually abstract, and always general, lacking the intense focus of a salient policy issue or a specific danger. It was usually wrapped up in, and overshadowed by, other national issues that divided the parties. As a result, whenever sectional anger appeared in the 1830s and early 1840s, it did not have the political force that its proponents wished it to have, as both the Liberty party's leaders and southern rights proponent John C. Calhoun frequently lamented.[59]

The ground began to shift in the mid-1840s. American involvement in foreign adventures helped transform what had been vague into something much more concrete and politically salient than it had been. This change did not happen suddenly or without a great deal of resistance. In fact, sectional political influences, while invigorated by the foreign policy conflicts of the 1840s, at first continued to be contained by the existing system of cross-sectional political division and discourse, which extended to foreign policy matters as well as domestic policy concerns. The Democrats, from the 1820s on, articulated a robust, often uncompromising foreign policy stance. America was always under imminent external threat, was their repetitive claim. Fortunately, the Democratic party stood on guard against aggression from both the nation's traditional and its newer enemies: Great Britain, Spain, and Mexico.

But the party's foreign policy was more than defensive and reactive. Under the leadership of Democratic president James K. Polk, there emerged in the 1840s a commitment to expand the nation's physical borders aggressively, regardless of consequences. Party spokesmen argued that under the Democrats' leadership America's "commerce whitens every sea" and "its flag is feared and respected by the most distant barbarians." The Democratic party had "presented to the Union Texas, and with it the command of the cotton supply, which . . . [was] so much more efficient than cannon balls in keeping manufacturing Europe on her good behavior." Under President Polk, "the national character has been elevated in the estimation of foreign nations to a degree never before known in the history of this republic."[60]

59. William Freehling, *The Road to Disunion: Secessionists at Bay, 1776–1854* (New York, 1990), and Joel H. Silbey, *The Partisan Imperative: The Dynamics of American Politics before the Civil War* (New York, 1985) explore the theme of sectional force and its limits in this era.

60. "Proceedings of the Democratic-Republican Convention of . . . Indiana" (1836) p. 5; "Papers for the People," p. 139; [Burke], "Taylor Whigery Exposed," p. 4.

But, predictably, such good intentions rapidly became the subject of intense partisan warfare. The Mexican War, which was opposed by many Whigs, had broken out, the Democrats argued, due to an "insolent foe who had dared to invade" American territory. Polk and the Democrats had repelled their audacity despite "the traitorous Whigs," who in their hesitation and outright opposition to the president's policies "reek with pestilent treason against their country" and are "aiding the cause of the enemy." Under Polk's leadership, and despite bitter opposition, the nation had acquired "the golden valleys of California and the silver mountains of New Mexico, and in them supplied . . . [the] country with a steadily improving tide of coin to meet and balance . . . [its] commercial fluctuations." Under a Whig president, in contrast, America had "truckled . . . to British power" in central America and "put our forehead in the dust before offended royalty" (the Spanish).[61]

Early on, in the 1820s, the National Republicans had been critical of the ability of the Democratic leaders to handle the nation's foreign policy, believing them to be a group of unproven politicians who lacked sufficient leadership skills and military leaders who were prone to violence.[62] In the 1840s, the Whigs were much less enthralled and exuberant than were their opponents about the flexing of America's muscles outside its borders. They had, as the Democrats claimed, spoken, campaigned, and voted against aspects of the war against Mexico. Whig congressman Abraham Lincoln's sharp questioning of the Polk administration's account of how the war between the United States and Mexico broke out was one part of a major Whig effort to draw the line against the president's foreign policy adventurism and to establish in the electorate's minds the extent of Democratic folly and "the lust for dominion" that was "now cherished by the democratic party." In contrast, Whiggery dared to "entrench itself across the path of national rapacity."[63]

The Whig presidential candidate in 1848, General Zachary Taylor, was "a friend of peace," while his Democratic opponent, Lewis Cass, was "an advocate of war." Whig leaders argued that Taylor "would stand upon our own soil to improve it." In contrast, they warned that Cass "would grasp at all the country around us." Cass, Daniel Webster claimed, believed "in the doctrine of American destinies; and that their destiny is to go through wars, and inva-

61. "Speech of Douglas, 1852," pp. 2, 7; [Burke], "Taylor Whigery Exposed," p. 2; "Papers for the People," p. 139.

62. "Conduct of the Administration," chap. 5.

63. "Address Adopted by the Whig State Convention at Worcester . . . September 13, 1848" (Worcester, 1848), p. 6; Horace Greeley, "Why I am a Whig: Reply to an Inquiring Friend" (New York, 1852), p. 6.

sions, and armies of aggrandisement." He was "a gentleman of rash politics, pushed by an ardent and rash party."[64]

In the early years of the next decade, the Whigs continued to oppose the exuberant expansionism of the Democrats in Central America as well as the latter's willingness to involve the United States in European affairs as a consequence of the revolutionary turmoil there. Expanding the arena of freedom outside America—as in the Democratic-fomented excitement over the appearence of Hungarian republican patriot Louis Kossuth in the United States in the early 1850s—was not, in the Whigs' view, America's concern. They were quick to criticize Kossuth's arrival under the auspices of the Democrats as an "unseemly interference with the peace and welfare of this country." They condemned the Democrats' attempts to whip up popular excitement in favor of the central European republican leader and blasted their rash willingness to confront Kossuth's European enemies directly and provocatively.[65]

These differences over foreign affairs were part and parcel of the normal realm of partisan confrontation. There was nothing new in such efforts in this partisan-dominated nation. But some of the dialogue that developed over the Mexican War had a much larger impact as well—in particular, as it involved the question of the expansion of slavery. Did slavery have the right to follow the American flag into the new southwestern territories acquired as a result of the war? A number of third parties took the lead in saying no and in resisting the expansion of slavery outside of its current boundaries. The Liberty party had challenged the existing partisan consensus in the early 1840s and attracted a number of votes at the margins of American political life with its rhetoric assailing the continuation of slavery on the American continent. In the election of 1848, the much larger Free Soil party added its voice to the partisan debates, demanding a major reordering of political priorities in the nation given significant disagreements over the future of the recent territorial acquisitions.

To Free Soil advocates, as with their Liberty predecessors, "minor topics" such as the tariff and the bank had now "sunk out of sight"; they were no longer relevant to the demands of the day. In their view, the old parties had become obsolete as the issues raised by the Mexican war and its aftermath had come to the political forefront. "Retaining their party names, which in years past have indicated a clear line of difference, the whigs and democrats now

64. "Address, Whig State Convention . . . [Massachusetts,] 1852" (Boston, 1852), p. 7; "Speech of the Hon. Daniel Webster on the Presidential Question Delivered at Marshfield, Massachusetts, September 1, 1848" (n. p., 1848), p. 9.

65. "The Contrast" (1852), pp. 22–23.

stand before the country without claiming as peculiar to themselves a single great measure of the slightest practical consequence. They propose to keep up the fight when nothing remains of their principles worth fighting for or against."[66]

The third parties' narratives indicated why this was so. They pointed to a moral failure in American life and the corruption of the older parties in the face of the moral conundrum they faced. To the minor party advocates, "neither Whigs nor Democrats *dare* look the great danger of the land in the face." New parties were needed, therefore, who would use the ballot to cleanse the republic of its failings and eradicate the dangers it now faced. Many of them were willing to use the force of government to change the way things were. They demanded that slavery "be excluded from national territories" newly acquired as a result of the Mexican War by action of the federal government. By the late 1840s, their particular weapon was the Wilmot Proviso, a congressional measure designed to prevent the further expansion of slavery into any part of the Mexican lands ceded to the United States by the peace treaty.[67]

These attempts to raise the sectional standard in place of the existing partisan confrontation did not, at first, have as great an effect as the Free Soilers and others wanted. To be sure, the Free Soilers did manage to make a dent in the normal course of American politics in 1848, with the great architect of the partisan political nation, Martin Van Buren, heading their ticket. But their efforts were largely frustrated by the strenuous efforts of the old parties to block the sectional debate and return to discussing the more traditional policy matters that divided them. These restorative efforts were at first successful. The partisan excitement over the Mexican War, and over Kossuth a few years later, reaffirmed and continued a confrontation between the parties that had become the political norm since the 1820s in the United States. The party battle that Americans had grown so accustomed to (and comfortable with) would continue on as it had done over twenty-five years, with no end possible so long as Americans in every part of the country remained as divided as they were over public policies and as willing as they were to confront those divisions at the polls on each election day.

66. "General Taylor and the Wilmot Proviso" (Boston, 1848), p. 3; "Cass and Taylor on the Slavery Question" (Boston, 1848), p. 4.

67. "To the People of Virginia (n. p., 1847), p. 8; "Address and Proceedings of the State Independent Free Territory Convention of the People of Ohio, Held at Columbus, June 20 and 21, 1848" (Cincinnati, 1848), p. 10. A useful survey of the evolution of political abolitionism and antislavery is Richard Sewell, *Ballots for Freedom: Antislavery Politics in the United States, 1837–1860* (New York, 1976).

"To Save and Exalt the Union"

A new phase of the nineteenth-century party battle burst onto the political landscape in the early 1850s, when new issues and a new major party came to dominate the American scene. The new party was totally unexpected by the leaders of the two major parties and, of course, they strongly resisted it. They continued to believe that the ideological conflict between the Whigs and the Democrats that characterized American politics in the generation after 1828 had an eternal quality to it, encompassing as it did the universal and everlasting conundrums of power, government, liberty, and responsibility. Party activists and their supporters assumed that because they were contesting such potent and unchanging issues, once the party system had been firmly implanted, its elements of discourse would remain the prime driving impulse of American politics.

"It is the destiny of associations to have a beginning and an end"

They were wrong. In the 1850s, the Jacksonian party system began to exhibit signs of aging and a need to change direction—signs that rapidly grew into a reality. New issues emerged that the existing major parties found difficult to integrate into their usual pattern of argument and operations. At the same time, the sectional impulse became so energized as to grow into a potent, and then the dominant, force on the national political scene. This time, the familiar partisan restorative efforts that had previously worked so well when cross-pressures erupted in American politics ultimately failed. The invigoration of issues that were largely outside of existing party discourse led to a potent voter realignment beginning in 1854 and the altering of the existing framework of party competition in a number of its critical components. From then on, the American party battle assumed qualities that led to a fundamental shift in its nature and direction: the emergence of two new national parties led to the disappearance of the Whigs and finally the triumph of the Republicans around a new central core of policy differences, largely sectional in nature.[68]

In this new era, much about the content and direction of American politics changed significantly. But much about the style, structure, and underlying

68. Michael F. Holt, *The Political Crisis of the 1850s* (New York, 1978); and William E. Gienapp, *The Origins of the Republican Party, 1852–1856 (New York, 1987)* are the best introductions to the political transformation of the 1850s.

substance of the election campaign rhetoric did not. The issues were new, and politically organized in new ways, and the rhetorical differences between the parties could not have been more pronounced along these new lines of conflict. But, even as the new party alignment took shape throughout the fifties, the earlier dipoles of conflict remained. Much of the partisan discourse continued to echo the basic ideological elements that were already embedded in American politics and that had been at play over the previous twenty-five years. The American party battle changed dramatically, but it also had a certain consistency. It continued to echo historical perspectives even as it was transformed by new and potent issues.

The political revolution of the 1850s did not originate solely with the sectional conflict, no matter how powerful that impulse later became in affecting parties, elections, and public policy. Rather, the first significant issue to roil the political waters was an old one: immigration and its consequences for the nation's future. Dormant on the national level for some time, this issue reemerged in the early 1850s with a new potency and became nationalized as it had not been since the Federalist-Republican conflict over aliens and sedition at the beginning of the century. Immigration, coupled with powerful religious and ethnic prejudice, became central matters of party warfare. The existing parties had differed over these issues earlier and continued to do so. But their expressed differences were not significant enough for some critics, who saw no alternative but to disrupt existing political habits and perspectives.

An emerging group of anti-immigrant and anti-Catholic nativists found their voice by condemning both the Democrats and the Whigs, who had, in their view, "been found wanting" in the strength of their commitment on this issue. In the nativists' view, the traditional parties "had become old [and] effete," indifferent to new dangers and increasingly alike in policy and in the way they behaved. With the members of both parties living only for patronage and to be reelected, there was no longer anything to choose between them. As one critic noted, "However wide apart might have been the points of the compass from which both parties had originally started, they had of late approximated so closely, that they had almost merged into the same homogeneous substance." Most dangerous was that, in their quest for votes and power, both parties had allowed foreign elements to become much too powerful politically. Both of them "were *the allies* of the alien faction, and too much under their thumb."[69]

69. "Principles and Objects of the American Party" (New York, 1855), p. 24; "A Few Considerations for Reflecting Voters" (New York, 1856), pp. 13, 16; Charles Gayarre, "Address to the People of Louisiana on the State of Parties" (New Orleans, 1855), pp. 2, 3, 8.

The threats to society were both real and critical, and could no longer be evaded by the political system. The decline of past republics had begun when the native population was "adulterated" by "too great an admixture" of foreigners. The evil effects of this trend were already evident. "The explosion of immigrants" entering the United States had led to vast increases in crime, pauperism, intemperance, and immorality, and, as a consequence, renewed dangers to the republic. "To what class of population are these [social pathologies] chiefly confined?" fearful critics asked. "Unquestionably," they answered, "to foreigners." Something had to be done to preserve American society, beginning with the recapture of the political system from its present leaders with one purpose in mind: "Americans should rule America."[70]

The Democrats received the most criticism from the nativists, especially because they generally supported the entry of Catholic immigrants, who were perceived by nativists to be the most dangerous element in the new tide. Nativists believed that, in the Democrats' support of Catholic immigration, the party had "degenerated into a *semi-papal* organization" that would do nothing to protect the nation from the resulting dangers. Unfortunately, the Whigs were no better. Though in the past they had often suggested their commitment to nativist beliefs and the preservation of a Protestant republic, the Whigs had slipped badly in the early 1850s, as the nativists saw it, and proved themselves miscreants to their previous commitment to cultural homogeneity. They had, nativists charged, "abandoned the old ground on which [they] had stood" to become a "counterfeit" of their opponents. Both parties, therefore, were now alike on this issue; a new party was needed.[71]

The Democrats had always been sensitive to the nativism issue and had always directly challenged the Whigs about it when it was raised. In 1848, for example, echoing familiar historical themes, they asked "our naturalized fellow-citizens" if they desired "to see the party elevated to power that proscribes you—the party that passed the infamous *alien* law . . . the party that openly leagues with the proscriptive native Americans to overthrow the democracy, who stand by your rights and privileges?" The "Puritan Federal party" (the Whigs) was, as before, trying to forbid entry to the foreign born with no legitimate reasons for doing so. Nor did this Democratic assault stop with the Whigs. When John C. Frémont ran as the first Republican presidential candidate in 1856, Democrats described him as "the representative man of caste, aristocracy, proscription, sumptuary laws, a meddling priesthood, and all that

70. Gayarre, "Address to the People of Louisiana," pp. 17, 30.

71. William G. Brownlow, "Americanism Contrasted with Foreignism, Romanism, and Bogus Democracy" (Nashville, 1856), p. 7; Gayarre, "Address to the People of Louisiana," pp. 2–3.

has so often proved itself at war with the principles of individualism, and the true progress of mankind."[72]

The Democrats, in contrast, Stephen A. Douglas stated clearly in 1852, made "no distinction among our fellow citizens." The party has "ever been just and liberal to all foreigners that come here," whatever their birthplace or faith. It "made this country a home for the exile, an asylum for the oppressed of all the world." The party's "creed is equal rights to all, both at the polls and in kneeling before the altars of God." Further, Democrats, again in contrast to their opponents, believed in letting people live their lives as they wished. The party was not organized "to act as a spy upon the private opinions or pursuits of men, or sit in judgment upon their consciences, or control even their outward conduct, except through the rightful actions of government."[73]

The nativist American party, or Know Nothings, as they organized and presented themselves in the national arena in the early 1850s, reiterated the narrative of political decline in order to establish their own beachhead against the dominant partisan system. To them, the country had lost its way amid the turmoil of the alien menace, was descending toward fragmentation and chaos, and was in extreme danger from the corrupting activities and failures of the major parties in the face of this overwhelming threat to American nationhood. Nothing could be expected from either of them. "Both parties have degenerated, have become unsound, and have lost the confidence of the people." Fortunately, an alternative existed that could reverse the decline. "The paramount and ultimate object of . . . [the] AMERICAN ORGANIZATION . . . [was] to save and exalt the Union."[74]

Amid this cauldron of social turmoil and loud claims about the parties' failure to deal with the dangerous problem of immigration, the sectional issue once more burst onto the scene, breaking through the bounds of conventional partisan confrontation to take over the political stage. When the issue reemerged in 1854, despite expressions that "this accursed agitation should cease" because it was "futile for good . . . and potent only for evil," its force

72. "Address of the National Democratic Republican Committee," (n. p., 1848), p. 3; Benjamin Barstow, "A Letter to the Honorable James Buchanan . . ." (Concord, N. H., 1857), p. 13; *Democratic Review* 38 (October 1856): 183.

73. "Speech of Douglas, 1852," p. 5; Richard Rush, "To the Democratic Citizens of Pennsylvania," (n. p., 1844), p. 8; "Proceedings and Address of the Democratic State Convention Held at Syracuse . . . 1856," (Albany, 1856), p. 9.

74. Gayarre, "Address to the People of Louisiana," pp. 2–3, 8; Brownlow, "Americanism Contrasted," p. 10.

was now too much to hold back.[75] Politics became complicated, then transformed, becoming more sectionalized than it had ever been.

The centerpiece of this sectional uprising was the emergence of the Republican party in the mid-1850s, as its members challenged increased southern aggression in the nation's western territories. The emergence of the party added powerful new currents to the nation's political debate—currents that moved the country further toward a confrontation about the expansion of freedom's universe. The leaders of the new party infused their rhetoric with the moralism of freedom, as had the Democrats and others before them; but they added to that a persistent and intense anti-Southernism. According to the Republicans, something had recently gone very wrong in America. The federal government no longer served everyone. It had become "the tool of the slaveholding power" and since the 1840s had continually promoted the aggrandizement of Southern interests at the expense of those of other Americans.[76]

The reason for that was very clear and very political. In William Henry Seward's words, "whatever has been at any time or anywhere done for the extension of Slavery within the United States, has been done by the 'Democratic' party." The Jacksonians were now and forever fully controlled by the slave power. If and when they controlled the federal government, their actions and policies always and unfairly benefited the South and its peculiar institution. This was unacceptable; the situation had to be confronted and actively dealt with. It was "time that the honesty of Government were renewed and its purity re-established." Republicans intended to do so and direct government toward the realization of "certain fundamental principles of right and justice," most particularly "absolute refusal ever to surrender another foot of free territory to slavery."[77]

In order to accomplish this, first, old party labels, habits, and commitments had to be overthrown. "It is the destiny of associations to have a beginning and an end," Republicans argued. They agreed with the Know Nothings that the "obsolete political issues of former years" had disappeared or lost

75. "Letter from Hon. Harry Hibbard to Stephen Pingry and Other Citizens of New Hampshire," (Washington, D.C., 1852), p. 7.

76. C. S. Henry, "Plain Reasons for the Great Republican Movement" (New York, 1856), p. 46.

77. William Henry Seward, "Speech of William Henry Seward at Oswego, New York, November 3, 1856" (n. p., 1856), p. 6; "The Man Who Doesn't Vote" (New York, 1860), p. 3; "Address of the Republican State Committee to the Electors of Rhode Island" (Providence, 1857), pp. 11, 18. The leading interpretation of the Republican ideology of freedom is Eric Foner, *Free Soil, Free Labor, Free Men: The Ideology of the Republican Party before the Civil War* (New York, 1970), but its conclusions should be compared to Gienapp, *Origins of the Republican Party,* especially chap. 11.

their centrality. Tariffs, banks, and the rest of the earlier political agenda, they claimed, were no longer at the center of affairs (although the Republicans had positions on all of them—largely reflecting those held by the Whigs). As a result of the shift in political issues, established parties could only "break asunder and dissolve when new exigencies bring up new and different policies and principles." That time had come. The existing political scene, in their eyes, reeks of a "demoralized atmosphere" that only the new Republican organization could overcome through their determination to use national power to restrict the further expansion of slavery.[78]

The Democrats vigorously countered, strongly denying their obsolescence and malfeasance, relying on their traditional themes of the necessity for limited government authority and the protection of individual liberties. They had never departed from their position, asserted to the American people as long ago as 1832, that "the only use of government, is *to keep off evil.* We do not want its assistance in seeking after good." That position, in their eyes, was relevant then and was even more so now, twenty years later. Since slavery in the United States was constitutionally recognized, Democrats argued that no one had the right to interfere with it, as the abolitionists in the Republican party were clearly endeavoring to do.[79]

But there was more than the question of constitutional rights and the power of government at stake in the 1850s. The Democrats were convinced that the Republicans posed a particular threat to the nation's safety. The new party was prepared to go beyond normal political confrontation, even to risk breaking up the Union, since the southern states would refuse to live under such threats as the Republicans posed. "The Black Republican party is most essentially the disunion party of this country," Democrats believed, with its intention to force its own conception of right on a resistant South. As such, they had no legitimacy, posed a massive danger to the Union, and had to be put down. In contrast, the Democratic party "has ever been the constitutional, and therefore the only national party. Its fundamental tenet of strict construction, affords the only security for the protection of the States and people." Therefore, in opposing any restrictions on slavery in the territories, it "is sustaining the glorious charter of our liberties."[80]

Despite all this tumult, as new and powerful issues emerged to reshape the

78. "The Parties of the Day. Speech of William H. Seward at Auburn, October 21, 1856" (Washington, D.C., 1857) pp. 4, 7; "Address . . . to the Electors of Rhode Island," p. 1; "Man Who Doesn't Vote," p. 3.

79. "Address of the Central Hickory Club," p. 7.

80. "The Great Issue to be Decided in November Next! Shall the Constitution and the Union Stand or Fall, Shall Sectionalism Triumph?" (Washington, D.C., 1860), p. 19; "Speech of Col. Jas. C. Zabriskie, on the Subject of Slavery . . . 1856" (Sacramento, 1856), p. 13.

institutions of political warfare and cause a massive confrontation between regions, many aspects of that political warfare remained as they always had been. Bernard Bailyn noticed a significant ideological transformation across time in the pamphlets of the American revolution.[81] In the ensuing century, a great many things on the political scene changed as dramatically as they had in the 1760s and 1770s. Certainly, Republican-Democratic confrontation in the late 1850s had distinct and transforming societal and racial dimensions, a fact that both parties recognized in all that they said about themselves and about the other side.

But the style, structure, and overall substance of the partisan arguments offered in response to new issues and new fissures in the 1850s did not change from what had been the norm. The discourse of the new two-party structure continued to echo the familiar themes of the immediate past political generation. The discourse of the 1850s remained, at least in part, firmly embedded in the same continuum of rhetorical style and substantive concern that now stretched over a generation of conflict, whatever changes in the external social and political environment had occurred. Beyond the specific focus on slavery, the territories, and immigration, the debates among Democrats, Know Nothings, and Republicans reawakened and stressed the earlier arguments about power, liberty, and the nature and future of the Republic. As the Republicans became the new second party in the United States, building on the ruins of the Whigs and the failure of the Know Nothings, they brought forward much that echoed past anti-Democratic rhetoric. The Democrats, in turn, found virtue in their traditional arguments and discourse against the old Federalist threat to rend the Republic apart, under whatever name the heirs of the Hartford Convention adopted.

"A NATIONAL GOVERNMENT *OF UNITY AND STRENGTH*"

These continuities persisted into the Civil War era. During the war, familiar echoes from an earlier time were frequently heard and continued to comprise the basic structure of partisan discourse. The war itself was both transformative and restorative, as far as the American party battle was concerned. It unleashed a vast storm of political controversy because of the pressures, problems, and initiatives it created. It was transformative in that these new pressures on society led to an unprecedented expansion of the reach and responsibilities of the government, an expansion that ultimately included the end of slavery by legislative and executive action. The national state, out of necessity,

81. Bailyn, *Pamphlets of the American Revolution,* pp. 90–202.

came to the center of affairs during the Civil War. The power of the federal government reached far beyond any of its earlier boundaries, both in its action and in terms of existing notions of the use of federal power.[82]

At the same time, wartime political conflicts were restorative in that much of the electoral battles that occurred between the Democrats and the Republicans were cast in terms of the traditional basic issues of liberty, power, and legitimacy. The exigencies of wartime and the revolutionary policies culminating in slave emancipation called, in the minds of many, for a vast exercise of power. But, unsurprisingly, notions of a powerful government and its consequences for the Republic and its people still fiercely divided American society and therefore its political parties. Republicans generally welcomed the unprecedented expansion of federal power that took place after 1861. What then happened went far beyond anything the Democrats would accept.

The result was a rekindling of many of the old issues that had divided the parties in an atmosphere undergirded by violence and the pressures of war, conditions that promoted the most extreme rhetoric, especially during the regular election campaigns that continued to be held. Whatever claims there were to this being a new era, with new subjects, elements and conditions, Democrats and Republicans readily continued their great debate about the nature and solidity of the Union, the powers of government, and the consequences to the nation of too much or too little of that power being exercised.[83]

The issue of which party best defends the nation against its enemies and counters the internal threats to its existence was debated once again with the same focus on iniquity—but with the contestants now reversed. The Republicans, with their Whig roots—in Democratic eyes, the heirs of Hartford Convention federalism and of the debilitating opposition to the Mexican War—were now the militant nationalists, insisting that secession and war had created a very different political environment, one that justified certain policies. First, the war provided the Republicans with a renewed basis on which to argue the need for effective national power in order to defeat the rebellion and save the Union. They took their stance quite seriously, vigorously drawing on a variety of familiar themes to make their case. To further their aims, they denounced as dangerous to the republic's survival any opposition to

82. The title of this section is from Abraham Wakeman, "'Union' on Disunion Principles! The Chicago Platform, McClellan's Letter of Acceptance . . . A Speech . . . November 3, 1864" (New York, 1864), p. 3. For general background, see Joel H. Silbey, *A Respectable Minority: The Democratic Party in the Civil War, 1860–1868* (New York, 1978), and Richard Bensel, *Yankee Leviathan: The Origins of Central State Authority in America, 1859–1877* (Cambridge, 1990).

83. Allan G. Bogue, *The Earnest Men: Republicans of the Civil War Senate* (Ithaca, 1981); Eric Foner, *Reconstruction: America's Unfinished Revolution, 1863–1877* (New York, 1988).

their wartime policies. "The stake in this war is no less than our country"; therefore, there could no longer be "divided counsels and irrelevant controversies." The question was no longer one of politics but rather "one of patriotism." Everyone's commitment had to be, as the Republican publicist Francis Lieber entitled one of his pamphlets, "no party now but all for our country."[84]

But their opponents, "the Peace Democracy, alias the Copperheads," went out of their way to resist efforts to save and restore the Union.[85] "One of the most singular anomalies which meets us in the present canvass," Republican pamphlet writers repeatedly underscored, "is the sympathy professed by those who call themselves democrats, with the authors and abettors of the rebellion." Of course, one writer suggested, "the so-called Democratic party is not, at this time, without distinguished and powerful allies: Jeff. Davis in Richmond, Louis Napoleon in Paris, Maximilian in Mexico . . . [and] the British merchants whose incomes have been swelled by the destruction of our commerce" during the war.[86]

The Republicans understood why this was so. The history they recounted of American politics continued to emphasize, as it had in the 1850s, slavery's long-standing control of the Democratic party. "Alike in victory or defeat, the Democratic party had for twenty years bowed to the slave propagandists." Whoever their leaders were, they had always, and voluntarily, engaged in the "low bending of the knee to the dark spirit of slavery." The results of that were seen clearly in the 1860s. "In the beginning, the Democracy invited secession, and, to the end, it encouraged rebellion." Two parties were, of course, welcome and necessary in a republic, "but an Opposition which, in a rebellion, takes sides with insurgents, forfeits for the future all claim upon public confidence."[87]

All of this was repeated incessantly by Republicans throughout the Civil War, their rhetoric becoming especially intense in the most critical of the contests held during the war in the North, the presidential election of 1864. The Democrats at that time were seeking an armistice with the Confederacy,

84. "Address of the Union League Club of Philadelphia . . ." (Philadelphia, 1864), p. 3; "A Few Plain Words with the Rank and File of the Union Armies" (Washington, D.C., 1863), p. 16; Francis Lieber, "No Party Now but All for Our Country" (New York, 1863), title page and p. 8.

85. The title of a Republican pamphlet published in Washington, D. C., in 1863.

86. "The 'Only Alternative.' A Tract for the Times (Philadelphia, 1864), p. 17; "The Great Issue. An Address Delivered before the Union Campaign Club, of East Brooklyn, New York . . . by John Jay, Esquire," (New York, 1864), p. 12.

87. "The Republican and Democratic Parties; What They Have Done, and What They Propose to Do. Speech of Hon. Henry Wilson, at the Republican Mass Meeting at Bangor Me., August 27, 1868" (Washington, D.C., 1868), p. 1; Henry C. Lea, "The Record of the Democratic Party, 1860–1865," (n. p., 1866), pp. 16, 39.

Republicans charged, "only to let the rebels recuperate." In their platform and in their leadership Democrats demonstrated that their real "treasonable purposes" are "the disruption of the union." The people should not be unsure of what was at stake. "Every other election has been trivial, compared with this. The choice is to be made by each one of us whether we wish that the Nation—the Great Republic—shall live or die." Fortunately the Constitution, "fairly and liberally expounded . . . does invest the government with all the power necessary to preserve itself and the nation."[88]

Preserving the union justified, in Republican eyes, the most expansive use of national power yet seen. They expounded a theory of government power unabashedly put forward to the northern electorate and worth quoting for its breathtaking sweep. "The war has taught us some valuable lessons of constitutional law," the pamphleteers of the Republican-controlled Union League of Philadelphia argued in 1864, "which plain men who are not lawyers, can understand. It had taught us that the government must have power to save the nation; that whatever is necessary to that end is constitutional; that the people are the nation, and that the constitution exists for the people; that the constitution belongs to us, the people of 1864, and that *we have a right to modify it to suit our needs according to our will.*"[89]

The Democrats were no more reticent about their position than were their adversaries. At first they were thrown off stride by the enormity of civil war and the insistent demands of their opponents that they forego political activity, but they recovered soon enough because their worst fears were, appallingly, coming true. The Democrats' distrust of national power and its consolidation at the center only grew as the Lincoln administration demonstrated how far it was willing to push to attain its ends. During the war the Republicans enacted an 1860s version of the old Whig program: a protective tariff, a central banking system, and government support for the building of extensive internal improvements. They instituted a military draft and engaged in wide-ranging efforts to control people's speech, political activities, and movements. Nothing any longer seemed beyond the reach of a vigorous and purposive central power.[90]

In the Civil War years, therefore, Democrats easily, if sorrowfully, articulated their familiar rhetoric to counter what they say as a renewed assault on

88. "Speech of Governor [John] Brough . . ." (Cincinnati, 1864), pp. 10, 12; Wakeman, "'Union' or Disunion," p. 31; "Address of the Union League Club of Philadelphia," p. 25.

89. "Address of the Union League Club of Philadelphia," p. 25. Italics added.

90. See Leonard P. Curry, *Blueprint for Modern America: Non-Military Legislation of the First Civil War Congress* (Nashville, 1968), and especially Phillip S. Paludan, *A People's Contest: The Union and the Civil War, 1861–1865* (New York, 1988).

the nation's values and liberties. They found unconscionable the abuses inherent in "the revolutionary policy of the [Lincoln] Administration," the threat to liberty and national survival it posed as it used its power to advance the most illegitimate and frightening ends. Federalism and its successors once more controlled the government and, as could have been predicted, their policies evinced that their main endeavor was going to be an assault on the liberty of all Americans, especially those who disagreed with them.[91]

The long-term results of four years of such Republican policies were clear to the Democrats. The Lincoln administration had "broken the Constitution shamefully and often." The Democrats believed that the Union was, once again (as the Republicans also insisted in their turn), in mortal danger. They expressed grave fears for its survival. As a consequence of Republican policies, the nation's present was despairing, and its future would be disastrous. "That the party of the Administration is both vicious and incapable, has been most abundantly proved." As a result, "we are literally drifting toward destruction." The Republicans' "odious policy" would extract its price, that is, "the liberty of the whole country," since "when did a ruler who had deprived his country of its liberties ever voluntarily restore them?"[92]

But there was more. According to the Democrats, the Republicans had gone beyond their claims to be only interested in restoring the Union. The Lincoln administration had reached even further, confirming Democratic fears about their opponents' unbridled appetite and uncontrolled determination to push beyond reason. "Representing radical and violent elements . . . among us," the Republicans had "changed the war into a humanitarian crusade outside of any constitutional or lawful object." The nation was now in the thrall of "Puritanism in politics." America was controlled by the social and political extremism of Puritan New England, with that region's incessant preaching of a "fratricidal hate" against its enemies. Its tenets had taken over the Republican party. The issue that the Democrats particularly connected to such extremism was race—that is, the emancipation of African slaves and the resolution of their eventual place in American society. Given Republican instincts, the Democrats were not surprised by their wartime efforts in this area, efforts that the Democrats greatly feared and stridently opposed.[93]

Lincoln and his congressional colleagues were following racial policies, the Democrats lamented, "which tend to social debasement and [the] pollution

91. "Congressional Address. By Members of the Thirty Eighth Congress, Politically Opposed to the Present Federal Administration . . ." (Washington, D.C., 1864), pp. 5, 11, 21.

92. Ibid., pp. 17, 18, 21, 27.

93. "Puritanism in Politics. Speech of Hon. S. S. Cox, of Ohio, before the Democratic Union Association, Jan. 13, 1863" (New York, 1863), p. 13.

of the people." The government was "established by white men and for white men and their posterity forever, and it is for the common advantage . . . that the exclusion of the inferior races from suffrage should be permanently continued." The races "should be kept distinct, socially . . . they should not blend together to their mutual corruption and destruction."[94] In its content, style, intensity, and savagery, such partisan political rhetoric infused the North's politics during the war in the same manner as its predecessors had in earlier years. To the Democrats, such discourse and resistance were necessary given what was at stake. To the Republicans, such Democratic behavior was to be expected, given the base and iniquitous desires of that party to resist what needed to be done to preserve the Union.

"A REVOLUTION IN OUR GOVERNMENT"

The debate between the parties that raged during the Civil War did not end with the defeat of the South in 1865. Democrats and Republicans violently disagreed over what was to follow the North's victory, both at home and in the surrendered Confederacy. Republican leaders saw the need to continue to use the federal government's authority with vigor and purpose to pursue a policy of reconstruction that included the advancement of the rights of the former slaves; the Democrats maintained their strenuous opposition to such authority and the purpose to which it was being put by the Republicans who were in control in Washington.[95]

In all that ensued in the election campaigns of the dozen years following the war, the focus and content of political discourse continued to be familiar. Republicans retraced the recent historical record to draw from it lessons and, particularly, warnings about their opponents. They began the postwar discourse by asking "is it not reasonable . . . to judge of the future of a political party as you should judge of the future of an individual—by its antecedent history?" They never let up on sounding the familiar warning: the danger to all Americans posed by the Democrats, given their record of support for slavery and the South before and during the Civil War. That party's history "recalls no inspiring ideas, no beneficent policies, no ennobling deeds for patriotism, for liberty, for justice, and for humanity. But it does recall images of slavery, . . . the slave power, . . . dark conspiracies, lawless rebellion, fields of blood . . . and the graves of the nation's dead."[96]

94. "Congressional Address . . . of the Thirty Eighth Congress," pp. 19–20, 22.

95. The best introduction to the Reconstruction era is Eric Foner, *Reconstruction: America's Unfinished Revolution, 1863–1877* (New York, 1988).

96. "Speech of George H. Williamson . . . San Francisco . . . 1868" (San Francisco, 1868), pp. 1, 8; "The Republican and Democratic Parties . . . Speech of Hon. Henry Wilson," p. 13.

The Democratic party remained "hostile in war and wrong in peace." One of the Republican pamphlets listed all of the "traitors" who had been in the last cabinet of a Democratic president and asserted that Democrats "justify and exult in the murder of Lincoln." As they organized for their presidential run in 1868, the Democrats were still "faithless and heartless," led by a "promoter and representative of disorder and anarchy" (former governor Horatio Seymour of New York) who was surrounded by similar "revolutionary and treasonable spirits." Voting for the Democratic candidates, Seymour and Blair, in 1868, Republican publicists warned, would open "the flood-gates of revolution and anarchy" in the United States. Such rhetoric, the Republicans believed, remained useful as a means of linking bad people with the Republic's recent experiences and its dangers.[97]

As to their own claims, the Republicans continued to make a strong case on behalf of national power, as they had done during the war. Their mission had not ended. Much remained to be done, especially in the South. As Republican senator Henry Wilson argued in 1868, the party had successfully developed "the nation's power" and advanced "its material interests" so that the United States now "stands on a higher plane than that of any political organization on the globe." And there could be no retreat from what they had done if the nation wished to maintain itself and what it has gained since 1861. The "unrepentant" South, allied with their Democratic colleagues, continued to resist the will of the nation. The danger, as always, was real. Southerners intended to restore themselves and their values to power as soon as they could so that "the malignant spirit of slavery and caste" could "rule again."[98]

The Democrats, of course, disagreed, using their familiar arguments of the danger to freedom and the desirability—the necessity—of limited government. Their "sordid and selfish opponents" had used the occasion of the war to take advantage "of the passions and delusions incident to the occasion" in order to impose their "views of finance, revenue, and the administration of government." In consequence, "a revolution in our government" had "been going on," whose tendency was "to vest in the General Government nearly every power that a government can possess over a people." The result was clear: Republicans had passed "repressive and not reconciliative" measures, measures that tended "to the destruction of the republic."[99]

97. "The Issues of the Day. Speech of Hon. Roscoe Conkling, at Utica . . . 1876" (New York, 1876), p. 15; "Treasonable Designs of the Democracy. The Issue before the People . . ." (Washington, D.C., 1868), pp. 3, 7, 8.

98. "The Republican and Democratic Parties . . . Speech of Henry Wilson," pp. 10, 13.

99. "Speech of S. S. Cox . . . August 30th, 1872" (n. p., 1872), pp. 7, 20; "The Principles and Policies of the Democratic Party . . ." (New York, 1875), p. 30; "Speech of Allen G. Thurman, at Cincinnati, Sept. 10,

Democrats devoted much of their rhetoric to the present and future condition of the emancipated slaves in the South and what (if anything) should be done by the federal government to help them in their transformation from slavery to freedom. As during the war, they were not happy about the direction and substance of their opponents' efforts. America was, no one should ever forget, "the country of the White race, given by the Almighty on which to build a great white nation." But the Republicans had opted to ignore this sacred trust in favor of their own policy of racial egalitarianism. The Democrats fiercely condemned Republicans' "malignant efforts to degrade the white inhabitants of the Southern states and place them at the mercy of an inferior race." Their policies would lead to the nation's "mongrelization" (a favorite Democratic word in the context of race issues in this era).[100]

"FOUNDATION OF OUR FAITH"

Reconstruction lasted until 1877, and its consequences were felt for a very long time thereafter. By the time President Rutherford B. Hayes ordered the last northern troops out of the South and presided over the final restoration of local control there, the parties had fully internalized the issues raised by the war and its aftermath and found ways to argue them that were infused with their previous approaches to American politics. In the 1870s, as before, although many of the specific details of American politics had changed over the past twenty years, the basic thrust of party warfare and tone of partisan rhetoric did not. Even with the rise of new issues in that decade, from civil service reform to monetary policies, neither party wavered in its basic course. The Democrats demanded that the government be reformed and restored, constantly reiterating their long-established commitment "to limit and localize government," which was now, as it was in the past, the "foundation of our faith." As they had been saying for a decade and more, "the necessities of war cannot be pleaded in a time of peace." It was time to restore the federal government to its previous limited role in national life.[101]

But there continued to be a serious problem. Under the Republicans, "the authors and abettors of administrative centralism," the federal government "is paternal, without limits and without well defined duties. It undertakes the

---

1870," (Washington, 1872), p. 1; "Speech of Hon. L. D. Campbell, at Delaware [Ohio] September 7, 1870, in Reply to Senator John Sherman" (Cincinnati [1877], p. 1.

100. *Illinois State Register,* Springfield, April 4, 1866; *Louisville Democrat,* November 20, 1867. This theme is discussed and analyzed in Forrest Wood, *Black Scare: The Racist Response to Emancipation and Reconstruction* (Berkeley, 1968).

101. *Official Proceedings of the National Democratic Convention . . . 1876* (St. Louis, 1876), p. 196.

care of the people—their morals, their industries, and their property . . . It legislates for every conceivable interest . . . It seeks to put a spy in every house and a constable at every elbow." As a result, Democrats continued to list the not unfamiliar issues of the day, from taxation, financial policy and the tariff, to radicalism, "republican disregard of the Constitution," the "Bayonet election law," and "our state governments belittled," among others, and ask, as they always had, whether faced by Federalists, Whigs, or Republicans, "Where is the old simplicity and purity" of the government?[102]

The time had come, the Democrats kept repeating, to reduce and reform the national government, and restore amicable relations between the sections. The election of 1876, August Belmont told the Democratic National Convention that year, "is a struggle between Democracy, representing union, progress and prosperity, and Republicanism, representing sectional strife, religious intolerance, and a continuation of financial and industrial prostration." The country remained endangered by the Republicans' control of national power. Only under the Democrats would the nation "return to the ark of the Constitution, to frugal expenditures, to the administrative purity of the founders of the Republic."[103]

The Democrats' opponents remained equally faithful to their existing discourse and ideological substance in the 1870s. Although "the cause of the Union and of freedom" had triumphed, the Republican publicists continued to point out that victory had come without the aid of the Democratic party. The latter, voters were once more reminded, was "debased by slavery and demoralized by Calhounism." Its members "had neither the courage, nor wisdom, nor patriotism to sustain the war which the nation waged in self-defense." Nothing had changed. In the 1870s, as in the past, the Democrats remained subservient "to the disloyal elements of the South," those who remained "unsubdued, defiant, hopeful, active and aggressive." The Democrats' presidential candidate in 1876, New York's Samuel J. Tilden, was "the man who did more than any other to precipitate the rebellion." He was "the most obnoxious person in the nation to all principles of order and good government."[104]

102. Ibid., p. 62; "The Danger and the Duty of the Democracy. A Letter to the Hon. Francis Kernan by Clarkson N. Potter of New York" (New York 1876), p. 9; "Peril of the Hour. Speech of General A. Saunders Piatt, Delivered at Mac-a-Check [Ohio], 18th September, 1876" (n. p., 1876), pp. 3, 15; "Speech of Hon. George Pendleton, at Loveland, O., August 22, 1871" (n. p., 1871), passim; "Grant or Greeley? Speech of S. S. Cox . . . 1872" (New York, 1872), p. 1.

103. *Official Proceedings of the . . . Democratic Convention . . . 1876*, p. 63.

104. "The Three Secession Movements in the United States" (Boston, 1876), pp. 17, 20, 24; "A Change to Democratic Rule; What It Means . . ." (n. p., 1876), pp. 6, 7, 8.

In contrast to the actions of their Democratic opponents, "the Republican party's deeds of usefulness, and acts of fidelity to the best interests of the people" were clear and positive, and, most important in the writer's view, were the proper policies for the nation. The Republicans' record was "no more to be compared to . . . [that] of the democratic party than light is to darkness, or loyalty to treason." And that record still counted although the war was over. Was the United States, Republican pamphlet writers asked, "sufficiently recovered from the effects of the war" so that it could "afford to put the high priest of secession at the head of the Government?"[105]

Through it all, the Republicans also continued to stress the power of the national government: "The nation not the states, is supreme," one writer argued, proceeding to underscore the theme of order and preservation through the use of federal power against the Democrats' disruptive degeneracy. The latter's "cry of 'centralism' is a mere fetch. The real danger is the other way. De-centralization, which means State Rights in the old pestilent secession sense is the real danger . . . 'Centralism' is a mere goblin . . . All the 'centralism' we have now, is a strong and stable government under which the nation prospers, with safety to property, labor, liberty, and life." In short, the Republicans' unrelenting message continued to be that "on one side [their own] is safe, tried, and stable government, peace with all nations, and prosperity at home, with business thriving, and debt and taxes melting away. On the other side [the Democrats], is a hybrid conglomeration made up of the crotchets, distempers, and personal aims, of restless and disappointed men. What ills might come of committing to them the affairs of the nation, no judgment can fathom, no prophecy can foretell."[106]

While the two major parties continued their warfare in the style and substance that had characterized them for half a century, there were glimmerings of new forces emerging onto the national scene in the 1870s. Most of these new impulses sought a home within the major parties.

Women had always played a role on the American political scene, but one that was largely informal, since they could not vote and were usually not encouraged to participate directly in nominating caucuses and other party activities. At the same time, women had repeatedly sought to expand their role, particularly by winning the right to vote. Like members of established political parties and proponents of various issues, women articulated their

105. "Address of the Republican State Convention Held at Little Rock, September 15, 1874" (Little Rock, 1874), p. 17; "The Three Secession Movements," p. 21.

106. "The Three Secession Movements," p. 24; "The Presidential Battle of 1872 . . . Speech of Hon. Roscoe Conkling at Cooper Institute, N. Y.,. . . 1872" (New York, 1872), pp. 36, 48.

perspective in pamphlets, adding their voice to the debates of the late 1860s and early 1870s. Like other reformers, they claimed to want to improve the Republic and enhance the freedoms of a significant part of the population within it. Leading suffragists, echoing the established style of political discourse, saw a clear distinction between the Republicans and their opponents. "We are willing," Massachusetts women argued in 1872, "to trust the Republican party" to follow through on the demand for voting rights by doing away with what the Republicans called restrictive "class" legislation, which defined suffrage in gendered terms.[107]

A powerful economic downturn in 1873, which seriously affected the whole country, provided the Democrats with an opportunity to break away from war-related issues and slash at their opponents along another familiar line of cleavage, the misbegotten economic policies of Federalist-Whig Republicanism. Although the Democrats, like their opponents, had significant internal differences over financial policy in the 1870s, specifically due to the vociferous demands of some Democrats that the government continue to accept paper money as legal tender and the resistance of others to what they thought was a dangerously inflationary policy, party leaders tried hard to play down their conflict and stress the basic differences between the parties over economic affairs.

To Democrats, the depression had been caused (unsurprisingly) by "the false policies of the Federal Government," with its "excessive" activities everywhere and the imposition of high taxes to pay for them. The period since the war "has been characterized by unsound public finances [and] . . . an extravagance in public and private expenditure." As a result, "labor finds scanty employment even at reduced wages. Incomes are lessened and fail altogether." Restoration of government frugality was an absolute neccesity. But it would never happen under a Republican Administration, as history abundantly demonstrated.[108]

The Republicans did not take the bait. They stated firmly that the real issues between the parties remained as they had been: the war, the preservation of the Union, the issues flowing from Democratic submission to the South, the Democrats' treasonable wartime behavior, and the inadequacy of

107. "Address of the Republican Women of Massachusetts" (Boston, 1872), p. 1. On the women's suffrage movement in this era, see Beverly Beeton, *Women Vote in the West: The Woman Suffrage Movement, 1869–1896* (New York, 1986).

108. "Governor Tilden's Letter of Acceptance, July 31, 1876," in *Official Proceedings of the . . . Democratic Convention . . . 1876*, p. 189; Samuel J. Tilden, "Finance, Taxation, and Reform" (Scarborough, Me., 1876), pp. 5,7.

that party's principles in every area. So far as the economic issues of the day were concerned, the Republicans blamed the Democrats for their succumbing to wild monetary panaceas that disrupted economic confidence. "It is my conviction," Rutherford B. Hayes wrote in his letter accepting the Republican party's presidential nomination, "that the feeling of uncertainty and insecurity from an irredeemable paper currency, with its fluctuations of value, is one of the great obstacles to a revival of confidence and business, and a return to prosperity." The longer such instability lasts, "the greater will be the injury inflicted upon our economic interests and all classes of society." The message was clear. The problem was, as always, the errors of the other side.[109]

This general pattern of blame and counterblame between the two major parties did not satisfy everyone. Some of the new participants who had appeared on the political scene challenged the hegemony of the major parties on behalf of their particular concerns. Some women's suffrage activists found both parties wanting and looked to third parties for redress. The economic distress of the early 1870s prompted vigorous third-party activity as well. A group of "independents," forerunners of what was to become the National Greenback Labor Party, joined the presidential contest in 1876 as the first of the third parties that were to become a prominent part of the political landscape in the last third of the nineteenth century. The Greenbackers argued for unorthodox financial policies, the issuance of paper money, and an income tax. They were forced to organize as an independent political movement, they said, because neither major party would do what needed to be done for the American economy.[110]

The Greenbackers' arguments echoed familiar themes and idioms that had long been heard in American political discourse. They, too, were in a "fight for the liberty of the American people" and, as a result, were engaged "in one of the greatest battles for reform that ever engaged the attention of man." American freedom was again in danger, this time from the concentration of economic power in the hands of a few, as well as "dangerously large fortunes," "foreign influence," and "corruption." Only through a Greenback victory at the polls would the wrongs perpetrated "against the rights and interests of the laboring, producing and commercial class" be corrected.[111]

109. Reprinted in in Russell B. Conwell, *Life and Public Service of Gov. Rutherford B. Hayes* (Boston, 1876), p. 305.

110. A still very helpful introduction to the Greenback movement is Irwin Unger, *The Greenback Era* (Princeton, 1964).

111. "To the Independent Citizens of Ohio" (Cleveland [1871]), p. 1; "Address of the New York County Committee of the National Greenback Labor Party" (n. p., [1876]), pp. 1–2.

Despite the familiarity of their expression and its compatibility with the existing style of political confrontation, neither women's suffrage nor the class-conscious economic demands of the Greenbackers gained much political authority in these years in terms of support from party leaders or from voters, although their emergence signaled some compelling changes on the horizon for a political landscape that was still dominated by partisan warfare rooted in republican values and issues engendered by economic development, individual liberty, and the role of the national government. But those changes remained in the future. The familiar still held sway as the years of Civil War and Reconstruction came to a close in the late 1870s.

New York's Republican senator, Roscoe Conkling, nicely invoked the power of the continuing confrontation between the two major parties in an address to his party's state convention in 1878. "The mission of the Republican Party is not ended," he began. "It has done much. It has put down a vast rebellion, freed 4,000,000 slaves, made a free Constitution, united the fragments of a shattered empire, managed war and finance to the amazement of mankind; it has carried railroads over deserts and mountains . . . it has made harbors . . . ; it has secured to every man who will have it a homestead of 160 acres of fertile land; it has stood for free speech, free labor, and freemen always; it has upheld the public credit; and its aims have been those of humanity and right."[112]

The Democrats ended the era in equally vigorous—and familiar—fashion. "The time is ripe," Samuel J. Tilden argued in 1876, "to discard all memories of buried strifes, except as a warning against their renewal; to join altogether to build anew the solid foundations of American self-government." There was much to do after too long a time under the sway of extremism and too much central power. The American people carried tax and other burdens greater even than those imposed by the immense and elaborate governments of Europe due to the policies of the Republicans, who had commanded the nation since 1861. They had built up "a more costly machinery than the imperial governments of the two richest and most powerful monarchies of modern times." It was now time to "make governmental institutions simple, frugal,—meddling little with the private concerns of individuals,—aiming at fraternity among ourselves and peace abroad,—and trusting the people to work out their own prosperity and happiness."[113]

112. "Speech of Roscoe Conkling, as President of the Republican State Convention, at Saratoga, [N.Y.,] September 26, 1878," (n. p. [1878]), p. 6.

113. Tilden, "Finance, Taxation, Reform," pp. 10, 27, 28.

"Consider Well . . . the Platforms . . . of the Parties Now Asking Your Suffrage"

America's political parties produced a mountain of words in the campaign pamphlets they published from 1828 to 1876. Their political battles had an extraordinary harshness and bite as well. Throughout, the pamphlets etched sharp contrasts and sounded warnings to never let up in this inevitable and serious conflict. Each party demonized the other by attacking its policies, its leaders, and its intentions in the most threatening and colorful manner. American political discourse was always one of excess.[114]

But these rhetorical excesses did not mean that the parties were only playing hostile games with each other—or with American voters. The monsters that they created in every campaign season in their narratives of America's past and present touched real and recognizable elements in the nation's political culture. The parties successfully articulated the basic nature of American politics as partisan leaders and voters understood it. Party leaders knew their audience well. Americans were concerned about the security and state of their society, and they had strong prejudices, fears, aspirations, and agendas, all rooted in their many experiences. But they were not in agreement about any of these. This half century was characterized not only by two-party dominance but also by a range of ideas and policies that remained essentially divisive and, depending on which side one was on, either positive or threatening to the nation and to the people's liberties.

Some scholars have lately been inclined to dismiss much of this partisan discourse as only electorally driven and therefore suspect as expressions of what its authors really believed (or what the voters they addressed really thought). As stated earlier, however, party activists were in fact deadly serious about their beliefs and what they wrote and distributed. A great deal of evidence challenges such skepticism as a misreading of a truly divided political scene. The parties went beyond rhetoric and differed from one another at every level of political confrontation. The Whigs (later the Republicans) and the Democrats espoused significantly different worldviews and repeatedly acted on those distinctions.

To be sure, the nation's political discourse in this era, rich in its language of conflict and divisiveness, always remained within particular ideological boundaries. Most political arguments do so. Neither side moved outside of the general framework that defined their society in its broadest terms. But

114. The quotation in the heading of this section is from "The Republican and Democratic Parties . . . Speech of Hon. Henry Wilson," 1868), p. 14.

that hardly made the debates the parties engaged in consensual, except at the outer boundaries of their confrontation. It is very hard to find any level of consensus in the highly charged expressions of both parties, except that each claimed that they were trying to achieve the same thing: the security and future of the nation.

One is also struck by the continuities in the style, structure, and content of writings of the various parties; all were remarkably stable over time. The parties used history to frame their arguments, to draw out telling examples, and to recount the critical moments that gave shape and direction to the present. They both used the vocabulary of classical republicanism and focused their attention on the fragility of republics in a hostile world, especially because of always-present internal dangers. They paid constant attention to the needs and the future of their economy and their society. Most of all, each party intensely and clearly argued that it was battling for the soul, the future, even the survival of the American experiment. The parties touched on all they themes in clear-cut, straightforward terms.

This discourse, though commonplace in much of its content, gave order and direction to its society and its political system. After fifty years of such widespread partisan articulation, no one who had paid any attention could doubt where the parties stood on the issues of the day or could ignore how much was at stake in these battles; that each voter had better attend to what was being said and act for himself and for the future of the country. Democrats and their Republican opponents, as Jacksonians and Whigs before them, stood for different things and represented different interests.

In fact, one can argue that two very different political cultures inhabited the same nation throughout these years, and that these cultures had quite different notions of proper policy, the nature of authority, and the definition of legitimacy. The reality of those differences is what gave the parties' campaign pamphlets their power. Neither the Republicans, nor the Whigs before them, sought to tyrannize the people of the United States, nor to degrade or destroy the nation—though Democratic audiences were not convinced of this. Simultaneously, in a dynamic nation undergoing rapid growth and facing unprecedented change, Democratic policies may have been more old-fashioned than their opponents thought helpful, wise, or legitimate; but the policies that the Democrats advocated were not as foolish, nor as treasonous, as the National Republicans, Whigs, and Republicans suggested.

The result was the continuation, from the Jacksonian generation into the years of sectional strife and beyond, of powerful political disagreements on the American landscape—disagreements that were thoroughly canvassed in the nation's many election seasons. The parties' ideological differences led to intense and unyielding partisan warfare that was well marked out and artfully expressed in the pamphlet literature produced by the leaders of the two major political parties as well as by those of the minor parties that appeared more fleetingly on the scene, but who spoke with the same intensity as the Democrats, Whigs, and Republicans, despite their more limited chances of electoral victory.

PART ONE

The Evolution of Party Warfare
1828–1838

I

Proceedings and Address of the New Hampshire Republican State Convention of Delegates Friendly to the Election of Andrew Jackson to the Next Presidency of the United States, Assembled at Concord, June 11 and 12, 1828 (Concord, 1828)

In June 1828 Andrew Jackson's New Hampshire supporters called a state convention in Concord, the capital. There the assembled delegates voted to issue an address to the voters that had been drafted by a committee of party leaders. The address, printed by the state's leading Jacksonian newspaper, the *New Hampshire Patriot,* presented in detail a harshly worded case against the Federalist-spawned John Quincy Adams and the corrupt Henry Clay. Andrew Jackson, in contrast, was linked to Thomas Jefferson and the long battle to preserve the nation's liberties. This document reflects the nature of the arguments that the Jacksonians were offering at this point on the current malevolence of political leadership and the consequent danger to the republic. It also suggests the emerging state of political organization that was necessary in order to put these arguments in front of the voters in a systematic, coordinated fashion.

Jackson captured 46 percent of the state's vote in 1828, and won the state in 1832.

To the People of New-Hampshire.

The history of all governments furnishes ample demonstration that in every country there have existed two great political distinctions or parties—that *might* has constantly been warring against *right*—that "power is always stealing from the many to the few." In despotic governments, it has ever been the policy of the few to keep the many in ignorance, so that power could be effectually grasped; and in governments controlled by the voice of the people, the exertions of the few have been untiring, first to cheat the people by every species of deception, and afterwards, gradually to impair those rights and privileges on which a free government is based.

Our fathers of the revolution successfully contended against the arbitrary rule of the mother country, whose government insisted on the right which the master exercises over the slave—on the right to tax us without our consent—on the right of the governor to perpetuate his power against the voice of the governed. The despotism of the few was then put down, and the rights of the people established by their valor: the invaders of our soil were repelled, and the shackles of a foreign tyrant were thrown off. The nation breathed the pure and unsullied air of freedom. But the evil genius of Aristocracy, which discovered itself in the abettors of British tyranny, the tories of the revolution, still lurked amongst us. Scarcely fourteen years elapsed after the close of the revolution, before the administration of the government of the people was in the hands of men who contemned the rights of the people—scarcely fifteen years had elapsed, before the rulers delegated by this free people, attempted by the passage of laws to throw around them those arbitrary restraints which, had they not been early arrested, must have created a tyranny at home not less destructive to all free principles, than the shackles which were contemplated by the tyrant from abroad.

It will not be denied by any republican, that the principles which characterized the administration of John Adams—an administration styled, by way of eminence, "the reign of terror"—were the same in essence as the principles contended for by the British parliament. The "Sedition law," which made it a crime punishable by fine and imprisonment, to call in question any act, or to speak, write or print any thing disrespectful, or in disapprobation of the President, was founded on the same arbitrary principle, as was that declaration by the British parliament of the right to tax us without our consent—to enact laws imposing arbitrary regulations on a people who were not allowed to have a voice in making those laws. The "Alien law," of the same administration, which invested the President with power, on his own mere motion, to banish any foreigner from the country who should be obnoxious to his displeasure, savoured not less of tyranny than the most arbitrary law of the most arbitrary despot. The same administration attempted to perpetuate its power by creating a host of useless officers, whose influence was intended and expected to operate through every grade of society—by creating a standing army in time of peace, which could have been intended only to overawe the people—by imposing taxes and heavy burdens on the people, intended to break down their spirit and to discourage their confidence in the value of our civil institutions—by holding up to public scorn and derision all who co[n]tended for economy and retrenchment of unnecessary expenses—and by forcing the people to wear that arbitrary badge of fealty to the powers that be, the "black cockade"!

In the Alien and Sedition laws of John Adams, the spirit of the Constitution was violated—the principles of free government were trampled upon.—Those patriots who stood by the principles of the revolution were persecuted and proscribed. But the people, alarmed by the encroachments of the men in power—alarmed that the tory adherents of Britain in the revolution had assumed the control, and that the best patriots of the country who had fought and bled to procure independence, were no longer cherished by the administration; the sovereign people arose in the majesty of their strength and expelled from office the men who had abused their trust. On the fourth day of March, 1801, John Adams retired from the Presidential office, amidst the frowns of an indignant people; and Thomas Jefferson, the man of whom John Adams declared in his letter to Cunningham in 1804, "I shudder at the calamities which I fear his conduct is preparing for his country"—was invested with the Presidential office. Under the new administration, a new order of things immediately commenced. Instead of a sedition law, free discussion, the liberty of speech and of the press were restored: the alien law was abolished. Instead of a useless standing army, a retinue of useless officers, and an increased public debt on *eight per cent.* loans; the public expenses were lessened and the debt was rapidly discharged—the standing army and the hordes of useless officers were abolished.

In his official communication to Congress, Mr. Jefferson held the following language:

"These views are formed on the expectation that a sensible, and, at the same time, *a salutary reduction, may take place in our habitual expenditures.* For this purpose, those of the civil government, the army, and navy, will need revisal. When we consider that this government is charged with the external and mutual relations only of these States; that the States themselves have the principal care of our persons, our property, and our reputation, constituting the great field of human concerns, we may well doubt whether our *organization is not too complicated, too expensive—whether offices and officers have not been multiplied unnecessarily,* and sometimes injuriously to the service they were meant to promote. I will cause to be laid before you an essay towards a statement of those, who, under public employment of various kinds, draw money from the Treasury, or from our citizens. Time has not permitted a perfect enumeration, the ramifications of office being too multiplied and too remote to be completely traced in a first trial. Among those who are dependent on *executive discretion,* I have begun the *reduction* of what was deemed unnecessary. *The expenses of diplomatic agency have been considerably dimin-*

ished. The inspectors of internal revenue, who were found to obstruct the accountability of the institution, have been discontinued. *Several agencies, created by executive authority, on salaries fixed by that also, have been suppressed,* and should suggest the expediency of regulating that power by law, so as to *subject its exercises to legislative inspection and sanction.* Other *reformations* of the same kind will be pursued, with that caution which is requisite in removing useless things not to injure what is retained. But the great mass of public offices is established by law, and, therefore, by law alone can be abolished. Should the legislature think it expedient to pass this roll in review, and try all its parts by the *test of public utility,* they may be assured of *every aid and light which executive information can yield.* Considering the general tendency to *multiply offices and dependencies, and to increase expense* to the ultimate term of burthen which the citizen can bear, it behooves us to avail ourselves of every occasion which presents itself for taking off the surcharge; that it never may be seen *here,* that after leaving to labor the smallest portion of its earnings, on which it can subsist, government shall itself consume the residue of what it was instituted to guard. In our care, too, of the public contributions intrusted to our direction, it would be prudent to multiply barriers against their dissipation, by *appropriating specific sums to every specific purpose susceptible of definition; by disallowing all applications of money varying from the appropriation in object, or transcending it in amount; by reducing the undefined field of contingencies, and thereby circumscribing discretionary powers over money;* and by bringing back to a single Department, all accountabilities for money, where the examination may be prompt, efficacious, and uniform."

Such were the doctrines of that great apostle of liberty, the illustrious Jefferson—doctrines which were long practised under his administration and those of his successors; but which now seem to have been forgotten by many claiming affinity to the republican party.

To trace the covert windings of the party which adhered to John Adams, from the reign of 1798 up to the present moment, would extend this address to a great length. At times, that party has taken the open field, and fought with a desperation bordering on madness, denouncing every thing republican—every act of our republican administration. The private character of Jefferson was assailed in vulgar prose and libidinous verse; and every stigma which falsehood could invent was laid on the *individual* to cast reproach on the *principles* for which republicans contended. But when those principles, when the glorious cause of democracy, became predominant, and so triumphant as to defy the open assaults of their enemies, the vindictive Aristocracy, under the pretext of laying down their arms, have waged against them a more successful, because a more insidious warfare. The name of federalist, under which the Aristocracy at first were proud to rally, became so obnoxious, even before Mr. Jefferson left the office of President, that other convenient names or appellations were assumed by this party, as the circumstances or the times would favor its views. When a British commander, at New-York, wantonly fired on an American vessel and killed the American seaman, Pierce, and when a British squadron attacked the American frigate Chesapeake, under the pretext of claiming British seamen, the Aristocracy were vociferous for war—they reproached the administration with pusillanimity—they declared "our government could not be kicked into a war"—they were then the avowed *friends of the nation's rights.* When the administration, forced to the alternatives of either paying tribute to Britain, of war, or an embargo, to save the remnant of our commerce, resorted to the latter measure, the Aristocracy were the *friends of free and unrestricted trade!* They would leave our ships and our seamen to take care of themselves. But when the nation, goaded and driven to the utmost verge of endurance—when thousands of our citizens, impressed on board of British ships, were compelled to fight her battles—when our ships and commerce were seized and confiscated under illegal orders in council—when the nation, driven to the last resort, was compelled to declare war; then the Aristocracy were the *friends of peace!* In this character these boasted friends of peace were guilty of deeds, at the recital of which their posterity will blush; and ever since that disgrace, they have renounced the name of *federalist,* as not less odious than that of *tory,* which fastened on the adherents of Britain at the era of the revolution.

An "era of good feelings" succeeded the treaty of Ghent, after the accession of James Monroe to the Presidency. This eminent citizen, like his predecessor, James Madison, had been peculiarly a subject of federal obloquy, ever since the year 1800: at that time governor of Virginia, he was reproached in all the bitter vindictiveness of ultra federalism; and during the last two years of the late war he was conspicuous, from the situation he held in the government, as a mark for the arrows from the quiver of the federal party. It was this abuse that greatly recommended him to the republicans as a candidate who could stem the torrent when Mr. Madison retired. After his inauguration, Mr. Monroe visited the Northern States; and strange as it may seem, such was the desire of the Aristocracy to conciliate the favor of the man whom they had recently abused, that they alone claimed the right to offer him their congratulations; and in many towns, indeed in all the towns where the federal party was predominant, the republican friends of Mr. Monroe, who had assisted to sustain the administration of which he had been a member, and the cause of the country, were studiously shut out of the committees appointed to do public honors to the President of the United States! The crafty Aristocracy, proclaiming an "era of good feelings,"* so contrived to manage the occasion of that visit as to place on the footing of strangers to Mr. Monroe, the old republicans with whom alone he could claim affinity of feeling, and who alone had encountered with him the bitter hate and animosity of his present flatterers. Strange, indeed, it may not be considered that the President was partially caught in a snare so artfully set: all appeared fair and smooth on the exterior, although there were many republicans who then perfectly understood what was meant. It would not be wise to conceal that these personal flatteries accomplished every thing the flatterers intended. Although the change of the administration was not immediate, the foundation was then laid which has since, in the election of the second Adams, restored to power the party which fell with the first Adams: a foundation was then laid for that craven "Amalgamation," which more effectually subserves the hidden purposes of mischief-making federalism than any other plot with which the Aristocracy have disgraced themselves since the termination of the "reign of terror."

Mr. Monroe, from that moment, looked with a more favorable eye on the men of the Hartford Convention. To that fallen party was then united all others in office or who desired office, whose object was more to serve themselves than the public: to that party was then united all such as would feed from the public crib; all who advocated sinecures and high salries; all who had adopted the doctrine that it was no sin to filch from the public coffers, and that the benefits of government were intended for the governors, and not the governed. Such is the materiel of which the present amalgamation party is composed—the almost entire body of the federal party, at least that portion of the federal party which is ready to resort to any means, even the most dishonorable means, to regain power, united with all that is false and unprincipled, all who would sell their political rectitude, for the loaves and fishes of office. Mr. Monroe, indeed, never fully gave in to the views of this party: he, probably, intended to sustain his democratic rectitude; but the fawnings and flatteries of his old political enemies, with the false show of oblivion to old party feelings which they took occasion to exhibit before the public, and especially before him, gave to his administration a complexion and a character which paved the way for that division in the republican ranks resulting in the formation of an administration of the highest Aristocratic character—an

**Extract from the Address of Hon. Thomas W Thompson, to President Monroe, in Concord, July* 1817.

"Upon this auspicious occasion, party feelings are buried, and buried, we hope, forever. A new era, we trust, is commencing. The leading measures of the General Government accord remarkably with the *views* and *principles* of all parties."

administration not less consonant to the wishes and desires of the Aristocracy, than was that of the first Adams.

Never was deception more artfully or more successfully practised, than that practised by the Adams family on the people of the United States. Participating in the revolution, being one of those who subscribed the Declaration of Independence in 1776, it was placed in the power of John Adams to take a conspicuous stand in the councils of our country as a Patriot and a Statesman. On a close review of his writings and his life, we are constrained to say that he *never was a friend to republican government*—that all his professions of attachment to republican men and measures were hollow-hearted and insincere. In saying this, we have no reason to doubt that he honestly opposed the tyranny of Great-Britain at the outset of the revolution: he, probably, desired independence: but he was one of those, who, having gained independence, wished a government of the well-born to be here instituted. Accordingly, we find him, while in Europe, even before our present Constitution was adopted, writing and publishing a book in favor of monarchy, in which he pronounced the British Constitution to be "the most stupendous fabric of human invention." In this work, entitled "A Defence of the American Constitution," he says—"In every State there are *inequalities* which God and Nature have implanted there," "particularly, inequalities of birth"—that "the people in all nations are naturally divided into *gentlemen* and *simplemen*"—that "the *poor* are destined to labor, and the *rich* are qualified for *superior stations*"—that "it is the true policy of the common people to place the *whole executive power in one man*"—that "the good sense of the people of the United States will dictate to them, *by a new Convention,* to make transitions to a *nearer resemblance to the British Constitution.*" We find him afterwards, while Vice President of the United States, declaring to John Langdon (as is proved by the letter of that deceased patriot to Mr. Ringgold,) that "*the people of America will not be happy without an hereditary Chief Magistrate and Senate, or at least for life.*" We find him, afterwards, while President of the United States, practising on these doctrines by introducing into his administration, wherever it was in his power, the paraphernalia of monarchical governments—by excluding from office many sterling patriots of the revolution, and by calling around him, as his advisers, the rankest aristocrats—by recommending and sanctioning laws encroaching on the rights of the people, calculated to restrain the liberty of speech and of the press, in discussing the conduct of public men and the character of public measures, and likewise calculated to perpetuate power in the hands of an overbearing aristocracy.

Writing to his relative, Cunningham, Jan. 16, 1804, John Adams, quoting another, says—"I have always been of opinion that in popular governments, the people will always choose their officers from the most ancient and respectable families. * * * If a family that has been high in office and splendid in wealth, falls into decay, from profligacy, folly, vice, or misfortune, they generally turn democrats and court the lowest of the people with an ardor, an art, a skill, and consequently, with a success, which no vulgar democrat can attain." Mr. Adams, although himself then an old man, did not think it too late, three years afterwards, seeing no prospect of promotion from the federal party, to bolt outright from his party. During those three years, himself and his son, who, we shall perceive hereafter, was faithfully educated in the school of his father, continued to express their contempt for sterling republican patriots: the latter, so late as 1807, wrote his famous vulgar verses ridiculing Mr. Jefferson, making as a subject of his raillery the purchase of Louisiana, against the acquisition of which, he had voted on every question brought before the Senate of the United States, of which he was a member.

The father and son turned democrats in 1807. John Q. Adams became an open convert (no "vulgar democrat,") in the latter part of that year, a few months after he presided at a Junto Federal Caucus in Boston, which nominated Caleb Strong as Governor, and Christopher Gore as Senator in Massachusetts; and he played his court to Mr. Jefferson and the people on that occasion "with an ardor, an art, and skill, and consequently with a success, which no vulgar democrat could attain." So great was his *ardor,* his *art* and his *skill* on that occasion, that even William B. Giles, of Virginia, one of the most sagacious men in the country—a politician who has scarcely ever mistaken any man's real character—acknowledges that he then believed him sincere. And if Mr. Giles was then deceived, as he now acknowledges, it cannot at all surprise us that the people were then deceived as to the real character of the Adams' conversion. The following extract from a late number of the Telegraph, published at the seat of government, under the eye of Mr. Adams, will furnish some idea of Mr. Adams' conversion:

> Gov. Giles, in his late patriotic address to the public, gives the following extract from a letter written to him by Mr. Jefferson.
>
> Mr. Jefferson said:
>
> "You ask my opinions on the propriety of giving publicity to what is stated in your letter, as having passed between Mr. John Q. Adams, and yourself. Of this, no one can judge but yourself. It is one of those questions which belong to the forum of feeling. This alone can decide on the degree of confidence, implied in the disclosure. Whether under no circumstances, it was to be communicable to others. It does not seem to be of that character or at all to wear that aspect. They are historical facts, which belong to the present, as well as future, times. I doubt, whether a single fact known to the world, will carry as clear a

conviction with it, of the correctness of our knowledge of the *treasonable views of the federal party* of that day, as that disclosed by this most nefarious and daring *attempt to dissever the Union,* of which the Hartford Convention was a subsequent chapter, and both of these having failed, consolidation became the first book of their history."

On the above, Gov. Giles, in a letter which appeared in a late Richmond Enquirer, among other things, thus remarks:

Hence the following facts evidently appear: that Mr. Adams made the disclosure to me, of his intending to desert the federal party the winter of 1807, 1808–to the best of my recollection, it was a short time previous to the first embargo. That it was made under the most solemn assurances of his patriotism and disinterestedness, and of entire exemption from all views of personal promotion by the party, to which he has proselyted. Mr. Jefferson states the grounds of this charge, as communicated by Mr. Adams himself, to be *the treasonable views* of the federal party, *and that these treasonable views extended to disunion.* All that now remains to be disclosed to the public, to give a full view of the whole ground of this eventful transaction is, to *designate the particular conspiracy on the part of the federalists of that day,* 1807, *which did induce Mr. Adams to charge them,* according to Mr. Jefferson's statement, *with treasonable views to dissever the Union; the particular foreign agents with whom it was carried on, the particular circumstances which gave rise to it, and the particular portions of the federalists implicated in the treasonable negociations then on foot.* Mr. Adams can state these facts to the public if he should think proper to do so; or if, which I should suppose impossible, he should deny them; then ought he to tell, what other political sins the federal party had committed, of so heinous a character as to justify his open, formal and sudden abandonment of them in their utmost need, and in his adhesion to their opponents—indeed, in the true spirit of proselytism, his going to the uttermost extremes in supporting his newly chosen associates, and his fulsome flatteries of Mr. Jefferson, through his extravagant commendation of this measure, and that too, not long after he had heaped upon Mr. Jefferson, all kinds of abuse, and even called doggrel verse, as is said, to his aid for the purpose. Now suppose it should turn out, that *no such conspiracy did exist,* and that *no treasonable negociations were carrying on, no treasonable views were entertained* by the federalists at that time, 1807, what must the world think of such treacherous charges against his old friends for his own personal aggrandizement, as is now rendered evident, directly against his own solemn avowals—(and I acknowledge I *was* deluded into a perfect confidence in his disclosures)—*I now sincerely believe, that the whole of these charges against the federalists* were unfounded, and consisted only in Mr. Adams' own mental misgivings and poetic licenses. For me, this conviction is sufficient; and I shall not vote for Mr. Adams for my President. Others, of course, will also act as they think best.

Those who have been in the habit of hearing the *free conversations* of Gov. Plumer of this State, who, whatever may have been his political changes, has always been as John Q. Adams was, and who cast a solitary vote for Mr. Adams, the only vote against Mr. Monroe in all the electoral colleges of 1820—must have heard him revert to this knowledge of Mr. Adams of the treasonable designs of certain leading federalists. But notwithstanding this knowledge of treasonable designs, the father in a letter to Cunningham, hearing date Dec. 13, 1808, more than a year after the family conversion, gives as a reason why John Q. Adams was averse to being run by the republicans of Massachusetts for the office of Governor—"Because it would produce an eternal separation between him and the federalists; at least, that part of them which constitute the absolute oligarchy."!

Mr. J. Q. Adams, it will not be concealed, is at this time a favorite of the federalists. His accusations made against the leaders of that party to Mr. Jefferson and Mr. Giles in a manner so serious and solemn as then to extort from them a belief in their truth, were either true or false. If *true,* what excuse can be offered for Mr. Adams in now taking to his confidence and his embraces the most incorrigible men of that party? If *false,* how can these federalists now follow their accuser as a leader, and fawn around the traitor who stabbed them in the dark? Mr. Adams offers no denial—no excuse or apology for his disclosure to Messrs. Jefferson and Giles: although he has frequently, while Secretary of State, and since he has been President, come before the public on more trivial subjects, he is silent on this. A more respectable authority could not be given as his accuser; yet we venture to affirm he will never further explain to the public his knowledge of the treasonable designs of the federal party!

In further proof that Mr. Adams' conversion to republicanism was hollow hearted and insincere, we quote the following charge: About the same time he made his communication to Messrs. Jefferson and Giles, "at the table of an illustrious citizen, he *lamented* the fearful progress of the democratic party, and of its principles, and declared that 'He had long meditated the subject, and had become convinced, that the only method by which the democratic party could be destroyed, was by JOINING WITH IT, and urging it on with the utmost energy to the completion of its views, whereby the result would prove so ridiculous and so ruinous to the country, that the people would be led to despise the principles and condemn the effects of democratic policy, and then (said he,) *we may have a form of government better suited to the genius and disposition of our country, than the present Constitution.*'"

We have said that Mr. J. Q. Adams was educated in the political school of his father: when he changed his politics and made pretensions of attachment to the republican party, he was not more republican than his father assumed to be. We have shown the aristocratic propensities of the father, as evinced in his writings and declarations. Those propensities have not been less marked with a decisive character in the writings of the son. The commencement of his political career, was in the same strain as that of the father. In a series of essays published in the Boston Centinel so early as 1792, he contended for the same aristocratic doctrines—that "*all the power of the people* ought to be delegated for their benefit"—that "the people of England *have delegated all their power* to the King, Lords and Commons," and that the British Government is *"the admiration of the world"!* If the conversion of J. Q. Adams in 1807, had been sincere, his subsequent declarations would prove that he has since returned to his first love for monarchy; for in his letter to Levitt Harris, written during the last war, and while he was charging and receiving for double outfits and salaries and for constructive journeys, he declared our republican government to be "*feeble and penurious*"; and after he had been placed in the office of President, in defiance of the expressed wishes of the people of Kentucky by the votes of the representatives of that State—after he had obtained that elevated situation by the "understanding" that if he should be elected President by the vote and influence of a Kentucky representative, that representative should be appointed the second officer in the administration—he advances, in his first message to Congress, the aristocratical doctrine, that the representative ought "*not to be palsied by the will of his constituents,*" lest it "*doom*" our government to a "*perpetual inferiority*" to "governments less blessed with freedom." From the year 1803, to the year 1807, he was in the United States Senate; and all that time he never gave a republican vote on any party question: he voted constantly against every question for adding Louisiana to the United States—he voted against a proposition to prevent the importation of slaves into that territory. In his writings, he called Jefferson the "Islam of Democracy," as much as to say he was an artful impostor; and but a few months before his conversion, he ridiculed in pitiful rhyme the author of the Declaration of Independence, on the false accusation of unlawful amours with "Dusky Sally." So far from regretting his old attachment to the aristocratic party—his opposition and abuse of the Democratic party—as late as 1822, in his correspondence with Alexander Smyth, he vindicated his votes on the Louisiana treaty, charged Congress with usurpation for legislating over that country, and maintained that it was unconstitutionally added to the United States!

Although it is a matter of sincere regret we are obliged to admit the fact, it is not the less important that fact should be stated, that artful demagogues who have changed sides, men who, yesterday, were flaming federalists, and, to-day, are *moderate* republicans, have found too much favor and been too hastily received into our ranks. Such men, having "turned democrats," have generally "courted the people with an ardor, an art, a skill, and consequently, with a success, which no vulgar democrat (that is, no democrat who acts purely from principle,) can attain." We have before us many living examples; and in the cases of men whose object has been the mere attainment of office, nine out of ten, he who has been gained to our cause has afterwards doubly injured us by the grossest duplicity and treachery. The case of John Q. Adams, now before us, is one of the most striking, being of a family more "high in office" than any which ever before apostatized from the federal party, his "art and skill, and consequently his success" have outstripped all other examples in this country. With the aid of his father, he has looked further ahead in all his plans of personal aggrandizement than any other political adventurer in this Republic.

His political life has proved that he has practised most successfully on the now fashionable doctrine of the federalists, that "all is fair in politics." The "art and skill" of his father, after the measures of his administration had become obnoxious to the people, in throwing the blame on Hamilton, Ames, Pickering and other federalists who participated in that administration, paved the way for the reception of both the older and the younger Adams into the republican ranks; and when the somerset was finally accomplished, the same "art and skill" are again visible in the choice made by the younger Adams of Pickering for an antagonist, when he fought himself into the favor of the democrats by seizing on a popular subject, and contending for that measure of the then existing administration which was intended to compel the British government to acknowledge American rights on the ocean. Whenever Mr. Adams' *republican* attachments have been doubted, his friends have deemed it a conclusive answer to refer us to his letter to Harrison Gray Otis, in answer to that of Timothy Pickering, in which he (Adams,) defended the Embargo, and to his review of the works of Fisher Ames, published about the time of his conversion, in which he only condemns those doctrines in the latter, which were consonant with the repeatedly avowed doctrines of his own family.

These devices, like that of the avowal to Jefferson and Giles of the discovering of a treasonable plot to dissever the Union among the leading federalists, were calculated to inspire confidence in the republicans as to the sincerity of the conversion of the Adams family. The younger Adams expected immediate payment for his apostacy to the federal party. But Mr. Jefferson was cautious and guarded and did not, during his administration, bestow any of those honors which Mr. Adams thought his disinterested services merited. Accordingly we find his father writing privately to his friend Cunningham, Feb. 14,

1809—"If his (John Q. Adams') talents and integrity *continue to be neglected,* as they have been insulted, *the fault is not his.*" And when, some time afterwards, after fruitless attempts to get some appointment, he obtained from Mr. Madison a mission to Russia, the father then writes to Cunningham—"Aristides is banished, *because he is too just:* he will not leave an honester or an abler man behind him" It is evident, that the family then considered no office, short of the first in the government, was sufficient to pay him for his apostacy. But Mr. Adams, "banished" as he was, made the best of this place, contriving at the same time he replenished his purse by holding on to double compensations, to stay in Europe until an opportunity should offer to embark, at home, in the line of "safe precedents." He returned from *banishment* and accepted the office of Secretary of State under Mr. Monroe. In this situation, he availed himself not only of the immense influence which the office gave him, but of a variety of other incidents, to further his ambitious views. He had been withdrawn from the agitations of the late war at home: he was not, therefore, obnoxious to the displeasure of the federal party on that account; while he claimed the favor of the republicans for his ardent zeal in their cause at the time of the embargo. He saw he was not a favorite of the great body of the republicans of the Union; and hence his first political act was to conciliate the men of the old Hartford Convention by appointing Benjamin Russell to print the laws of the United States—a man who had stigmatized the illustrious patriots, Jefferson and Madison, as "French citizens," and "disciples and fellow-laborers in the same cause with their friend, the imperial butcher of the human race!" His only hope was to "divide and conquer" the republican party; and hence, while he kept himself aloof, his friends, the federalists, threw into Congress the fire-brand which was calculated to arouse the North against the South—to awaken a mutual jealousy and hatred as unforgiving and cruel as the grave, among the slave and non-slave holding States. The Missouri slave question carried the hostile feeling to the highest pitch, for two or more sessions of Congress; and when the asperity was stilled by the admission in favor of Missouri, that Congress had, by the Constitution, no right to interfere, Mr. Adams himself, to conciliate his friends in the slave-holding States, authorized the informal admission, that he too was of opinion it was beyond the authority of Congress to legislate on the subject! An "art and a skill" was manifested on this subject by Mr. Adams and his friends, which, while it left no responsibility on him, innoculated that poison into the public mind which was calculated to subserve fully the objects of the Websters, the Hopkinsons and other politicians, who, at first, artfully kindled the flame.

The plan to "keep up the division" was artfully pursued during the whole of the last four years of Mr. Monroe. Jefferson, Madison and Monroe had each been successively designated for the office of President at open meetings of the republican members of Congress; and this method was relied on by those who were sincerely desirous of continuing the unity of the republican party. The example had been sanctioned by Mr. Adams himself, who attended the meeting of Senators and Representatives soon after his conversion, which first nominated Mr. Madison; but such a nomination, at this time, did not suit the convenience of Mr. Adams—he declared against this mode of nomination—that he would not accept the office, if designated as a candidate by a caucus of the members of Congress. A combination was immediately entered upon by his friends and the friends of other sectional candidates, to prevent any nomination by the members of Congress: the New-Hampshire delegation was called together by Mr. Senator Bell, and each was required to give the other a pledge that he would not go into convention to designate a candidate for President. It was boldly avowed, in the papers friendly to Mr. Adams, that their object was to prevent the choice of any candidate by the people, and to bring the question to be ultimately decided by the House of Representatives by States, where thirty-six representatives would have it in their power to control the votes of two hundred and thirteen representatives—and where the one representative of Missouri would have the same weight as the thirty-four representatives of New-York—where, in fine, as was predicted by the friends of Mr. Clay in Kentucky, the question might ultimately be carried by "bargain, intrigue and management."

It is worthy of remark here, that it was the friends of Mr. Adams—nay, it may be said to have been Mr. Adams himself, who first put forward Andrew Jackson as a candidate for the Presidency; for it was his own authorized Journal at Washington which then advocated the cause of the General—a paper which now daily pours the vilest abuse on the head of the hero "who has filled the measure of his country's glory." Mr. Adams and his friends did not suppose, when they at first set forward General Jackson, that he would be a formidable rival to him—he was set up to "divide and conquer" in those States where Mr. Adams could obtain few votes against Mr. Crawford—he was set forward to prevent a choice by the people; and, such was his popularity with the people, although the station was unsought by Gen. Jackson personally—such was the high estimation in which he was held, that those who set him forward, as we have good reason to believe, deplored the effects of their own trick: indeed, what they intended as a *ruse de guerre,* was taken by the people, after Mr. Crawford's lamented illness, so much in earnest, that the friends of Mr. Adams trembled for the result. Jackson obtained ninety-nine unbought electoral votes, while Adams himself obtained only eighty-four; and of these twenty-six were given in New-York by a "bargain" in the Legislature of that State with the friends of Henry Clay, without consulting the wishes of the people of that State.

It is believed the proceedings of the friends of Mr. Adams, in and out of Congress, to frustrate a choice of President by the people, to be without a parallel in the history of our elections; and to accomplish this object the management at Washington was as constant and untiring, as it was unprincipled. The influence of the existing administration was directed against Mr. Crawford, and in favor of Gen. Jackson only so far as to prevent the ultimate success of Mr. Crawford. It was a game of calculation on the part of Mr. Adams and Mr. Clay, who was each for himself. Up to the time of the voting of the Electoral Colleges, these two gentlemen had been most bitter personal and political enemies. The publications of both the gentlemen in 1822, under their own signatures, prove that there was a secret hatred existing between them while negociating the peace at Ghent: Mr. Clay then promised the public that he would, "at some time more propitious than the present, lay before the public a narrative of those transactions as *he* understood them;" and Mr. Adams answered, that as Mr. Clay's narrative may "*chance to be postponed* until both of us shall have been summoned to account for all our errors, before a higher tribunal than that of our country, I feel myself now called upon to say, that let the appropriate dispositions, when and how they will, expose the open day and secret night of the transactions at Ghent, the statements both of fact and opinion in the papers which I have written and published, in relation to this controversy, will, in every particular, essential or important to the interests of the nation or to the character of Mr. Clay, be found to abide unshaken, the test of human scrutiny, of talents of time." Mr. Clay, in his published article, had hinted at some "errors" of Mr. Adams, ("unintentional no doubt";) and the tenor of both publications left us not without the inference that there was a deep grudge between the two statesmen. But the evidence developed by a recent investigation before the Senate of Kentucky, proves that the hatred of Henry Clay towards Mr. Adams could not be excoeded even by his present horrible aversion for Gen. Jackson. This evidence proves that at the very moment Mr. Clay was insinuating the "unintentional errors" of Mr. Adams, the western papers were teeming with the most injurious charges against Mr. Adams, instigated by Mr. Clay's own tongue, or coming from his own hand!

During that investigation, Mr. Wickliffe, a devoted friend of Mr. Clay, asserted in his place, that Mr. Clay never did entertain any ill feelings towards Mr. Adams, in consequence of the transactions at Ghent; in proof of which he adduced Mr. Clay's declarations to himself; and he defied the friends of

Gen. Jackson to prove the contrary, by the evidence of any respectable man. Samuel Daviess, Esq. then arose in his place, and stated that the gentleman himself had, by his speeches and votes in 1824, affirmed the truth of the charges against Mr. Adams; and he, moreover, produced a series of numbers, signed "*Wayne,*" which were published in the "Liberty Hall and Cincinnati Gazette," at Cincinnati, Ohio, early in the fall of 1822, averring that they were written in Kentucky, sent to Mr. Clay, and by him directly or indirectly forwarded to the State of Ohio, for publication; the proof of all which he declared he had at hand. Mr. Wickliffe sunk to his seat, overwhelmed at this prompt exposure, and no man dared again to say that Mr. Clay had no objections to Mr. Adams on account of the Ghent negociations. These numbers had passed through the hands of Mr. Clay, before the date of his publication accusing Mr. Adams of "unintentional errors," and were, at that very moment, republishing in the Kentucky papers. In these numbers he charges Mr. Adams with "an unfeeling policy," "which would crimson our fresh fields with the blood of our border brethren, and light the midnight forest with the flames of their dwellings"—with "giving our wives and children for *fish,* and bartering the blood of our citizens for *money.*" The proposition to yield the navigation of the Mississippi, for the right of taking fish, contended for at Ghent by Mr. Adams, Mr. Clay declares to be a "fatal project," an "atrocious proposal," as "strange as it is alarming;" and that, but for his own exertions, "the seeds of war might now have been sowing, along our western borders, which, at no distant day, would have produced an abundant harvest of tears and blood."

About the same time he wrote accusing Mr. Adams of "unintentional" errors, and declining a controversy with Mr. A. lest *his motives* should be misconstrued, he called on his friend, the Editor of the Argus, published at Frankfort, Kentucky, for the purpose of correcting an error relative to the principles assumed at Ghent, which had brought upon that editor and Mr. Clay the severe censure of Mr. Adams. He gave this friend a narrative of the proceedings at Ghent, and convinced him of his error. The editor then took up the publication of Mr. Adams, and reviewed it in a series of numbers addressed to John Quincy Adams. After these letters had been published in the Argus, Mr. Clay offered the Editor fifty dollars, towards defraying the expense of their republication in pamphlet form. Finally, one thousand copies were printed in Lexington, by Mr. Tanner, and Mr. Clay paid one hundred dollars—about one half the expense—out of his own pocket, as the publisher lately testified before the Senate of Kentucky. By this act, Mr. Clay adopted these letters, and made them his own. He made himself responsible for all the statements they contain—if he be not, in substance, their author. In these letters Mr. Clay charges Mr. Adams with "bearing false witness against his neighbor;" with "falsehood" in relation to the navigation of the Mississippi—almost with the massacre of one of his own "near connexions;" with "weighing dollars against blood;" with "falsehoods" relative to the extent of the fisheries, contested at Ghent; with "knowingly violating the very letter of his instructions;" with pursuing "a course wholly sectional;" with attempting to make the Western people pay an exclusive tax of rivalship, war and blood, for the security of those fishermen who frequent British waters;" with "manufacturing facts;" with asserting "opposite principles;" with gross "absurdities, inconsistencies and contradictions;" with injustice to his colleagues of the minority; with a policy promoting Indian wars and massacres; with "a deadly hostility, or a culpable indifference to the interests of the Western country;" with hostility to the annexation of Louisiana to the United States; with "adding insult and mockery to abandonment and injustice;" with being "an *artful sophist,* a *clumsy negociator,* and *vindictive man;*" with "views TOO ERRONEOUS, FEELINGS TOO SECTIONAL, AND TEMPER TOO VINDICTIVE, *for the Chief Magistrate of a free people!*"

It has been, moreover, proved on Mr. Clay, that another great objection urged against the elevation of Mr. Adams to the Presidency—an objection urged with untiring industry in the papers in the interest of Mr. Clay in Kentucky and Ohio—was the danger which threatened our institutions from a *perpetuation of the Cabinet succession*—that the uniform practice of electing the Secretary of State to the office of President, was assimilating our government to monarchy, in which each Chief Magistrate appoints his successor. The following extract from the Kentucky Reporter of July 15, 1818, a paper edited by Mr. Smith, a connexion and devoted friend of Mr. Clay, taken from among many others, proves the hostility of Mr. Clay to the line of "safe precedents:"

"Mr. Adams is designated by the President and his presses, as the heir apparent, the next successor to the Presidency. Since the principle was introduced, there has been a rapid degeneracy in the chief Magistrate; and the prospect of greater degeneracy is strong and alarming. Admit the people should acquiesce in the Presidential appointment of Mr. Adams to that high office; who again will he choose as his successor? Will it be Josiah Quincy, H. G. Otis, or Rufus King? An aristocrat, at least, if not a TRAITOR, will be our portion."

Such was the bitter hostility of Henry Clay towards John Q. Adams up to the time he was excluded from the House of Representatives by the votes of the Electors as one of the three highest candidates—a hostility, certainly not less inveterate, not less unforgiving, than that now manifested by Mr. Clay towards Gen. Jackson—a hostility not only to the person, but to the principles of John Q. Adams. Yet, after Mr. Clay was himself excluded, in defiance of his own declarations and principles, on the understanding that he should be Mr. Adams' Secretary of State, by his controlling influence over five of the Western States, he made Mr. Adams President!

Much has been written and published to prove and disprove a bargain between Mr. Adams and Mr. Clay. We do not consider it at all necessary to labor this point. In his zeal to divest himself of the charge, Mr. Clay has proved too much: one single fact demonstrates how indefeasible is his case. While he has produced the affidavits and declarations of his friends to prove that he had decisively made up his mind to vote for Mr. Adams, long prior to the time, he has himself declared in his speeches and his conversations that as late as the latter part of December prior to the election, he had not made up his mind to vote for Mr. Adams! The Hon. John Floyd of Virginia testifies that so late as the month of January, or the latter part of the preceding month of December, Mr. Clay made to him, in substance, the following declaration: "When I take up the pretensions of Mr. Adams, and weigh them and lay them down—then take up the pretensions of Gen. Jackson, weigh them and lay them down by the side of those of Mr. Adams—I never was so much puzzled in all my life, as I am to decide between them." Abundant other evidence is presented of the declarations of Mr. Clay, that he himself stood wholly uncommitted. In his address to his constituents, after the election, he informs them of the deliberation which it cost him to make up his mind, after he found himself excluded from the House of Representatives: he says, "I found myself transformed from a candidate before the people, into an Elector for the people. *I deliberately examined the duties incident to this new attitude, and weighed all the facts before me,* upon which *my judgment was to be formed or reviewed*" Yet the "Diary" of the Hon. William Plumer, jun. of this State, declares the opinion of Mr. Clay, as given to him, to have been unalterably fixed as early as the winter session of 1823–4! And Mr. Clay himself, notwithstanding his *grave deliberation,* now says his mind was decisively made up not to vote for Gen. Jackson, almost three months before the period of this deliberation!

The truth is, Mr. Clay, whether he had made up his mind or not, had determined that his influence in the election should go for his own personal advantage: he intended that all the candidates should understand that he "stood uncommitted" until he ascertained what was to be done for *him;* and accordingly so soon as the sworn enemies, Mr. Adams and Mr. Clay, met (according to letters then written to this State by Mr. Plumer, jun. to his father,) *the bargain was completed,* and Mr. Adams' friends then, and not till then, understood that the election of Mr. Adams was certain. Mr. Francis Johnson, one of the Kentucky representatives, asked by one of his constituents, how he came to vote for Mr. Adams? answered that he thus voted to "*get Mr. Clay made Secretary of State.*" And Mr. David Trimble, another Kentucky representative, said on various occasions, as is proved by numerous witnesses, "*it was distinctly ascertained that Mr. Adams would make Mr. Clay Secretary of State, and that Gen. Jackson would not.*"

Resolutions instructing the Representatives of Kentucky to vote for Gen. Jackson, had passed the Legislature almost unanimously: Mr. Clay had received those instructions, and said that he stood uncommitted. Yet he voted for Mr. Adams against Gen. Jackson; and when asked why he disregarded the voice of Kentucky, he has only to say, "THE REASON IS MY WILL"—as early as October, 1824, I had taken a "fixed resolution"—my resolution was "unalterably fixed"—I had come to a "fixed and unwavering decision" not "in any event" or "under any possible circumstances" to vote for Gen. Jackson!

The bargain between Adams and Clay is best proved by those events which are matter of notoriety—by the fact that Mr. Clay and his friends voted for the man whom Mr. Clay had characterized as possessing "views too narrow, feelings too sectional, and a temper too vindictive, for the Chief Magistrate of a free people, "for the very office of Chief Magistrate—by the fact that he thus voted against the almost unanimous instructions of the Legislature of his own State, and that he was rewarded for that vote by the man of "temper too vindictive" with the appointment of Secretary of State. The proof of corruption also exists in the fact, that Scott, of Missouri, who carried the vote of that State for Mr. Adams, and who had confessed that not one in twenty of the citizens of the State were friendly to his election, after he had lost a re-election by the people in consequence of that vote, was rewarded by a more lucrative appointment, that of inspector of land offices in the West, from the hand of Mr. Adams: proof also exists in the case of Cook, of Illinois, who also voted against the wishes of his State, and who, when he lost his election in consequence, was sent on a secret diplomatic errand, undoubtedly with a compensation much larger than that of representative, by the administration which his vote had made!* The bargain is further proved by the fact that the election of Mr. Adams was ascertained even before the balloting took place, and was

*It having been denied in the newspapers printed "by authority," that Mr. Cook received any such appointment, we subjoin the following extract from the report of the committee on retrenchment, made to the House of Representatives, May 15, 1828, and published among the official documents of Congress:

"In the appendix, it will be seen, that your committee received a communication apprising them, that the late Daniel P. Cook, late member of Congress from the State of Illinois, had received the sum of $5,500 for some services connected with the foreign relations of the country. As no record appeared of this item on foretold in letters received in this State from members of Congress. It has also been charged by respectable testimony—and has never been denied by Mr. Webster, that he exhibited, as an inducement for the federalists to support Mr. Adams, a WRITTEN PLEDGE, *corrected by the hand of Mr. Adams himself,* that in case he should be elected President, the federal party should be provided for, as it has been provided for in the case of Rufus King and others. This pledge was exhibited to members of Congress and others by Mr. Webster: at least, he has been charged with the exhibition, and has never denied it. And Mr. Walsh, the devoted friend of Adams and Webster, has virtually admitted the existence of this written pledge.

Considering every circumstance—the previous hostility of Mr. Clay, and his subsequent appointment as Secretary of State—the protection given by the President to Scott and Cook—the pledge to Webster for the federalists;—if the case be not made out that the last Presidential election was brought about by "bargain, intrigue and management," we conceive it to be difficult, nay, impossible, that any case of bargain can be made from evidence.

It is no matter of "special wonder" that Mr. Adams, and the friends of Mr. Adams, should have anticipated an opposition to an administration thus corruptly formed. It was, in the very nature of things, to have been expected that his re-election would have been opposed by all who had not participated in

---

any of the accounts transmitted either from the Treasury or the Department of State, your committee called on the Secretary of State to inform them, if,in point of fact, Mr. Cook had been so employed, where they were to look for the settlement of the account. This call resulted in an overture on the part of the Secretary of State, to make to the Committee "*a confidential communication* respecting this expenditure, which he neither admitted or denied." On full consideration, your committee decided to decline receiving a communication burdened with such an obligation, as they desired to make no report to this House, which might not be common to the people, whose trustees and servants we are.

"That Mr. Cook, after the adjournment of Congress in the Spring of 1827, received an appointment from the President, connected with our foreign intercourse; that one thousand dollars were paid to him in advance, and in part compensation for his services; that he actually embarked from New-York for Cuba, towards the end of April, (which it appears was the place of his public destination;) that he arrived early in June at St. Louis, Missouri, on his return home; that he was in exceedingly critical health and in doubtful condition to attend to any business, more especially, of a diplomatic character, requiring so much labor and anxiety; that *he did not understand the language of the people among whom he was sent,* probably as a secret agent; that he must have been less than one month in Cuba on this service; that he was to receive, and probably has received, a further sum than the amount of the advance made him in remuneration for his services, and that this remuneration came out of the secret service fund, are facts which your committee think abundantly appear from the testimony in the appendix. They coerce, on their face, the solemn enquiry, why Mr. Cook, under such circumstances, was appointed a *secret* agent, and why he was paid out of this fund? Whilst your committee feel the force of this question, they feel it likewise their duty to leave it where they find it, with the remark that such payment, made from such a fund, *finds no sanction from the precedent of an agency to Cuba,* instituted during the Administration of Mr. Monroe, which was filled with eminent ability by Mr. Thomas Randall, and whose compensation was paid with specification, out of the contingent fund of foreign intercourse, and audited under the ordinary circumstances of official notoriety at the Treasury."

the first choice; and such is the jealousy in this free country of the purity of our elections, that he ought to have anticipated that a very large portion of his own supporters at the polls would so have condemned the means by which he was, in the end, elected, as to withdraw their support. Tramelled with bargains and pledges as Mr. Adams was at the time of his election, he has deemed it to be expedient and necessary to pursue the same system to support a sinking cause. A course of electioneering, of attempts to operate on the State elections, has been adopted, which is believed to be without example in this free government. Professing to belong to no political party, this administration has used its official influence to purchase the support of the unprincipled of all parties. Where its adherents supposed themselves to be strong in point of numbers, proscription has been the order of the day: where they were few, the patronage of the men in power has been held out as an inducement to come over. Political apostates have been rewarded with public patronage; and those political knaves who, having opposed the election of Mr. Adams, afterwards became his flatterers, are now most warmly caressed.*

*To name one instance, the patronage of the administration, has been heaped upon John Binns. The printing of the Custom House, *by order from Washington,* was taken from a widow to a soldier of the revolution, and given to John Binns; and the same Binns has been appointed printer of the laws of the United States.

BINNS'S PROFLIGACY.—Reader! If you wish a specimen of political profligacy and baseness, that has no parallel in the history of mean and unprincipled actions, read the following extract from the Democratic Press of 1815, and then contrast it with the daily sheet of the author of the extract, who is employed in heaping upon the head of ANDREW JACKSON every species of malignant abuse, denouncing him as a *murderer,* violating the quiet of his domestic retirement, and lacerating the feelings of the partner of his cares and toils, by the most infamous falsehoods; and after you have read the article, if you shall ask, why the author of it has become the reviler of the brave defender of his country, you will find the answer in two words—"*Presidential patronage.*"—Judas betrayed his master for thirty pieces of silver. This man lives upon the *crumbs* that fall from the executive table.

From the Democratic Press, March 28, 1815.
EDITED BY JOHN BINNS.

Before the attack on Orleans, the Federal Republican assailed the character of Gen. Jackson, but he soon found he was gnawing a file. The halo of glory which has surrounded this *distinguished* CHIEFTAIN, has struck dumb the slanderers, and he is, of all our warriors, first in the hearts of our countrymen. That he should be *envied* and *hated* by the *British,* is right and *reasonable,* but that any *Americans,* even *skulking, trembling cowards,* who, in the battle day never saw the enemy, but were safe under the shadow of Jackson's valor and foresight, that such men with a dastardly and malignant spirit should, shrouded in darkness and at thousands of miles distant, attempt to assassinate the fair fame of Gen. Jackson, may be permitted to excite some wonder. But Gen. Jackson repulsed the enemy with great slaughter. He is a *republican,* and *therefore* must be vilified. "Be thou as pure as snow, as chaste as ice, thou shalt not escape calumny."

We have avoided, as far as duty would permit, any remarks upon the federalists who held distinguished commands in the army; but our forbearance and that of the Republicans generally, appears to be attributed to any thing rather than a generous contempt for men who reflected so little honor on the military character of the nation. The remark is now extorted from us, but it is as true as the bravery of Gen. Jackson is indisputable:—*Every glorious military event of the war, whether of attack or defence, was achieved under the command of a Republican officer.*

On a review of the course of Mr. Adams, it is not at all surprising that he has become a favorite of the federal party; for where has there been an instance of apostacy from democratic principles that has not recommended the apostate to the favor of the federalists? He is likewise endeared to that party by an adherence to the doctrines of his father—by his strong desire to consolidate power, that power which belongs to the individual States, and the hands of the federal government. The profuse expenditures of his administration also strongly recommend him to that party which, ever since 1800, has fed on corruption as its best aliment, and which looks on every encroachment on the rights of the people as a gain to its cause.

In the administration of Mr. Adams, we see the old principle of Aristocracy warring against the principle of Democracy. The public documents, the reports of the Treasury Department, prove that in the three first years of his administration, in a time of general peace, the expenses have exceeded, by more than EIGHT MILLIONS of dollars, the expenses of the last three years of Mr. Monroe. If it be asked how this money has been expended; as a sample, it may be answered—large sums have been paid to favorites and dependents, for which adequate services have not been rendered: witness, more than $5000 paid, contrary to law, to John A. King for about sixty days service—$1,940 paid to J. H. Pleasants, one of Mr. Adams' editors, for carrying despatches to Buenos Ayres when he never went—$1,205 paid to Mr. Clay's son for carrying a packet to Mexico, when the service would have been as well done for $200—$2,388 extra paid the Attorney General for attending to certain law business of the United States during five months, at the same time his salary of $3,500 was going on—$1000 paid to prepare for making pictures of John Q. Adams to send among the Indians. This is barely a sample of the manner in which the contingent and other expenses in nearly every department have been improvidently enlarged. The constitution has been greatly warped, if not expressly violated, for the purpose of catching the opinions of different districts or particular States, and sending swarms of government officers, charged with the prosecution of local improvements, with the government funds, and having also a special charge of the votes of the people.

During this administration, the President has asserted that he alone had the right, without the consent of the Senate, to institute foreign missions, and under him missions have been attempted, and favorites appointed on those missions, which experience has condemned, and the policy of the country has forbidden.

During this administration, while the Heads of the Departments, particularly the Secretary of State, have been travelling the country, making electioneering harangues, as if determined sooner to "annihilate heaven and earth than fail of carrying their point," the public interests have been grossly neglected; an important trade with the colonies of England and France in the West Indies has, in one case, been destroyed, and in the other endangered by over-diplomacy in the one instance, and utter neglect in the other.

During this administration, whilst a great public question (the Tariff,) has been perverted to political uses, and very large and exclusive pretensions set up for political effect, that great subject has been neglected in the official recommendations of the President, and has been voted against by some of his immediate political and local friends and supporters.

During this administration, its friends and abettors have incessantly attempted to array the prejudices and the worst passions of the people of the North, against their brethren of the South, by repeating the old epithets of "*slave representation,*" "*negro votes,*" "*southern aristocracy,*" "*slave-holders of the South,*" "*white slaves of the North,*" so often used by the federalists fifteen years ago—thus setting at defiance the sacred injunction of Washington to "frown indignantly on the first dawning of every attempt to alienate any portion of our country from the rest, or to enfeeble the sacred ties which now link together the various parts."

During this administration, the most glaring attempts have been made to interfere in the local and State elections directly from Washington. Witness the journey of Slade, a Clerk in the employment of Mr. Clay, to Vermont, at the time of the last election of U. S. Senator in that State, receiving more than $1000 as a compensation for distributing laws, *a part of which he never delivered,* while his pay as Clerk was going on at home. Witness the journeys to Kentucky of Mr. Clay himself on the eve of her elections, and his electioneering speeches before the people. Witness the thousands of misrepresentations and falsehoods, sent from Washington, under the official frank of members of Congress, before the late election in this State. Witness the official misrepresentations and falsehoods of the War Department, relative to the trial and execution of the six mutineers at Mobile during the last war, and the attempt to impose the lie on the people, that the time of service of those mutineers and deserters had expired. Witness the circulation, from Washington, of the most unfair and unjust attacks upon the character of Gen. Jackson—the gross perversions of his views, and the most calumnious misrepresentations of his conduct, prepared under the eye of the Cabinet, profusely circulated by members of Congress, the confidential agents and advisers of the administration, who, for these purposes, have prostituted their official franks.

Having shewn, 1st, the objection to Mr. Adams on account of his political doctrines; 2d, on account of the manner of his election; and 3d, an account of the conduct of his administration; the question presents itself,—*Why is he entitled to the support of Republicans?* There are those, who contend that, being still a republican, Mr. Adams ought to be considered the republican candidate. To such, it is a sufficient answer to say that Mr. Adams bore testimony, in his first official message to Congress, against continuing the former political distinctions, and his policy has ever since been to break down the republican unity by creating local parties in the various sections of the Union. While he has professed a wish to do away the asperities of party, he has encouraged and countenanced the proscription and persecution of men of the old republican family: he has, in fact, merged all distinctions of principle, and made the question of opposition or support of his measures and his re-election, the dividing line between the parties. His partisans and retainers have allowed no freedom of opinion in discussing public men and measures—they have tolerated neither opposition nor neutrality, but required unequivocal approbation of all measures, right or wrong—they have revived the exploded doctrine that "the King can do no wrong;" and by a system of favoritism to flatterers and fawning sycophants, and of persecution of all others, they have attempted to force this doctrine on the people. It is evident, therefore, that as a republican, Mr. Adams has no claims on the old republican party for support.

Nor has he, on the score of personal pretensions, greater claims on the suffrages of the people, than thousands of others. He has been better paid for his services than any other man. In less than eight years he received about $120,000, being at the rate of $15,000 per year; and for services during two years, including the last year of the war, when he was uttering the reproach that our government was "feeble and penurious," he received from $40,000 to $65,000, much of it contrary to law, and in dereliction of patriotism. As he has received a higher compensation, so it has been alleged that his talents and qualifications are superior to those of other men. We look in vain to any acts of his present administration for evidence of those superior talents and qualifications. True it is, he received much of his education in a foreign land, near the courts of hereditary princes; true it is, that his father presented a bill of charges for a part of the education of his minor son while abroad, which was disallowed by Congress: but we, as republicans, cannot yield to the opinion that a princely education in and near the despotic courts of foreign governments, better qualifies the statesman and the patriot, than the plainer modes of education in our own country.

Would the friends of Mr Adams claim for him support as the republican candidate, why do they contemn the republican usages in electing a republican President? Why do they call, in aid of his re-election, the support of the enemies to republican principles? It cannot be pretended that at any time Mr. Adams has been the favorite of any considerable portion of the republican party out of New-England: and whatever may have been the case previous to the last election, it will not now be pretended that he is the choice of the republicans of New-Hampshire. With all the array of sectional prejudices which has been brought to bear on this question, it must be admitted that not one republican voter in six, in this State, now favors the election of Mr. Adams. Heretofore it has been deemed factious in the minority of any party to unite with the opponents of that party to defeat the voice of a majority: the punishment of all unprincipled men has awaited those who have assisted to "divide and conquer" by means like these. The public indignation has long pointed at those who, by treachery, have wounded their own cause in the house of its friends. The "republican friends of Mr. Adams," if, indeed, there be any republicans left in this State who are still determined to adhere to him, must either admit that their conduct is factious in supporting a candidate against the wishes of a large majority of the republican party, or, waiving all pretensions as republicans, they must identify themselves with that party now supporting Mr. Adams in this State, which has always been opposed to republicans. And if the doctrine of amalgamation which is now so fashionable with the Adams party, be indeed adopted—if there be now no difference either in the *principles* or the *merits* of those who were formerly designated by the names of federalists and republicans—why continue to claim as a merit that a candidate for office has been formerly a republican? why do federalists keep in the back ground, and put forward before the public none but those formerly called republicans? why did the administration party, whose meetings before the last election were composed of at least four-fifths federalists, nominate a ticket for Governor, Counsellors and Senators, exclusively of the men who had acted with the republicans? why do the federalists make an array of republican names as the supporters of Mr. Adams in this State, and in all cases, where they can be found, elect delegates to the Adams Conventions, men who call themselves republicans? If there is no difference in the parties, why do *they* make the distinction? If they do not consider there is still a difference, why do they make a difference in the selection of their candidates? Base and degrading must be that duplicity, that hypocrisy, which, while it insists on the oblivion of former party distinctions, keeps up those very distinctions, doing voluntary penance to the principles it hates by nominating only those men as candidates for office, who formerly professed the doctrines hated, but are now ready to become traitors to those doctrines, to conciliate the favor of their former opponents! Such is the present degraded condition of the party adhering to the fortunes of John Q. Adams—nay, such is the double degradation to which Mr. Adams himself is reduced!

The shameless effrontery with which men, high in office, have exercised not only their individual influence, but the influence of their official patronage to control the State elections, finds no parallel in this country. The conduct of Henry Clay, the first Cabinet officer of President Adams, having been as barefaced and shameless, as it is alarming and revolting to the friends of free elections, challenges the public reprobation. It has been urged by his friends that the arduous duties of his office have affected his health. If so, there is the less excuse for his conduct; for it may, in truth, be alleged, that his electioneering efforts alone would have been sufficient for the labors of any one man. Indeed we have good reason to believe that the subject of the next election has almost exclusively occupied his attention. Why was the British trade with the West-Indies lost to the United States—lost, too, purely from neglect because the Executive has since offered to take the precise terms proffered by the British government? It was lost, because Mr. Clay, after a minister had been appointed instead of taking a little time to write his instructions, was spending that time in making electioneering harangues at barbecue dinners to influence the elections in Kentucky. Mr. Clay has pursued his system of electioneering with an "ardor, an art, and a skill" hitherto unprecedented: he seems determined "rather to annihilate heaven and earth, than fail in carrying his point." His most extraordinary effort, was the last of which the public have any account, to wit: his dinner speech at Baltimore; in which he whose very life forbids the idea of morality and religion—he who deliberately attempted, even since he held his present office, to take the life of a Senator, for the exercise of the liberty of speech guaranteed by the Constitution—publicly invokes the Deity, and puts up the prayer: "If, indeed, we have incurred the Divine displeasure, and it be necessary to chastise this people with the rod of His vengeance, I would humbly prostrate myself before Him and implore His mercy to visit our favored land, with WAR, with PESTILENCE, with FAMINE, with any scourge other than *military* rule, or a blind and heedless enthusiasm for mere *military* renown"!

In this mixture of shocking impiety and madness, it is but too plain that Mr. Clay's objection to Gen. Jackson now, has the same moving cause as had his hostility to Mr. Adams prior to the latter part of 1824—it is HIMSELF, and not his country, that called forth his vehemence and zeal. In the anticipated failure of Mr. Adams and himself, he sees the triumph of the People over the cause of the unnatural and unholy Coalition; he sees his own prospects, his only hope of arriving at the highest office in the Republic in his own marked line of "safe precedents," forever blasted. But

> Is there not some chosen curse,
> Some hidden thunder in the stores of heaven,
> Red with uncommon wrath, to blast the man

who would rather that any curse—that even the three direst calamities that can be named, should fall on his whole country, than that he should fail to carry his point!

It was Mr. Clay, personally, who first raised the outcry of "Military Chieftain," as applied to the candidate of the people—it was Mr. Clay who was foremost in creating an alarm: and it is Mr. Clay and his creatures who have attempted not only to strip the hero of his laurels, but have conjured from the abodes of infamy, by all the ingenuity of fraud and falsehood, the materials to deceive and alarm the people. Therefore are we, on this occasion, justified in naming the most formidable, the most persevering, the most bitter and vindictive enemy of Jackson.

The term "Military Chieftain" will apply to any civilian as well as to Gen. Jackson. There is something due to him on the score of military renown; but, like WASHINGTON, more is due to JACKSON, that he is an honest man, an inflexible patriot and republican, a man of sound and ripe judgment, of excellent discrimination, and of practical knowledge of the genius and spirit of our free institutions, than to any mere military exploit. Who can fail to admire the honest soldier, who has fought the battles of his country, whether in poverty or affluence? Is there any danger that these shall have too much of our sympathy? Is there danger of him who, regardless of life and propty, has fought and bled for the liberties of his country, that he will turn traitor to the very freedom and independence he has assisted to establish? Rather should we not suspect the patriotism of the mere civilian, who, forever fed and pampered on the public treasury, has yet never been satisfied with the quality or the amount of the feeding? Shall we reject, as a dangerous "Military Chieftain," him who fed upon acorns, who pledged his whole estate, his own life, for his country when that country was in danger; and prefer him who, while his country was bleeding at every pore, was receiving double outfits and salaries, and at the same time uttering the reproach, that our government was "feeble and penurious"?

The character of Gen. Jackson is not such as to bear comparison with that of any dangerous "Military Chieftain." The genius of our Constitution, not less than the intelligence and virtue of the people, which constitute the stamina of that Constitution, forbid the idea of danger from any military man. The President, in no case, personally leads our armies; and if he did lead them, they are a body of enlightened freemen not less than interested than all others to preserve our civil institutions. If the muskets could be wrested from the hands of our yeomanry, as they have been under despotic governments—if, after they are thus wrested, the command, even of so small a standing army as twenty thousand men should be given to any man—there would be more real danger of that man, than there ever can be of a President of the United

States, surrounded as he must be with all those counteracting checks which cannot fail to foreclose every avenue to encroachment on the people's rights.

But it is not military men who have been the most dangerous men: it is true, before the light of knowledge was extensively diffused, military men have been usurpers: A Bonaparte has trodden over the liberties of mankind; but it was such "practised statesmen" as Mirabeau, and Danton, and Marat, and Robespierre who "destroyed the democratic party" in France, by "joining with it and urging it on" in headlong enthusiasm, till the people became sick of self-government and ready to yield it into the hands of a "Military Chieftain" as the only means of safety. So and this country, there is more danger to our civil liberties from the artifices of one such man as John Q. Adams or Henry Clay, ready to stretch the Constitution to any dimensions, so it may suit their purposes of patronage; ready to seize on any precedent as a pretext, and to do any violence to right and justice, even on mistaken precedents; than from the combined efforts, in that capacity, of all the military men that have lived, now live, or will live in this country for a century.

But our object is not simply to present a question of individual preference in the choice of candidates for President. It is to prevent the recurrence in the next election of that state of things, which, at the last election, took the choice of President from the hands of the people, and placed it in the hands of a minority of a House of Representatives, scarcely one in twenty of whom were chosen by the people with a view of being called upon to decide that question. It is important that we have a good man and a sound patriot to be our Chief Magistrate; but it is more important that the man, whoever he may be, should be the choice of the people. It has been the constant object of the few, the vindictive Aristocracy, to frustrate the wishes of the people; and especially of that portion of the people which, in trying times, rallies under the standard of republicanism. This party now knows that ANDREW JACKSON, as was THOMAS JEFFERSON in the great contest of 1800, is the candidate of the Republican party; and hence the desire to amalgamate with the Aristocracy a sufficient number from the republican ranks, to place the power in their hands. Hence the desperate efforts of Mr. Adams, Mr. Clay, Mr. Webster and their friends, to destroy old political distinctions, inviting men of all parties to their standard, calling in the aid of sectional prejudice, and on all unprincipled men, to form an union assimilating to that formed by Aaron Burr twenty-eight years ago.

Despairing of all means to prevent a choice, as was prevented four years ago, and aided by the immense means and patronage in their hands, the most daring and desperate efforts have been made, are now making, and will continue to be made by the Coalition, to prevent the election of ANDREW

JACKSON. Believing that the great mass of the people cannot be corrupted—believing that calumny has already done its worst, and that deception is fast passing away—believing that the character of Andrew Jackson as an honest man, as a pure and incorruptible patriot, as a prudent, discreet and sagacious statesman, cannot be shaken—knowing that a great majority of the people are firmly attached to the principles of the revolution—we have full faith that the cause of the people, the cause of truth and freedom, WILL PREVAIL.

WILLIAM BADGER, *President.*

FRANCIS N. FISK, *Secretary.*

THOMAS E. SAWYER, DUDLEY S. PALMER, *Assistant Secretaries.*

Concord, June 12, 1828.

2

The Virginia Address (Richmond, 1828)

As with the previous document, this address was the product of a state convention, this time of John Quincy Adams's supporters. (Adams had come in a distant second to William H. Crawford in Virginia in the election of 1824, but ahead of both Jackson and Clay.) The document is notable for its extensive defense of the president against the distortions and calumnies of his opponents; its admission that there were policy differences in the Adams ranks, but that those were less significant than the "offences committed by General Jackson, against the most sacred principles of our Government"; and, finally, the assertion that it was they, Adams's supporters, not the Jacksonians, who were fighting to preserve "republican simplicity and virtue" against "military pomp and glory." The quality, character, and background of leadership was what counted if the Republic was to go on, not minor differences of opinion over a few specific policies. Despite these arguments, Virginia voted substantially for Jackson in 1828 and 1832.

A Convention of Delegates, appointed by Public Meetings in the several Counties of the Commonwealth of Virginia, for the purpose of adopting measures to prevent the election of GENERAL JACKSON to the Presidency, assembled, to the number of 220, in the Capitol, in the city of Richmond, on Tuesday the 8th of January. The Convention, being organized, proceeded to the discharge of the interesting duty for which it had assembled, and continued to sit, from day to day, deliberating on, and maturing, the requisite measures, until Saturday, the 12th, when the Committee appointed to prepare an Address, (comprising several of the ablest and most eminent men in the State,) reported the following ADDRESS and Resolutions, which, having been read through, were unanimously adopted as follows:

To the People of Virginia.

Having been delegated, by those who oppose the election of Andrew Jackson as President of the United States, and having assembled in the City of Richmond, pursuant to our appointment, and formed an Electoral Ticket, we feel it due to ourselves, to those who deputed us, and to our country, to submit a brief exposition of our views on the very interesting subject which has brought us together.

It is no ordinary occasion, which, at this inclement season of the year, has brought so many of us from our business and our homes. We believed that the dearest interests of our country were at stake; that her character, her peace and happiness, and even the permanence of her free institutions, were in peril. We feared the most pernicious consequences from the election of General Jackson, and we have come to consult about the means of averting this calamity from our country. We believe that the only means of effecting this great object is the re-election of the present Chief Magistrate, and have formed an Electoral Ticket for that purpose, which we earnestly recommend to the support of the People of Virginia.

We know that many of you strongly disapprove [of] some of the leading measures of the present Administration,—have not confidence in it, and would be exceedingly unwilling to sanction the principles of construction applied by the present Chief Magistrate to the Constitution of the United States. But we do not perceive, in these circumstances, any sufficient reason for withholding your support from the ticket we have recommended. We ourselves are not agreed upon these subjects. While some disapprove these measures, want confidence in the Administration, and are unwilling to sanction the principles of construction adopted by the President,—most of us approve the general course of the Administration, have confidence in its virtue, its patriotism, its wisdom, and see nothing to condemn in the President's interpretation of the Federal Constitution. Yet we do not discuss among ourselves, and we will not discuss before you, the grounds of this difference. We waive such discussion, as wholly inappropriate, and postpone it to the time when there may be some choice offered us, that might be influenced by it. Now there is none such. We are left to the alternative of choosing between Jackson and Adams: and however we may differ in opinion as to the merits of the latter, we heartily concur in giving him a decided preference over his competitor. The measures which some disapprove in the present Administration, none would hope to see amended under that of General Jackson: the distrust in the present Chief Magistrate, entertained by some, is lost in the comparison with that which all feel in his competitor—and the Constitution, which we would preserve from the too liberal interpretation of Mr. Adams, we would yet more zealously defend against the destroying hand of his rival.

While, however, we decline a discussion of those subjects, on which we differ in opinion, and pretermit any general vindication of the Chief Magistrate, his Cabinet, or his measures, we cannot pass unnoticed some topics connected with the last election, and some acts of the Administration, in relation to which, we think, the public mind has been greatly abused.

The friends of General Jackson have confidently held him up, as the favorite of the People—have insisted that, in the last election, his plurality of votes proved him to be the choice of the nation—and have bitterly complained, that *that* choice was improperly disappointed by the Representatives in Congress.

Never was there a more direct appeal to those prejudices and passions, which, on all occasions, the good should disdain, and the wise should repress; never was a complaint more utterly ungrounded; and never one more characteristic of that disregard for the Constitution, which has been manifested on more occasions than one, when its provisions stood in the way of General Jackson's march.

Whether General Jackson is the People's favorite, is to be tested by the event, not assumed as the basis of the pending election. That his plurality of votes proved him to be the choice of the nation at last election, we confidently deny. It may, perhaps, be found, upon examination, that, while General Jackson had a plurality of electoral votes, Mr. Adams had a plurality of votes at the polls; and we are confident, that if Mr. Crawford and Mr. Clay had been withdrawn from the canvass, and the contest had been single-handed between General Jackson and Mr. Adams, the election would have resulted as it has done, in the choice of Mr. Adams.

But this is not the light in which this question deserves consideration. The minds of the People ought not to be influenced by such extraneous considerations; and above all, the principles of our Constitution ought not to be abused, by admitting, for a moment, that the plurality of votes given to General Jackson, should have governed the choice of the House of Representatives. We do not mean to say, that a proper respect for the wishes of the nation, fairly ascertained, ought not always to be observed by its Representatives. But we do say, that the present Chief Magistrate holds his seat by the will of the People of the United States, regularly expressed, in the only way in which an expression of that will has any authority. They have willed, in the most solemn form—in the form of a Constitution, which they declare shall be the supreme law of the land—that a plurality of votes shall not constitute an election; that, when there is such plurality, the Representatives shall elect, voting by States—thus withdrawing from the People that equality of influence which is given them in the first vote, and transferring it to the States in the second. This provision of our Constitution is in the true spirit which pervades the whole of it, and which marks it the result of a conference between States, surrendering in part, and retaining in part, their political equality. Shall this spirit be appealed from, on every occasion in which it was intended to soothe and conciliate, and the spirit of faction be invoked, to expose our magistrates to unjust prejudice, and bring our institutions into discredit? These things are revolutionary in their tendency, and ought to be discouraged.

Of like character is the complaint against the Kentucky delegation, for disregarding the instructions of their Legislature. We have too much respect for the Legislature of Kentucky to suppose that they meant to bind the delegation by an instruction. We can only suppose that they meant to furnish the best information in their power, of the opinions of the People on a question which had never been submitted to them. Such information was entitled to the respect due to intelligent opinion, and no more. It was not the constitutional organ through which the will of the People was to be conveyed to the Representative. The Representatives in Congress were directly responsible to their Constituents, not to the Legislature. And an attempt of the Legislature to control the immediate Representatives of the People. would be a usurpation upon the rights of the People—an act, which, instead of deserving obedience, or even respect, required resistance and even reprobation. The faithful Representative will obey the instructions of his constituents whenever constitutionally given. He will pay a respectful attention to their wishes, and every evidence of their wishes. But, when not bound by instruction, he will look beyond the imperfect evidences of their will, informally conveyed, he will rest upon the conclusions of his own mind, formed from the best lights he can obtain; will consult his country's good, and firmly meet the responsibility of those acts, he deems proper for its attainment. This we believe the Kentucky delegation did. They were not instructed—they did not choose to shelter themselves from responsibility, under the cover of a legislative recommendation; consulting their own judgments, they preferred the man thought most capable of advancing the interest of his country; and there is no question, that Virginia then concurred in the opinion, and approved the act.

This vote, which, if honestly given, is an affair chiefly between the Representative and his Constituents, would not have been obtruded on your attention, had it not been connected with a charge of grave import, made upon the purity of the election, impeaching the integrity of the Chief Magistrate of the Nation, and the first member of his Cabinet. This charge, in its strongest form, imports that, at the last election, the vote of the Kentucky delegation was in the market, for the highest bidder; that it was offered to one candidate, and, being refused by him, was sold to the other; and that the consideration of the vote, was the office of Secretary of State, bestowed on Mr. Clay. If this were true, we should not hesitate to affirm, that it stamps infamy on the characters of the guilty, and renders them forever unworthy of public trust.

This charge, not so strongly, however, as has been here stated, was made, for the fist time, pending the Presidential election. It was promptly met, and challenged by Mr. Clay, and deserted by its supporters. They rallied again, after the election, gave it a form somewhat varied, drew to its aid some imposing circumstances, and, at last, gave it the public sanction of Gen. Jackson's name. Mr. Clay again publicly denied it, called for the proof, and challenged inquiry. No proof has appeared to sustain it, no inquiry has been instituted, and now, in all its phases, it stands reprobated, by a body of proof, so strong and so convincing, as to require, from the least charitable, its open disavowal, and, from the most suspicious, a candid acknowledgment, that they have done injustice in even thinking it probable.

It may not be unworthy of notice, as one of the means by which the public mind has been prejudiced and inflamed, that opinions, the most offensive to a Republican People, have been unwarrantably and uncandidly inferred from some of the President's communications to Congress, and gravely imputed to him, as doctrines in his political creed. He has, on one occasion, not perhaps with strict rhetorical propriety, used the expression, "palsied by the will of our constituents"—in reference to duties enjoined by the Constitution.

This phrase has been torn from its context, misinterpreted, and used as the authority upon which the President is charged with the heresy, that a Representative owes no obligation to the will of his constituents. On another occasion, incautiously taking it for granted that every one would understand that the high obligation of an oath was derived from Heaven, he has again, perhaps, without much felicity of phrase, made an obvious, though not avowed reference to his oath of office, as imposing an obligation above all human law—and this reference is tortured into a public avowal of the odious doctrine, that his political power was *jure divino.* If these had been the taunts and the railing of anonymous newspaper scribblers, they would have been deemed unworthy of this public notice. But when such charges are seriously made and reiterated, by men holding high stations in the Government, and exercising some influence over public opinion, they cannot be too strongly condemned.

Mr. Adams, it is said, is friendly to a regulation of the tariff of duties, with a view to the encouragement of American manufactures, and this is clamorously urged against him, as a serious objection, by those who support the election of Gen. Jackson.

This objection seems to have been treated, before the public, as if Mr. Adams were the founder of a new and odious doctrine, and the father of the measures to which it had given birth. Nothing can be further from the truth. Not a single act of the Government, on this subject, has its date within his administration. And so far is he from being the founder of the doctrine, that it is traced to the earliest and purest times of the Republic, avowed and acted upon from the foundation of the Government, when the Father of his Country presided over its destinies. Before the adoption of the Federal Constitution, the power of regulating commerce, and imposing duties on imports, belonged to the State Governments; and such of them, as deemed it expedient, so regulated their tariff of duties as to give encouragement to their manufactures. The Constitution transferred to the Federal Government, by express provision, the power of regulating commerce, and of imposing duties. An act, passed at the first session of the first Congress, held under the Constitution, advocated by James Madison, and signed by George Washington, on the 20th of July, 1789, contains the first tariff of duties on imported goods laid by the General Government, and its preamble recites, that it was "necessary for the support of Government, for the discharge of the debts of the "United States, *and the encouragement and protection of manufactures.*" This doctrine was acted upon, by every succeeding Administration, by the elder Adams, by Jefferson, by Madison, and Monroe. The policy of protecting and encouraging manufactures was recommended by them all; the tariff was increased from time to time, with a view to that object; and yet, no champion of the Constitution, though many and bold and able there were, always at their posts, ever challenged the authors of these measures, as invaders of constitutional ground; until, during the administration of the last President, when the fathers of the Constitution, having most of them retired from the field of action, a member from Virginia suggested, in Congress, the want of constitutional power to give protection to manufactures.

On this question we forbear to enter the field of argument; and content ourselves with saying, that the power of Congress to regulate the tariff of duties, so as to give protection and encouragement to agriculture, manufactures, commerce, and navigation, cannot be denied, without denying to the letter of the Constitution its plain import, and to its spirit its most obvious and essential attributes; without affirming that those who have administered the Government, from its foundation to the present day, have either misunderstood the charter of their powers, or wantonly and habitually violated it; without coming to the extraordinary conclusion, either that a power which existed in the State Governments, and was frequently exercised by them, before the adoption of the Federal Constitution, was annihilated by the secret and magical influence of that instrument, or that such power does not properly pertain to the Legislature of any free People.

The exercise of this power is necessarily referred to the sound discretion of Congress, to be justly and impartially employed for the common benefit of all—not to be perverted to the purpose of advancing the interest of one class of the community, or of one part of the country, at the expense of another; and, whatever some of us may think as to its abuses under a former administration, or of the danger of such abuses under the present, all must concur in the opinion, that the remedy is not to be found in the election of General Jackson; but, if sought at all, should be looked for in the vigilance and exertions of faithful and able Senators and Representatives in Congress.

The opinions of Mr. Adams, and his recommendations to Congress, in relation to internal improvement, are unpopular in Virginia, and have been urged against him with much earnestness, and perhaps with some effect, even though it cannot, with any color of reason, be contended, that his competitor, Gen. Jackson, is not exposed to precisely the same objection. We do not vindicate these opinions, or discuss them, because they fall within the interdict we have imposed on ourselves—we differ in opinion concerning them. But we will remind you, that these opinions, whatever may be their merit, have produced but few and unimportant acts, during the present Administration: and we will avail ourselves of the occasion to appeal to the good sense and good feeling of Virginia, and invoke its influence in tempering the asperity of party politics, and in securing to every subject of national interest, a deliberate and candid consideration. We beg leave also to remind them, that the questions of Constitutional law, and State policy, connected with this subject, are important, delicate, and of acknowledged difficulty; that there are arrayed on either side of them, Statesmen of approved patriotism and talent, whose opinions should be examined with great consideration, and whose measures, if deemed wrong, after being judged with candor, should be opposed with reason, not with passion—with firmness, not with violence;—that those among us, who deny the Constitutional power, and condemn the policy, should entitle our doctrines to respect, by the fairness of our views, and the force of our reasoning, and give weight to our opposition, by its temper and its dignity; while those who affirm the power, and approve the policy, should observe the most respectful deference for the opinions of the many and the wise, who differ from them; should consult the public interest and tranquility, by confining their measures to objects of acknowledged and general interest, by infusing into them a spirit of the most exact justice; and by observing, in all things, scrupulous care in the exercise of a power so delicate, and so much controverted.

Thus far, we have endeavored to correct error and disarm prejudice, that reason might be left free to estimate fairly the present Administration, and its principal measures. We have offered no panegyric on the present Chief Magistrate;—we cheerfully leave you to estimate the value of his long and varied public services, his great experience, his talent, his learning, and his private virtues,—and to set off against them, whatever your fancy or your judgment may find to blame, in his private or public life. When you have done this—reflect on the character of the office you are about to fill—inquire what feelings, what temper, what talent, what acquirements, what habits, are best suited to the discharge of its high duties; and then carefully compare John Q. Adams with Andrew Jackson, in reference to the great question, Which of them is best qualified for the first office in the nation—which most likely to preserve to us the distinguished blessings we enjoy—from which is most danger to be apprehended to our peace and happiness, our lives and liberties?

It is not in wantonness that we speak; but, in the sadness of our hearts, we are compelled to declare, that, while we yield our confidence to the present Chief Magistrate in very different degrees, we are unanimous and unhesitating in the opinion that Andrew Jackson is altogether unfit for the Presidency, and that his election would be eminently dangerous; that, while we cheerfully accord to him his full share of the glory which renders the anniversary of the 8th of January a day of joy and triumph to our land, we must, in the most solemn manner, protest against a claim to civil rule, founded exclusively upon military renown; and avow that nothing has occurred in the history of our country so much calculated to shake our confidence in the capacity of the People for self-government, as the efforts which have been made, and are yet making, to elevate to the first office in the nation, the man, who, disobeying the orders of his superiors, trampling on the Laws and Constitution of his country, sacrificing the liberties and lives of men, has made his own arbitrary will the rule of his conduct.

In stating an opinion so unfavorable to a distinguished man, who has rendered valuable services to his country, a proper respect for ourselves and for you, requires that we should declare the reasons which compel us to withhold our confidence from him.

Capacity for civil affairs, in a country like ours, where the road to preferment is open to merit, in every class of society, is never long concealed, and seldom left in retirement. General Jackson has lived beyond the age of 60 years, and was bred to the profession best calculated to improve and display the faculties which civil employments require; but the history of his public life, in these employments, is told in a few brief lines—on a single page of his biography. He filled, successively, for very short periods, the office of Member of the Tennessee Convention, which formed their State Constitution; Representative and Senator in Congress; Judge of the Supreme Court of Tennessee; and again, Senator in Congress of the United States. Here was ample opportunity for distinction, if he possessed the talent, taste, and application, suited for civil eminence. But he resigned three, and passed through all of these stations, acknowledging his unfitness in two instances—manifestly feeling it in all—and leaving no single act, no trace, behind, which stamps his qualifications above mediocrity.

For civil government—and in no station more emphatically than in that of President of the United States—a well-governed temper is of admitted importance. General Jackson's friends lament the impetuosity of his, and all the world has evidence of its fiery misrule.

To maintain peace and harmony in the delicate relations existing between the Government of the Union and the various State Governments and our Confederacy, requires a courtesy and forbearance in their intercourse, which no passion should disturb. Let the spirit of domination displayed in General Jackson's celebrated letter to Governor Rabun, warn us of the danger of committing to his keeping this precious deposite—sacred to the union of our Republics, and to the freedom of mankind.

Military men should never be allowed to forget, that the obligation to obey being the sole foundation of the authority to command, they should inculcate subordination, not by precept only, but by example; that profound respect for the Laws and Constitution of their country, is an indispensable guarantee of their worthiness to be entrusted with the sword which is drawn to defend them; that they should lose no fit occasion for manifesting that respect, by practical illustrations of the principle, sacred in every well ordered Republic, which proclaims the military subordinate to the civil power; that mercy even to the guilty, and humanity always to the conquered and the captive, are part of the law of God and man, found in every civilized code, written in every human heart, and indispensable to the true glory of the Hero.

General Jackson has been unmindful of these truths. Though he has enjoined subordination by precept, and enforced it by authority, he has not recommended it by example. He has offered indignity to the Secretary of War, in the very letter which assigned his reasons for disobeying an order to disband his troops; he has placed his own authority and opposition to that of the War Department, by a general order, forbidding the officers of his command to obey the orders of that Department, unless they passed through the channel which he had chosen to prescribe; and he disobeyed the orders of the Government in his military operations in the Spanish territory.

He has been unmindful of the subordination of military to civil power, and has violated the law and the Constitution, by declaring martial law at New Orleans, and maintaining it, of his own arbitrary will, for more than two months after the enemy had been beaten and repulsed, and all reasonable apprehension of their return had ceased; by surrounding the hall of the Louisiana Legislature with an armed force, and suspending their deliberations; by seizing the person of Louaillier, a free citizen of Louisiana, and member of their Legislature, and bringing him to trial before a military tribunal, for having the boldness to denounce, through the public press, the continued arbitrary reign of martial law; by disapproving the acquittal of Louaillier upon his trial, when, to have condemned and executed him, would have exposed the actors in the fatal tragedy to the legal pains of death; by suspending, of his own arbitrary will, the writ of *habeas corpus,* when the Legislature of Louisiana had refused to suspend it on his application, when no law of Congress authorized it, and no imminent danger pleaded its apology; by arresting and imprisoning Judge Hall for issuing the writ of *habeas corpus* to relieve Louaillier from illegal confinement, and arresting and imprisoning two other officers of the law, for appealing to civil process against his tyrannic rule; by the arrest, trial, and execution, of six militia men, who were guilty of no other offence than the assertion of their lawful right to return home, after their legal term of service had expired; by organizing a corps of volunteer militia, and appointing its officers, without any warrant for so doing, and against the provisions of the Constitution, which expressly reserve the appointment of the officers of the militia to the States respectively; and by making war upon the Spanish Territory, seizing and holding Spanish posts, in violation of the order of his Government, and whilst peace existed between Spain and the United States.

That mercy and humanity may unite with the offended Law and Constitution, in accusing General Jackson of being unmindful of their voice, and in refusing to his laurel crown the rays of true glory will be acknowledged by impartial posterity, when they review the history of his Indian campaigns, and especially when they read the stories of the cold-blooded massacre at the Horseshoe; of the decoyed and slaughtered Indians at St. Mark's; of the wanton and unexampled execution of Ambrister, an Englishman, found fighting, it is true, in the ranks of the Seminoles, but taken prisoner, tried, doomed to a milder punishment, and executed by order of the commanding General, against the sentence of the tribunal appointed by himself; and of the still more injured Arbuthnot, another Briton, not bearing arms at all, only found among the warring Indians, a trader, and an advocate for peace.

We have done with this sickening catalogue. You have now a brief summary of the evidence, on the authority of which we regard General Jackson as wholly disqualified for the Presidency, and look to the prospect of his election with the most gloomy forebodings.

You think, perhaps, we pay a poor compliment to the virtues of our People, and the strength of our institutions, by indulging in apprehensions of danger from the encroachments of military power, in the youth and vigor of our Republic, and in the midst of profound peace. We should, indeed, do great injustice to the virtue of our People, the circumstances of our country, and the value of our Government, if we indulged in the idle fear, that an open attack upon our liberties, made with any military force, which General J. could probably command in the course of his administration, would bring us under the yoke of his power. These are not our apprehensions; we would bid a proud defiance to his power, if he should so dare our liberties. Nor will we do him the injustice to charge his ambition with any designs, at present, on the liberties of his country, or withhold our acknowledgment, that, if they were assailed by others, we believe he would promptly and boldly draw his sword to defend them.

But we have no security for the continuance of peace, in whatsoever hands the Government may be placed: and it is not unreasonable to think, that, in the hands of a man of military pride and talent, and of ungovernable temper, the danger of war will be increased. A foreign war may come, may rage with violence, and find General Jackson at the head of the civil government, and commander-in-chief of the land and naval forces. Dissentient views among the States may arise: controversies grow up between the State and Federal authorities, as dissensions and controversies have heretofore arisen; and who, then, we pray you, can answer for the consequences of that spirit which said to Governor Rabun, *When I am in the field, you have no authority to issue a military order?* Reflect on this question, we beseech you—on the peculiar structure of our Government; on the collisions of opinion, and the threatened collisions of action, both in peace and war, which have already occurred between the State and Federal authorities—and then tell us, whether the fear is altogether visionary, that the first foreign war, seriously waged against the United States, with General Jackson their chief, would bring danger of civil discord, dissolution of the Union, and death to the hopes of every free government in the world.

We say nothing of the danger of civil discord, even when no foreign war should afflict us—though the retrospect of a few short years would teach us that such danger is not imaginary—and that the slightest want of tact, in its management, the least indulgence of temper, on the part of the chief Magistrate, might inflame the whole nation, and light the funeral pile of freedom.

There are dangers of another kind. If we are correct in the detail of offences committed by General Jackson, against the most sacred principles of our Government, what will be the moral effect of the direct sanction given to these offences, by rewarding the offender with the first honor of the nation? Can we preserve our love and reverence for institutions which we suffer to be violated, not only without censure, but with applause? Will not our affections and our veneration be transferred from the despised Laws and Constitution, to the honored Hero who has abused them—from republican simplicity and virtue, to military pomp and glory? Will you not, in fine, by such example, lay the sure foundation of that moral depravity, and admiration of arms, which must soon reduce us to the condition in which Greece was enslaved by Alexander: Rome, by C\\ı,37\\sar; England, by Cromwell; France, by Bonaparte; and in which we will assuredly find some future Jackson, not too fastidious to accept the proffered crown, and erect a military despotism on the ruins of the last Republic?

We appeal to the People of Virginia, to say what there is in the present party politics, so alluring on the part of the Opposition, so frightful on the part of the Administration, as to seduce them to the fraternal embrace, or drive them under the protection, of such a man as Andrew Jackson? We ask an answer to this question, not from their offended pride, nor from the prejudice which attachment to party never fails to beget; but we ask it from their love of country, their love of truth and virtue; we ask it, after a deep and dispassionate consideration of the true state of the question; after a candid estimate of the little to be possibly gained by the rejection of Mr. Adams, the incalculable mischiefs which may probably attend the success of his rival. If you indulge the faint hope, that, under the Administration of General Jackson, the tribute which agriculture will pay for the encouragement of domestic industry and enterprise, will be somewhat lighter than at present—we ask you, first, whether the hope is not groundless? and next, whether it is wise to insist on enjoying the profits of your estates in the uttermost farthing of their fancied value, at the risk of having your free allodial lands converted into military tenures or fiefs of the crown? If you are fighting the battles of General Jackson, in this political contest, with the vain hope that victory will conquer from your adversaries some barren spot of constitutional ground—we ask whether you will wage such a war with your countrymen, at the hazard of laying all your conquests, and all your former possessions—the Constitution itself, and the freedom it was intended to protect—at the feet of a despot? This does not become the character of Virginians!

In the ancient state of political parties, when federalists and republicans contended for ascendancy, there was something in the great questions of foreign policy, in the leading principles of construction applied to the Constitution, bearing strongly on the essential character of the Government, and worthy of a generous struggle between the statesmen, who, on the one hand, sought to guard against a dissolution of the Union, by strengthening the Federal bond, and, on the other, endeavored to avert consolidation, by establishing more firmly the State authorities. But this state of things has passed away, and the feelings and doctrines to which it gave rise, though not entirely forgotten, are almost unknown in the party distinctions of the day. Federalists and republicans mingle together in the ranks of the Opposition—and, together, rally around the standard of the Administration. There will be no great principle of political doctrine to distinguish them, unless the Opposition, following too closely the footsteps of those who trample on the Laws and Constitution of the country, should give to the supporters of the Administration some claim to be the champions of civil rule and constitutional law. Shall our parties be hereafter founded on local interests, and marked by geographical boundaries, arraying the North against the South, the East against the West—losing the generous enthusiasm which is always inspired by a contest for principle, for honorable distinction, for pre-eminence in the service of our common country; and acquiring the bitterness of spirit, acrimony of feeling, narrow policy, and sordid views, which ever characterise the contests of men, striving, not for the promotion of the common good, but for the advancement of their own peculiar interests—and which must lead, inevitably, to the entire subjugation of the weaker party, or a dissolution of the Union?

We know well, that the People of Virginia will never countenance any such distinction. Their generous sacrifices in the cause of their country, their uniform devotion to civil liberty, and their noble daring in the defence of freedom, from whatever quarter assailed, is the sure guarantee that they will not be slow to follow where the path of duty leads; and on that guarantee we repose with confidence, that, in this hour of danger, sacrificing all minor considerations, they will go forth in their strength, and save the Temple of Liberty from pollution.

1. *Resolved,* That JOHN QUINCY ADAMS, of Massachusetts, be recommended to the People of the United States, as a fit person to be supported for the Office of President.

2. *Resolved,* That this Convention approve the nomination of RICHARD RUSH, of the State of Pennsylvania, for the Office of Vice President, made

by the Convention at Harrisburg, and recommend him to the People of Virginia as a fit person to be supported for that office.

3. *Resolved,* That the President of this Convention be requested to transmit a copy of the proceedings and address of this Convention to each of the gentlemen who have been nominated on the Electoral Ticket, and inform them of their several appointments.

4. *Resolved,* That the following persons be appointed a Central Corresponding Committee, with the authority to fill any vacancies which may occur within their own body, or in the Electoral Ticket in favor of the election of John Quincy Adams, as President of the United States, and Richard Rush as Vice President, viz: Judge William H. Cabell, Judge Dabney Carr, Judge John Coalter, Mr. Robert Stanard, Reverend John Kerr, General J B. Harvie, Mr. Peyton Randolph, Mr. John H. Pleasants, Mr. Charles Copland, Mr. Thomas Brockenbrough, Mr. E. W. Rootes, Mr. J. H. Eustace, Dr. Thomas Nelson.

5. *Resolved,* That the Corresponding Committees, which have been appointed by the meetings opposed to the election of General Jackson as President of the United States, in the various Counties and Corporations of this Commonwealth, constitute the Corresponding Committees of said Counties and Corporations, with authority to add to their numbers, and fill any vacancies which may occur in said Committees.

6. *Resolved,* That the Central Corresponding Committee be authorized to appoint corresponding committees in the several counties and corporations which have not appointed them; which committees shall have authority to exercise the same powers as those which have heretofore been appointed.

7. *Resolved,* That it be recommended to the Convention that each member should pay the sum of five dollars to the Secretaries, to be deposited in the Bank of Virginia to the credit of the Chairman of the Central Committee, to defray the expenses of printing and circulating the documents directed to be published by the Convention, and such other publications as may be thought advisable by the said Central Committee, for the purpose of distribution among the citizens of the Commonwealth, and all other incidental charges.

8. *Resolved,* That at least thirty thousand copies of the proceedings and address of this Convention be printed and circulated, under the direction of the Central Committee, through the several counties and corporations of the Commonwealth.

9. *Resolved,* That the Central Corresponding Committee be requested to publish, in pamphlet form, as many copies of the address of the Hon. Henry Clay, with the accompanying documents, as they may deem expedient, and that they cause to be published such other documents as, in their opinion,

will sustain the facts and principles set forth and the address of this Convention.

10. *Resolved,* That the Central Committee be requested to make to the officers of the Senate and House of Delegates who have attended upon this Convention during its session, such compensation as they may deem proper, to be paid out of the fund provided by this Constitution.

11. *Resolved,* That this Convention entertain feelings of unfeigned gratitude for the facilities offered, and the spirit of accommodation manifested, by both Houses of the Virginia Assembly and their officers, to this Convention, in the prosecution of their duties, and that the President be requested to tender the thanks of this Convention to both branches of the Assembly and their officers, for their kindness and liberality.

12. *Resolved,* That the Editors of the several newspapers printed in Virginia be requested to publish the proceedings of the Convention, together with their address to the People of Virginia, in their respective papers.

3

Proceedings of the Antimasonic Republican Convention of the State of Maine, Held at Hallowell, July 3rd & 4th, 1834. For the Nomination of a Candidate for Governor, "and the Transaction of Such Other Business as the Success of Anti-Masonry May Require" (Hallowell, Me., 1834)

The Antimasonic party operated largely in the Middle Atlantic and New England states. This pamphlet, produced by the party's state convention in Maine for the off-year election of 1834, typifies the style and substance of the group's assault on the dangers posed to the nation by the secret Masonic order and, in their view, the startling indifference of the major parties to those dangers. In similar fashion to the main parties that they criticized so strongly, the Antimasons feared that the Union was in sharp decline, its revolutionary "inheritance" now "wasted" and "squandered" by the actions of the petty and dangerous men running the nation. Also like the main parties, the Antimasons believed that the nation had to be purified of its internal dangers; their opponents had to be demonized because they were part of a vast conspiracy to bring down the republic; and the electoral process was the most effective way to solve the nation's difficulties.

Hallowell, July 3, 1834.

Agreeably to the call of the State Committee, delegates from different towns in the State of Maine, assembled at the town hall at 11 o'clock A.M. to organize the Anti-masonic State Convention . . .

Mr. Farwell from the committee to report a statement of facts relative to the abduction and murder of Wm. Morgan and the conduct of Masons in preventing the due execution of the laws against the offenders, made the following report, which was accepted.

The committee appointed to report a statement of facts relative to the abduction and murder of William Morgan, and the conduct of Masons in preventing the due execution of the laws against the offenders, ask leave to report the following statement, compiled from the judicial evidence which has been given in courts of Justice, and from well authenticated documents relative to those extraordinary transactions, by the Hon. Mr. Whittlesey of New York, and by him as chairman of a Committee reported to, and made part of the published proceedings of the United States Antimasonic Convention, held at Philadelphia Sept. 1830. Your Committee have full confidence in the authenticity of the facts stated, as they have been many times sworn to in Courts, and reportedly ascertained and stated by investigating committees, and have become matter of so well authenticated history that they will never hereafter be questioned. [See Whittlesey's Report.]

Mr. Gibbs, from the committee to report a short view of Freemasonry, showing its principles and tendency from the oaths and ceremonies of the institution, made the following Report, which was accepted.

The Committee appointed to report a short view of Freemasonry, shewing its principles and tendency from the oaths and ceremonies of the institution, ask leave to report.

By the aid of masonic writers we learn that all the Freemasonry now existing in the world emanated from the Lodge in the Apple-tree tavern in Charles street, Convent garden, London, where it assumed its speculative form and character on the 24th of June 1717—prior to which time there were societies of working masons, but they admitted none but actual craftsmen, and were styled masons.—So that *Freemasonry* did not exist prior to the above date. The pretensions of Freemasons to the great antiquity of their order are therefore false, and only intended for effect on the weak and ignorant.

This society has, until since 1826, enjoyed the countenance and favor of a large portion of the people of this country, who took upon trust, masonic professions of charity and benevolence. In the autumn of that year, a free citizen of New York, and a royal arch mason, bravely dared, for the benefit of posterity, to disclose to the world the secret abominations of Freemasonry. And for this offence, without suspicion or pretence of any other, masons of high standing in society kidnapped him, transported him 150 miles, confined him in a fort of the United States, and finally murdered him, or in masonic language "executed upon him the penalty of his obligations."

Some of the oaths, obligations and principles of masonry which led to, and justified the murder of Morgan, are presented in the following synopsis.

The entered Apprentice swears, that he will always hail and never reveal any part * * * * of the secrets of Freemasonry, which he has received, is about to receive, or may hereafter be instructed in, &c. The fellow craft swears, that he will support the constitution of the Grand Lodge—and "conform to all the by-laws, rules, and regulations of this or any other Lodge of which he may become a member"—And that he will obey all regular signs and summons, given, handed, sent or thrown to him by the hand of a brother fellow craft, &c.

The Master Mason swears, "I will not give the grand hailing sign of distress except I am in real distress &c. * * * and should I ever see that sign given, or hear the word accompanying it, and the person who gave it appearing to be in distress, I will fly to his relief at the risk of my life, should there be any greater probability of saving his life than losing my own. I will not speak evil of a brother master mason, neither behind his back, nor before his face, but will apprise him of all approaching danger, if in my power. "Furthermore do I promise and swear, that I will not violate the chastity of a master masons wife, mother, sister or daughter, I knowing them to be such, nor suffer it to be done by others, if in my power to prevent it. A master mason's secrets given to me in charge, and I knowing them to be such, shall remain as secure and inviolable in my breast as in his own, before communicated to me, murder and treason excepted, and they left at my own election."

The Mark Master swears to support the constitution of the General Grand Royal Arch Chapter of the United States of America, also the Grand Royal Arch Chapter of this State, under which this Lodge is held and conform to all the by-laws, rules and regulations of this or any other Lodge &c. That, I will obey all regular signs and summons, given, handed, sent or thrown to me from the hand of a brother Mark Master Mason, or from the body of a just and legally constituted Lodge of such, provided it be within the length of my cable-tow.

The Royal Arch Mason swears "I will aid and assist a companion Royal Arch Mason, when engaged in any difficulty, and espouse his cause so far as to extricate him from the same if in my power, *whether he be right or wrong.* I will promote a companion Royal Arch Mason's political preferment in preference to another of equal qualifications. A companion Royal Arch Mason's secrets given me in charge as such, and I knowing them to be such, shall remain as secure and inviolable in my breast as his own, *murder and treason not excepted.* All of which I most solemnly and sincerely promise and swear, with a firm and steadfast resolution to perform the same, without any *equivocation* or mental reservation in me whatever; binding myself under no less penalty than that of having my scull smote off, and my brains exposed to the scorching rays of the sun, should I ever knowingly or wilfully violate any part of this my solemn oath or obligation—So help me God and keep me steadfast in the performance of the same.

From the first obligation of the illustrious knight of the cross, the candidate receives under oath the following injunction: "Should you know another to violate any essential point of this obligation you will use your most decided endeavors by the blessing of God to bring such person to the strictest and most condign punishment, agreeably to the rules and usages of our ancient fraternity, and this by pointing him out to the world as an unworthy vagabond, BY DERANGING HIS BUSINESS, BY TRANSFERING HIS CHARACTER AFTER HIM WHEREVER HE MAY GO, AND BY EXPOSING HIM TO THE CONTEMPT OF THE WHOLE FRATERNITY, AND OF THE WORLD.

Besides the regular degrees, many honorary degrees, as they were called, are appended to the system. Among them is that of "Secret Monitor." The oath of this degree binds the candidate by express words 'to prefer a brother in business—to assist him in trade—and to warn him in making a good or bad bargain, according to circumstances, either by sign, grip, or word.' This degree has for its particular object the power to dupe the simple, who do not belong to the order, for the benefit of the crafty who do. To the oath of this and all the degrees are annexed penalties of the most sanguinary and ferocious character.

Such are some of the principles of masonry, expressed in the language of the craft, and proved to be genuine by a mass of testimony of various kinds, too clear to admit of the shadow of a doubt, and not denied by masons themselves. These obligations it will be perceived compel such as acknowledge them to passive obedience—to warn each other of *all* approaching danger—to conceal each other's crimes—to extricate each other from difficulty, right or wrong—to support each other's reputation in *all* cases—to oppose the interest, derange the business, and injure the reputation of unfaithful brethren—to sacrifice the traitors of Masonry—to give each other unjust preferences in trade and business over those who are not Masons, and to advance the brethren to political preferment.

And is it possible that reputable, discerning and virtuous men should adhere to such detestable principles? No: men of this description who were once masons, are silent seceders. The virtuous and enlightened of the craft, after having been duped into a few of the first degrees, abandon the lodge in disgust; and hundreds of this number have also had the moral courage *openly* to come out from the polluted thing, and pronounce it to be a cheat, thus leaving the ranks filled only with weak and wicked men,

> "Fit for treasons, stratagems and spoils."

And why should not the good abandon an institution, which has nothing to hold it together but its secrecy, and that now no more? "A virtuous mind cannot delight in secrecy. Its joy is in communion. We are sociable by nature. Our best affections and highest faculties equally indicate it. As social beings, if we discover useful facts, or important truths, we desire to communicate them to all who are susceptible of benefits from their application. As all the principles of science, charity, and religion are susceptible of beneficial application to the whole human race, good men and good governments will impose no artificial restriction upon their universal diffusion."

We charge Freemasonry with being opposed to free enquiry. Witness the thousand mobs and riots that have been excited by the craft to put down lectures and discussions on the subject. Witness the shameful subserviency and silence of the press. Witness the bitter persecution and slander to which all editors of antimasonic newspapers are doomed.

We charge masonry with having the power to counteract, by its secret organization, the salutary operation of the laws. And it will not be denied that this power has been repeatedly exercised, in various parts of the country. The most remarkable instances of its exercise are recorded in the history of the Morgan trials in the western part of New York.—After the consumation of the first great crime against the laws of God and man, the fraternity in that region set themselves to work to screen from merited punishment the vile kidnappers and murderers of Morgan, and to suppress the publication by Miller, of Morgan's disclosures. The secret machinery of the lodges and the efficacy of masonic oaths triumphed over nearly all the attempts of the civil authority to bring the conspirators to justice.—Sheriffs and juries were corrupted. Witnesses sometimes refused to testify, and sometimes committed wilful perjury, and in other instances were spirited away from the reach of compulsory process. Accused individuals were rescued from the officers of justice—money was appropriated by masons individually and by lodges, in aid of convicted persons, and for the employment of standing counsel for the accused. In short, obstacles of almost every kind were thrown in the way to prevent indictments and convictions. These are not mere suggestions of the imagination, but matters of sober history, of great notoriety in the vicinity of the outrages and attested to *us* by multitudes of credible witnesses.

The rites and ceremonies of the institution are scarcely less objectionable than the oaths. The representation of Moses and the Deity in the burning bush—the mock prayers and irreverent reading of the scriptures by professed infidels who happen as they often do, to be placed in the master's chair, and at the same time the ludicrous appearance of a half naked and haltered candidate—the raising of the body of the fabled Grand Master, Hiram Abiff—and the drinking of the cup of "double damnation" out of a human skull, with the excessive mirth occasioned by the effect which some parts of these farcical proceedings produce on the mind and feelings of the candidate, are well calculated to produce levity and irreverence for holy things, to lead the christian into labyrinths of scepticism and infidelity, and to undermine and destroy the sanctity and binding effect of all oaths.

Mr. Herrick from the Committee to report on the evidence of the truth of the disclosures of Freemasonry, reported as follows, which report was accepted.

The Committee appointed to examine and report on the existing evidence of the truth of the Morgan disclosures, and those contained in a book published by Elder David Bernard, entitled "Light on Masonry," report,

That the solemn attestation of respectable seceders from Masonry is of itself sufficient to convince any candid mind of the truth of the disclosures referred to. Among a multitude of high minded and virtuous men who have thus confirmed these disclosures are Henry D. Ward, Master Mason, New York; Lebbeus Armstrong, Grand Elect Prefect and Sublime Mason, N. Y.; Rev. Moses Thatcher, Royal Arch Mason, Mass.; Abner Morse, Master Mason, N. J.; Ezra Sliper, Royal Arch Mason, Md.; Calvin Barber, Mark Master Mason, Conn.; Noble D. Strong, Royal Arch, Conn.; Col. Pliny Merrick, Royal Arch, Mass.; Herbert A. Read, Knight Templar, &c. &c. N. Y.; Gen. William Wadsworth, Knight Templar, N. Y.; Elder Withcrell, Royal Arch. N.Y.; Soloman Southwick, Mark Masters, N.Y.; Cephas A. Smith, Knight Templar, N. Y.; Cadwalader D. Colden, Royal Arch, N. J.; Sheriff Sumner, Royal Arch, Boston.

The character of these witnesses for intelligence and veracity, and their undoubted means of knowing the facts—the want of inducement to testify, falsely—the the certainty of their being exposed and rendered infamous if they had so testified—and the general acknowledgment of virtuous and respectable Masons that these men are not imposters, strongly confirm the disclosures.

The abduction and murder of Morgan by the Masonic fraternity, for the alledged and only offence of revealing masonic secrets, is confirmation "strong as holy writ" that the revelation was true—and the fraternity have thus stamped the transaction with martyrdom, and sealed the truth of the disclosures with blood.

In addition to the evidence above alluded to, there is abundant legal proof of the disclosures on record, in courts of justice and legislative investigations. Particular cases might be named where verdicts of juries have pronounced the evidence plenary and satisfactory—but your committee forbear. The evidence, intrinsic and extrinsic, direct and collateral, is so strong and irresistible that no candid man can hesitate a moment in pronouncing the Morgan disclosures, and also the further revelations contained in Bernard's "Light on Masonry" to be authentic and unquestionable.

Your committee find further evidence of the truth of the disclosures of masonic secrets, if indeed further be wanting, in the fact that a statement of specific charges was presented by the Antimasonic State Committee of the State of Massachusetts, to the Grand Lodge or Grand Chapter, or to any individual of that State, against the masonic institution with a request for either of those bodies, or any of their individual members to deny the truth of any or all of the charges made, and charge those who made them with falsehood. The State Committee pledged themselves, if they should comply with this request, immediately to commence an action of libel against those who should thus charge them with falsehood, and thereby each party would be entitled to the benefit of compulsory process to compel the attendance of witnesses, and thus they would be enabled either to substantiate or disprove the allegations made against the institution. Notwithstanding these charges were made by responsible men, and for the express purpose of testing their truth by judicial investigation, no masonic body, or individual mason, has ever dared to meet the issue. This, your committee conceive to be conclusive evidence of the truth of the allegations; because they cannot conceive, nor indeed is it possible for them to believe that any man or body of men, who are innocent, would sit down under such serious and specific charges, affecting as these do not only the character of the masonic institution, but of individual masons, and make no attempt to refute them. The following are the charges preferred on which the Antimasons wished to make up an issue.

Allegations against Freemasonry

The Declaration, signed by about twelve hundred Freemasons, "of Boston and vicinity," denies, unequivocally, *all* the allegations against Freemasonry, and Freemasons, that have been made, during the last five years. Some of the most material of these allegations, which the State Committee (in behalf of the Antimasonic State Convention) are prepared to prove, are the following. We allege,

1. That the kidnapping and consequent murder of William Morgan, was preconcerted in Lodges and Chapters, and carried on with their knowledge and co-operation, and that none but Freemasons were concerned in that outrage.

2. That the only motive for this crime, was the disclosure of Masonic secrets, by Morgan.

3. That the penalty imposed for a violation of Masonic oaths is *death,* and *death* only.

4. That the Masonic construction of Masonic penalties, is *death* for a violation of Masonic law; and that no ceremony, lecture, or injunction in Masonry, previous to 1827, explains away this plain literal construction, but that the whole tenor of all such authorities enforce it, in the strongest terms.

5. That the manner of the infliction of death, imposed by these penalties, in eight of the degrees, beginning with the first, is—cutting the throat and tearing out the tongue—tearing out the heart—severing, quartering and disemboweling the body, and burning to ashes—tearing the breast open, and throwing the

heart on a dunghill to rot—smiting the scull off, and exposing the brains to the sun—pulling down the house to the offender, and hanging him on one of its timbers—striking the head off, and placing it on a lofty spire—tearing out the eyes, chopping off the hands, quartering the body, and throwing it among the rubbish of the Temple.

6. That Freemasonry, by the legitimate operation of her principles, and the literal construction of her oaths, has prevented the detection, indicting and conviction of kidnappers and murderers.

7. That Masonic jurors have refused to indict or to convict Masonic offenders, and that Masonic witnesses have refused to testify against them.

8. That in the contest of five years, between the legal tribunals of New York and Freemasonry, but two verdicts and three pleas of guilty have been obtained against the kidnapper, and murderers, though well known; and the whole amount of punishment that has been inflicted for these outrages, committed by a large body of men, has been five years and five months imprisonment in county jails, distributed among five convicts!

9. That no "partial and inflammatory representation" of these offenses, committed by Masons, has been made, beyond what the facts, as judicially established, fully warrant.

10. That these offences grew out of the legitimate construction and application of the oaths, principles and engagements of Freemasons.

11. That the five Masons sentenced for participation in the crime, eighteen indicted, and many others implicated, have ever remained in full fellowship with Lodges and Chapters, and that some of them have been since advanced to high Masonic honors.

12. That these convicts and kidnappers are held in full communion by Masons in Massachusetts, because the principles of Masonry require all Lodges and Chapters to receive and fellowship Masons, so long as they retain membership in any Lodge or Chapter.

13. That the perpetrators of the violence on Morgan were not "a *few misguided men,*" but were men comprising the most active occupations and professions, as respectable in the communities where they lived, as the twelve hundred signers of the Declaration are in this community.

14. That at least three hundred and fifty Masons were accessary to the outrage, or principals in the crime, and that it became known, Masonically, to at least five hundred more Masons, in New York, soon after it was committed, and, as there is no doubt, to acting Masonic bodies generally, throughout the United States.

15. That Lodges and Chapters concealed the criminals, contributed money to protect them from justice, and to enable one of the actual murderers to escape from the country.

16. That forty-three of the most active criminals, whom we can name, were men of high respectability and standing, comprising officers of justice, and be-

longing to almost every occupation and trade, and to three of the learned professions, and that the murderers themselves were men of no mean consideration.

17. That Masonic principles, oaths and engagements are, in every essential particular, the same in Massachusetts as in New York.

18. That a knowledge of the crimes of Masons in New York, by Massachusetts Masons, soon after those offences were committed, is fairly inferred from the introduction of a check test, or oath here, from New York, established to exclude from the Lodges those who studied the disclosures made by Morgan.

19. That the Masons of Massachusetts, when called upon formally, in 1830, by the State Antimasonic Convention, to disfellowship the Masonic bodies in New York, which cherished the Morgan conspirators, declined to do so, or to deny, as a Masonic body, the truth of the disclosures against Freemasonry, or to renounce the system, or to disapprove the murder.

20. That Masonic newspapers, Masonic officers, and Masons of great responsibility, embracing even Ministers of the Gospel, in this State and in Rhode Island, have justified the murder of Morgan, and declared he had met his just desserts, for a violation of his Masonic oaths!

21. That in repeated instances Masonic oaths have proved to be stronger, and more binding on the consciences of Masons, than civil oaths, in trials and examinations before judicial and legislative tribunals.

22. Them Masonic oaths, as administered in New York and Massachusetts, impose solemnly upon those who take them the following among other obnoxious and criminal obligations, viz:

1. To conceal and never reveal, except to a brother Mason of the same degree, any of the secrets of Freemasonry, under any circumstances.
2. To obey all Masonic signs and summonses, given by one Mason to another, or by a Masonic body.
3. To obey the grand hailing sign of distress, at the hazard of life, and to apprize a brother Mason of *all* approaching danger.
4. To keep a brother Mason's secrets of every description, when communicated as such, murder and treason only excepted, and they left to the election of the Mason receiving such secrets; and that this specific exception of only two crimes which may be disclosed, plainly enjoins the concealment of all other crimes.
5. Not to violate the chastity of the female relatives of a Mason, *knowing* them to be such, but enjoining no such restraint towards other females.

   To keep *all* secrets communicated by a Royal Arch Mason,—or all secrets without exception,—or murder and treason not excepted.
7. To assist a royal Arch Mason, espouse his cause, and extricate him from difficulty, whether he be right or wrong.

8. To travel forty miles, barefoot, and on frozen ground, if required, to relieve the necessities of a worthy Knight Templar.
9. The drinking of wine out of a human scull, and imprecating the sins of the person whose scull that once was, upon the head of the candidate, as the Savior bore the sins of the whole world, should the person who takes this oath violate any of his Masonic oaths.

23. That the Master Mason's oath extends to the concealment of all crimes but *two,* and therefore, if an oath to conceal *all* secrets, murder and treason not excepted, be indefensible, an oath to conceal all other crimes but these two, is not less so.

24. That if adhering Masons can construe away their oaths which enjoin the concealment of each other's secrets, except, or including but two crimes, (murder and treason,) then, by the same process, they can construe away the injunction in the same oaths, to conceal any of the secrets of Freemasonry; and hence, that if an adhering Mason discloses such secret of a brother Mason, he is just as guilty of violating his oath, as the seceding Mason is who discloses all the secrets of the Craft.

25. That these facts prove Freemasonry to be "at variance with the fundamental principles of morality, and incompatible with the duty of a good and faithful citizen."

26. That the Declaration of the twelve hundred Masons is not only false in its denials, but false in its assertions, because—

27. The candidate is *not* "made acquainted with the nature of the obligations he is required to assume," previous to taking his oaths, but he is required to promise to conform to the usages, and customs of Freemasonry, without knowing what they are, and, by the Massachusetts book of constitutions, he is only permitted, before taking the oath, to see the charter and by-laws of the Lodge, and a list of its members, all of which contain no reference whatever to the oaths and obligations he is required to assume.

28. Because, the intimation from the Master, that the oaths will not interfere with the religion or politics, is a deception, and no explanation of their nature, because it is not a part of the oath and because the terms of the oaths, if they are to have any meaning at all, do interfere directly with religion and politics, and are nowhere explained, by any equally binding and concurrent authority, to mean anything different from their plain, literal import.

29. Because, if under such circumstances Masons who profess to regard their oaths as binding at all, can explain away the literal import of their Masonic oaths, they may, by the same reasoning explain away the literal import of their civil oaths.

30. Because, obedience to the civil magistrate, and being true to the civil government, and just to the country, are not requisite to retain Masonic fellowship and membership of a Lodge, inasmuch as the book of Constitutions lays

down the maxim, that though a brother be a rebel against the State, yet "*if convicted of no other crime, they cannot expel him from the Lodge, and his relation to it remains indefeasible.*"

31. Hence, that by Masonic law, and practice, *treason* and *murder* are not offences which are deemed of sufficient magnitude so authorize expulsion from the Lodge.

32. That it is not true that Freemasonry secures its members in the *freedom of speech,* because she fetters and hoodwinks them, and makes them swear to have their *throats cut,* and their *tongues torn out,* if they indulge in *freedom of speech,* touching any of the mysteries taught them by this pretended patron of freedom of speech; and because her books of constitution, monitors and orators, enjoin *silence* and *secrecy;* to be "cautious in *words,*" to *manage* a discourse, and to "be voluntarily *dumb,*" in order to avoid freedom of speech.

33. That these exclusive and selfish oaths, and the whole principles and practices of Freemasonry, do necessarily interfere with the dictates of conscience and the acts of Masons in matters of religion and politics, and disqualify men, under their influence, from conducting towards the rest of mankind with the same impartiality, in the capacity of jurors, judges, officers or legislators, as can be exercised by men who acknowledge no other than civil, moral and religious obligations.

34. That if Masonry does disdain the making of proselytes, *Masons,* nevertheless, have repeatedly urged men to join the Lodge.

35. That so far from admitting only those whose characters "are unspotted by immorality and vice," one of the inducements held out in her books of highest authority, to become a Mason, is, that it will introduce you to the fellowship of corsairs, pirates, and marauders, who will treat you as a brother.

36. That she not only admits men of the vilest character, into her Lodges, but retains in full fellowship the profligate, the abandoned, the worthless, the intemperate, the profane, and does not expel men guilty of kidnapping, murder, and treason!

37. That so far from being the handmaid of religion and virtue, she is the offspring of skepticism and vice—excluding revelation and the name of the Saviour, from her seven first degrees; admitting the Bible of the Pagan and Mohammedan to a concurrent authority with the Bible of the Christian, as "Holy Writings," and practising secret rites and ceremonies, tending to bring the resurrection and the miracles of revelation into contempt.

38. That the pretended "charitable uses" of her "accumulated funds" received "in sacred trust," is deceptive; because no person likely to require charity, is, by her constitution, permitted to be initiated: because her system of charity is merely a scheme of mutual assurance, rarely, if ever, paying out in charity what is received in fees, and appropriating to parades and processions, idle ornaments and *gorgeous temples,* the very funds pretended to have been received in sacred trust for charitable uses.

These are the allegations which make up the most material counts in the indictment of the people against Freemasonry and Freemasons, and on these the State Antimasonic Convention, through their Committee, tender a distinct issue to the Twelve Hundred, or the Grand Fraternitics in this State, in any form best adapted "*to establish truth and expose imposition.*"

(Signed,) *By the State Committee.*

Mr. Patterson from the committee on the influence of masonry in judicial tribunals, &c. made the following report.

The Committee appointed to report on the influence of Freemasonry upon our judicial tribunals, and its tendency to corrupt the fountain, and poison the streams of justice, have attended to that subject, and now report as follows:

Freemasonry has been abundantly proved, by a great mass and variety of testimony to be an association of men, holding out to the world as their object, the works of charity and brotherly love to the whole human family, but practicing these virtues with but a very sparing hand, and exclusively among themselves. It has also been fully proved, by the declaration of seceders, and by legislative investigations, and judicial trials, that the fraternity impose oaths, binding their members to fly to the relief of a brother whenever he is in distress, and to extricate him from all difficulty whether he be *right or wrong*—to keep a brother's secrets, *murder and treason not excepted*—to promote the political preferment of a brother—to punish such as are unfaithful to their masonic obligations, by deranging their business, and pointing them out to the world as unworthy vagabonds and transferring their character after them wherever they may go. Which oaths are guarded by the most sanguinary penalties, extending to the taking of life, in the most cruel and unheard of forms. The rites and ceremonies of the craft too, are proved to be of the most revolting character, bordering on blasphemy, and turning the forms of religion into ridicule.

These, among a multitude of other objectionable traits in the character of the institution, as described by a great number of respectable seceders, and drawn out from adhering masons, in judicial trials, are alone sufficient to stamp the institution with a corrupting influence on judicial proceedings. But the tree is known by its fruit—and the history of some of the fruits of masonry shows, that it is admirably adapted to the corrupt object of thwarting, evading and defeating the otherwise sure and salutary operation of our judicial tribunals. Cases almost innumerable can be referred to, where, in legal trials, masonic influence has turned the scale in favor of the brethren of the craft. But the Morgan conspiracy, with the perjury and masonic management consequent upon the first great offence presents in the strongest light the influence and power of the institution whenever exigencies occur to call them forth. The majesty of the law was there humbled in the dust before masonic power—juries were packed by masonic sheriffs, masonic witnesses refused to testify or violated their civil oaths in order to be faithful to their masonic obligations—masonic funds were liberally applied to the relief, comfort, and countenance of masons who had been convicted of kidnapping Morgan. Let any unprejudiced mind view the legal proceedings which the Morgan trials present. Let him observe Sheriff Eli Bruce, who was afterwards convicted and punished for being concerned in the abduction of Morgan, summoning, term after term of the Courts, grand juries, a majority of whom were masons, and instructing his deputy, Hiram B. Hopkins, also a mason, to be particular in this respect. Let him note the manner in which these grand juries proceeded in their investigations—permitting no questions to be put to witnesses, except such as had been written down, and could be answered without implicating Bruce. Let him observe the great number of facts and circumstances elicited and divulged in the various stages of these trials, shewing that the great body of the fraternity felt, spoke and acted as parties in the trials, and interposed every obstacle in their power to prevent the prosecuting officers from coming at the truth, and when convictions were effected, did much by caressing, encouraging, comforting and aiding the convicts, while suffering the sentence of the law in prison, to ward off its effect, and make the offender respected; and the conclusion will irresistably force itself upon such inquirer after truth, that masonry necessarily and unavoidably tends to polute our courts of justice, and render the rights of the uninitiated unsafe. This tendency flows from the very nature of the institution, and has been abundantly exemplified and proved, not only by the Morgan trials, but in other instances of recent date. The Royal Arch Mason swears that he will extricate a brother from all difficulty, whether he be right or wrong, under the penalty of having his scull smote off, and his brains exposed to the scorching rays of the sun. He cannot be faithful to such an oath when acting as judge, juror or prosecuting attorney, consistently with his duty in these stations, provided one of the parties to be a mason. That the oaths of masonry are held to be binding by those who take them, and even paramount to all other obligations is evident, from the fact, that high and intelligent masons have, in the Morgan trials and elsewhere, repeatedly refused to testify on the stand, where masonic secrets would be endangered, and have suffered fine and imprisonment rather than do so. In confirmation of this position, your committee would recite the two following instances of refusal to testify. The first was on the trial of a case against Harvey Cook, a mason in New York in 1830. In this case Erastus Day being called as a witness, and asked if he was a mason, peremptorily told the court that "they would not be able to get any thing out of him about masonry." The court decided that the question was proper, and the witness must answer it. He then testified that he had taken seventeen degrees in masonry. He was asked if he had taken the usual oaths or obligations, from the entered apprentice's up to the royal arch. He refused to answer, though told by the court that he must—said "he considered his masonic oaths binding, and would not violate them for *any court.*" As to obeying signs, summonses and tokens, flying to the relief of one giving the grand hailing sign of distress; also as to aiding, assisting and extricating a companion from difficulty, right or wrong, he wholly refused to answer, and said he *could not* without criminating himself. He would not answer as to keeping secrets, murder and treason not excepted, and told the court he considered his masonic oaths superior to the oath he had just taken in court! Sylvanus Cone was next called, to whom the same questions were put, and also some others, and he *wholly refused to answer,* although told by the court that they were proper and he must answer them. Elisha M. Forbes was sworn, and said "I'll tell any thing that isn't masonry, but any thing that is, I won't." He was asked as to keeping secrets, helping out of difficulty, &c. and peremptorily refused to answer any of them. *John T. Carr, Samuel T. Bush* and *Luther Bavin* stubbornly refused to be sworn.

The other case alluded to was that of Ezekiel Jewett, one of the Morgan conspirators, where *Orsamus Turner,* being introduced as a witness refused to answer questions, for which the court imposed a fine of $250 and ordered him to be imprisoned thirty days. *Eli Bruce, Sheriff,* and *John Whitney,* both refused to be sworn, and Whitney was fined $250, and each were imprisoned thirty days for this contempt.

Others have committed wilful perjury to avoid a disclosure of Masonry. Others again, have solemnly declared that no consideration would induce them to divulge the secrets, and have openly justified the murder of Morgan, saying he was "a perjured wretch, and ought to suffer death, agreeably to the penalty of his obligations." A newspaper published by a Royal Arch Mason, in Groton, Mass. soon after the Morgan affair, openly declared this sentiment.

If the masons generally, or even a large portion of them, believe the oaths to be of such binding force, does it not necessarily follow, that so far as such masons are connected with our courts, they must corrupt the streams of justice?

In vain do masons endeavor to paliate and justify the nature of their oaths, by saying the candidate is told by the master who administers them, that there is nothing in the oath which will interfere with his religion or politics, and charged to be a quiet and peaceable subject, true to the government. &c. so long as the oaths themselves contain no such provision, but *do* contain the concluding phraise, "*All this I promise and swear with a fixed and steady purpose of mind in me to perform the same, without any equivocation, mental reservation, or self-evasion of mind in me whatever.*" And the solemn appeal, "*So help me God, and keep me steadfast in the same.*" The *guilty* meaning is impressed in clear and strong language, in the oaths themselves, but what masons, who attempt to defend them, would have us believe is the *innocent* meaning, arises from a construction diametrically opposed to the common import of the language, and founded on what they call lectures and charges given after the oath is taken, and forming no part of it, and even sometimes wholly omitted. Masons who are strongly armed in virtue may, and probably do, disregard the import of the oaths, but multitudes of intelligent and high standing masons in New York, understood and practiced upon them avoiding to their literal meaning, when they conspired against the liberty and life of Morgan, and violated their civil oaths, to screen the immediate perpetrators of that foul deed.

Mr. Swett from the committee on Political Antimasonry made the following report, which was read and accepted.

The Committee appointed to consider and report on the reasons in favor of political Antimasonry have attended to that subject and would now offer their report.

Freemasonry is now extensively believed by Americans to be an institution, fraught with danger to their liberties. More than a hundred thousand of our citizens have expressed this opinion at the polls. Their reasons are briefly these: The institution in this country numbers from one to two hundred thousand individuals, leagued together by oaths of secrecy, enforced by penalties of the most cruel and sanguinary stamp, and requiring by their literal tenor the performance of acts clearly inconsistent with morality, and in direct and manifest collision with civil oaths and duties. In obedience to which oaths, masons of intelligence and good standing in society, in the state of New York, effectually conspired against the liberty and life of a fellow citizen, and without any pretence of cause, except a violation of masonic law in divulging the secrets of the craft. This offence against the civil government was countenanced, to a considerable extent, by the fraternity in that State—if the combined efforts of the lodges to aid and comfort the conspirators, after the fact, by voting them money from the funds of the lodges, employing and paying counsel for defending them in courts, and supporting in prison those who had been convicted, be such. To prevent the conviction of individuals charged with that offence, masonic witnesses have refused to testify, jurors have violated their oaths of office, Masonic sheriffs have corruptly packed and otherwise tampered with juries.—And while these outrages were going on, the American press, that boasted centinel on the watch tower of liberty, was found to have been, either bribed or lulled into profound slumber, or awed into silence; and even down to the present time it is believed this charge is to a fearful extent, true. If masonry is the same in its laws and general features throughout the country [as its high dignitaries have declared] and if such as above described be some of its features, all who are not infatuated with its gaudy trappings and farcical ceremonies will, at least in their sober and candid moments, confess that it is a political evil of great magnitude. And shall we, (as moral antimasons would have us) confine our efforts to extirpate it to moral persuasion? Shall we only repeat the same warfare against the institution, which proved so fruitless in the days of Pritchard and professor Robinson? If masonry were only a moral evil and not entrenched in secrecy and guarded by oaths, signs and grips, public sentiment might perhaps be made to reach the case without resort to a political organization. But its acts in numerous cases and the whole structure of its laws and machinery shew it to be more of a political engine than a charitable society. It has the most sovereign contempt for public opinion, so long as it is suffered to retain its organization, and power to gull the uninitiated, and hold nearly all offices of honor or profit in the government.—and it will always be able to do this, unless attacked by the constitutional weapon which freemen rightfully wield at the ballot box. The great but ineffectual excitement produced by Pritchard's disclosures, called "Jachin and Boaz," and the more recent writings of Barruel and Professor Robinson, shew that without political action antimasonry will be wholly inefficient. Aware of this, masons cry out proscription! whenever we resort to the ballot box. But is it proscription to apply a constitutional remedy to a political evil? The charge is false. As well might every political party in the country charge its opponents with proscription. We refuse to vote for masons, because we believe their adherence to masonic oaths disqualifies them for civil trusts. They have sworn allegiance to masonic government, and cannot be true to this and civil government at the same time in matters where they come in conflict—which is often the case. Civil government requires of a witness in Courts to tell the truth, the whole truth and nothing but the truth, but the masonic government requires of its members to "keep the secrets of of a brother, *murder and treason not excepted.*" And yet masons have the consummate impudence and absurdity to set up and implied claim to the vote of antimasons, by whining about proscription. They have established a government and laws of their own, which thwart and contravene the government and laws of the land, and yet they claim to be entitled to the confidence of the people as suitable candidates for office, and clamoursly charge antimasons with fanaticism and persecution in refusing to vote for them. Verily, Sir Knights, these are pretentions as extravagant as the boasted antiquity of your order. First, renounce your right by "prerogative" to govern the world by arbitrary mandates, issued from midnight secret conclaves, and place yourselves on a level with the people. Till this is done your claim to their confidence is preposterous and vain.

Mr. Farwell from committee to nominate a State Committee made a report which was accepted, and the following gentlemen were elected the Antimasonic State Committee for the ensuing year.

Hon. JOSEPH SOUTHWICK, Augusta, Kennebec
NEAL DOW, Esq. Portland, Cumberland
THEODORE ELWELL, Esq. Buxton, York
Col. JOEL HOWE, Nobleboro', Lincoln
Hon. JOSEPH C. SMALL, Newport, Penobscot
JAMES WHITE, Esq. Belfast, Walde

ELIAZER COBERN, Esq. Bloomfield, Somerset
JOHN MOULTON, Esq. Portor, Oxford
TIMOTHY WHITING, Esq. East Machias, Washington.

The committee to enquire whether masonry and antimasonry are "minor considerations" made a report, which was ordered to lie on the table.

Mr. White from committee on resolutions made a report which was laid on the table.

Report of the committee on the National Convention was laid on the table by Mr. Richardson.

Voted to adjourn to meet at nine o'clock to-morrow morning.

JULY 4.

Met according to adjournment.

The following report from the committee on the 6th resolution, yesterday laid on the table was read and accepted.

The committee to whom was referred the inquiry whether Masonry and Antimasonry are *in fact* "Minor Considerations" at the ballot box, ask leave to Report,

That, on the 24th of June, 1825, W. F. Brainard, a Masonic orator of high standing in the Lodge and in society at New London, Connecticut, before the Union Lodge of that place, on the recurrence of a fabulous anniversary of the institution, thus describes Masonry: "What is Masonry now? IT IS POWERFUL. It comprises men of RANK, wealth, office and talent, in power and out of power, and that in almost every place where POWER IS OF ANY IMPORTANCE; and it comprises among other CLASSES of the community, to the lowest, in large numbers, active men, united together, *and capable of being directed by the efforts of others,* so as to have the FORCE OF CONCERT *throughout the civilized world.* They are distributed too, with the means of knowing one another, and the means of keeping secret, and the means of co-operating, in the DESK—in the LEGISLATIVE HALL—on the BENCH—in every *gathering of business*—in every *party of pleasure*—in every ENTERPRISE OF GOVERNMENT—in every domestic circle—in PEACE AND IN WAR—among enemies and friends—in *one place* as well as in *another*—so POWERFUL indeed is it at this time, that it fears nothing from *violence,* either public or *private,* for it has *every means* TO LEARN IT IN SEASON TO COUNTERACT, DEFEAT AND PUNISH IT."

Such were the sentiments in 1825, not of Mr. Brainard only, but of a whole lodge (who adopted them by thanking Mr. B. and ordering the address to be published) in the enlightened State of Connecticut. The scenes enacted the succeeding year in New York, but too well confirm the truth of this picture of Masonry. There masonry was indeed "*powerful.*" The civil arm of government was palsied and the force of the law evaded by its superior tact and management. There masonry was in possession of "*office, and talent, and power*" in every place where these "*were of any importance.*"—There masonry was found to comprise "*large numbers of active men united together so as to have the force of concert.*" There masonry was found to have the "*means*" (and the disposition too) "*of co-operating on the bench, in the legislative hall*" and elsewhere, and the means of silencing the public press.—There masonry feared nothing from its enemies, for it had the means to "*counteract, defeat and punish them.*"—And there masonry, with these attributes, conceived, planned and executed (not from malice or revenge, but in accordance with the literal tenor and import of its fundamental laws—not through the instrumentality of a "few misguided and ignorant men," but by the concerted agency of numerous lodges, spread over a large territory, and with the knowledge, and at least silent acquiescence of nearly the whole fraternity in that great State) a conspiracy and murder against a citizen, not charged with, or suspected of any other crime than that of divulging masonic secrets. And there too these characteristics of masonry were found effectual against the utmost exertions of the civil authority, to ferret out and punish the murderers of Morgan, though the immediate executioners of this bloody deed became well known to the whole community.

That masonry is substantially the same in all parts of the country, and that it acts under secret laws, rites and ceremonies of a grossly immoral nature and tendency, have been conclusively proved in Courts of justice and elsewhere. And that instead of being, as its votaries pretend, a charitable institution, it is in fact a combination of mercenary and ambitious men, (principally, to say the least) for selfish objects—political preferment forming no small part of its views and purposes, your committee have no doubt. These are some of the reasons why Antimasons refuse to vote for the adherents of masonry. Whether they are "minor considerations," let freemen judge.

That both of the other political parties of the day are, to a considerable extent, under the dominion of Masonry, is evident from the fact, that they are continually cally on Antimasons to "give up these minor considerations," and unite with them against their opponents. Masonic Jacksonmen say to us, "the United States Bank will cheat us of our liberties and ruin the country, come over and help us to destroy the *monster.*" The Masonic Whigs, alias Nationals, exclaim, "the constitution is violated, the laws are trampled upon, the country is lost—*aye, in the midst of a revolution!* Dear Anties, just lay aside your party organization and help us right the ship, or we sink."—Both parties in their blind zeal assuming as a fact that Antimasons were originally on their side, and would again act with them, but for Antimasonry. But who does not see the miserable absurdity of such a call, and its direct tendency to restore masonry to its former prosperity and splendor? It carries on its very face an insult to antimasons. It supposes them insincere in other professions of belief that masonry is the greatest political evil of the day, and far more dangerous to our liberties than the worst dogmas of either of the other parties. It cannot be listened to by antimasons without a total abandonment of our own principles. Our motto, "PERSEVERE," would thus be disregarded and lost, and nothing is more obvious than that a general defection of this kind in our ranks would be neither more nor less than the complete disbanding of the party. And shall we be seduced by masons and the friends of masons, under the guise of pretended patriotism, to give up our organization, and submit to be governed by the secret, irresponsible power of a blood-stained institution? No, your committee confidently believe that Antimasons will, to a man, spurn these insiduous attacks, and press onward in the great cause of equal rights, until they have prostrated that secret power behind the laws, that is greater than the laws themselves.

Report of the committee on resolutions, yesterday laid on the table was taken up and accepted.

1st. *Resolved,* That it is a right recognized by our constitution, "for the people at all times to assemble in an orderly manner, to consult on the common good;"—but when questions of great importance, to the safety of our country, or the purity of our republican institutions arise, it then becomes not a *right* merely, but an imperative duty, which we owe to our country, ourselves and posterity, thus to assemble and adopt such measures, as shall tend to promote the general welfare.

2d. *Resolved,* That the disclosures which have been made public touching the character and conduct of the masonic institution—its ceremonies, oaths, and appaling penalties, and more particularly the daring acts of wickedness, and violation of law and justice with which it has been proved guilty, afford abundant cause for the people frequently to assemble to consult on the most judicious means to suppress and abolish this institution.

3d. *Resolved,* That all associations which are not rendered responsible to the people, the true source of all power, for their acts, are dangerous to our liberties and ought in no case to be encouraged, supported, or tolerated, by a free people.

4th. *Resolved,* That, inasmuch as Freemasonry is protected and sustained by legislative enactments, by receiving civil charters with extraordinary privileges and immunities from our Legislature, and inasmuch as our Legislature has refused to divest it of this peculiar protection, and thereby let it rest on its own merit, but continues to protect it, the only way by which the people can reach the institution is by political action—by returning such men to our Legislature as will withdraw from masonry the support which our laws now afford it.

5th. *Resolved,* That the more reflection we give the subject, the more strongly are we confirmed in the belief, that the principles on which our party is founded, are entirely sound and correct, and that by bringing the question directly to the ballot box, is the only way in which we can hope for the destruction of the masonic institution.

6th. *Resolved,* That possessing the most undoubted confidence in the correctness of our principles, we are determined to maintain and persist in our organized opposition to masonry, so long as the organization of masonry shall exist.

7th. *Resolved,* That every new development of masonic secrets serve to strengthen our conviction of its dangerous tendency and alarming power,—of its anti-republican and anti-christian principles, and of the absolute necessity of its entire abrogation in order to secure even-handed justice to all our citizens, and the supremacy and wholesome operation of the laws.

8th. *Resolved,* That the "dignified silence" or refusal of Freemasons to defend the principles and practices of their institution from the serious, and appalling charges of wickedness and crime which have been in the most solemn manner preferred against them, amount, in fact, to an acknowledgment that those charges are TRUE and UNANSWERABLE.

9th. *Resolved,* That the pretence which has recently been made, that masonry is dead, is only a deceptive artifice, invented by the fraternity for the purpose of inducing Antimasons to give up their opposition to an institution which its friends have neither the courage nor the ability to defend.

10th, *Resolved,* That our warfare is with principles and not with men. That the masonic institution being an empire, a distinct and independent government, exercising jurisdiction over the liberty and *lives* of its members, who having sworn allegiance to its empire, they have to all intents and purposes disfranchised themselves as citizens of the U. States, consequently the barbarous and sanguinary oaths taken by a Freemason preclude him from holding any office of profit or trust, until he renounces his allegiance to that empire, which is at war with every other government on earth.

11th. *Resolved,* That the evidence exhibited to the public, by numerous and respectable witnesses show, that Freemasonry, instead of being the "handmaid of religion" is a wicked and infamous institution, dangerous to the peace of society, setting the laws of the land at defiance, marking out and sacrificing its victims at pleasure and with impunity—and is a wicked conspiracy against the laws of God and our country; and ought to be extirpated immediately by the use of all peaceable and constitutional means in our power.

12th. *Resolved,* That we pledge ourselves to use our efforts to deliver our State and Country from the influence of Freemasonry, one of the foulest stains and deadliest curses ever permitted to afflict the human race.

Mr. Rice, from the Committee to prepare an Address to the people, reported the following, which was adopted:

CITIZENS OF MAINE: At a season of general excitement and alarm, when strife and bitterness have usurped the place of calm deliberation in the halls of legislation, and the echoing voices of excited partizans are responding to every note of alarm, from the very extremities of our political domain, when self-interest and vile idolatry are viewing with each other in language of adulation and recrimination in order to drown what cannot be silenced,—it is hardly to be expected that the voice of modest truth and sober reason will find many attentive auditors. The all-engrossing topic of the day—the angry contest between a powerful moneyed institution and the executive power of the Union—as it occupies men in power, and swallows up the important time of Congress, so it gives tone and utterance to all the fierce and angry passions of the body politic; and unfits the minds of the people for that calm consideration, and sober investigation which are the inlets of truth, and the safeguards of our political institutions. The search for political truth is strained too far: it is simple—it is near at hand—it is within the reach of ordinary vision. It depends on no abstruse principles; it requires no metaphysical abstraction.

But what means are to be used to withdraw the astonished and affrighted gaze of the public eye from those airy flights to which it has been raised by the designing master-spirits of the age? Grown giddy by super-republican elevation, their disturbed imaginations are revolving in excentric orbits;—how, then, shall true republican gravitation be applied to produce an equilibrium?

The machinery set in motion at the present day to manufacture public opinion—the apparatus used to mystify and encloud what otherwise plain common sense would comprehend at a glance—the mighty efforts of mighty geniuses to reach above ordinary comprehension, and to persuade common minds contrary to their honest convictions of truth, present barriers which might well seem to us insurmountable.

But as friends of truth, we cannot be silent. As Republicans, we owe it to our country to declare our sober and honest opinions. As friends of equal rights, we have a duty to perform when we see those rights in danger; and if there ever has been a time since our birth as a nation, when those rights were endangered, we believe the present to be that time. Though we are no less interested than others in whatever affects the currency of the country, we are led to consider that a subject of secondary importance, and but one of a train of evils which have their origin in one general cause. We are disposed to stand aloof from *such* a contest, conducted in *such* a manner, guarding, as well as we can, against the effects of mistaken policy, and interested; crafty, and intriguing management.

The causes of what we suffer—the antecedents of these consequents—can be ascertained from propositions less complex than are generally used. As a people, we are not what our fathers left us. Freedom and equality were our inheritance; but where are they now? Wasted, squandered, their place usurped by proud aristocratical combinations. *They* left us competence and happiness;—we have sought for wealth and power. *That wealth,* instead of general diffusion, has been monopolized by a *few; that power* has been silently accumulating in the hands of *certain classes* in society; and though nominally we are still free, and enjoy the shadowy attributes of freedom, yet when we attempt to exert our liberty, we find that we are restrained and shackled in its exercise.

Fellow Citizens—at this important crisis, shall we be permitted to recur to first principles, and invite your attention to the simple but firm basis on which our Republic is founded. Shall we be permitted once more to call to mind that commodious fabric which our fathers reared, but which has grown up into splendid elegance, and in which, for convenience, labyrinthine windings, and interminable passages have been substituted? *Time was* when there was nothing interposed between the laws and the people; the laws were simple and their execution unobstructed. *Time was* when puplic opinion bore rule, and the laws and their execution were subject to its influence. *Time was* when the right of free suffrage was freely accorded, and freely exercised. *Time was* when it was permitted to every man freely to think, freely to speak and freely to act; amenable only to the laws of his country; laws to the framing of which himself was a party. But times have changed. Justice is now entangled in her net of law, and the execution of the laws is obstructed by difficulties insurmountable. Our Legislators have given birth and maturity to a corporation—*imperium in imperio*—which successfully resists all legislative, judicial and executive power. The hand of justice is arrested—the innocent suffer without an avenger, while the guilty—though their guilt be manifest as light—escape with impunity. Under certain circumstances, the trial by jury, becomes a mere farce, and the administration of a judicial oath is but solemn mockery. Our Judges still occupy the bench; Juries fill the boxes; and witnesses are sworn to "tell the truth, and the whole truth;" but what avail these ceremonies while Judgement is turned aside, Justice paralized and truth suppressed? It is but a prelude to anarchy, or an introduction to oppression, which renders it doubly oppresive. It deceives us with hopes of justice, which add pangs more bitter to disappointment.

The time has come when the *public opinion* that bears rule is manufactured by a few ambitious individuals—Caucus dictation must be obeyed under severe pains and penalties; and for a man to presume to think for himself, and act from his own convictions of right, is thought, and rendered punishable. Office is prostituted to reward partizan zeal; and he who scrambles and manages most adroitly—no matter how dishonorably if he be successful—bears away the richest of the spoils. The right of free suffrage—that vital principle of political liberty—is virtually denied to be of common right. "Regular nominations" must limit its exercise; and even those nominations must be made by particular parties. *We* are called on to relinquish our preferences, and to fall in with those of the favoured few. The reasons on which *our* opinions are based, must be vacated, unless they are satisfactory to those who have assumed the censorship of public opinion—the right of testing political orthodoxy, and of punishing heretics. They flatter us with words smooth and deceitful in praise of liberty; they, have much to say about free institutions. But Liberty, in *their* vocabulary, consists in following *their* dictation, and free institutions are those that promote *their selfish interests.*

> They call it public good, but mean their own.

Must thus the fate of our Republic identify itself with the fates of those free States that have preceded it? Must the interests of the *whole people* be thus absorbed by the interests of a *few individuals?* Must interested combinations subvert the Constitution, and change the laws intended as our safeguard and protection, into chains, and fetters of oppression! Fellow citizens, the answer is with you. It is for you to say whether, tamely and supinely you will resign your rightful prerogative, and be the dupes of an imposition so degrading, or whether you will arise and crush whatever interposes to deprive you of your equal and unailenable rights; whatever rises between you and the free exercise of your republican privileges. Every possible effort has been made, and is now making to deter you from investigating this subject with that attention which its importance demands. Your prejudices have been bespoken against it, by representations false and malicious. You have been told that Antimasonry rests on no principle;—that it is an excitement got up by disappointed ambition to make it a stepping stone to office. That Masonry is a harmless affair—a charitable institution—a blessing to the unfortunate—a resource for widows and orphans. When such representations have failed of effect, you have been told that it is already extinct—and that it is idle to fight a shadow. Again, it is said to be absurd to oppose masonry politically. Fight it morally—show it to be a moral evil;—but beware how you touch it with politics; asserting that it has no connexion with them, nor any influence upon our political institutions.

If you are disposed to give full credit to these assertions, you are at liberty so to do; but if you are disposed to investigate the subject, you will be willing to follow us through this address attentively; and thereby you will be able to understand some of the facts and principles from which we draw the conclusions which determine us to make our opposition to Masonry, political as well as moral. A vast field opens before us, and we shall necessarily be brief where volumes might be written.

In the first place, we propose to consider *the evils of Freemasonry, and how it affects our political institutions.*

In the second place, *to show that political opposition to the Masonic institution is, not only justifiable, but that it presents the only effectual means of counteracting the evils it has occasioned, and of preventing its future encroachments upon our equal rights.*

The evils of freemasonry are so numerous that we shall only be able to take up such as fall under a few general heads, and leave the minute detail of them for a more proper mode of consideration.

1st. *The Masonic Institution is subversive of the true principles of charity and Christian benevolence.* Professing to be a charitable institution, thousands have contributed liberally to its funds, who would otherwise have given the same sums in private charity; and have never once mistrusted they were not charitable in so doing. The sums thus received have been expended in building and furnishing Masonic Temples, Chapters and Lodge-rooms; in procuring refreshments, such as brandy, wine, table luxuries, &c.; in enabling criminals to escape the punishments due to their crimes, and in softening for them the rigor of deserved imprisonment. We are not disposed to question that relief has sometimes been worthily afforded to innocent sufferers. No imposition would be successful without some show of virtue. But for every dollar thus expended, thousands have been lavished as before mentioned. Had the immense sums thus worse than wasted, been given in private charity, many a tear that has fallen would have been wiped away. Many a heart that destitution and neglect have broken, would have been comforted. Besides, it turns even the charities it does bestow into particular and unnatural channels;—passing by the most worthy sufferer not a mason, to bestow favors upon the most guilty wretch, if he has chanced to have been graced by the cable-tow.

2d. *The direct tendency of the Institution is to counteract the principles of the Gospel of Christ.* The precepts of our Divine Religion—the commandments and ordinances of God, as contained in the New Testament, breathe a spirit of holiness, forbearance, forgiveness, and peace, as opposite to the levity, profaneness, vindictiveness and mockery of Freemasonry, as light is to darkness. "Swear not at all" is the language of the Gospel, while masonry fills the mouth of the candidate for light, with oaths most horrid, sanctioned by penalties at which the feelings of a cannibal must revolt. "Love your enemies," is a Gospel precept. "Pursue them with malignity and bring them to the most condign punishment," is the voice of Masonry. We might pursue these contrasts, but must leave them for your own examination. By its ceremonies and mock representations of scripture scenes, blended with fable; by its awful profanities, and personifications of the Deity, and by its absurd application of passages from Holy Writ, it tends not only to bring religion into disrepute, but to enfeeble the force of the divine and solemn impressions, which its ceremonies are calculated to inspire. The repetition of such ceremonies on trivial occasions, the quoting of scripture texts in light conversation, and their application to matters of trifling importance, cannot fail to be detrimental to the cause of religion. Yet to induce Christians, and especially clergymen, to lend their influence to the institution it has been held forth as the "Hand-maid of Religion!" No one who investigates its character and ceremonies, will hesitate to pronounce it antichristian in its principles and tendency, leading directly to infidelity.

3d. *By the administration of extra-judicial oaths, it not only interferes directly with the administration of justice in our Courts, by binding its members to concealment and eternal silence, inconsistent with the rights and security of civil society, but also indirectly by rendering the mind familiar with oaths in the name of God—oaths conceived in terms and sanctioned by penalties, which, addressing themselves to the senses, inspire horror rather than awe: and, substituting a nearer for a more remote evil, impair those solemn sanctions which ought ever to be preserved and cherished to secure truth from violation in all Judicial Tribunals.* Every person acquainted with the operations of the human mind, must be convinced that it may become so familiar with the most terriffic scenes on earth, that they will fail to inspire any dread. The soldier long conversant with the scenes of blood and slaughter, ceases to shrink from the field of carnage. The shrieks and the groans of the dying cease to move him, and the horrid din of battle becomes to him no more than is the field of toil to the husbandman. The ear may become accustomed to sounds at first exceedingly painful, until they cease to have a painful effect. Thus the youthful and virtuous mind, when first it witnesses scenes of dissipation and profanity, shrinks from the contamination of vice and crime. But soon, too soon alas! that dread is lost—

> For, "seen too oft, familiar with her face,
> We first *endure,* then *pity,* then *embrace.*"

Such is the influence of the frequent administration of oaths. They never should be resorted to on trifling occasions, and never be administered but in a legal and judicial manner.

Many instances have occurred within a few years, that show beyond question the alarming fact, that masonic oaths are considered by many of its members as paramount to the oaths administered in our courts. Witnesses have refused to testify when under oath, merely because they had sworn to keep masonic secrets, and have been committed and punished for contempt of the process of court. These are facts that may well alarm us for the consequences which must result from such a state of things.

It has been said that these oaths are mere forms, never intended to be binding when they conflict with the laws or the established forms of Justice. What does this argue? Either these oaths are binding or they are not. If they are binding, they directly conflict with the laws of the land. If they are not, they are too profane even for pirates, or the fiercest banditti. Can such language—such forms and ceremonies,—be used without effect? Impossible. The majority of mankind are much more affected by outward forms, and external appearances, than by the real nature of things. Divest a man of his garments, hoodwink him, invest his neck with a halter, lead him round a lodge room, and make him feel abashed by every insult you can offer him, then cause him to kneel at the altar, and, with his hands on the Bible, swear under awful penalties to do or not to do,—think you it will pass on him as an idle farce, or a meaningless ceremony? By no means, is it possible. Ages could not efface the impression from his mind.

Compared with such a ceremony, how simple is the language, how impressive are the formalities of a judicial oath! How much more vivid in the remembrance will be the impressions of horror that result from the former, than the simple awe which accompanies the latter! Let these facts and principles be attentively considered and we do not hesitate to affirm that every rational mind must be convinced of the evil tendency of masonic oaths and penalties.

4th. *It tends directly to subvert Republicanism by introducing a privileged class among us, thereby giving birth to Aristocracy.* A moment's examination will convince every unprejudiced mind, that no necessity ever introduced masonry into the United States. It has no congeniality with our free institutions. It is an anomaly. The protection of our laws was ample, and the broad shield of our excellent Constitution was interposed to secure free and equal rights to each citizen. Where then could be found the least plea for such an institution? Was it needful for purposes of charity? Could not benevolence be exercised in a free country without the aid of bloody oaths and sanguinary penalties? 'Twas no necessity which brought it here. Foreigners introduced it to counteract that spirit of liberty, which no foreign oppression could subdue. Britain withdrew her armies from our shores, but she left what she well foresaw would be more effectual in overthrowing the freedom she wished to destroy, than the sword of the conqueror, or the arms of her heroes. Freemasonry is the planting of her right hand. It sprang up and flourished unsuspected and therefore unwatched. Ere long it began to concentrate wealth and power. Almost all important offices were soon in the hands of its members; and it seemed to hold almost unlimited sway in the councils of the nation. "Whom it would, it thrust down, and whom it would, it set up." At length it dared to set the laws at defiance; murdered an unoffending citizen; and proudly contemning the laws of the land, screened its agents in that dark affair from the punishment due to their crimes, in violation of the most sacred principles of human justice. And when an indignant people attempted to bring to light the dark transaction, threats and reproaches, scolls and vituperations were lavished on them, from every side. The press was silenced. Its most cautious whispers were rebuked. Never had it been seen on this wise before. In vain was it attempted to lift the curtain. Mystery and darkness shrouded the whole affair. Investigation was suppressed—courts of justice were paralized—legislative authority was set at naught, and executive power *neutralized.* For almost eight years has this secret, aristocratic combination withstood the power of the nation, and defied the laws of the land. And more than this, such is its popularity—such its influence in the nation—that scarcely a legislative body in the Union has dared to say aught against it, or to repeal the laws that have given it power thus to triumph. To oppose it in its destructive course, is to expose one's self to unpopularity and vituperation. Is there no cause of alarm with such a state of things in the Republic? When combinations against law succeed and prosper, and when it is accounted criminal to attempt to enforce the eternal and invariable principles of justice, are we to fold our hands and be silent? Should we not rather arise in the true dignity of Republicanism, and crush an institution that has thus trampled on the laws, and violated the rights of our citizens?

Unworthy are we of liberty, if for a moment we can hesitate to assert the supremacy of the laws, and to defend them from so gross a violation. Unworthy are we of the inheritance left us by our fathers, if from fear of scoffs or censures, we shrink from the responsibility of vindicating the rights secured to us by their blood and privations.

Who will say that Freemasonry has no tendency to Aristocracy? By the very oaths administered to its members on their admission, they are bound to give political preference to a brother mason. By the same oaths they are bound to promote his special interest, and ever to conceal his crimes, and to espouse his cause whether he be right or wrong. And further, they are bound, in effect to be accessories to each other's crimes, and to save each other harmless.

5th. Hence it follows that *there can be nothing so well calculated as the Masonic institution for purposes of conspiracy against individuals, or against government.* All is secret—all is dark. Every preparation can be made, and not the least suspicion excited, until, like the springing of a mine, it bursts forth with a tremendous explosion. Such was the Morgan conspiracy. But it is said that the institution is made up of virtuous and respectable members so that no danger need be apprehended. The truth of this statement we fear has not been found universal. We know what its members *have* done, and we are aware of the truth of the old adage: "*What man has done, man may do.*" When trust has been grossly abused, it is apt to become a little sensitive. Masonry has abused our confidence; how, then, are we certain that it will do so no more?

But admit that the assertion is true. Have we any assurance that it will remain so? How susceptible is the institution of change, shrouded as it is in secrecy! We are no friends of irresponsible power. We wish to have the repositories of power open to inspection. We know that its tendency is to make the head giddy; and its irresponsible possession has ever led to its abuse. We wish to know what moves the wires, that give it operation. Let a light shine into darkness that darkness cannot comprehend. If Masonry be innocent, it will not shrink from public scrutiny. If it be guilty and corrupt, scrutiny is necessary. Liberty and equal rights are too valuable to be resigned to chance and uncertainty.

Fellow citizens! guard well your rights. If you preserve them, they will be preserved. If you leave them to the care of others, you may, perhaps, be deceived. Remember there is in existence among us, a corporated society—chartered by our laws—that binds its members to secrecy by revolting oaths. Money and influence are at its command, and all its operations are carried on in secret. You well know what such associations *have done*—what they are well calculated *to do.* Is it, then, safe to cherish such an institution? More especially should we fear now, for all its more virtuous members have withdrawn from it, and it is managed by the desperate who bid defiance to public sentiment. Do we well to rest incautiously, and to permit them to proceed unchecked and unmolested?

Thus much of the evils of Freemasonry. We have entered into no detail of particulars, nor have we transcribed the oaths, or given particular descriptions of the ceremonies of the institution. If any one pleases to controvert any of these statements, or inferences, we are prepared to defend them. The details are before the public, and within the reach of every inquiring mind. Suffice it to say as a summary—its oaths are profane, and its ceremonies revolting. We envy not the insensibility of the man who can read the penalties which the candidate invokes upon himself in default of his oath, without feeling his blood curdle in his veins. Impious, heaven-daring and shocking in the extreme, they are revolting to every religious feeling of the heart.

We now proceed to consider the second proposition, to wit: *that political opposition to the Masonic institution is not only justifiable, but that it is the only effectual means of counteracting the evils it has occasioned, and of preventing its future encroachments upon our equal rights.*

This leads us to examine the nature of the institution, and the relation it bears to our political institutions. If in its ORIGIN and CONTINUANCE, it is distinct from these, and stands wholly unconnected with political power; and if it never, directly or indirectly, interferes with the political affairs of the State or Nation, then it is absurd to oppose it politically. But if, as we promise to show, it owes its corporate existence, without which it could have no power, to legislative favor, and if it interferes, both directly and indirectly, with our political affairs, then our point is gained, and it will be manifest as light, that political Antimasonry is both right and expedient. Whatever owes its existence to the exercise of political power, is properly amenable to political tribunals. And whenever in a republic one legislature enacts a law which is unsatisfactory to a portion of those there represented, it is considered a fair test of the question to refer it to the result of the next election. This is precisely the present question. Here is an incorporated institution, of a known character, which must have originated by an exercise of political power. Having become satisfied that this institution is an evil, we petitioned the Legislature of this State to have it placed under certain restrictions. Our petitions were rejected. Thus aggrieved, where are we to seek redress? May we not be permitted to vote for State officers who will be disposed to regard our wishes? If not, where is our political liberty?

But as to the origin of Freemasonry in the United States. "The first Masons' Lodge in America, was held in Boston, July 30th, 5733, [1729,] by virtue of a commission from the Right Honorable and Right Worshipful Anthony Lord Viscount Montague, Grand Master of England. The Massachusetts Grand Lodge was first established on December 27th, 5769, [1765,] and descended from the Grand Master of Scotland. On the 19th of June, 5792, [1788,] a Grand

Masonic Union was formed by the two Grand Lodges, and all distinctions between ancient and modern masons abolished."—[Massachusetts Register, 1807, etc.]

Thus it appears that while these States were yet provinces, dependant on Great Britain, the Grand Master of England, holding authority from Parliament by which the Grand Lodge of England was incorporated, issued his commission, and extended his authority into the Boston Colony; and that the Grand Master of Scotch Masons afterwards, to wit: in 1765, extended his dominion into the same Colony;—and that in 1788, these two rival sects, which by their contests have since that time caused so much bloodshed in the Mexican Republic, coalesced in Massachusetts.

Before American Independence was established, Masonry had taken deep root in most of the thirteen Colonies; and being established on Parliamentary authority, grew up and flourished in a fertile soil. The dawn of peace and independence gave a new impetus to their progress; and while the Cincinnati was watched with a jealous eye, the Masonic institution rapidly extended itself, fostered and cherished by legislative protection. Acts of incorporation and charters were granted with promptitude; and no pains were taken to ascertain whether the institution were good or bad. It was enough that it *professed* to be a charitable institution.

Thus it went on from strength to strength until 1826. Such was its audacity at that time, that, by its orators, it had defied the "world in arms to put it down." Acting in this assuming attitude, the Morgan outrage, the particulars of which need not be detailed here, was committed. So gross a violation of right awoke a spirit of indignant inquiry. How was that spirit of inquiry met? By insolent threats, by insult and contumely.

The press, ever ready to circulate facts on any other subject, refused to admit facts and inquiries relative to that dark affair. It became necessary to establish an independent press, and it was found impossible to support one without forming a distinct party. Antimasonry was dragged into politics, necessarily, but reluctantly; because it was denied the usual channels for the circulation of light which it was labored to suppress. And down to the present time, the general press of the Country—the Newspapers of other parties, political and religious, not only exclude the truth, on this subject, from their columns, but endeavor to destroy its force when disclosed through other channels. Thus it first became political,—and thus has it been continued so. Whenever the press shall become disenthralled, and masonry shall cease to hold control over other political parties, so soon as the supremacy of the laws is restored, and the rights of our citizens are secured—when the power of Masonry shall cease to be sustained by our laws in violation of their most sacred provisions, then Antimasonry will cease to be political.

Ever since the disclosures of 1826, and those that followed, Antimasons have been petitioning the Legislatures of several of the States, to have some measures adopted to guard the rights of the people against the encroachments of masonic power. They have petitioned for laws to prevent the administration of extra-judicial oaths, and to repeal Masonic Charters; but for the most part without success. In two of the States they have partially succeeded. In this State, as is well known, the subject was referred to a committee of the Legislature; but the question was evaded by the committee, and their doings were approved by that body. Consequently nothing was effected.

When a horrid tragedy disclosed the true character of Masonry, and that disclosure was confirmed by a revelation of principles, the friends of equal rights calculated on the prompt aid of the Legislature in checking its dangerous power. When they saw the laws set at defiance, and the sacred rights of the citizens trampled upon; when they saw Masonic Judges and jurors disregard their oaths, and banish Justice from the Courts; when they saw witnesses refuse to testify under oath, holding their masonic oaths more sacred than those administered according to established forms of justice, they looked to the guardians of public liberty for redress. But they have looked in vain. Petitions and remonstrances, though offered in language the most mild and conciliating, have been disregarded, or noticed only to be made a subject of mockery by the servants of the public. How, then, are we to attempt a reform of these public abuses, but by electing men to office who will listen to our complaints, and see that the State receives no detriment? How can we hope to counteract the mal-influence of a rich and powerful institution, sustained by men in power, unless we place the power in hands that will dare exercise it for the public safety? Those who can see inconsistency in this, may well be suspected of a selfish interest to uphold Masonry.

They manifest a temporizing disposition—a slavish fear unworthy of republicans. For ourselves we dare the mighty contest. Appealing to Heaven for the rectitude of our intentions, we have taken our course; and *that* course we are resolved to pursue until we see freedom and equal rights predominant; until we once more witness the supremacy of the laws, and the putting down of arrogated, unconstitutional power, which has risen to subvert our free institutions.

And not only do we trace its origins and continuance to a political source, and to political protection, but we have had repeated instances of its direct interference in political contests. Grand Master Russell's famous summons to his brother Masons in behalf of Mr. Brooks when a candidate for Governor of Massachusetts, and Deputy Grand Master Jenks' Address to the Masonic Fraternity previous to the election of De Witt Clinton in New York, in 1824, are instances of open interference on the part of masons to promote each others' political advancement. And these are far from being the only instances of the kind. Many more might be cited were it necessary. But open interferences are not so congenial with its character as those partaking of that secrecy which is the spirit of the institution. And it is not to be expected that these instances bear any comparison to the secret influences which have been exerted almost without exciting suspicion. Political preference for a brother mason is a part of the obligation, as before mentioned. And many were the instances, when masonry flourished, that political advancement was held forth by masonic orators as an inducement to young men to join the lodges. And how is it possible in any other way to account for the fact that almost all the important officers in the United States were in the hands of Masons, when they constituted but a small proportion of the population and talent of the Nation. This alone is sufficient to fasten the charge of direct interference with politics upon the institution. Indeed when we consider the constitution of the human mind, we can hardly deem it possible that, with so strong a temptation before it, it should always show itself *purely disinterested.*

Men of aspiring minds, in seasons of high political excitement, could hardly meet in a guarded conclave without thinking that a favorable opportunity for promoting some favorite plan, was presented; and *thinking* could hardly fail of *prompting* to *some effectual action.* We have not—we *cannot* have a doubt that such opportunities have been improved to *private* advantage; and that it is owing to this that so many offices have been bestowed upon masons.

Again, why is it that each State must have its Grand Lodge, and as soon as a State is divided, the Grand Lodge must be divided too? Why is it that the Grand Convocations must always take place during the Sessions of the Legislatures, and whenever the seat of Government is changed in any State, the meeting-place of the Grand Lodge follows? These circumstances with the facts above adduced, prove to us beyond question, that Masonry has had *much* to do with politics, and has *often* interfered with elections.

If these facts and inferences can be shown to be without foundation, let it be done. But our opposers far rather whine, and cry out "*excitement, persecution* and *proscription,*" than attempt the hopeless task of answering these charges. They know that it is impossible to answer for one of a thousand of these things; therefore they shrink from investigation. They would hide its deformity by maintaining a "dignified silence." When its horrid deformity is dragged forth to the light, immediately they cry out that it is extinct,—that it has lost all power for good or for evil. But how does this appear? Why does the Grand Lodge hold its regular convocations? why are officers, "*most excellent, most worshipful, most puissant,*" annually chosen? And why do many of the subordinate lodges begin again to hold stated meetings? Why is there so much sensitiveness if there is no life? Many such deaths has masonry suffered, and her ghost has afterwards appeared to inhabit the high places of the earth.

If Masonry is dead, let us keep it so. But we are jealous of an institution that has so grossly, abused powers which it still retains, and which it is by no means disposed to resign; especially so, as it is still protested by the shield of legislative favor.

But that masonry still lives, and lives to exert an interfering influence on political questions is proved beyond question by recent movements among political parties. No one has forgotten the singular manœuvre in Vermont of the last year, by which an amalgamation was offected between the Nationals and Democrats; in which a party that for years had been predominant, submitted to the degrading terms of adopting a candidate of opposite political sentiments, supported by a feeble minority, for the sole purpose of defeating the Antimasonic candidate, whose political views were coincident with their own. What effected *such* an amalgation, for *such* a purpose, if masonry is extinct? When John Quincy Adams, a man deservedly admired for superior talents, and distinguished for most important public services, and who had repeatedly received the almost unanimous support of Massachusetts for the Presidency of the United States, was candidate for Governor of that State, what influence set up Mr. Davis in opposition to him, for no possible cause but because Mr. Adams was an Antimason, if Masonry is no more?

And let it not be forgotten,—though we remember it with feelings of deep mortification, for its effect on the reputation of a statesman, who has been honored with many important offices in this State and nation,—that, after the lamented William Wirt—the amiable, the godlike Wirt;—the exalted statesman—the sound, discriminating, eloquent Lawyer—the accomplished gentleman and scholar, and most devoted Christian,—had been regularly brought before the people of the United States, as a candidate for the Presidency, in opposition to General Jackson;—a leading National Republican from this State, at the convention which nominated Mr. Clay for the same office, though a political, and, as we are informed, a personal friend to Mr. Wirt, so far overlooked the distinguished merit of that statesman, as to presume that Mr. Clay would "receive the undivided support of all who were opposed to the election of Andrew Jackson." What but the influence of masonry could have so blinded him to the merits of one, with whose name it would honor Mr. Clay to have his associated in honorable competition? No person acquainted with the candidates for the Presidency of the last canvass, can for a moment hesitate to pronounce that Mr. Wirt was the most suitable and worthy man to fill that high and responsible office. Yet such was the influence of masonry that he was thought to be unworthy of the notice of the Clay convention; which seemed to opine that the American people, had not so much as heard that such a man existed, add that they would wholly disregard his nomination by as respectable a convention as has for many years assembled in the United States.

Other instances might be cited, some even in our own State, but we forbear. *Masonry is not dead.* It is the policy of the institution to quiet the public mind by such pretensions, until the present justifiable excitement subsides. But be assured that it only waits a favorable opportunity again to obtrude itself upon the world, in all its pomp and circumstance. Power once attained, will never be resigned without an effort to retain it. And while a majority of our legislators are the abettors of Masonry; while they refuse to do or say any thing tending to obstruct or oppose its power, we may depend upon it, *that power will be re-*

tained. If our rulers venerate that proud institution, nothing short of a change of rulers can prevent its soon being venerated by the imitative multitude. If in the day of its greatest adversity, it holds our statesmen in awe, what are we to expect when its adversities shall have passed away?

Fellow Citizens, beware. Be not deceived by false appearances. There are doubtless, a few masons who are willing that masonry should go down. But a large majority of its members are calculating on its future success and triumph. They cleave to it with the tenacity of life. We entreat you to investigate this subject with the same unprejudiced attention you would bestow on any other subject of equal importance. If you do this, you cannot fail to be convinced that it is the safer course to crush the masonic institution while it is in your power. Give it time to rally its scattered forces, and concentrate its power and influence, and who will be answerable for the consequences. The check it has received will only inflame its love of domination. It will hasten to avenge the "durance vile" in which it has been held; and this nation will hereafter be convulsed by throes more agonizing than any it has yet experienced. We profess no second sight;—no spirit of prophecy ever enlightened our minds with visions of futurity. Yet we venture to predict—and we call you to witness, fellow citizens, that we predict—if Antimasonry does not gain that single triumph to which alone it aspires—the abolition of secret societies—the time will come when this nation will be torn and rent asunder by the influence of such associations. While patriotism and private virtue are the ornaments of the times, such societies can effect little. But when, as it happens with all nations, ambition and self interest gain the ascendency—when many are aspiring to what few can attain—when every other consideration is absorbed in a desire for power, such advantages as are offered by secret, oath-bound associations will not be unimproved.

The impression made on the public mind by the late outrages and disclosures,—though now powerful,—unless followed up, will soon begin to weaken. Time will gradually efface it. By degrees, as that impression becomes more feeble, Masonry will revive. Unless you wish it to flourish as it has flourished, take measures to remove it entirely by throwing it from the pale of the laws, which it has so grossly violated. Suffer it no longer to deceive the unwary by its false pretensions. Let public favor be withdrawn from it; let this sanctuary of crimes be demolished; and let nothing interpose to prevent the operation of the laws; nothing interfere with the free exercise of equal rights.

But it is said to be proscription and persecution to exert the right of suffrage in opposition to the masonic institution. How so? It is no proscription for a friend the bank to oppose a candidate for office who is opposed to the Bank, nor for an anti-tariff man to refuse to vote for a tariff advocate. A Jackson man may withhold his vote from Mr. Clay, nor is a Clay man obliged to vote for Mr. Jackson. All this is rational and consistent. But when an Antimason refuses to vote for an upholder of Masonry, he is without the rule, and is guilty of an unheard of crime. But, we ask, what principle is violated? what right is infringed by the Antimasons? We have ever believed that offices in this Republic are the free gifts of the people; that they are not a right to be demanded, but merely a right to be conferred. The right is with the people—a right freely to be exercised.

No man has any grounds to complain because others may receive the votes he had hoped for—The people are their own judges; and we had humbly supposed that it might be permitted them to be governed by their own convictions. We acknowledge no right in any mason or friend of masonry, or in any other man or class of men, to limit us in the exercise of the right of suffrage. We have as good right to oppose, and we have set forth as important reasons for opposing it to the masonic institution as other political parties can for exerting it in opposition to each other. If freedom be anything more than a name, we have an equal right with other parties to select and support candidates for office, whose principles and practice we approve.

Again it is said that Antimasonry rests on no political principle. If by this assertion it is meant that it does not rest on principles of Jacksonism or Clayism, it is very true. If it is meant that it is not founded on tariff or anti-ariff, bank or anti-bank principles, it is equally true. On all such questions Antimasons are at perfect liberty to think and act for themselves as individuals, and may agree or disagree without any violation of the distinctive principles of Antimasonry. But if by the assertion it is meant Antimasonry rests on no distinctive principle whatever, it *is false.* Its distinctive principle is as broad as the basis of our Republic. It is no narrow, exclusive, or selfish principle. It is rooted in the deepest, firmest foundation of civil liberty. Its principle is that the supremacy of the laws, made pursuant to the Constitution of our Country, should be maintained; that the equal rights of our Republican citizens should never be violated with impunity; that "the best government is that in which an offence against the humblest citizen, is an offence against the whole nation."

In view of such a principle the ephemeral distinctions of other parties may well dwindle into insignificance. This principle has been violated; and Freemasonry, both in principle and practice, is a perpetual violation of it. And so long as it remains an incorporated body among us, so long as its organization and privileges continue, so long shall we owe it *to ourselves, to our country, and to our God,* to overlook *minor* considerations and distinctions, so far as it is necessary to *unite as common friends, in a common cause, against a common enemy*! Far distant be the day, when, in such an emergency, there shall be no fearless patriots to throw themselves into the breach, and expose their all, to save from ruin our excellent institutions.

The principles we advocate are founded in reason and truth, and are the dictates of plain common sense. It requires no mighty stretch of the reasoning powers to comprehend them. These violated, there is an end of government—

an end to the laws. When there is a power which violates the supreme authority of the laws, and prevents their execution, there is no security—no true liberty. And such a power masonry has shown itself to be. It is in vain to disguise the truth—in vain to resist it.

And now, Fellow Citizens, shall we in vain appeal to your patriotism, to your love of liberty, to your sense of the value of equal rights and republican privileges, on behalf of a cause which rests on principles so important—principles violated before the eyes of men in power, who have been elevated by your suffrages, and by whom such violations are deemed unworthy of notice? To you we appeal from the slanders of those who are interested to misrepresent us and our views. We invite you to reject the shackles with which it is attempted to bind you, and enlist under the broad banner of Freedom and Equality. Will you unite with us in asserting the dignity of our laws—in maintaining, inviolate our sacred institutions? With us will you sustain the principles of Liberty when assailed by a haughty aristocratic combination, that what we inherited from our forefathers, we may hand down to posterity unimpaired and unscathed,—as the richest legacy which can be bestowed upon them?

The candidates selected by the Antimasons, and offered for the suffrages of the People, are men against whom even malice can say no evil. They will bear the most rigid scrutiny of comparison with those presented by other political parties.—They are above reproach; men of integrity, piety and patriotism;—as statesmen, amply qualified to discharge, with honor to themselves and advantage to the State, the duties of the important offices for which they are named. They are men of principle, of experience, of information, of native and acquired talents; of virtuous minds, and above all the rest of the supporters, the firm and fearless supporters of equal rights; and are ready with unshrinking fortitude, and frank independence, to vindicate the "SUPREMACY of the LAWS."

With *such men,* fellow citizens, to preside in the councils of our State, our institutions will remain inviolate, and our rights secure. Far more conducive to the prosperity of this State would be the election of such men to office than to continue, as for several years past, to elect only warm partizans, who study the interest of the *party,* forgetful of that of the *State.* Far more creditable than to elect those who make offices the rewards of political zeal in sapping the foundations of republicanism, by deceiving the minds of the people; and misleading them to a disregard of their own true interests. Far more prudent than to elect the Past Grand Master of the Grand Lodge of Masons in this State; for by so doing there would be manifested an indifference to a dangerous institution, indicative of a want of caution in guarding the republic from the appearance, at least, of evil.

We entreat you, Fellow Citizens, to give this subject a calm investigation, unbiased by prejudice,—uninfluencec by favoritism. We doubt not of your candor in examining the reasonings and facts embraced in this Address; and we cannot but expect your favourable decision. So important, indeed, these principles appear to us, that on their maintenance, we believe depends the integrity of our free institutions. Let them prevail, and our destiny will be happy, and our REPUBLIC IMMORTAL.

In Convention at Hallowell, July 4, 1834.

4

To the Electors of Massachusetts (Worcester? 1837)

IN THE MID-1830s, the Whigs had not yet become as united and as well organized as their opponents. Although they campaigned vigorously in the presidential election of 1836 (supporting four different candidates, each in a different part of the country), I have not been able to locate any of their pamphlets for that year. A year later, however, the Massachusetts Whigs offered a powerful rendition of their party's basic policy argument. Pointing out that they faced state elections in 1837, they stressed that "the great questions which now engage the public mind, are questions of National concern." A great economic crisis was besetting the country, and its origins lay in the disastrous financial policies of the Democrats, beginning with Jackson's veto of the Bank recharter and continuing in the wildly destructive state bank policies of the current president, Martin Van Buren, "followed by other acts equally impolitic and equally arbitrary." In addition, all of the Democrats' policies had a quality besides their foolishness: they were "an abandonment and abdication of all of the powers" that the Constitution gives to the national government to help the people. In short, both their specific policies and the Democratic approach to government were dangerous and could only lead to further national disaster.

At a Convention composed of the Whig members of the Legislature and of delegates from cities and towns not represented by Whigs, held at the State House on the 15th day of March last, the subscribers were appointed the State Central Committee for the present political year; and by this appointment the duty was imposed on them of addressing their fellow citizens on the subject of the approaching Annual Election.

In the discharge of this duty, we shall make but little reference to the individual candidates who are presented to your support. Principles rather than persons, measures rather than men, claim now and always the chief regard of Republican Voters. And now, perhaps, more than ever before in the history of our own Republic, does this claim demand of us all a primary and paramount attention.

In the political contest which is now agitating the United States, principles are at stake which reach at once to the property and the liberty of the people, and measures which deeply involve both public rights and private prosperity. In such a contest individual Candidates, however distinguished by their abilities or their virtues, are justly the subjects of but secondary consideration, and so long as the fitness of their selection cannot be questioned, their peculiar qualifications or comparative claims are left to tell their own story. We shall accordingly confine ourselves on this topic of our Address, to a simple transcript of two of the Resolutions adopted by the Convention by which we were appointed;—assured that the character of the individuals of whom they make so honorable mention, will need no other testimonial with the great majority of the citizens of Massachusetts:—

> RESOLVED: That the members of this convention, in conformity with Republican usages, do hereby unanimously recommend and nominate
>
> His Excellency EDWARD EVERETT
>
> as the Whig candidate for Governor of this Commonwealth for the ensuing political year; that we have marked with continued approbation the whole course of his official conduct as Chief Magistrate; that we entertain undiminished confidence in his long tried political integrity; and that, as citizens of Massachusetts, we feel the same honest pride as at first, on account of the purity of his private character, his eminent attainments in all useful knowledge, and the practical ability with which he has discharged that public duty.
>
> RESOLVED: That this Convention unanimously nominate
>
> His Honor GEORGE HULL
>
> of Sandisfield in the county of Berkshire, as the Whig candidate for re-election to the office of Lieutenant Governor, and that they cordially recommend him to the support of the people of Massachusetts, as a pure and patriotic citizen, a faithful and capable public officer, and a firm and unwavering whig.

With the recital of these Resolutions, unanimously passed at a convention of delegates from every part of the State, we leave all consideration of the candidates submitted to your choice.

Nor do we propose to enter upon any detailed examination of the particular State policy which these officers have for two years past pursued, and which, if again elected, they may be expected to pursue in future; or to contrast it, at any length, with that which the candidates nominated in opposition to them, are pledged, in case of their success, to substitute. Were there not other topics of a more engrossing interest at the present moment, such a course of remark, we are sensible, might be adopted with great advantage to the cause committed to us. We might point you, on the one hand, to the steady and successful efforts which have been made under the administration of our present Executive, for improving the condition of our Free Schools, for raising the character of our Militia, for simplifying the processes and rendering plain the precepts of our Laws, and for increasing the efficiency and extending the usefulness of all those Institutions, which were established by the foresight of our fathers, for the education, the defence and the general welfare of the people. We might recount to you, on the other hand, the disorganizing and destructive doctrines which have been so often directly avowed, or indirectly sanctioned, by the opposing Candidates, during their protracted struggle for promotion—doctrines, which are the very watchwords of the party by which they are supported, but which are as widely variant from the principles of a true Democracy, as they are incompatible with the existence of any republican government. We might exhibit to you the untiring efforts of that party to break down within our own Commonwealth some of the most valued safeguards of society, and to abolish some of the most solemn sanctions of justice. We might refer you to the almost unanimous vote of its representatives in the last legislature, refusing to concur in the remonstrance against a bill introduced into the Congress of the United States to violate what is commonly known as the Compromise Act, to reduce the Tariff, and to destroy at once that protecting system, under which the Manufactures of New England have hitherto prospered, and to which Massachusetts in particular owes so much of her population and wealth.

Indeed, upon this last manifestation of the policy of our opponents we cannot refrain from indulging in a single remark. We will not pause to inquire what would have been the condition, actual or prospective, of our national treasury, if that short-sighted proposition *"to reduce the revenue to the wants of the country,"* (falsely so called,) had been sustained, and if its operation had been such as was intended by its author and advocates. Bankrupt as that treasury already is, it may not be important to discover to what greater degree of bankruptcy, to what lower depth of destitution, it might have been reduced, if those who had charge of the ways and means of the country, had followed out and fulfilled their designs. But what, we do ask, would have been the condition of our own commonwealth, if this vote of the Van Buren representation in her last Legislature could have taken effect, and the bill, to which it related, had become a law;—if, besides all the disasters which the mad financial measures, of which we shall presently speak, were then bringing upon her citizens, the duties upon foreign manufactures had been, at the same moment, greatly decreased, and this new disturbing element had been added to the causes which were already pregnant with the existing Crisis;—if this new impulse to importation had been superinduced upon that wild spirit of speculation which even then was menacing her with ruin, and the unchecked competition of foreign labor had been united with the influences which are now so fearfully depressing her domestic industry?

We cannot believe, fellow citizens, that you will forget or forgive, at the approaching polls, the treachery to Massachusetts interests and Massachusetts principles which this vote involved, nor that you will fail to secure yourselves against such a misrepresentation of your sentiments and such a perversion of your delegated powers in future.

But we forbear further comment on the policy or the measures of our opponents, so far as they are peculiar to the affairs of our own Commonwealth. The great questions which now engage the public mind, are questions of National concern. Upon these, at this moment, parties are every where divided, and upon your judgment of these, the approaching election will, doubtless, depend for its result.

During the last six or seven months, the people of this Commonwealth, in common with their fellow citizens throughout the Union have been suffering under an amount of pecuniary embarrassment which has absorbed all attention, and which must continue to do so until relief is afforded. Whether this embarrassment is to be attributed, in whole or in any considerable part, to the measures of the National Administration, or whether it has been the result of causes over which Government has had no control, is a question of vital interest to the prosperity of the country and of every one of its citizens, involving, as it directly does, the more practical inquiry, *from whence is relief to be expected.* If the sufferings we have been doomed to experience are the mere result of private rashness and individual mismanagement, it is unreasonable to visit the vexations which they have caused upon our political rulers, and vain to look beyond ourselves for the remedy. But if they are the unavoidable consequences of Executive Measures, begun, continued and ended in the face of all the financial experience of the country, and in direct defiance of the most solemn warnings of the very events which have now occurred, the authors of those measures are justly the subject of our rebuke, and from them, or from their removal from power, can we alone hope for redress. The causes and the remedy of the existing crisis being thus intimately connected, we ask your attention to a brief investigation of the one, before we venture to make any allusion to the other.

And at the outset of this investigation, we are not unwilling to admit the justice of the remark, in the late Presidential Message, that it is *"hardly to be expected that those who disapproved the policy of the Government in relation to the currency, would, in the excited state of public feeling produced by the occasion, fail to attribute to that policy any extensive embarrassments in the monetary affairs of the country."* But while we acknowledge the justice of this idea in the negative application which is here given to it, we cannot forbear to suggest that there is another and more positive application of the same general sentiment, which may, with no less justice, be commended to the author and his supporters. If it be true, that those who have disapproved the late policy of the National Government in relation to the Currency, are too ready to find in that policy the fruitful source of existing monetary embarrassments, how much more true is it, that those who have not only not disapproved but supported that policy, who have not only supported but instigated it, who have not only instigated it in its origin and supported it in its progress, but who are still pledged, in their own persons, and beyond possibility of retreat, to sustain, carry on, and complete it, are quite ready enough, to say the least, on their part, to ascribe those embarrassments to any and every other source, and to conjure up all manner of causes for their existence which may divert the attention of the people from their own acts! Were there any doubt of the general justice of this position, the document from which we have made the foregoing quotation, and to which we shall have occasion to make further allusion hereafter, would furnish ample evidence of its entire applicability in the present case.

The Political Party of which we have the honor to be the organ in this Commonwealth, consider it, we do not hesitate to aver, their highest claim to public confidence and support, that they have, from first to last, by their own votes at the polls, and by the votes and voices of their Delegates in the National Legislature, opposed the financial policy of the late President of the United States. They have opposed every act by which that policy has been advanced, and every principle on which it has been advocated. They have opposed the unprecedented abuse of the Veto—thrice put forth in the prosecution of this policy. They have opposed the arbitrary and irresponsible exercise of the Appointing Power—so flagrantly displayed in one of its most critical stages. They have opposed the outright usurpation of Executive control over the currency, manifested through the medium of those Treasury Orders by which that policy was recently consummated. And had no disasters resulted from these acts, had they been attended by all the blessings which were promised by their advocates, instead of being followed by the unmingled curses which are now upon us, we should no less eagerly have asserted our uniform and unqualified opposition to them. As unwarrantable and tyrannical acts, adopted and pursued in violation of the whole spirit of our Constitution, and tending directly to the concentration and consolidation of all the powers of the Government in a single hand, they deserved, without regard either to their results or their motives, the unhesitating reprobation of every friend to Liberty and the Republic.

But it is by no means true, as the Presidential paragraph which we have cited, was doubtless intended to imply, that the opponents of this policy of the Government in relation to the currency, are now for the first time opening their eyes to the positive pecuniary evils with which it was fraught;—or that the reference of the present commercial disasters to these acts, as their origin, is only an afterthought, prompted and stimulated by personal disappointment or political rancour. On the contrary, the Congressional records and the popular journals of the last six years every where attest, that the Whig statesmen in their public places, and the Whig party, at their primary meetings, distinctly predicted these very evils and disasters, even to their ultimate catastrophe in the suspension of specie payments, while yet that policy of the Government was only in its conception. The speeches of your own Adamses and Websters are full of these predictions. They and their colleagues in both branches of Congress, foretold the very crisis that is upon us, as certain to be produced sooner or later, by the prosecution of such a policy; and, in the same breath in which they denounced the acts by which it was carried on, as illegal and arbitrary, they declared their conviction that it could only end in the entire derangement of the currency, and the utter prostration of credit.

The reference of the present Crisis to Executive policy, then, fellow citizens, has been no mere wisdom after the event;—no artful wresting of existing, accidental circumstances into grounds of accusation against political adversaries;—nor even, to use the softer and more insinuating terms of the President's Message, has it emanated from *"an excited state of public feeling, produced by the occasion."* It has been a judgment in advance of that occasion,—conceived long before that excited state of public feeling existed,—uttered in no spirit of taunt for what was done, but in a tone of deprecation for what was proposed to be done,—a judgment founded upon dispassionate, unchanging principles, confirmed by past experience, and, we may now add, verified by present results. And had that judgment been seasonably regarded, had those clear and distinct predictions, instead of being slighted off as the empty ravings of splenetic partizans and seditious panic-makers, been candidly heard and heeded, our country might have been spared the overwhelming agonies of the present hour. But we are anticipating the result of the investigation which we proposed to attempt, and to this, without further preface, we again invite your attention.

Let us go back, for this purpose, to the first step in that series of Executive measures, which by common consent has received the title of the *Experiment,* or rather to that step, which taken, perhaps, without looking to consequences, made it necessary that some experiment should be tried. We refer to the denunciation and Veto of the Bank of the United States.

We will not detain you by attempting to assign the motives of the Administration for adopting this measure. Whether it originated in an honest and well-considered scruple of the Constitutionality of the charter or of the utility of the institution itself, or whether it was instigated by the mortifying but well-merited repulse which had been sustained, in the notorious effort to make that institution an instrument of executive patronage and power, can make no difference to the present issue. The fact, in either case, is the same. An institution which first came into existence under the auspices and by the deliberate assent of George Washington, and which, after the expiration of one charter, received its second call into being from the lips of James Madison, was denounced as unconstitutional corrupt, dangerous to liberty, by Andrew Jackson, and the bill, which had passed both branches of Congress to give it a prolonged duration, vetoed.

It is not too much to assert, fellow citizens, that by this single blow was struck open the salient spring of all the calamities we are now enduring. At the moment it was dealt, no nation on the face of the globe possessed a better currency than these United States. Redeemable in specie at sight, or convertible with equal readiness into bills of unbounded circulation, it united the convenience and cheapness of paper, to the uniformity and soundness of coin. The domestic exchanges of the country, now embarrassed and deranged almost beyond the power of mercantile negotiation, were then transacted at rates greatly below the natural standard—the price of transporting and insuring specie—and a circulating medium was thus supplied to the whole trading community of the Union, absolutely more uniform than specie itself.

But we need not resort to the inferences and arguments which these and other facts so abundantly furnish, for the proof of our position. *Experience* is a readier as well as more satisfactory kind of evidence, and we happen to have had not a little experience in precisely the same case. The Bank of the United States had been suffered to expire before. Its original charter terminated in 1811, and it was not revived until 1816. And what was the result of that expiration? We do not ask simply, what was the history of that interval. Every one knows the embarrassment, distress, convulsion, with which it was crowded—

never exceeded, never equalled, but by those of the present moment. Every one knows, too, the overbanking and overtrading, or as the message entitles it, *"the overaction in all departments of business," by which they were preceded, and the fatal catastrophe by which they were followed*—the suspension of specie payments in all parts of the country except New England. But how much of all this was the consequence of the dissolution of the Bank of the United States? We appeal to one, whose historical accuracy will be as unsuspected, as his financial ability is unsurpassed. Albert Gallatin, who during a portion of the time of which he writes, was in the immediate confidence and cabinet of President Madison, shall answer this question.

"The creation of new state banks," says he in accounting for this very suspension of specie payments, *"the creation of new state banks, in order to fill the chasm, was a natural consequence of the dissolution of the Bank of the United States. And, as is usual under such circumstances, the expectation of great profits gave birth to a much greater number than was wanted.* * * *From the* 1st *of January* 1811 *to the* 1st *of January* 1815, *not less than one hundred and twenty new banks were chartered, and went into operation with a capital of about forty, and making an addition of near thirty, millions to the banking capital of the country.* * * *And as the salutary regulating power of the Bank of the United States no longer existed, the issues were accordingly much beyond what the other circumstances already mentioned rendered necessary.* * * * * IT IS OUR DELIBERATE OPINION THAT THE SUSPENSION MIGHT HAVE BEEN PREVENTED, AT THE TIME WHEN IT TOOK PLACE, HAD THE FORMER BANK OF THE UNITED STATES BEEN STILL IN EXISTENCE. *The exaggerated increase of state banks occasioned by the dissolution of that institution would not have occurred. That bank would, as before, have restrained within proper bounds and checked their issues."*

Such is the account given by Mr. Gallatin of the consequences of the dissolution of the first Bank of the United States—an account written for the express purpose of warning the late Administration from the measures it was preparing to pursue—and how precisely does it correspond with the results of the destruction of the second! Has there not been exhibited throughout the country the same eagerness and the same excess in creating new state banks, *to fill the chasm,* and have not those banks, when created, been enabled to indulge in the same improvident and unchecked issues? The *same* did we say? The extravagance of these creations and the improvidence of these unchecked issues have as far surpassed those between the years 1811 and 1816, as the ruin which is around us now, exceeds that which Mr. Gallatin described.

The late Presidential Message, itself, contains a partial statement of the facts upon which this assertion is based. But a report of the Secretary of the

Treasury in January last furnishes the particulars in full. And by that report it appears, that between the 1st of January 1830—a date shortly subsequent to the original denunciation of the United States Bank, and when the effects of its impending destruction first began to be developed—that between this date, and the 1st of December 1836, three hundred and fifty-seven new banks, besides one hundred and forty-six branches were created, making an addition of more than one hundred and seventy-nine millions of dollars to the banking capital of the country; while, during the same seven years, there was an increase in the issues of paper money of more than one hundred and twenty-four millions, and an increase of bank loans and discounts of more than three hundred and ninety millions of dollars!

Some of the peculiar circumstances by which these various augmentations were swollen so disproportionately to those detailed by Mr. Gallatin will presently demand notice. But when we examine the two periods in our financial history, and perceive in each of them events so entirely similar and differing in nothing but the degree of their development, we cannot fail to ascribe them to that only cause which we know to have existed in both cases—the destruction of the National Bank, and the tempting opportunities for over-banking of all sorts, which the removal of that great regulator of the currency so manifestly offered. And when, fellow citizens, we reflect on the pecuniary distress and personal misery which these circumstances have produced, how forcibly are we reminded of the remark of President Adams, in his Speech on the removal of the deposites, that if the pamphlet of Mr. Gallatin from which we have quoted, and in which these results were so clearly pointed out, "had been honestly read, in the pure pursuit of truth, by the Statesmen whether of the parlor or the kitchen who rule this nation, many an awful foreboding of ruin, many a bitter cry of distress, many a deep and agonizing execration of wretchedness, would have been spared to our Constituents and to our own ears." What a tenfold emphasis, at this moment, has that assertion of his, which, even when it was made, was fully justified by the circumstances of the times, that "no man with a mere human portion of malignity, or with any portion short of that of a *fiend,* could have read that pamphlet, and then rushed headlong upon the experiment under which the country now writhes in torture."

But neither the prediction of these results, not the history of those which had followed the dissolution of the former bank, were confined to Mr. Gallatin's pamphlet. The same history was narrated and the same results were foretold, by the most distinguished statesmen in all parts of the Union. And they all but embodied that experience which the authors of this measure had themselves lived long enough to enjoy, and but predicted those results, which, with the ordinary faculty of employing the history of the past for the interpretation of the future, they might themselves have foreseen. In the wanton disregard of that experience, in the wilful neglect of that foresight, they *did* "rush headlong on that experiment under which our country now writhes in torture." Those awful forebodings of ruin have been realized, those bitter cries of distress, those deep and agonizing execrations of wretchedness are now ringing anew and in redoubled accents in our ears. The prosperity of the Country and the welfare of the People have been *vetoed* for many years to come!

But the veto of the bank charter was but the preparatory process of the *reform* to which the Executive was pledged, and but the primary cause of the evils which have ensued. It was not sufficient that the Bank should be doomed to dissolution at the expiration of its existing term. It must be instantly robbed even of those powers and privileges which, during that term, its charter had seemingly secured to it. The revenues of the government, for the collection and custody of which it was mainly created, must forthwith be filched from its vaults, and be placed where they may better subserve the ends of Executive influence. Congress, indeed, had pronounced them safe where they were, and had expressly refused, upon deep deliberation, to authorize their removal. But fortunately for the freedom of Executive action, Congress did not remain in session quite all the year through. It had now adjourned, and, until it should be again convened, some degree of discretionary authority over these deposites, was legally devolved on the Secretary of the Treasury. To that authority the President appealed for their removal. But the individual who at the moment enjoyed it, saw no occasion for its exercise, and refused to accede to the President's wishes. His fidelity to the public service was instantly deemed worthy of a different sphere of exhibition, and he was promoted to the post of Secretary of State. A new Secretary of the Treasury was now appointed for the express purpose of executing the President's plan. But he, too, could not find it in his conscience to perform this deed. But, though General Jackson had thus, by the confession of his own acts, no power to remove the Deposites, he had, or at any rate claimed to have, and consequently exercised, the power of removing refractory Secretaries, and to this power he again resorted. Mr. Duane was dismissed, in disgrace, from his three day honors, and another individual was placed over the treasury department, who could be relied on to affix his name to any order which the President might dictate. The confidence, this time, was not misplaced. The President assumed the responsibility. The Secretary signed the order. And, between the two, the public treasure was removed from the vaults where Congress had left it in safety, and scattered over the country at Executive will.

In this arbitrary proceeding, fellow citizens, we have a second and an auxiliary cause of that enormous increase of bank capital and bank issue which we have detailed, and of the distresses which are now resulting from it. The creation of new State banks was stimulated not only to *fill the chasm* which the destruction of the United States Bank would create, and to take advantage of the license of unchecked issues which would follow, but, also, to secure some portion of the spoils which had been plundered from it in anticipation of its end. These spoils were yearly growing greater and more valuable. The land bill of Mr. Clay, by which that portion of the revenues accruing from the sale of the public lands was to be annually distributed among the people, was condemned by General Jackson to the same fate with the charter of the Bank. He professed to believe that the great domain to which it related, and which had been purchased by the blood and toil of the *old* States, had, by some miraculous and invisible transfer, become the unalienable property of the *new!* He pronounced it palpably unconstitutional to distribute a superfluous portion of the public revenues among the whole people of the Union, and yet regarded it entirely constitutional to distribute the whole source of those revenues among a small portion of that people! At all events, he *vetoed* the Land bill as he had done the bank, and the rapidly increasing revenues of the country were thus permitted to accumulate unchecked in the vaults of their new protectors. These constantly accumulating deposites, for which no interest was paid, and which were too often obtained in mere consideration of the party fidelity and zeal of those who applied for them, could not fail to form the basis of a most lucrative business to the selected banks, and it thus became a matter of direct pecuniary interest to every citizen in the country to obtain a share in their management. It is not to be wondered at, that, under the impulse of such an interest, new banks were everywhere created, and the capitals of old ones enlarged. The promise, the expectation, the hope, the chance, the mere possibility of securing a portion of these deposites, for which nothing but principles and votes were to be paid, and from which untold amounts of substantial profit might be received, was enough to engender a Banking Mania throughout the Union. And thus the revenues of the nation became not only one of the readiest means of an unlimited political corruption, but one of the most efficient causes of that exaggerated increase of bank capital and bank issue which is now overwhelming us with its results. The property of the people was thus, at the bidding of an arbitrary Chief Magistrate, converted into an Engine of destruction, at once to their rights and their interests, to their liberty and their prosperity!

In the positions which we have thus far advanced, fellow citizens, may be seen the fallacy of the argument, so plausibly set forth in the late Presidential message, and so unceasingly urged by our political adversaries, by which it is attempted to screen the administration from a just responsibility for its measures, by ascribing the present crisis primarily and exclusively to overtrading and overbanking. That these have been among the causes of this crisis we do not hesitate to admit. But no one can fail to perceive, from the facts we have now adduced, that they have been but *secondary* and *derivative* causes, and that they have been themselves the direct and inevitable consequences of the Executive Experiment. Rashness on the part of the people has, undoubtedly, conspired with that on the part of the President, in producing the result. The passions of private citizens have, undoubtedly, yielded to the temptations which the Executive held out, and to the opportunities which he created. But without those temptations and without those opportunities, this Crisis could never have occurred. Had the Bank of the United States been permitted to remain in its original relation to the government, in that relation which it had sustained for forty, out of the forty-eight years of our constitutional existence, holding the revenues of the country in its vaults and distributing such part of them as accrued from the public domain, to the people to whom they belonged, agreeably to Mr. Clay's bill, all might now have been well. "The exaggerated increase of state banks, occasioned by the dissolution of that institution, would not have occurred, and that bank would, as before, have restrained and checked their issues." Enterprise would not have been stimulated to excess, nor credit expanded to explosion. *The Suspension of specie payments might have been prevented.* Private distress and public bankruptcy might alike have been avoided. And the Nation might still have been advancing along the tried Constitutional track to new degrees of prosperity and honor.

But the measures which we have thus far alluded to, were not the only ones, which, adopted by the Executive in direct opposition to the deliberate action of Congress and without any warrant of Constitutional authority, have resulted at once in aggravating distress and in cutting of all ordinary means of relief. The destruction of the Bank, the removal of the Deposites, and the distribution of the revenues among a few, favored agents of the Administration, were destined to be followed by other acts equally impolitic and equally arbitrary. An attempt had been made at an early stage of the Experiment to render it more palatable to the people, by a pretence that it was to terminate in the utter extirpation of paper money and in the complete substitution of a metallic currency. Yet every step which had been thus far taken hard, as we have seen, produced the direct effect of increasing that paper money in amount, and of rendering its redeemability in specie tenfold more conjectural than before; while not an additional dollar of silver or gold had yet found its way into circulation. Congress had indeed passed a law to alter the relative legal value of these precious metals, and a slight increase of one of them may thus have been effected, though probably at the expense of the other. But the Executive now resolved on making a desperate effort to introduce them forcibly into the country. The allowance of our long unsettled European claims gave some opportunity for the attempt, and the remittance of these claims was forthwith ordered to be made in gold. But that was, after all, only a small sum and came slowly, and the Deposite Banks were therefore appealed to, on their allegiance, to aid in the effort. Holding the rich prize of the public monies entirely at Executive will, they of course could not fail to comply with Executive wishes. And thus, at the very time when our trade with the old world, under the influence of a vastly expanded credit, was extending itself beyond all former precedent, the balance against us was augmented by the immense sum of *forty millions* of the precious metals, imported forcibly, artificially, and contrary to all the courses of commerce, for the mere gratification of an Executive whim. The history of the Crisis affords no instance of overtrading in any way comparable to this overtrading of the President himself in gold and silver.

Still it did not find its way into circulation. No man's purse *"jingled"* with it. No man's pocket was distended with it. Paper money was more abundant, more convenient, and would buy bread and meat as well; and not even the sturdy vociferation of *rag-money* which was kept up by a distinguished portion of the Executive partizans, could procure its rejection. The imported gold and silver slid noiselessly into the vaults of the banks which had bought it, most of it without even the ceremony of re-coinage, *forming the basis of still new and new emissions of paper* while it was there, but ready to be drawn out for re-exportation to Europe, whenever the great pay-day should arrive, and the country should be called on to settle its balances abroad.

In the mean time, the proceeds of the Public Lands, bought up by the township, in that spirit of reckless speculation which the measures we have described were so well calculated to excite, had reached an amount exceeding thirty millions of dollars. And this vast deposite, held at the feudal tenure of Executive favor, and constituting one great Electioneering Fund, had become a subject of just alarm throughout the whole country. A proposition for its distribution was accordingly introduced anew into Congress, and, after some modification, was adopted with such unanimity in both branches, as to compel the Executive to lay aside his brandished veto, and to give it "a reluctant assent." But, though by his own signature, the Distribution Bill had now become a law, immediate evidence was given of a design to embarrass and defeat its operation. As long as the proceeds of these lands were permitted to accumulate in the vaults of the selected banks, their rapid sale had been regarded with undisguised satisfaction. Certainly, no effort whatever had been made to retard it. But no sooner was the distribution among the People resolved on, than this wild speculation became in the last degree monstrous, and instant measures were taken to put an end to it. Could this be effectually accomplished, and the annual expenditures of the Government be made to exceed by only a few millions, the enormous amount to which this *economical* Administration had already carried them up, the distribution among the People might still be prevented. Congress would come together again before the act providing for that distribution would go into operation, and under such circumstances would not fail to suspend it.

Such, fellow citizens, are believed to have been the original views under which was issued that infamous Treasury Circular, by which payment for public lands was thereafter to be received in nothing but gold and silver—a measure which ought not to be named without arousing the universal indignation of the people, fraught, as its operation has been, with embarrassment and disaster to the whole Union. Doubtless, there were other views which aided in its dictation. In checking the sale of the *public* lands, it would throw the monopoly of this whole subject of speculation into the hands of *private holders,* some of the largest of whom are believed to have been not a great way off from the very council chamber of the Executive. Nor would it only enrich these private holders. It would enable them, also, to pay over the money with which they had speculated to the deposite banks of whom it was borrowed, and without which these institutions might fail of being ready to pay over, in their turn, the surplus revenue to the people should the Distribution Bill be ultimately insisted on. It would, moreover, have the certain effect of driving specie to the West, and thus of destroying the facility of its re-exportation to Europe, whenever Exchange should turn against us and our mercantile balances abroad should be called for. The desperate chance of a metallic currency would thus be prolonged, and General Jackson might at least have an opportunity of getting out of his office with honor, before all the gold and silver which he had imported, had actually got out of the Country.

But, let the motives of this measure have been what they may, it was utterly unwarranted on the part of the Executive by any Constitutional authority, and was in direct contravention of the recently expressed will of Congress, to whom alone its consideration belonged, and in one of whose branches it had already been rejected by the votes of all the members save *one.* But the same arbitrary power, which had disregarded these circumstances before, and assumed the responsibility of removing the deposites from the Bank, was prepared to disregard them anew, and assume the responsibility of removing the specie from the sea-board. A subservient Secretary signs the order, and the consequences are immediate. Those millions of gold and silver which had been forced into the country, contrary to all the courses of business, and against all the impulses of trade, and which, when here, had been made the basis of excessive issues of bank paper, are now driven into new and still more arbitrary channels. They leave the great reservoirs where the Commerce, and Industry, and Enterprise of the country demand their aid, and are found struggling over the Mountains to form the clumsy medium of a ruinous speculation. The domestic credit, to which they had given expansion, and of which they had formed the basis, is suddenly contracted. The foreign balances, which their importation had in great part created, and for the settlement of which they had been relied on, are called for. And the whole business community is subjected to distress both from abroad and at home, which they alone are capable of relieving. But the Order is persisted in. Congress, indeed, by great majorities in both branches, annul it. But the Executive Veto again prevails. The bill by which it was annulled, instead of being returned to Congress with the reasons of the President, is sent to the office of the Secretary of State with the reasons of the Attorney General! The relief which it provided, is denied to the people, and ruin now rushes unobstructed over the land.

Nor was this the only operation of the Treasury Circular. Besides drawing off from the banks of the great commercial Cities, the specie upon which their issues had been based, and thus compelling a sudden and ruinous contraction of those issues, that Circular proclaimed, in language not to be misunderstood, to the whole people of the country, not merely the general hostility of the Government to bank paper, but their particular distrust of its immediate value. It was, in effect, an Executive indorsement of all the *slang*, which had emanated from the administration presses for months before, against the solvency of the State Banks, and an open declaration that their issues were not considered worthy of further credit at the National Treasury. Confidence in the existing currency was thus disturbed. The private bankruptcy which was daily occurring, increased the distrust, and a general panic soon ensued. A run upon the banks by the People, was the natural result of that which had been commenced by the Government. And the suspension of specie payments in the great Commercial Metropolis of the Union, gave instant origin to the same deplorable catastrophe from Maine to Florida. And thus the Experiment ended. And thus was fulfilled to the letter the prophecy of our illustrious Senator with regard to its end:—"UNDER A PRETENCE OF A DESIGN TO RETURN TO A CURRENCY WHICH SHALL BE ALL SPECIE, WE ARE LIKELY TO HAVE A CURRENCY IN WHICH THERE SHALL BE NO

SPECIE AT ALL. WE ARE IN DANGER OF BEING OVERWHELMED WITH IRREDEEMABLE PAPER—MERE PAPER—REPRESENTING, NOT GOLD AND SILVER,—NO, SIR,—REPRESENTING NOTHING BUT BROKEN PROMISES, BAD FAITH, BANKRUPT CORPORATIONS, CHEATED CREDITORS, AND A RUINED PEOPLE!"

And here, fellow citizens, let us examine that all-sufficient and impregnable defence which the administration of the country have recently undertaken to set up against these and all other arguments, by which any portion of the existing Crisis is ascribed to Executive action. What is it? It is, to use their own words, that *"evils similar to those suffered by ourselves, have been experienced in Great Britain, on the Continent, and indeed, throughout the commercial world; and that in other countries as well as in our own, they have been uniformly preceded by an undue enlargement of the boundaries of trade, prompted, as with us, by unprecedented expansions of the system of credit."* And again they say, *"two nations* (Great Britain and the United States,) *the most commercial in the world, enjoying but recently the highest degree of apparent prosperity, and maintaining with each other the closest relations, are suddenly, in a time of profound peace, and without any great national disaster, arrested in their career and plunged into a state of embarrassment and distress. In both countries we have witnessed the same redundancy of paper money and other facilities of credit; the same spirit of speculation; the same partial successes; the same difficulties and reverses; and, at length, nearly the same overwhelming catastrophe."* And *"in view of these facts,"* says the late Executive Message, *"it would seem impossible for any sincere inquirers after truth to resist the conviction that the causes of the revulsion in both cases have been substantially the same."*

Now, without arrogating to ourselves, or to the Party in whose behalf we speak, any exclusive claim to the title of "sincere inquirers after truth," we instantly admit that so far from resisting, we have conceived and cherished this conviction from the beginning. The causes of the revulsion, such as it has been, in both the Countries here alluded to, and in all the Countries in which it has in any considerable degree occurred, have undeniably been substantially the same. But the great question still recurs,—*What have those causes been*—not the derivative and secondary causes, but the original, exciting causes of this great Crisis—what have they been? Have they, or have they not been, that same series of highhanded Executive Measures which we have just described, and which, though projected and pursued within the little round of the American Capital, have extended and exercised their influence over the whole sphere of American Commerce? This is the exact question at issue. And the answer to this question, contained in the foregoing paragraphs of the President's message, is about as satisfactory as the logic of one, who should adduce as irrefragable evidence that the Asiatic cholera had not its primal seat and original source in the region from which it takes its name, the well-known fact, that the same disorder has committed its terrible ravages "in Great Britain, on the Continent, and, indeed, throughout the commercial world."

It is plain, that in order to give validity to either argument, it is essential to prove that there has been no such influence as *contagion* at work. And without wasting words on the possibility or impossibility of *medical* contagion in this or any other case, we presume no one will have the hardihood to dispute the constant existence and operation of what may well be called *mercantile* contagion. Who does not know that Commerce, and its great ingredient, Credit, are sensitive, to a proverb, to the slightest foreign touch, and that they fluctuate, like the very element on which their principal operations are transacted, before the merest breath of external influence? Finding a way wherever a plank can float, or a wheel run, or a foot tread, and meeting occupation and instruments wherever there are wants to be supplied or materials to supply them, they push their enterprise along every meridian, and leave no latitude uncrossed by the track of their ceaseless circuit. And yet throughout that whole circuit, there is not one point which is not affected to a greater or less degree, by the same adverse or prosperous influences which are brought to bear upon any other point. There never can be a Commercial Crisis which shall begin and end on the same soil.

But not to dwell upon this obvious, abstract position, let us suppose, for the sake of argument, that the views we have presented of the origin of the present Crisis, wherever it has appeared, are admitted to be correct, and that our adversaries have, for a moment, acquiesced in their truth. Is there anything, the world over, which has yet transpired, which is at all inconsistent with this hypothesis? Is it anything unnatural or extraordinary that the spirit of speculation which had been excited here, and which was obliged to cross the ocean for materials and means to gratify its insatiate rapacity, should have lighted up something of a kindred spirit in the bosoms of our brethren abroad? Is it wonderful that the forced and artificial importation of forty millions of the precious metals into the United States, should have disturbed the pecuniary equilibrium of Great Britain and France, from whom it was drawn, and so much of whose circulating medium is composed of these metals? Is it entirely unaccountable that, when under the influence of this speculating spirit and of this importation of gold and silver, an enormous Commercial Debt had been contracted by our citizens, and had become due and payable to their correspondents and creditors in these foreign countries, and when, by the derangement of our currency and the prostration of our credit, all power and possibility of paying this debt had been cut off or postponed—is it, we repeat, entirely unaccountable, except upon the supposition of independent contemporaneous causes, that these foreign countries, under such circumstances, should have experienced, in the persons of such creditors and correspondents, severe pecuniary embarrassments? In other words, can debtors become bankrupt, or in any way fail of making punctual payment of their dues, without communicating loss, embarrassment and failure to those by whom they have been trusted? And is not this the whole history of the revulsion, such as it has been, in foreign countries?

We say *such as it has been.* For, fellow-citizens, we must not be understood to admit all that is implied or even all that is expressed with regard to this revulsion elsewhere, in the Executive paragraphs we have just quoted. *It is not true* that the same revulsion has been experienced in other countries, or in any other country, which has occurred in this. *It is not true* that "we have witnessed in Great Britain the same redundancy of paper money and other facilities of credit; the same spirit of speculation; the same partial successes; the same difficulties and reverses; and at length, nearly the same overwhelming catastrophe." And, in making these assertions to account for the present Crisis, the Chief Magistrate of the United States has assumed as arbitrary a dominion over *facts* as his predecessor usurped over the *laws,* in taking the steps by which that Crisis was produced. An intelligent and discerning People, before they can give a true verdict in the case submitted to them, or do any justice to the parties concerned, must rescue both laws and facts from so manifest and flagrant a perversion.

It would protract this Address beyond all reasonable bounds, to enter into a careful comparison of all the causes, symptoms and effects of the Crisis which the Executive Message has pronounced the same in the two countries. Nor is it necessary to do so. No one whose eyes are not completely coated over with the most impenetrable film of party prejudice, can fail to perceive the falseness of the assertion. It is a mockery of the sufferings which have been experienced in the United States to speak of them in the same breath with those which have taken place elsewhere;—a mockery which could only have been anticipated from those who had wantonly inflicted them. What "overwhelming catastrophe" has Great Britain met with? Has its commerce been convulsed and paralyzed in every limb and muscle as ours has been? Has its whole system of domestic exchanges been annihilated? Has its currency been plunged back into the chaos from which centuries of experience and wisdom had been required to redeem it? *Have its Banks been compelled to suspend specie payments?* This alone is the difference of life and death to Commercial Credit, of wealth and bankruptcy to the National Treasury. And this is the difference which is slurred over and almost suppressed, in the Executive expression *"nearly the same"!*

The pecuniary disasters which have occurred, "in Great Britain, on the Continent, and indeed throughout the commercial world," fellow citizens, are mainly those which might have been expected and even calculated beforehand, from the existence of our own. And wherever they have occurred, they have been so regarded and so spoken of. How was it in Great Britain in this respect? For what class of her monied men, her manufacturers and her merchants, were fears felt in advance, and on what class of them did the main crush of the Crisis ultimately fall? Was it not the American Houses, the American Bankers, and those who manufactured for the American market? Was it not on account of these, and such as were known to be dependent on these, that every arrival from New York was waited for with such solicitude on the London Exchange, and even some of the Packets waylaid before their arrival, and robbed of their mailbags by chartered Steamers? Was it not to bolster up American bankers, until the whole extent of the "American Crisis" should have been developed, that the Bank of England abandoned its accustomed sphere of action, and employed such unwonted resources? As it has been in Great Britain, so has it been elsewhere. With other countries our mercantile connections are less intimate, and in other countries the reaction of the American Crisis has been proportionably less disastrous. With Great Britain, as the Message truly states, we maintain *"the closest relations,"* and there that reaction has been most severe. And, maintaining such relations, it would have been as complete a miracle had the commerce of the United States been prostrated, as it has been, without seriously embarrassing the commerce of Great Britain, as it would be for the waters of the Gulf Stream to be evaporated to the winds or quenched upon the central fires, without leaving the British Navy, high and dry, in the bed of their own Channel!

The existence of commercial calamities elsewhere then, furnishes no new facts for our consideration, and not only no answer but a positive corroboration to the arguments already adduced. That the American Crisis may, in some of its stages, have developed seeds of disaster already existing in other countries, and such as always exist to a greater or less degree in every commercial soil, is undoubtedly true. But that there has existed any where any great exciting and original Cause, similar or dissimilar, antecedent, contemporaneous or subsequent, which, producing, within the past year, the same or "nearly the same" overwhelming catastrophe with that which has been witnessed in these United States, may be taken as a safe, dispassionate expositor of our own Crisis, is utterly untrue. And in relying upon such premises for their only vindication and defence, the National Administration have pronounced and ratified their own sentence of condemnation.

And now, fellow citizens, the condition of our Country being such as it is, and the causes of that condition such as we have stated, what is the *remedy* which has been proposed by those upon whom such a proposition officially devolves, and by whom alone any proposition can be effectually made? The Administration by which the ruinous policy we have described was carried on, has changed its ostensible head. But substantially, we know, it is the same. There has been some shifting of places, and some change of names. But it is supported by the same party and has the same responsible and irresponsible advisers. It has now called together the National Legislature, by special proclamation, to consider "great and weighty" matters. It has opened its budget. And what does that budget contain? Is there anything of manly confession of mistake, or of honorable purpose of amendment? Anything of regret at the calamities it has occasioned, or of anxiety to minister to their redress? Any thing of an abated tone in the delivery of exploded dogmas, or even of a willingness to waive them for the relief of the community? And what do these great and weighty matters turn out to be? The rescue of the currency from chaos? The restoration of the exchanges to uniformity and order? The reconstruction of that great regulator of the circulating medium whose overthrow has been twice signalized by an almost immediate suspension of specie payments? The resuscitation of credit and confidence among the people? The deliverance of Industry in all its departments from that incubus of embarrassment which is destined to crush it even more fearfully than it yet has done, if not speedily removed?

It might have been expected, certainly, that a few syllables of an Executive Message prepared under such circumstances, would have been spared to propositions of this kind. And the expectation was encouraged and strengthened by the example which had been given by an Administration of former days. We have before alluded to the condition of our country in 1811–16. And we have alluded to the fact that James Madison, who it is hardly to be admitted was less pure in his patriotism or less fervent in his democracy, than the self-styled democratic leaders of the present hour, and who it is well known opposed the creation of the first Bank of the United States and once vetoed the charter of the second, reconsidered his opinions and retraced his steps in view of the exigencies of his country, and gave to that second charter his official assent and signature. It is important to state the language of Mr. Madison upon some of these occasions, as his opinions upon this question have been so grossly misrepresented in the Address of the late Van Buren

Convention at Worcester. The Records of the Nation will attest, that at the opening of Congress, December 5th, 1815, President Madison used this language:—"The absence of the precious metals will, it is believed, be a temporary evil; but until they can again be rendered the general medium of exchange, it devolves on the wisdom of Congress to provide a substitute, which shall equally engage the confidence, and accommodate the wants of the citizens throughout the Union. If the operation of the State Banks cannot produce this result, *the probable operation of a National Bank will merit consideration.*" And the same Records will attest, that at the opening of Congress on the 3d of December, 1816, previously to which he had actually signed the Bank charter, after speaking of the measures which had been adopted for "the restoration of an uniform medium of exchange," he added: "*The Bank of the United States has been organized under auspices the most favorable, and cannot fail to be an important auxiliary to those measures.*" Nay, in the very Message in which he vetoed this charter as originally proposed to him, we find him, at the outset, expressly *"waiving the question of the constitutional authority of the Legislature to establish an incorporated Bank, as being* PRECLUDED, IN HIS OPINION, *by repeated recognitions, under varied circumstances, of the validity of such an institution, in acts of the legislative, executive, and judicial branches of the Government, accompanied by indications, in different modes, of a concurrence of the general will of the Nation."*

Three and twenty years have elapsed since this language was uttered by Mr. Madison under circumstances of the most solemn responsibility. And since it was uttered, too, *his own Executive Acts* have been added to those by which the validity of such an institution was previously recognized, and twenty years of new existence have been given to that institution by his personal recommendation and assent. And yet so far is the denial of the constitutional authority of the Legislature to establish an incorporated bank from being regarded as *precluded,* by those who pretend to be the lineal inheritors of Mr. Madison's democracy, that it has become a leading article of their political faith and practice, and "the authority of Mr. Madison's own name" is declared to be in their favor! Infamous imposture! which wields the sacred influence of a venerated name, in a cause which its owner had so solemnly renounced. Pitiful fraud! which charges upon one dead, sentiments which it had never dared to ascribe to him living. Infatuated meanness and folly! which imagines that, in the age of the printing press, the lapse of a single generation can have effaced all records of the *truth.*

We had thus, fellow citizens, some right to anticipate that an Administration, professing to be Democratic in its character and creed, would have sacrificed something of its preconceived opinions and feelings to the wants and necessities of the people. Whether that sacrifice should have been manifested in precisely the same mode with that of the former Administration to which we have referred, we do not undertake to pronounce. We are not so wedded to the idea of a National Bank, that we should not have hailed with unalloyed satisfaction the proposal of any adequate substitute, if any such could have been devised. But, that some proposal would be made, in a spirit of concession and with a purpose of relief, the people of the country had a right to expect, and did expect. And how has that expectation been gratified? Self-justification for the past, self-will for the present, and self-security for the future, may be declared, without exaggeration, and without suppression, to be the sole dispositions and designs which are exhibited in the late Executive Manifesto.

Having voluntarily convoked the Constitutional Representatives of the people, having called them all directly from among the people, and many of them with the freshest tokens of popular favor and the latest evidences of popular feeling, the first business of its author has been, to lecture these Representatives upon the will of the people, and to lay down instructions for their action, derived from stale manifestations of favor to himself, or from the most doubtful indications of assent to his opinions. Professing a desire to do everything to remedy existing evils consistent with the principles of the Constitution, he has, next, taken care to assert and maintain that precise construction of the Constitution, which precludes the adoption of the only remedies, which experience, here and elsewhere, has proved to be effectual,—a construction, which pronounces almost every year which has elapsed since that Constitution was ratified, to have been a year of unconstitutional action; and which pushes out from the hallowed circle of Constitutional Patriotism every one who has been called to preside over the destinies of the Country, except himself and his illustrious predecessor!

And what is the policy which he has concluded by recommending? It is one, which, under the canting cry of divorcing Banks and State, will divorce rulers and people—erecting the former into a separate rank of privileged masters, while it sinks the latter into a common herd of dependent subjects. One, which under the paltry pretence of discarding corporations as fiscal agents, will create the whole army of office-holders into one great Corporation, with the Treasure of the Nation for its Capital, and their own irresponsible will for its Charter. One, which, if fairly fastened on the country, will change its whole face, will reverse its whole destiny, will put fetters on its industry and rivets on its enterprise, will unpeople its cities and unfertilize its fields, will corrupt all that is left of its virtues, will destroy all that is left of its liberties, and will leave the whole great work of our Fathers to be done over afresh.

What, fellow citizens, are the three leading measures which the administration have recommended and proposed? Let us look at them for a single moment, and see if we can discover a *clue* to the Policy which embraces them all.

First, we have the Act to exempt the Secretary of the Treasury from paying over to the States the fourth instalment of the surplus revenue. We will not spend time in detailing the obvious objections to this act—the suspicion it will cast upon all acts of a Government which thus unceremoniously discharges itself from an obligation so solemnly incurred—and the inconveniences to which it will subject the People, who, relying on the performance of this obligation, have entered into a thousand contracts, which, if it be not fulfilled, must in their turn also be violated. Certainly, both of these are serious considerations, and the latter has justly characterized the act, as one of fresh oppression, instead of one of relief, to the community. But incomparably the most alarming feature of this measure is found, not in the immediate consequences which must follow its enactment, but in the manifest motives which have prompted its proposal—in the eager lust which it exhibits on the part of the Administration to avail itself of the first shadow of pretence for grasping anew at the treasure of the country, and for bringing back under its own dominion what had been so lately and so laboriously wrenched from it. Owing to the peculiar circumstances of our currency, it is not pretended that this money can be applied to the present necessities of the Treasury Department, and it is admitted that its distribution among the people might be accomplished with no very considerable delay or loss. But there is a plausible ground for retaining it under the orders of the Executive, and it is accordingly so arranged.*

Next, we have the Bill to authorize the emission of twelve millions of Treasury Notes. What a consummation of a series of measures which, hardly six months ago, were declared by their advocates to be on the eve of resulting in the entire extirpation of paper money, and the complete substitution of gold and silver! What an ending for the old Experiment, what an opening for the new!

And lastly, there is what is called the Sub-treasury System, which is nothing else than the legal surrender of all the revenues of the country, collected and to be collected, now and hereafter, to the unconditional keeping of Treasury Agents.

The two latter measures are, certainly, fit counterparts of each other. We

*Since this was written, this Bill has become a law, and the payment of the 4th Instalment of the Surplus Revenue is postponed to the 1st of January, 1839. It is well understood, and it was so stated substantially by Mr. Adams and others in their remarks against the bill, that though a date for the payment has been named, the postponement is intended to be indefinite and perpetual.

need not say that both bear ample testimony to the same design, which is so clearly stamped upon the first of the three—that of placing and retaining the whole monies of the Nation under the sole control and custody of the Executive.

Yes, fellow citizens, trace this new policy of the Administration to its sources, strip it of its disguises, drag it out from its concealments, and what do you find it? What, but a new attempt to convert our Constitutional Republic into that "simple machine," which has been the subject of such constant eulogy for the last eight years? What, but a more daring effort to consolidate all the means and attributes and authorities of government into that 'unit' of power, in furtherance of which the present incumbent of the Presidency resigned his post in the cabinet of Gen. Jackson, when he first aspired to the rule of this nation? What, but a more desperate determination to bring about that fearful union of purse and sword, which is the very definition of despotism?

The public monies, according to this policy, are, indeed, to be distributed among a thousand—more likely—among a hundred thousand hands. But of them all, only ONE will be elected by the People, while all the others will owe their offices and emoluments to the direct appointment of that ONE. True, there is the check of the Senate. And the time was, when that check might have been safely confided in against a world of Executive Corruption. But alternately defeated and defied, as it has been by the last Administration, there are now none so poor to do it reverence. The *removal* of these thousands of monied minions will be made by the President without the Senate, and their *appointment* by the President in spite of the Senate! What a pecuniary machine is this! What an organ of patronage, what an engine of power! And proposed, too, by those who are prating, in the same breath, about "the concentrated money power" of a National Bank. Fellow citizens, call this contrivance what you will, hide it up under what terms of ingenious imposture its projectors may coin or counterfeit, IT IS ITSELF A NATIONAL BANK, and *such an one* as the Freemen of this nation ought never to submit to have established.

But we are considering this policy only from a political point of view. From that alone, we find it full of fearful omens to our country and its liberties. But what will be its effect upon our Currency and Exchanges? Will it do anything for their uniformity or soundness? Will it reanimate credit? *Will it restore specie payments?* It does not even profess to be intended for any such object, and none such can it possibly effect. Its first principle is to abandon these affairs to their own direction, and its first operation will be even worse than this. Instead of promoting the uniformity of exchanges and currency, it will perpetuate their want of it. Instead of restoring specie payments, it will entail upon the country forever the frauds and abominations of irredeemable paper. It will create one currency for the people, and another for their rulers—secure specie to the latter, but give only depreciated paper to the former. Salaries and taxes will thus be raised, a handsome per centage pocketed by those who receive them, and a perpetual interest planted in the bosom of the Office-holder to make that per centage larger, by increasing the difference in value between the people's paper and his own gold.

Fellow citizens, we should utterly exhaust your patience, if we have not done so already, were we to attempt to enumerate all the enormities with which this new Experiment of the National Administration is fraught. Regarded from any point of view, it is alike odious and fearful. It has no redeeming feature. Morally, it is a return to *strong boxes* and *iron chests,* and will bring along in its train all those temptations to fraud, peculation, robbery and murder, which have ever hovered over the known receptacles of gold and silver. Economically, it will cost the Country new millions for salaries, and will stake its whole treasure upon the casual honesty of successful office-hunters. Politically, it will augment the patronage of the President beyond that of any king in Europe, and place in his hand a sceptre of power second only to that of the Autocrat of Russia. And Constitutionally, how is it *Constitutionally?*

It is a virtual abandonment and abdication of all the powers of that Sacred Instrument, so far as any object of general welfare is concerned;—a preservation and maintenance of them only for private, official, partizan ends. And in favor of this project, the Administration and its friends have had the effrontery to appeal to the history and the principles of that Constitution and its Framers! A Constitution, the first impulse to whose formation was notoriously found in prostrated commerce, in depressed industry, and in disordered finance, and whose earliest effort and operation was to give new life to that commerce, new nerve to that industry, and perfect symmetry to that finance, is now, in this nine and fortieth year of its organized existence, discovered to contain not a single authority for any such purpose, and its very authors and finishers are summoned from their shrouds to prove it!

Sanction this construction of your Constitution, fellow citizens, and you seal the doom of this Republic. Confirm this policy, and you surrender your own birthright. It is now plausibly stated, artfully couched, ingeniously disguised, and there may be fascination in some of its appearances. But once adopted, and it will unfold itself in a thousand coils of destruction to your interests and poison to your principles. Commerce will not be its only victim. That will serve but to flesh its fangs. Manufactures were long ago marked out for its prey. And Agriculture, secure and even smiled upon as it may now seem, will enjoy but the miserable satisfaction of being struck down last. Where is the interest, so insulated from every useful art and industry of society, so single in its nature, so separate in its operation, so selfish in its end, so independent of all influences but those of God and nature, as to live and prosper under so contracted, so corrupt, so treacherous a policy? You may find it in the breast of some absolute officeholder. You may find it in the career of some savage outlaw. Tyranny and anarchy alike, may furnish examples of its existence. But no such interest can be found in the honest hearts or among the peaceful pursuits of a civilized, Free, Republican People. Already has this policy, in its earliest struggles into being, blotted out from the page of Constitutional Power almost the whole catalogue of Internal Improvements—once the cherished object of National appropriation, and the anticipated source of National prosperity and pride. Already has it doomed to destruction every shred and patch of a Protective Tariff which has been hitherto grudgingly spared to the necessities of our Domestic Industry. And now, it denounces, as matters pertaining to a particular class of the people, as exclusive in their nature, and unworthy of regulation by a government which was instituted for the general protection and welfare, the entire system of Exchanges, Currency, and Credit. Where next will it find the objects of its proscription? We should rather ask, where will such a policy not find them? Carried out to its legitimate conclusions, it would extinguish every light along your shores that now sheds safety upon the midnight mariner, and leave your Navy and your Merchantmen to wreck themselves together on the ruins of your beacons and break-waters. It would raze to the dust every Custom house on your coast, and send an armed exciseman into your shops and granaries, your cellars and closets, to exact the means of paying for a Government which provided no protection in return. It would disband every regiment on your National Frontiers, and leave fields to be ravaged, and firesides to be desolated, at the alternate will of savage and civilized marauders. Why, it would ask, should such exclusive and separate interests as these be regarded? It is expecting "too much of the government," and losing sight of the ends for which it was formed. True, all these interests have hitherto been provided for, and all these ends have been hitherto happily accomplished. But sounder principles are beginning to prevail, and a sounder policy must now be established. And that policy would only find its perfect consummation, when the severed symbols of triumphant *Nullification* should have supplanted the banner of Union and Liberty, upon every flagstaff and cupola in the Country!

But that policy will not be confirmed. That construction of the Constitution will not be sanctioned. Better hopes are before us. Better auspices are around us. The Country is aroused to the danger of this new Experiment, and wherever opportunity has yet occurred, has given glorious pledges to resist and defeat it. Maine, Rhode Island, the great West! What cheering voices have we heard from them all, assuring us that though the People may be cajoled and deluded for a while, they cannot permanently be robbed of their senses, or spoiled of their rights, and that our Laws and Liberties will finally be rescued from overthrow by the intelligence and virtue and patriotism of the Nation!

Massachusetts has no steps to retrace. She has held on through good report and evil report, through discouragement, defeat, despair, every thing but *dishonor,* to the true principles of the Constitution and the tried policy of the Country. She now beholds with something of conscious pride as well as of unfeigned delight, her Sisters, far and near, returning to the good old path, and joining in the march of Republican Reform. She sees one of her cherished sons, the never failing supporter of those principles and that policy, and under whose lead her course has been proudly maintained, receiving the reward of his fidelity and patriotism in the respect and gratitude of his fellow citizens throughout the Union, and already designated in more than one direction for the highest honors in their gift. But, at such a moment as the present, she will indulge in no selfish or sectional feelings. Yielding up to the decision of a majority of the States, in convention duly assembled, the free selection of persons, she will be satisfied herself with an unyielding support of principles—those Principles whose triumph will be the true triumph of the People, and whose defeat, the certain downfall of Constitutional Liberty.

We cannot close this Address, fellow citizens, too long as it has already detained you, without a brief allusion to another topic of high National concern. We refer to the proposition which has recently been made in some quarters of the country, to enlarge the American Union by the annexation of Texas.

We do not propose to recount the origin of Texan insurrection or to narrate the history of Texan independence. Nor can we do more than mention the imminent perils both to our domestic harmony and our foreign peace with which such an extension of our National Territory would be attended. These are all, undoubtedly, momentous considerations, and full of import to the honor and welfare of our Country. But were Texan patriotism of unspotted, unsuspected integrity, and the history of Texan independence worthy to be inscribed on the same page with that of our own, there is another aspect of the proposed measure which assures us that Massachusetts will never be accessary to its adoption.

The Legislature of Massachusetts, at their last session, by an almost unanimous vote in both branches, adopted Resolutions vindicating the Rights of Petition and Discussion from the arbitrary assaults which had been made upon them both by the administration majority in the National House of Representatives. Those Resolutions, having received the signature of the Executive, became the legitimate language of the whole Commonwealth. And it is believed that no part of them more truly expressed the unfeigned and heartfelt opinions of both Legislature and People, than that which pronounced the institution of *slavery* to be "a great, moral, political, and social evil." Nor is such an opinion new to the citizens or the councils of the State. It has been entertained, expressed and acted upon from the time of the Revolution.

It is not to be believed, under such circumstances, that Massachusetts will give any thing but united and uniform opposition to a measure, whose adoption would add a vast slave territory to the Union. The Constitution of the United States, as it is, she is determined to abide by, in respect to slavery and in every respect. She will infringe none of its guaranties, violate none of its compacts, overstep none of its limitations. The Union, as it is, she will cherish and cling to, to the last, as the best bond of Peace, the best bulwark of Liberty. May its banner over us be love forever! But she will enter, voluntarily, into no new alliances, which have either for their design or their effect, to extend or perpetuate the institution of slavery. And she will regard such an event, should it be destined to occur, as one of the greatest evils which could befall this Republic.

Such, fellow citizens, we believe to be the sentiments of the entire people of Massachusetts. We will not accuse even our political adversaries in this Commonwealth, with differing from us materially upon this subject.—Certainly, if they do, they disguise and even deny such a difference.

But is there no reason to apprehend that while they entertain and avow the same repugnance with ourselves to the proposition before us, every vote which they cast will produce the very opposite influence? We have before alluded to the fact, that parties are every where divided upon questions of National Legislation. It is notoriously and exclusively so in our own Commonwealth. While not a single National Officer is to be chosen at the approaching polls, it is not less true that every vote which is thrown, will give encouragement and support to one or the other of the two great parties which divide the nation, and to one or the other of the particular policies which they are respectively pursuing. Indeed, the very principle on which our adversaries organized themselves at their recent Convention at Worcester, was that of unqualified defence and support to the *financial* policy of the National Administration.

But is it entirely certain, fellow citizens, that their votes to the coming election will give support and countenance to no *other* policy of the National Administration? We know well, from the freshest experience, the adroitness with which that Administration can interpret to their own intents, the purposes of all who, from any cause, cast votes in their favor. We have seen the head of that Administration in his late Message to Congress, torturing into an expression of assent to a particular creed which he had been pleased to espouse, every ballot which was thrown for him as President, and even as Vice President of the United States. Is there no danger that the ballots which are thrown in favor of his supporters, in this State, at the approaching election—taking place, as that election will, at a moment when the subject of Texas is at the heart of the whole country—may, one day or other, be quoted as indisputable evidence that so many of the People of Massachusetts were in favor of its admission to the Union?

Are we asked, what reason there is to believe that the National Administration is itself friendly to this measure? Gladly, most gladly, would we believe otherwise. But when we remember that as Vice President of the United States, Mr. Van Buren gave his casting vote in favor of a bill to subject the contents of every mail bag to an inquisition, with authority to suppress and destroy whatever, in the discretion of the Postmaster, might be deemed of an incendiary character; and when we remember too, that in his Inaugural Speech, as President, he so far violated the decency and dignity of his position, as to menace the Representatives of the People with a Veto, should they venture upon any legislation ever so remotely affecting the existence of slavery—we cannot fail to fear that, if he is opposed to the annexation of Texas, it is not from any indisposition to further the peculiar views or to favor the peculiar institutions of the Slave States.* And, when we remember also, the unbecoming haste with which the qualified authority of Congress was taken advantage of by General Jackson, to recognize officially the independence of Texas, and the entire absence of all explanation or expression upon the subject in the late Executive Message, it is impossible to repress the conviction,

*To avoid all possibility of misunderstanding in this matter, we subjoin the following extract from Mr. Van Buren's Inaugural Speech—"Perceiving, before my election, the deep interest this subject was beginning to excite, I believed it a certain duty fully to make known my sentiments in regard to it—and now, when every motive for misrepresentation has passed away, I trust that they will be candidly weighed and understood. At least they will be my standard of conduct in the path before me. I then declared that, if the desire of those of my countrymen who were favorable to my election was gratified, 'I must go into the Presidential Chair the inflexible and uncompromising opponent of every attempt, on the part of Congress, to abolish slavery in the District of Columbia, against the wishes of the slave holding states; and also with a determination equally decided to resist the slightest interference with it in the States where it exists.' I submitted also to my fellow citizens, with fullness and frankness, the reasons which led me to this determination. The result authorizes me to believe that they have been approved, and are confided in by a majority of the people of the United States, including those whom they most materially affect. *It now only remains to add, that no bill conflicting with these views can ever receive my constitutional sanction.*"

that the National Administration is decidedly in favor of the measure. Indeed, it has been openly avowed by its supporters on the floor of Congress, that negotiations upon this subject are at this moment pending between the Governments of Texas and the United States.*

What a solemn responsibility do these considerations give to our votes at the coming election! Those votes are now in our own hands. Let us be careful that they be so cast, that no man shall be able to interpret them, at his pleasure, into evidences of assent to so abhorrent a measure. The existence of Texas as an Independent Nation, coming into that existence on the principle of perpetuating slavery, cannot be sufficiently deplored. But while it is a separate nation, the people of the United States are, at least, not partakers of its guilt. And, if it remain a separate nation, it may even be the means—not certainly means of our own choosing—of effecting the diminution, perhaps the ultimate disappearance, of Slavery within the boundaries of our existing Union. Its vast extent of luxurious soil will afford far greater temptations to the southern planter than any portion of our present territory. And thither the slave may be removed. But once let it be annexed to the American Union, and the idea of seeing that Union free from this great evil, will only exist in the hopeful vision of some pious philanthropist, or in the desperate design of some mad fanatic.

Rarely, fellow citizens, has it happened in the history of any people, that they have been called on to give judgment, at one and the same time, upon two

*After this Address was in the press, the documents upon this subject, communicated by the President to Congress, in pursuance of their call, were received here. They consist of a letter from the Texan Minister (General Hunt) to our Secretary of State, in which the *annexation* is directly proposed, of the reply of the Secretary, and of a rejoinder of the Minister. The whole substance of the Secretary's reply, which abounds in expressions of respect and friendship for Texas, is contained in the following sentences:—"Whether the Constitution of the United States contemplated the annexation of such a State,and if so, in what manner that object is to be effected, are questions, in the opinion of the President, it would be inexpedient, under existing circumstances, to agitate. So long as Texas shall remain at war, while the United States are at peace with her adversary, the proposition of the Texan minister plenipotentiary necessarily involves the question of war with that adversary. The United States are bound to Mexico by a treaty of amity and commerce which will be scrupulously observed on their part, so long as it can be reasonably hoped that Mexico will perform her duties and respect our rights under it. * * * * The inducements mentioned by General Hunt for the United States to annex Texas to their territory, are duly appreciated; but, powerful and weighty as certainly they are, they are light when opposed in the scale of reason to treaty obligations, &c. &c." It is manifest that this reply does not in any degree alter the view we have presented. The proposition is at best postponed. The inducements to the annexation are declared to be "powerful and weighty," and "Treaty obligations" alone are objected to it. Should Texas obtain a Peace, or the United States be embroiled in a War, with Mexico—or even should the Executive cease, from any cause, to have "reasonable hopes that Mexico will perform her duties and respect our rights," all these objections will vanish. It is evident that they will not last long. Indeed, the letter in which they were stated, was dated in August, and to the rejoinder of the Texan Minister, in which they were answered, no reply is given. From the recent avowal on the floor of Congress, to which we have alluded in the Address, it is feared they have already evaporated.

such momentous propositions as those which are now before us. It is fortunate, that, with a large majority of the Citizens of Massachusetts, this double judgment will involve no conflict of principles, no clashing of duties. By the same vote they can condemn them both. And though the objects to which they relate are so widely different in their nature, the propositions themselves are by no means unworthy of being coupled in the same sentence of condemnation. If the one would extend and perpetuate slavery among a class of the People, the other would create and establish a despotic power in a branch of the Government. If the one would endanger the existence of our Peace, our Union, and our Liberty, by an unnecessary and unjust *extension* of the limits of our National Territory, the other would put a stop the prosperity and progress of our Country, and annihilate the whole value of its Constitution, by an unwarranted and arbitrary *contraction* of the limits of its Legislative Authority. And both, both would be attended, in their adoption and operation, with fearful, fatal tendencies to the entire corruption and overthrow of our present Republican System. As we love and honor and value that System, then, as we would live under it and die under it ourselves, and leave it unimpaired to our children, let us enter our Solemn Protest against both these propositions at the approaching polls. And thus, while we secure for ourselves a pure and faithful administration of the affairs of our own Commonwealth, we shall do all that is in the power of the people of a single State, to preserve and perpetuate our UNION AS IT IS—ITS CONSTITUTION WITHOUT DIMINUTION—ITS TERRITORY WITHOUT ADDITION.

PART TWO

The Jacksonian–Whig Synthesis 1838–1854

5

To the Democratic Republican Party of Alabama (n.p., 1840)

THIS ADDRESS was written by some of Alabama's most prominent party leaders, a group of Democratic congressmen and U.S. senators. One of them, William R. King (1786–1853), would become his party's successful vice presidential candidate in 1852. Here, in 1840, King and his colleagues introduced into the two-party discourse the dangers posed by the rise of antislavery societies in the North in the late 1830s, and these organizations' aggressive petition campaign against the South's peculiar institution, a campaign that had deeply roiled Congress, and that continued to do so. The most notable thing in the argument presented here was the close tie that the authors argued existed between the antislavery agitation and the Whig party in the North, which combined traditional party concerns with sectional ones particularly strongly. The pamphlet does not assail the North as a section, but adds the abolitionist threat to all of the other issues associated with the Democrats' partisan enemies as part of a broad litany of dangers that Southerners, and Americans generally, faced.

FELLOW-CITIZENS: The extraordinary exertions which [our opponents] are making to mislead the public mind on the approaching Presidential election, and, which, we are informed, have extended to Alabama; induce us to address you on the propriety of adopting a political organization in every county throughout the State, which shall insure a union of effort in defence of our principles, as effective as that with which they are assailed. The two great parties, which have always divided the country, are again in the field struggling for mastery; *we,* under our appropriate name and principles, contending for a strict construction of the Constitution, which shall protect the rights of the many against the encroachments of a privileged few; while *our opponents,* under the hope of concealing their political identity, have assumed the new name of Whigs, but are true to their old principles: That ours is a Government not of equality, but of *privilege;* and that under the Constitution, Congress can confer on favored individuals not only the exclusive privilege of manufacturing a paper currency for the whole Union, but the right to convert the whole revenues of the Government into so much bank capital, to be used and loaned out for their individual benefit. This is the true issue which is involved in the present contest of political parties, and, to insure another signal triumph to the republican cause, it is only necessary that the question should be fairly understood. The great body of the people, who have no favors to ask but an honest and equal administration of the Government, are, and ever have been, essentially republican. If any portion of them have adhered with stricter fidelity than all the rest to these cherished principles, it has been the southern people. With them, republicanism is not merely a sentiment, consecrated by education and their earliest political recollections, it is to them a citadel of defence against the encroachments of the stronger sections of the Confederacy; a fortress for all their rights and institutions against the assaults of a tariff, a bank, or their still more formidable enemy, abolition. With what propriety, then, can the southern people, unless under a most woful misconception of the contest, be expected to throw their strength against the re election of a Chief Magistrate, who, by his unflinching support of republican principles, has been designated by his opponents, "*A northern President with southern principles.*"

But, fellow citizens, in relying on the justice of our cause, and the strength of our principles, let us not underrate the efforts of our adversaries to mislead and deceive the people. It is not Gen. Harrison's popularity we have to meet; it is not the naked face or the naked weapons of our old Federal opponents we have to contend against; it is their still more powerful allies which are to give heat and violence to the contest. *The whole banking power of the country,* with a very few honorable exceptions, has taken up arms against the present Administration. The number of these institutions is above eight hundred, dispersed through every State and Territory in the Union. To judge of their power and influence, it is sufficient to say; that, at the period of the general suspension of specie payments, there was due to them from the people, the enormous sum of five hundred millions of dollars. What a weight of influence is this to throw around the consciences and opinions of men in a contest, by which the banks are struggling to regain their lost power and privileges! Is it to be wondered at, that four-fifths of the political press, the citadel of popular rights, have surrendered at discretion to this immense power, and are doing its bidding by writing up General Harrison and writing down Mr. Van Buren? Need we be surprised at the books, pamphlets, documents, essays, speeches, caricatures, and lives of General Harrison, with pictorial representations, which are pouring in upon a central committee of members of Congress at this place, who frank them off in the proportion of *wagon-loads* to the *bushels* sent by the Republican members? Need we wonder at the perfect organization of this party throughout every State, and in every county in the Union? That this central committee have found their way to almost every post office in Alabama; and that every human means are used to cause the people to ground their arms before these potentates of the paper system, and the political party with which they are allied. Need we wonder, that when the makers of paper money have so much at stake in the coming elections, they should avail themselves of a pecuniary pressure in England, still more intense than exists in this country—a pressure which the board of trade of the great manufacturing town of Manchester have proven conclusively to be produced by the joint action of the Bank of England and British bankers—a pressure which has reduced our cotton in English markets to the lowest price;—need we be surprised, that this moment should be seized on as a favorable one, to increase the pecuniary sufferings of the people, with a view of furnishing ground of accusation against the present Administration? Need we be surprised that travelling emissaries of bank power should be sent abroad to preach to the people, that the hard times are produced by the Sub-Treasury policy of the Administration, before that policy has been either adopted or put in force.

In reply to this clamor of hard times, we put the question to the banks;—why they, who have the exclusive privilege of furnishing a bank-paper currency, have not furnished the country with a sufficient and sound paper medium? We hold them to their responsibility, and demand an answer to the question. The Sub-Treasury, which they affect to dread, has not been put in force, and the banks are, from the necessities of the case, to a great extent the depositories of the public money. The bills of all specie-paying banks are still received in payment of public dues. The legislatures of the several States have imposed no disabilities on them. On the contrary, it has been matter of exultation on the floor of Congress, and in the opposition press, that democratic legislatures have shrunk from the responsibility of enforcing any measure of restriction or forfeiture on the suspended banks. In this condition of exemption from all legislative interference on the part of the States or the Federal Government, why do not the banks relieve the present pressure? If *able*, where is their apology for not doing it, except a determination to drive the people, by suffering, against the present Administration? If *unable*, does it not prove the utter worthlessness of these institutions, and of bank circulation? Why should they throw the blame on the Government, which has no control over the question, except in the collection of its own revenues, which it now does in bank paper, and which the present Sub-Treasury bill does not propose to discontinue for years to come? If the banks, *when they have every thing in their own way,* are not able or willing to furnish a sufficiency of sound currency for the demands of the country, they might as well be abolished, and let us return to a metallic currency at once.

The first manifestation of relief under the present pressure has been, not from the banks, but from private capitalists. Money is now abundant in New York on good security, at *less than the legal rate of interest;* and we have the authority of the Whig correspondent of the National Intelligencer, that in that city, the difficulty is not in finding *lenders* at legal interest, but sound *borrowers;* so utterly has the bank system destroyed anything like sound credit.

But, fellow-citizens, whatever are the odds against us in this contest, we look with confidence to the people, as the only power which can triumphantly sustain the cause of equality, against the powerful foes by which it is assailed. It is a question for the industrious producing classes—mechanics and sturdy agriculturists of the country—how far they will degrade the pursuits of labor, by giving to the manufacture of paper money an ascendency, which shall make labor still more tributary to the exactions of the paper system. From the beginning of time, a perpetual war has been waged by *privilege on popular rights.* The same struggle is still going on, for the purpose of giving to the cormorant appetite of the banks, a larger slice from the loaf of labor; and it is for this reason, we urge on you, to take timely means to *arm the people, in defence of the people.* Let them but know that the banks have been for three years urging a doubtful battle with the Government, for the possession and use of the public purse, and for the privilege of having a factitious credit given to their notes, by being received in exclusive payment of the public dues. Let them know that this has been avowedly the ground of dispute between political parties ever since the time when, by a general suspension, these faithless depositories reduced the Government, with a redundant Treasury, to temporary bankruptcy; let it be known that, for resisting this claim of bank privilege, Mr. Van Buren has been the doomed victim of bank vengeance; let them know that the party sustaining the insolent pretensions of these purse-proud corporations, have brought forward General Harrison as a candidate for the Presidency, with the avowed intention of restoring these privileges to the banks; let it be known who constituted the convention by which he was nominated—how little the great productive classes, who fill the ranks of the Republican party, had to do with that nomination; let them, in short, comprehend, what we believe to be the true issue, whether the banks or the people are to govern this country, and we have no fear of the verdict, which the popular voice will pronounce.

But, fellow-citizens, we cannot close this communication, without bringing to your notice, what we honestly believe to be another element of Gen. Harrison's strength, which, though not as powerful as the one already mentioned, is, perhaps, still more dangerous to the South. We will not stop to inquire what are the opinions and feelings of General Harrison on the absorbing subject of abolition. We will, for the present, suppose, as his friends urge, that he is free from the infection of this foul fanaticism; but we cannot help reflecting, that public men are more or less under the control of the party by which they are brought into power; and that it is often more important to examine the principles of that party than of the individual they propose for office. This is more particularly just, in relation to a Presidential candidate, and the party by which he is sustained, for his success invariably brings that party into power and office. To test General Harrison by this rule, what are his claims on the South. It will be recollected that, in the convention by which he was nominated, he received not a single vote from any slaveholding State. The southern portion of the convention, after being outvoted, acquiesced in the nomination; but not until by a decisive vote they had expressed their preference for another. So irreconcilable were the opinions of that convention, they adjourned without adopting, in the form of a public address, any exposition of their principles, or the principles of their candidate; and, from that day to this, the opinions of both the convention and the nominee on this vital question, have been purposely kept from the public. More recently, a great national convention of Whig young men, purporting to represent every portion of the Union, assembled in Baltimore, and numbered, according to their own accounts, twenty thousand persons: and yet this immense assemblage of the party passed off without adopting any address, or avowing a single political principle, except their determination to place themselves in power. If there was no contrariety of feeling, why did they not publish an address; and if General Harrison owes nothing to the support of the Abolitionists, why does he not come out boldly, and denounce them and their wicked designs. In striking contrast to the policy of our opponents, in not trusting the people with an avowal of their principles—a policy new in the history of parties in this country, and based upon a feeling of mistrust toward the people—the Democratic convention which nominated Mr. Van

Buren on the fifth of the present month, among other resolutions defining their principles, and to which we are proud to call the attention of the southern people;—unanimously

> *Resolved,* That Congress has no power, under the Constitution, to interfere with or control the domestic institutions of the several States, and that such States are the sole and proper judges of every thing appertaining to their own affairs, not prohibited by the Constitution; that all efforts of the Abolitionists, or others, made to induce Congress to interfere with questions of slavery, or to take incipient steps in relation thereto, are calculated to lead to the most alarming and dangerous consequences: and that all such efforts have an inevitable tendency to diminish the happiness of the people, and endanger the stability and permanency of the Union, and ought not to be countenanced by any friend to our political institutions.

The Democratic State Convention in Ohio, and most of the Democratic Legislatures, have openly denounced abolition and the Abolitionists. We challenge our opponents to show *when a Whig convention, a Whig Legislature, or any other Whig association in the non slaveholding States, have uttered a sentiment of disapprobation of the Abolitionists or their incendiary schemes.* Mr. Van Buren has not failed to respond to every call which has been made on him in relation to this question, by expressing his determination to use the powers with which he is invested by the Constitution, in opposing every project of these incendiary agitators; and yet General Harrison, from considerations which none can mistake, closes his lips on the subject.

If the silence of General Harrison, taken in connexion with the circumstances under which he obtained his nomination in preference to Mr. Clay, the idol of the Whig party, did not sufficiently disclose the abolition agency by which he is presented for the Presidency, a secret circular issued from Albany, by S. Dewitt Bloodgood, a leading Abolition Whig, has been brought to light, and republished for some weeks without its authenticity being questioned, so far as we know; which fully discloses the means by which it was effected. This secret circular, it was said, was sent to the Whig delegates in the non slaveholding States, as soon as they were nominated to the convention; and, among many reasons why General Harrison *could* be elected, and Mr. Clay *could not,* the circular says of Mr. Clay, *"the Abolitionists generally will oppose him,"* while General Harrison was represented as a candidate *"free from these objections."*

But the following paroxysm of abolition extacy from the Emancipator, the abolition organ in New York, in the incautious moment of receiving the first news of General Harrison's nomination, is conclusive:

The Harrisburg Convention.—Well, the agony is over, and Henry Clay is—laid upon the shelf. And no man of ordinary intelligence can doubt or deny that it is the anti-slavery feeling of the North which has done it, in connexion with his own ostentatious and infamous pro-slavery demonstrations in Congress. Praise to God for a great anti-slavery victory. A man of high talents, of great distinction, of long political services, of boundless personal popularity; has been openly rejected for the Presidency of this great Republic, on account of his devotion to slavery. Set up a monument to progress there. Let the winds tell the tale—let the slaveholders hear the news—let foreign nations hear it—let O'Connell hear it—let the slaves hear it—a slaveholder is incapacitated for the Presidency of the United States. The reign of slavocracy is hastening to a close. The rejection of Henry Clay by the Whig Convention, taken in connexion with all the circumstances, is one of the heaviest blows the monster slavery has received in this country.

Again, read the following exultations of the notorious Garrison:

From Garrison's Liberator

Nomination of General Harrison.—The National Whig Convention, assembled at Harrisburg on the 6th instant, nominated William Henry Harrison for the office of President of the United States. On the first and second ballot, the vote stood—for Henry Clay, 103; for Harrison, 94; for Winfield Scott, 57. On the third ballot, the vote was—for Harrison, 148; for Clay, 90; for Scott, 16. *All the slave States went for Clay.* We regard this as another important sign of the times—*as a signal defeat of the slaveholding power in this country.* Had it not been for Abolitionism, Henry Clay would undoubtedly have been nominated. *We have faith to believe that no slaveholder will ever again be permitted to fill the Presidential office in this Republic.*

The Le Roy Gazette, once edited by Mr. Gates, a Whig Abolition Member of Congress from New York, says:

Very much alike, indeed! The editor of the Ohio paper abandoned the Whigs *because they nominated the Abolitionists, and joined Loco Focos because they went for the dough-faces; while we left the Jackson party because it adhered to slavery, and united with the Whigs because they supported abolition!*

The following extract of a letter from the same Mr. Gates shows further the hopes of the Abolitionists from General Harrison's election:

> You will have seen by the last Philanthropist, that General Harrison is actually a member of an Abolitionist society, and, in 1822, claimed not to be in favor of slavery at all, and excused himself for his vote on the Missouri and Arkansas questions, on the ground of constitutional objections, which, consistently with his oath to support the Constitution, he thought he could not disregard. He also claims that he was the first member of Congress to propose the prohibition of slavery for ever in the Territory above Missouri. He says, while he has been means of *liberating many slaves,* he has never *placed one in bondage.*
>
> Whether these explanations, taken in connexion with the fact that his Vincennes speech was delivered at a time when the principles of modern abolition were imperfectly understood in Ohio, will render him so far acceptable to Abolitionists in your section, as to induce them to vote for him in preference to Van Buren, who has thrown himself so fully into the embraces of the South, to secure the slaveholding influence, I am of course unable to predict.

In a letter from a Mr. Hance, a Whig Abolitionist, published in the "Philanthropist" of March 17, the writer says:

> *Have the Abolitionists not already reason to congratulate themselves on the concessions made to their violence in the nomination of General Harrison? Most assuredly, they have. Who is there that can believe that General Harrison would not have been the Whig candidate, had it not been for Clay's anti-abolition speech in the United States Senate last Spring?* IS NOT THE HARRISBURG NOMINATION A GREAT ABOLITION VICTORY, ACQUIRED WITHOUT A SINGLE DIRECT EFFORT OF OURS? *And what does this promise us in future, if we only remain true to our first principles.*

If the length of this address would permit, we could multiply proofs of this identity of the abolitionists with the Whig party of the North, to an extent which would astound the southern people, and perhaps none more than those; who, by clamor and the activity of our opponents, have without due reflection declared for General Harrison, and who we know to be as decidedly opposed to the Abolitionists as we are ourselves. Most of these we are certain have avowed their preference for General Harrison with but a limited knowledge of his character or his principles, and with no other feeling than that of opposition to Mr. Van Buren, thus furnishing another instance of the reckless extent to which embittered party feeling sometimes carries the most patriotic and worthy. We are greatly deceived if the dissemination of information as to the views of the Abolitionists, and the purposes they expect to secure by the election of General Harrison, does not cause thousands in the South to pause, and, ultimately, to retrace the steps into which they have been inconsiderately hurried.

To that portion of General Harrison's supporters, who live by banks, and the profits of making paper money, and who have joined in the warfare against Mr. Van Buren, for no other purpose than to maintain the paper system, we have little doubt that even abolition itself, has fewer horrors, then the prostration of bank power and the loss of bank privileges.

In short, we believe the election of General Harrison would be the triumph of northern Federalism, bankism, and abolitionism; that it would bring into power a political party whose ascendency would be fatal to the rights and institutions of the South; that it would be followed by a strong Federal Government, a high tariff, a mammoth Federal bank, a system of internal improvements by the Federal Government, and by all the concomitants of Federal usurpation, which are subversive of the rights of the States and the liberties of the people.

WM. R. KING,

C. C. CLAY,

DIXON H. LEWIS,

DAVID HUBBARD,

REUBEN CHAPMAN.

6

Address of the Liberty Party of Pennsylvania to the People of the State (Philadelphia, 1844)

THE ANTISLAVERY Liberty Party first ran a national presidential campaign in 1840, winning relatively few popular votes. In 1844, faced with the specter of both major party candidates being slaveholders (not, of course, for the first time), they came back to the electoral lists with renewed vigor. The Pennsylvania Liberty men told a new story in American politics: the long domination of national affairs by the "slave power". Each action, each piece of legislation, the whole direction of government, reflected that power, which was derived from the South's control of the national parties and from a distribution of congressional seats that favored the Southerners unfairly. If the nation was to be "free in reality, as in name," independent political action was the only way to achieve such an end and honor the United States.

FRIENDS AND FELLOW CITIZENS.

At a Convention of Delegates of the Liberty Party of the Eastern section of Pennsylvania, held in Philadelphia, Feb. 22, 1844, and of the Western section, held at Pittsburg on the same day, the undersigned were made the chairmen of committees appointed to address you upon the great cause which we are laboring to promote. We now, therefore, proceed to set before you, our views, our principles, and our aims; to state the means by which we believe those aims will be accomplished; and to invite your cordial and earnest co-operation with us, to secure such results as, we are sure, will be for the best good both of our State and of our country.

Principles of the Party

In the first place, then, we would state, that the Liberty Party, though new in its organization, is not new in its principles. It is, in the great elements of its character, only an old party revived. It is, in its principles, the same party as that which, in 1776, rallied around the Declaration of Independence, and "pledged their lives, their fortunes, and their sacred honor," to maintain the noble sentiments avowed in that instrument, that "all men are created equal, and are endowed by their Creator with the unalienable rights of life, liberty, and the pursuit of happiness." It is, in its principles, the same party as that which, in 1787, formed our own federal Constitution, the great object of which, as set forth in the preamble, is "to establish *justice*—to promote the *general welfare*—and to secure the *blessings of liberty*." It is, in its principles, the same party that, in the same year, in the Congress of the old Confederation, passed, unanimously, that ever-to-be-honored Ordinance, in which it is declared that the whole territory of our country North and West of the river Ohio, should never be trodden by the foot of a slave.

Such, fellow citizens, are the principles of our party. We cherish the same views as Washington, who wrote these very words,—"there is but one effectual mode by which the abolition of slavery can be accomplished, and that is *by legislative authority*, and this, so far as my SUFFRAGE will go, SHALL NOT BE WANTING." We cherish the same views as Patrick Henry, who declared "that we owe it to the purity of our religion, to show that it is at variance with that law which warrants slavery." We cherish the same views as Robert Morris, who, in the Convention for forming the Constitution, pronounced slavery to be "a nefarious institution." We cherish the same views as William Pinckney, who said in the House of Delegates of Maryland, in 1789, "by the eternal principles of natural justice, no master in this state has a right to hold his slave for a single hour." We cherish the same views as Jefferson, who uttered these memorable words, "I tremble for my country when I reflect that God is just, and that his justice cannot sleep forever." We cherish the same views as Dr. Rush, who declared slavery to be "repugnant to the principles of Christianity, and rebellion against the authority of a common Father." And we cherish the same views as Madison, who said in the Convention of 1787, that it was "wrong to admit into the Constitution even the idea that there could be property in man."

Yes, fellow citizens, these men of former days, and many more that might be named, saw and felt the evils of slavery. They saw that it must be a curse to any country; and they saw the great inconsistency of cherishing it in our own. They saw, too, that if they themselves had any right to resist unto blood for a pound of tea, the slave had an infinitely higher right to make the same resistance for an infinitely higher object. This, one of these patriot spirits had the candor to express, declaring "that in such a contest the Almighty had no attributes which could take sides with the master." The men of those days looked forward, confidently, to the speedy extinction of slavery. In the Conventions of several of the States that met to ratify the Constitution, these opinions were unequivocally expressed. In the Convention of Massachusetts, Judge Dawes remarked, that "slavery had received its death wound, and would die of consumption." In the Convention of Pennsylvania, Judge Wilson, himself one of the framers of the Constitution, said, "the new States which are to be formed, will be under the control of Congress, in this particular, AND SLAVERY WILL NEVER BE INTRODUCED AMONG THEM." And that great man, whose illustrious example can never be too often held up to us for imitation—Gen. Washington—wrote to John Sinclair, "the abolition of slavery must take place, and that too at a period NOT REMOTE."

Such, fellow citizens, were the opinions of the men who laid the foundations of our republic; men of high, noble, wide reaching views; and who feared that nothing would so endanger the permanency of the fair fabric which their wisdom had reared, as the continuation of slavery. Far different, indeed, felt and spoke and wrote those men, from many of our modern, so-called statesmen: far different from the Calhouns and the McDuffies, who declare "slavery to be the corner-stone of our republican institutions:" far different from Henry Clay, who has proclaimed, unblushingly, that he is opposed to "any emancipation, immediate or gradual;" and pronounced the opinion of Madison, "that man cannot hold property in man," to be a "visionary dogma:" far different from Martin Van Buren, who pledged himself before election to veto any bill that Congress might pass to abolish slavery in the District of Columbia: and far different from many other prominent men of our times, whose highest ambition, we feel constrained to say, seems to be, to cringe to the slave power.

We will now, therefore, proceed to set before you, historically, and in a very succinct manner, these

Changes and Their Causes

Very soon after the formation of our Constitution, the slaveholders saw the great political power which, for the sake of peace and union, its framers had given them; and they determined to use it for their own aggrandizement. Whether there was any express understanding, or any secret compact among them, that in all questions touching slavery, they would go together as one man, can never be known. Be this, however, as it may, the fact that they have done so remains, and it is clear to every one who knows any thing of the history of our country. No matter what other questions, apparently of momentous interest, have distracted different parties; here the slaveholders, true to their instincts, have presented but one undivided front.

District of Columbia

In the year 1790, Congress accepted from the States of Maryland and Virginia the territory of ten miles square, now the District of Columbia, for the purpose of locating there the capitol of the nation. When these states ceded this territory to Congress, they "relinquished the same to the government of the United States, in full and absolute right and exclusive jurisdiction,"* and all the state laws that before had existence there, became of course, by that very act, null and void. The very act of Congress in that year, in relation to this subject, shows this truth most conclusively; for that act ordained that the laws of Maryland and Virginia should continue in force until otherwise ordered. To pass an act for their continuance, is of course a full admission that they would not continue without such an act. That act, therefore, is precisely the same as if Congress had enacted an entire new code for the perpetuity of slavery there. Had it any right to do this CONSTITUTIONALLY? Clearly not. To argue that it had, would be to argue against the sun. The constitution gives no power to Congress to establish slavery. The men who framed that instrument would not allow the word slave to be inserted in it. Its preamble declares one of its objects to be to "secure the blessings of liberty," not the curse of slavery; and article fifth of the Amendments reads thus: "no person shall be deprived of liberty without due process of law." The act of Congress, therefore, that was framed to introduce slavery into the District of Columbia, was a plain, open, total violation of the constitution. But the slave power went unitedly for it, and the deed was done. But every man, woman, and child, there held as a slave, is at this moment virtually free; and the Supreme Court of the United States would doubtless so decide, were it not for the fact, to which we shall soon particularly allude, that a majority of its judges are from the slave states.

And now we ask you, fellow citizens, to look at this subject for one moment longer. Look at the capitol of our nation, over which Congress, in the words of the Constitution, "exercises exclusive legislation in all cases whatsoever;" look at it, transformed into a slave market, the most extensive and

*See act of the State of Maryland, passed December 19th, 1791.

loathsome of any in the world. See there, the domestic slave trade vigorously and unblushingly carried on in open day, a trade, which Judge Cranch and eleven hundred other citizens of the District, in a memorial to Congress in 1828, declare to be "more cruel in its operations and more demoralizing in its effects, than the African slave trade itself." See there, in the daily papers, standing advertisements for the purchase of men, women and children. See there, every two or three weeks, cargoes of human beings shipped on board vessels for a Southern market, like so many beasts. Like beasts, did we say? Aye, worse; for horrid as it is, *they are* FETTERED, TWO AND TWO, IN IRONS; and should any accident happen to the vessel, they have not even the chance of making an exertion for their safety; but, as in that awful case that lately occurred near the mouth of the Ohio, may see others saving themselves, while they, helpless and unpitied, must go at once, with their heavy irons fastened about them, deep, deep, deep to the bottom.

And how, fellow citizens, think you, these slaves are kept in security, until they can be safely shipped? We will tell you. To a considerable extent in jails, built by your money, supported by your money, protected by your money. These, with the private prisons, are the receptacles for the safe keeping of husbands separated from wives, and wives separated from husbands; of children from parents, and parents from children; until, as they term it, "a cargo can be made up." Men of Pennsylvania! ye who enjoy the blessings of freedom unmolested; ye who can look around on the happy faces at your own fireside, and feel that, in subjection only to the Providence of God, they are all your own, and that no spoiler's hand can snatch one of that endeared group away, will you not feel in a case like this? Aye, and will you not act, too? How, you may say. How? By giving your vote for such men to fill all our public offices, from the highest to the lowest, as will exert all the power that they can, to put an end to this abomination; to this deep, foul, national disgrace. If the Slave states, in order to prop up a little longer their heaven-daring system, will send men to Congress to legislate FOR Slavery, will not you have the humanity as well as the manliness, to send men who will legislate AGAINST it?

But we cannot enlarge upon this subject, full of interest though it be, but will next, in historical order, advert to

The Purchase of Louisiana in 1803

Fifteen millions of dollars of the people's money were paid to France for this territory, and when the purchase was made, French law, which before had obtained there, ceased, and it was the duty of Congress to adopt the same measures in relation to this territory, as it adopted in 1787 in relation to the North West Territory, namely, TO MAKE IT FREE. But no, this would not suit the slave holders, and it was not done; and thenceforth that vast territory was to have its rich soil moistened with the tears and blood of the slave. The consequences are already seen. Three states have already been formed out of it, having now ten votes in the House of Representatives, and six votes, *almost one-eighth,* in the Senate of the United States. Here you see another of the monstrous encroachments of the Slave power upon constitutional liberty. Next in order, we will introduce you to

The Purchase of Florida in 1821

This was purchased of Spain; and again it became the duty of Congress to make such provisions, that a slave should never tread its soil. Slavery, we know, is not a state of nature, and the right to hold a slave is not a natural, but a legal right. Slavery is a creature of positive law, and exists within those limits, and within those limits ONLY, where the laws that sanction it have force. The second clause of section second, article fourth, of the Constitution, says, "Congress shall have power to make all needful rules and regulations respecting the territories belonging to the United States;" and Article fifth of the "Amendments," reads, "No person shall be deprived of liberty without due process of law:" while the preamble declares one of its objects to be, "to secure the blessings of liberty."

Now, what are the facts? We all know them, and know them too well. there are now, according to the last census, in the territory of Florida, twenty-five thousand seven hundred and seventeen human beings held in slavery there, in utter, shameless defiance of the Constitution. And what have been the consequences to this nation? Since 1836, more than FORTY MILLIONS of dollars have been expended on the Florida war, for the special benefit of the slaveholder, to drive the red man from his native forests, and from the graves of his fathers, that he might not be able to give shelter to those who should fly to him for protection from the hand of oppression and tyranny. We first purchase Florida for FIVE MILLIONS, and then expend FORTY MILLIONS MORE, that the slaveholder may hold his victims with a more secure grasp. But the money, enormous as is the amount, and coming home as it does to every man in the country, is nothing, and less than nothing, when we look at the lives sacrificed, the miseries endured, the cruelties practised, and every principle of honor and justice and humanity outraged and trampled on. Men of Pennsylvania! have you not SOMETHING to do with slavery?

Missouri Struggle in 1820–22

The next instance of the alarming extension of the Slave power, and one ever to be remembered, was the admission of Missouri into the Union as a slave state. In 1820, the "District of Maine" petitioned for admission into the Union. It was proper that she should be admitted; she had all the requisite qualifications, and no objections could be made to her on independent grounds. But the Slave power, with Henry Clay, then Speaker of the House, at their head, declared, unequivocally, their firm and determined hostility to the admission of Maine, until Missouri should have been admitted as a Slave state. The struggle was long and severe. The debate on the subject was protracted through two sessions, and the experiment throughout the country was intense. The representatives from the Free states showed more spirit, more manliness, and a firmer determination to defend the Constitution from violation, than they have ever done since; and one of our own representatives. John Sergeant, delivered, on that occasion, a speech to which Pennsylvanians will ever be proud to refer. At first, the friends of freedom were in a majority. But the slaveholders, never for a moment relaxing in their vigilance, continued to move on in solid column; and soon gained over enough of Northern votes to turn the scale, and thus that execrable project was finally carried, in utter defiance of every principle of natural justice, and of the letter, as well as of the general spirit of the Constitution.

Lastly, but six months ago, a most nefarious plot was matured by the President and the Southern members of his cabinet, in a manner as mean from its secrecy, as the measure itself was daring in its wickedness—A PLOT TO ANNEX TEXAS TO THE UNITED STATES.

Such is one class of facts, in the history of our country, to show the alarmingly increasing influence of the Slave power in the councils of the nation. Let us now proceed to another class of facts.

Preponderance of the Slave Power in All the Most Important Offices of Government

I. PRESIDENTS

Since the organization of our government, the Slaveholding states have had six Presidents, who will have served, at the end of this term, forty-three years and eleven months; the Free states, four, who have served twelve years and one month: and one of these four, Martin Van Buren, was elected on the ground of his being "a Northern man with Southern principles." And be it remembered, that no President from the Free states has ever been elected for a second term.

II. SECRETARIES OF STATE

Next in importance to the President, is the office of Secretary of State. He it is, that has the management of all the business and correspondence with foreign courts; that instructs all ambassadors, ministers, commissioners, and consuls; and that negotiates all the treaties. Of the sixteen Secretaries of State since the formation of the Constitution, the Slave states have had TWELVE, the Free states, FOUR.

III. THE JUDICIARY

In the Judiciary, the very balance wheel of our government, and which has continually before it the most important questions of which man can take cognizance; questions of constitutional law; questions of chartered rights and privileges; questions involving millions of property; and above all questions that are to decide the LIBERTY OR SLAVERY OF MAN; here, we say, the preponderance of the slave power is still more alarming.

First, look at the Districts, and see how unequally, how unjustly they are divided. Vermont, Connecticut, and New York constitute one District with one Judge. They have forty two Representatives in Congress, and a free population of 3,030, 826; while Alabama and Louisiana, with but eleven representatives, and with a free population of but 521,183, a little more than ONE SIXTH of the former, constitute another District, with another Judge. Then compare, where the comparison comes more home to ourselves. New Jersey and Pennsylvania constitute the third District; Mississippi and Arkansas the ninth. The former has TWENTY NINE Representatives in Congress, and a free population of 2,096,601; the latter, but FIVE Representatives in Congress, and but 258,079 of free population.

Second, look at the manner in which the bench of the Supreme Court of the United States has ever been, and still is constituted. Of the twenty seven Judges of that Court, since the adoption of the Constitution, the Slave states have had SEVENTEEN, the Free states but TEN: and of the eighteen Attorneys General, the number has been against us in the still greater ratio of THIRTEEN to FIVE. Within the last nine years, six appointments have been made to the bench of the Supreme Court, and *all these from the Slave states;* and that, too, men of Pennsylvania, when we had within our own domain such men as Binney, and Dallas, and Chauncey, and Sergeant, and Rogers, and Gibson; men whom we know to be equal to any, and superior to most of those who now occupy the seats of that high tribunal. Is there not something deep, dark, designing in all this? Does not the Slave power mean to keep, if it can, a majority of the Judges on *their* side, to decide *their* way in all questions involving human liberty? Who, with his eyes open, can for one moment doubt it?

IV. SPEAKERS OF THE HOUSE

But the Slave power is not content with all this. It is determined, if it can, to give its own complexion to our national legislation. To this end, it has so managed, generally, that the Speaker of the House of Representatives shall be identified with its interests. He it is that appoints all the Committees of the House. These Committees report on the various subjects committed to their charge, and their reports are printed in large numbers, and sent abroad on the wings of the wind, all over the land. Look back, then, into the history of our national legislation, and you will find that in thirty elections for Speaker of the House of Representatives, the Slave states have secured their man TWENTY ONE times, or for *forty* years; the Free states, NINE times, or for SEVENTEEN years. With the exception of Mr. Taylor, of New York, who served three years, THE FREE STATES HAVE NOT GIVEN A SPEAKER TO THE HOUSE SINCE 1809. Then go over to the other side of the capitol, and you will find that of the seventy six Presidents of the Senate, *pro tempore,* the Slave states have had SIXTY, the Free states SIXTEEN.

But we have neither space nor time, fellow citizens, to take up all the Offices and Departments of our Government, and to comment upon each separately. We will therefore select a few, and place them in a tabular form, comparing the number of those furnished by the Free states, with those furnished by the Slave states, and leave you to make your own comments.

	Free states	Slave states
Presidents,	4	6
Secretaries of State,	4	12
Judges of the Supreme Court,	10	17
Speakers of the house,	9	21
Presidents of the Senate, *(pro tem.)*	16	60
Ministers of all kinds to foreign powers,	52	80
	136	232

We said that we would leave you to make your own comments. We cannot, however, but remark, that whenever Northern men have been elected or appointed to any of these high offices, Southern men, whose vigilance is worthy of a better cause, have always been very careful first to see, that the persons thus selected have a "fellow feeling" with themselves on the subject of slavery. In 1841, six persons, ALL FROM THE SLAVE STATES, had been nominated to diplomatic stations, previous to the nomination of Edward Everett, of Massachusetts, to the Court of St. James, and all were confirmed without hesitation; but his nomination was laid on the table. For what reason? Because he was unfit for the station? No! for no one doubted that in every intellectual qualification he was immeasurably superior to all the rest. But—and mark it well, fellow citizens—because he was thought by the Southern senators not to favor sufficiently their "*peculiar institutions;*" a soft phrase which they use, we know, for *slavery,* when conscience, paying thus an involuntary tribute to justice and virtue, would cause the latter term to stick in their throat. At the rejection of such a man, a few Northern editors did, for a time, shake off their mouse-like spirits, and speak out like men. The nomination was at last confirmed, but—and mark this, too—not until some of the Northern friends of Mr. Everett had the meanness so far to cringe to the Slave power, as to send letters to Washington to assure their "Southern friends" that he was not tinctured with "abolition sentiments." And within this year, of six nominations sent on one day to the Senate of the United States to fill important public stations, five were from the Northern and one from a Southern state; all from the Free states were rejected, while the one from Virginia was confirmed; though he had been a second in a duel, which, in a moment, made a wife a widow, and a family of children, orphans.

The Slave Power Controls the Great Interests of Our Country

Having thus shown you, fellow citizens, the vast preponderance of the Slave power in all the important offices of our government, we will now proceed to set before you a few other facts, which prove, conclusively, how it has extended its power and exerted its influence in every possible direction, to the greatest injury of our country's best interests.

1. THE NAVY

Ever since the glorious act of England, in emancipating all the slaves in her West Indies colonies—an act which, from the most happy results that have followed, seems to be held up to the world as a signal example that it is always safe to do right—the Slave power has been most vigilant in securing a preponderance in the Navy. The "Home Squadron" has been a favourite measure with them, that they might have protection for their infamous coastwise slave trade, as well as protection for their sea coast. A guilty conscience sees a thousand threatening dangers where an honest man sees none; and the slaveholder seems to have continually flitting before his distempered vision, scores of vessels, laden with armed free blacks from the West Indies, approaching our Southern shores, to avenge the cause of their brethren in bonds. Hence they have taken special care to have a majority of the officers of the Navy from their own states, and to have the Naval Bureaus at Washington under their own control.

Of the forty-three officers in the Navy Department in Washington, *thirty-one* are from the Slave states, and but *twelve* from the Free states; and of all the officers of the Navy, whether in actual service or waiting orders, Pennsylvania, with a free population more than double that of Virginia, has but *one hundred and seventy-seven,* while Virginia has *two hundred and twenty-four.* The late Secretary of the Navy, Judge Upshur, in the first year of his office, appointed thirty-two midshipmen, of whom fifteen were taken from Virginia, and the other seventeen from Maryland, Delaware, and the District.—We might extend this train of remark to a great extent, but we have not space. The facts, however, show the deep, well-laid design of the Slave power to be, to secure the services of the Navy for the defence of Slavery, and, in the event of a war, to secure the possession of the Navy itself.

Look, now, fellow citizens, at the appropriations for the fiscal year ending June, 1844. They are—for the Army, more than two millions: for the Fortifications, &c., more than four millions; for the Navy, more than eight millions, and for the Peace establishment, not quite seven millions of dollars. Here, in a time of profound tranquility, the expenses for war are more than double those for peace.

But why so much, you may ask, for the Navy? We will tell you. The "Home Squadron" is to consist, this year, of SIXTEEN vessels. Yes, fellow citizens, to protect our own coasts, an establishment is to be kept up of three frigates, six sloops, two steamers, and five brigs and schooners. Do you ask the reason of all this array of military force? Let the late Judge Upshur, the Secretary of the Navy, himself from Virginia, answer. In his late Report he speaks of "those incursions from which so much evil is to be apprehended." Again: "the effect of these incursions, on the Southern portion of our country, would be disastrous in the extreme." And again: "the *Southern* naval stations, MORE ESPECIALLY, require a large force for their security. A large number of arms is kept in each of them, which, by a sudden irruption of the class of PEOPLE *who are not citizens,* might be seized and used for very disastrous purposes."

Here, fellow citizens, you have the whole of it. Here you see that we of the free states are to be taxed to an enormous amount, and that the power of the General Government is to be used, to keep the slaves of the Southern states from insurrection! The question will not now, we think, be asked by you—"What has the North to do with Slavery?"

II. THE POST OFFICE

Scarcely any one of the great elements of modern civilization is productive of more happy results to a country, than the post office system, when properly conducted; that system, by which a Government takes upon itself the obligation to give to its subjects or citizens the power of communicating one with another, at any distance, throughout its whole domain. But that this system may do the most good, two things are essential; namely, SECURITY and CHEAPNESS. The farmer, or the merchant, or the tradesman, who wishes to learn the state of the markets—the mechanic or laborer, who desires to know the rate of wages—the friend, who is anxious to hear of the welfare of a friend, from whom he has long been parted—the mother or the father, who wishes to hear from an absent child—the emigrant who has left the home of his youth, and gone out into the far West, but who yet wishes to gain frequent tidings from that spot he has left behind, so dear to his memory;—all these should be able to communicate with each other, *freely* and *safely,* indeed, but CHEAPLY. THE GREATEST, THE STRONGEST CEMENT OF OUR UNION, WOULD BE A CHEAP RATE OF POSTAGE. In Great Britain, a Monarchy, a friend can send a letter to a friend to any part of the kingdom for TWO CENTS: while in republican America it would cost him, in most cases, from *six to twelve times that sum.*

Now, fellow citizens, let us tell you that *the great obstacle to a* SAFE *and* CHEAP *postage, is the Slave power.* In 1835, Amos Kendall, the Postmaster General, to please the citizens of Charleston, South Carolina, wrote to the Postmaster there "so far as I can prevent it, no anti-slavery pamphlets or papers, shall be circulated through the public mails;" and the citizens of that city met, and passed a series of resolutions, in which they declared themselves determined to resist, by FORCE any attempt to send through the mail, what they termed "incendiary pamphlets;" and actually opened a number of LETTERS, and *burnt a large number of papers and pamphlets!!* But this is not all. In the same year, the Postmaster of New York, "assumed the responsibility" of suppressing such papers as he thought proper, and of refusing the mail to such citizens as had sent to him some copies of the Anti-Slavery Reporter; and in the year 1838, a large number of the "Baltimore Religious Magazine," containing an article on "Bible Slavery," which did not please the slavebreeders in Petersburg, Virginia, were taken from the Post Office, and burnt in the street, in *the presence, and by direction of the Mayor and Recorder!!* Such outrageous violations of the Constitution need no comment.

You thus see, fellow citizens, how the Slave power tramples on the *sacredness* of the mail. I will now show you by figures, how and why same power has thus far opposed, and successfully opposed all reduction of our present enormous rates of postage.

According to the last Report of the Postmaster General, the excess of revenue over the expenditure in the Free states, is $552,066; while the excess of expenditure over the revenue in the Slave states is $545,262; that is, while the Free states are a GAIN to the department of more than half a million of dollars, the Slave states are a LOSS to the department of over a half a million of dollars; in other words, Northern freemen pay the postage of Southern slaveholders. Compare our own state, fellow citizens, with Virginia, and the contrast is still more striking. In Pennsylvania, the excess of revenue over the expenditure is $147,409; in Virginia the excess of expenditure over the revenue is $50,777; so that our citizens, besides paying our own postage, pay the postages of Virginia, and then have enough to make up the deficiencies of Maryland, South Carolina, and Mississippi. No wonder the Slave power has opposed all reduction of rates. The present system suits them exactly. And what do we get in return, for thus paying their postage? We have told you. We have *our letters opened, and our papers burnt.*

III. PUBLIC LANDS

Whenever there is to be any distribution of money, fellow citizens, the slaveholders always manage to get the "lion's share." This they did in the "Distribution Bill," which was passed in 1841, to distribute the proceeds of the public lands among the several states. They secured their object, by having the distribution based upon "federal numbers," that is, according to their representation in Congress, where three fifths of the slaves are represented, and not according to free population. Supposing the proceeds of the public lands to be three millions of dollars, Pennsylvania, with a free population more than double that of Virginia, by 142,349, instead of receiving more than double the amount, will receive $74,521 less; and with a free population equal to that of Maryland. Virginia and North Carolina, received $94,330 less. Had our Representatives in Congress had any just sense of what is due to the dignity, the honor and the interests of their own state, they would have withstood, to the very last, a bill so grossly and palpably unjust. And let us tell you, fellow citizens, that you never will have Representatives in Congress of the right character, until you make an effort to elect them. To secure the end, you must adopt the means.

IV. SURPLUS REVENUE

Of the same character was the Bill passed in 1836, to distribute the surplus revenue in the Treasury of the United States among the several states. The Secretary of the Treasury calculated that there would be twenty-two millions of dollars to be distributed, and that, too, in the words of the Bill, "in proportion to the representation of the states in the Senate and House of Representatives." By this method of distribution the Slave states, with 3,789,674 free inhabitants, received 9,428,580 dollars, while the Free states, with 7,003,239 free inhabitants, received but 12,571,420 dollars. Had our states received in proportion to our number of free inhabitants, instead of twelve millions and a half, we should have received eighteen millions. The state of Virginia received 1,721,090 dollars; Pennsylvania, 2,244,900 dollars; but had the whole amount of surplus revenue been proportioned as it should have been, we should have received 3,125,927 dollars, or nearly one million more. Or, to place the injustice of this measure in a still broader light, a Virginia slaveholder, with an hundred slaves, receives as much as SIXTY ONE freemen of Pennsylvania. We need make no further comments, fellow citizens, on a Bill so palpably unjust.

V. RATIO OF REPRESENTATION

Immediately after the last Census of the United States had been taken, it became the duty of Congress to fix a new ratio for Representation. The subject was before the House of Representatives for a long time, and a variety of numbers were proposed, that should be entitled to one Representative. At last they agreed that there should be one for every 50,189, which would have given 306 members to the House; and they sent the Bill to the Senate. That body, however, which, of the two, has ever been most subservient to the Slave power, saw that this would not do. They saw that this Bill would give the Free states a majority of 68 in the House. They knew, indeed, that our states must have, in any case, a majority; but they also knew that they could better manage and break down a small majority than a large one, and immediately they set themselves to work, to see how they could weaken us the most. They therefore sent back to the House a Bill, giving one Representative to every 70,680 of federal population, and which would *reduce* the House from its then number, 242 members, to 223; and give the Free States a majority of 47 instead of 68. But why that odd number 680! We will tell you, fellow citizens. It deprives the four great states of the North, namely, Massachusetts, New York, *Pennsylvania* and Ohio of one member each. Take that number off, and let it be 70,000, and all the *other* states would have *precisely the same* number of Representatives It would injure no one to take off the 680; but put it on, and it gives to the great states we have mentioned one Representative less.

And then, too, look at the fractions unrepresented. While all the Slave states have but 140,092, the Free States have 218,678, a difference of 78,586. The fraction of Virginia is 2, that of Pennsylvania is 27,687, besides, that she is deprived of one member in the House. And the House, to their shame be it said, concurred in this Bill, so clearly and designedly lessening their influence. Even the correspondent of the New York Herald could thus write, at the time:—"The Senate Apportionment has robbed the North of at least one quarter of its practical influence in the Union, when regarded in its full extent; and the members of the Free states who voted for it, have thus yielded and surrendered the rights of their constituents, and violated their trusts."

The Slave Power the Chief Cause of Our Financial Embarrassments; or, in Plainer Words, of "Hard Times"

1. BY CONTROLLING THINGS ABROAD

If you will take the pains, fellow citizens, to look into our commercial treaties with foreign nations, you will find that the great majority of them are made with reference to the products of Slave labor. All our ambassadors to foreign courts have ever been particularly instructed in this respect. The cry has been continually, *cotton,* COTTON; *tobacco,* TOBACCO; *rice,* RICE. For very many years after the formation of our government, wheat and flour, the products of the Free states, constituted the chief articles of our export. We hardly need tell you, that these were years of unexampled prosperity to our country. But in later times, and particularly since the signal overthrow of the friends of freedom in the Missouri struggle, down to that ever-to-be-remembered and disgraceful letter of instructions, written by Daniel Webster to Mr. Everett, at London, respecting the slaves shipwrecked in the Creole, the Slave-power, by uniting with one or the other of the two great parties of the North, has managed so adroitly, by securing all the important offices of the Government to itself, that the foreign markets for free labor produce have been growing less and less, and those for the products of slave labor have been constantly enlarging. We have seen England, France, Austria and Russia, one after another, induced, by the incessant persuasions of our General Government, to modify or remove their onerous duties on COTTON and TOBACCO; while not an effort has been made to induce England to alter her corn-laws; or to persuade France, or any other European power so to modify their tariffs, as to favor the importation, into those countries, of the wheat, the provisions,* the products of the fisheries, the forests, and the mines, or any of the various manufactures from the free states of the North or the West.

II. BY CONTROLLING THINGS AT HOME

Here, fellow citizens, we have to speak of a subject, which we have all, within the last ten years, more or less severely felt—the influence of the Slave power in producing our embarrassments in commerce, in agriculture, and in all the arts and employments of life. Looking, always, with a most jealous eye upon the prosperity of the North, and knowing that, with the indomitable energies of free labor, it can adapt itself to almost any system, *provided it be permanent,* the object of the Slave power has ever been change, *change,* CHANGE.

Very many years ago, foreign commerce found no favor in its eyes, but domestic manufactures were loudly called for. Well, domestic manufactures were established. But scarcely had the North begun to put forth its giant strength in them, when the South felt that its locks must be shorn, and demanded a return to free trade, under the threat of dissolving the Union, unless this demand were complied with. All the changes that have been made in the tariff, that have operated unfriendly to Northern interests, (and such changes have taken place every few years,) have been made by the South; and "the great compromiser," Henry Clay, has always managed to "compromise" but one way—*against free,* and FOR SLAVE labor.

But, above all, look at the enormous losses which the North has sustained from its Southern trade. It has found, by its own sad experience, that there is more than one Grand Gulf at the South; that the whole South is but ONE GRAND GULF, constantly calling for, and swallowing up the free capital of the free states. This, the failure of the U. S. Bank; this, the losses of thousands

*England has lately made some alteration in her tariff as regards "provisions;" but no thanks to the powers at Washington.

of merchants, and manufacturers, and mechanics throughout our Free states, affecting every where so injuriously the great farming interests, most conclusively prove.

It is computed that the Slave states owe the Free states, at the lowest estimate, THREE HUNDRED MILLIONS OF DOLLARS; while some have reckoned it as high as FOUR HUNDRED AND FIFTY MILLIONS. In 1837, New York and other cities at the North and East, lost ONE HUNDRED MILLIONS of dollars in Southern debts. In 1838, Maryland, Virginia, and Kentucky lost EIGHTY MILLIONS of dollars, because Mississippi, that "*chivalrous*" state, refused to pay for the slaves she had illegally imported. But this loss fell ultimately on the Free states, who received in payment for the debts due to them from the *slave selling* states, paper endorsed by the banks of the *slave buying* states—the banks at Mobile, Vicksburg, Grand Gulf, and New Orleans.

And now, fellow citizens, let us come home to ourselves. You all remember, too well, the fall of the United States Bank, and the other banks in Philadelphia, a few years ago; and how many banks in the interior, by having more or less of the stock and other obligations of these institutions, were materially crippled. And you remember, too, the utter failure of many of our best merchants; and the great, though not destructive losses of many more. Why, and whence all this? We will tell you,—connexions with the Slaveholding states, by speculations in cotton, by giving long credits to Southern merchants for goods, and by purchasing the stocks of their banks, and rail roads, and other companies, to enormous amounts. The United States Bank has now due to it from the Slave states, debts to the amount of at least TWENTY MILLIONS OF DOLLARS; and the merchants of Philadelphia, including all who purchased Southern stocks, lost from the year 1834 to 1839, at the lowest estimate, THIRTY MILLIONS OF DOLLARS, in the Slave states, of which they will never receive one cent.

Here then, we have an amount of FIFTY MILLIONS OF DOLLARS utterly sunk. The distress which these losses occasioned, you all, fellow citizens, well know; and many, too many of you most deeply feel. How many a person in the decline of life, who had retired from business, how many an orphan, how many a widow, had their ALL laid up in that *mammoth institution,* in the fullest assurance that it would yield them a sure and regular return, while life should last. And at its fall, how much sorrow, how much distress, how much real, bitter, pinching poverty did it bring with it. How many a hearth was made cold and cheerless, how many a mansion made desolate, how many were thrown upon the cold charities of the world. Nor were the losses confined to Philadelphia. By no means. They reached every corner of the State—every log house beyond the mountains. Can FIFTY MILLIONS OF

DOLLARS, be sunk in a city, the great emporium of trade and commerce—the great receiver and distributor of the products of labor, and the loss not be felt along every road, and highway and canal that leads to it? Can a central, vital function of the body be diseased, and the derangement not be felt throughout every vein and artery of the system? Impossible.

Our Object

And now, fellow citizens, you may ask, what is our object in thus exhibiting to you the alarming influence of the Slave-power? Do we wish to excite in your bosoms feelings of hatred against citizens of a common country? Do we wish to array the Free states against the Slave states, in hostile strife? NO, fellow citizens, NO, NO. But we wish to show you, that, while the Slave states are inferior to us in free population, having not even one half of ours; inferior in morals, being the region of bowie knives and duels, of assassinations and lynch law; inferior in mental attainments, having not one-fourth of the number that can read and write; inferior in intelligence,* having not one-fifth of the number of literary and scientific periodicals; inferior in the products of agriculture, and manufactures, of the mines, of the fisheries, and of the forest; inferior, in short, in every thing that constitutes the wealth, the honor, the dignity, the stability, the happiness, the true greatness of a nation, it is wrong, it is unjust, it is absurd, that they should have an influence in all the departments of government so entirely disproportionate to our own. We would arouse you to your own true interests. We would have you, like men, firmly resolved to maintain your own rights. We would have you say to the South,—if you choose to hug to your bosom that system which is continually injuring and impoverishing you; that system which reduces two millions and a half of native Americans in your midst, to the most abject condition of ignorance and vice, withholding from them the very key of knowledge; that system which is at war with every principle of justice, every feeling of humanity; that system which makes man the property of man, and perpetuates that relation from one generation to another; that system which tramples, continually, upon a majority of the commandments of the Decalogue; that system which could not live a day, if it did not give one party, supreme control over the persons, the health, the liberty, the happiness, the marriage relations,

*And here, in this connexion, we would remark, that if Northern freemen had a proper sense of their own dignity and rights, they would say to every editor of a newspaper or magazine, who cringes to the Slave power, if you choose rather to favour that region so devoid of intelligence, to that region go; and we will support those journals that "know their rights, and knowing dare maintain."

the parental authority and filial obligations of the other; if you choose to cling to such a system—cling to it; but you shall not cross our line; you shall not bring that foul thing here. We know, and we here repeat it for the thousandth time, to meet, for the thousandth time, the calumnies of our enemies, that while we may present to you every consideration of duty, we have no right, as well as no power, to alter your State laws. But remember, that slavery is the mere creature of local or statute law, and cannot exist out of the region where such law has force. "It is so *odious,*" says, Lord Mansfield, "that nothing can be suffered to support it but *positive* law."

We would, therefore, say to you again, in the strength of that Constitution under which we live, and which no where countenances slavery, you shall not bring that foul thing here. You shall not force the corrupted, and corrupting blood of that system into every vein and artery of our body politic. You shall not have the controlling power in all the departments of our government, at home and abroad. You shall not so negotiate with foreign powers, as to open markets for the products of slave labor alone. You shall not so manage things at home, as every few years to bring bankruptcy upon our country. You shall not, in the apportionment of public moneys, have what you call your "property" represented, and thus get that, which, by no right, belongs to you. You shall not have the power to bring your slaves upon our free soil, and take them away at pleasure; nor to reclaim them, when they, panting for liberty, have been able to escape your grasp; for we would have it said of us, as the eloquent Curran said of Britain, the moment the slave touches our soil, "the ground on which he stands is holy, and consecrated to the Genius of UNIVERSAL EMANCIPATION."

Thus, fellow citizens, we come to

THE GREAT OBJECT OF THE LIBERTY PARTY

It is, in the words of the Constitution, "TO ESTABLISH JUSTICE; TO SECURE THE BLESSINGS OF LIBERTY." It is, ABSOLUTE AND UNQUALIFIED DIVORCE OF THE GENERAL GOVERNMENT FROM ALL CONNEXION WITH SLAVERY; and we would, therefore, here utter our solemn protest against the nefarious doctrine avowed by HENRY CLAY, in the Senate of the United States, in January, 1839, that "this Government is bound to protect the domestic slave trade." We would say, in the eloquent language of that noble son of freedom, CASSIUS M. CLAY, of Kentucky, "Let the whole North in a mass, in conjunction with the patriotic of the South, withdraw the moral sanction and legal power of the Union from the sustainment of slavery." We would employ every CONSTITUTIONAL means to eradicate it from our entire country, because it would be for the highest welfare of our entire country. We would have liberty established in the District, and in all the Territories. We would put a stop to the internal slave trade, pronounced, even by Thomas Jefferson Randolph, of Virginia, to be "worse and more odious than the foreign slave trade itself." We would, in the words of the Constitution, have "the citizens of each state have all the privileges and immunities of citizens in the several states;" and not, for the color of their skin, be subjected to every indignity, and abuse, and wrong, and even imprisonment.* We would have equal taxation. We would have the seas free. We would have a free and secure post office. We would have liberty of speech and of the press, which the Constitution guarantees to us. We would have our members in Congress utter their thoughts freely, without threats from the pistol or the bowie knife. We would have the right of petition most sacredly regarded. We would secure to every man what the Constitution secures, "the right of trial by jury." We would do what we can for the encouragement and improvement of the colored race, and restore to them that inestimable right, of which they have been so meanly, as well as unjustly deprived—the right of suffrage. We would look to the best interests of the country, and the *whole* country, and not legislate for the good of an Oligarchy, the most arrogant that ever lorded it over an insulted people.† We would have our commercial treaties with foreign nations regard the interests of the Free states. We would provide safe, adequate, and permanent markets for the produce of Free labor. And, when reproached with slavery, we would be able to say to the world, with an open front and a clear conscience, our General Government has nothing to do with it, either to promote, to sustain, to defend, to sanction, or to approve.

Thus, fellow citizens, you see our objects. You may now ask, by what means we hope to attain them. We answer, by

Political Action

What is political action? It is, *acting in a manner appropriate to those objects which we wish to secure through the agency of the different departments of Government.* He, for instance, who desires Congress to charter a national bank, or to pass a highly restrictive tariff, will do what he can to send to Congress such

*Read the memorial of citizens of Boston, to the House of Representatives, on the imprisonment of free citizens of Massachusetts by the authorities of Savannah, Charleston, and New Orleans.

†The slave-holders, at most, do not number over 250,000; not so many as there are inhabitants in the city and districts of Philadelphia. How humialiating, that such a set of men should govern such a country.

men as are known to be favorable to those objects. So he who is interested for the freedom of millions of the human race; who desires that our general government may be entirely divorced from all connection with slavery; who wishes to see our country governed by "just men," will, if consistent, adopt measures appropriate to secure such ends. What are those measures? There is but one answer. The only way in which he can act *constitutionally*, is, to go to the ballot-box, and there, silently and unostentatiously, deposit a vote for such men as will do what they can to carry out those principles which he has so much at heart. This is POLITICAL ACTION, or action in political affairs; and is as pure, in itself, as action in domestic, or mercantile, or ecclesiastical affairs. We grant that not the purest associations have been connected with the phrase, because good men have too often stood aloof from political action, and have left the great affairs of government to be managed by not the most worthy; by those who make politics a sort of trade.

But we now, fellow citizens, propose to you a sort of political action in which you may most ardently engage without being soiled. It is the same political action which was enjoined more than three thousand years ago. "Moreover thou shalt provide out of all the people able men, such as fear God, men of truth, hating covetousness, and place such men over them to be rulers."* This, fellow citizens, we have done, and this we ever intend to do, and in this action we now invite your aid.

In saying this, we do not intend to underrate moral suasion. Far, very far, from it. None can value it more highly. We are always using it, and we hope ever to use it till slavery is overthrown. Moral power is, indeed, *the* great power. But as in most other cases, so here, this power must have a lever which it can grasp and wield, in order to be effectual. That lever is POLITICAL ACTION. Why? Plainly, because Slavery is the creature of "political action," and how else than by "political action" can it be abolished? The laws that sustain slavery are not the laws of God, but in total violation of His laws. Neither did they make themselves; and they cannot annul themselves. They were made by men, and by men only can they be repealed. But they were made by selfish, unjust men; by men regardless of the rights of their fellow men. They must therefore be repealed by men of a character totally different: by men who regard justice and equal rights: by men who have no sympathy with the proud oppressor: by men who will dare to do right: who will meet any obloquy, and face any danger in the course where duty leads. And how are such men to be placed in office? We answer, of course, BY VOTES, fellow citizens. There is no other constitutional way. The case is as clear as any axiom in mathematics.

*Exodus xviii.21.

We ask, then, how can any good man—any true friend of his country's best interests—any lover of justice and humanity—for a moment doubt what his duty herein is? Will he withdraw from all action in the questions of the deepest public interest, and leave every thing to be managed by those who make politics a trade? And if he makes no effort, in the way the Constitution provides, to remedy great evils, with what face, we ask, can he complain of the continuance of those evils? But you may ask why we adopt a

Separate Organization

We answer, because we believe this to be the only effectual mode to accomplish our object. For years and years, we tried both the two great political parties; but all in vain. Henry Clay himself said in the U.S. Senate, "It is not true, and I REJOICE that it is not true, that *either* of the two great parties in this country, has any *design or aim at abolition.* I should *deeply lament* if it were true." Of the great number of candidates, therefore, whom we would question as to their views in relation to our great objects, some would not answer at all; some would answer in a manner insulting to our feelings; and some would answer, like the oracle at Delphi, as profound as unmeaning. A very few would answer favorably to secure our votes, and then after they were elected by our votes, would turn around, and laugh at our credulity. A sense of what is due to ourselves, and to the best good of our country, has compelled us, therefore, to the course we have taken.

At the approaching election, fellow citizens, you will have before you the candidates of three parties, from which you are to choose. The candidate of the Whig party for the Presidency is

Henry Clay

It is painful to us, fellow citizens, at any time, to speak against the character of any one. But in a case like this, when most unworthy candidates are presented for your suffrage by two of the parties feeling must yield to duty, and we must tell you *why* they are unworthy of your confidence.

There are some features of the moral character of HENRY CLAY which we have not the least desire to discuss. From the time that he first entered upon public life at Washington, until within a very few years, unless common fame has done him the grossest injustice, his moral character could not but meet the reprobation of every good man. Had he given any evidence of sincere repentance, we would be the last even to allude to these things. That he is utterly unworthy of the suffrages of the friends of liberty, however, we need hardly tell you. That a man who will say in a speech before the Colonization Society, that he is utterly opposed to all emancipation of the slaves, either "immediate or gradual, without their removal;" that a man who exerted all his influence for the admission of Missouri into the Union, as a slave state;* that a man who declared and the Senate of the United States, February 9, 1839, that "that is property which the law declared to be property"—"that two hundred years of legislation have SANCTIFIED negro slaves as PROPERTY;" who, in the same speech, pronounced the opinion of Madison, that "man cannot hold property in man," to be a "visionary dogma;" and who had the awful blasphemy to compare men, held as slaves, with other "LIVE STOCK;" that such a man has no claims to a freeman's vote, we need, certainly, take no pains to prove.

But that which should render HENRY CLAY still more odious, if possible, in the eyes of every good man, is the fact, that HE IS THE GREAT DUELLIST OF THE LAND. The first affair of murder in which he was engaged was with Colonel Daviess, of Kentucky, in 1805. A challenge was given and accepted, and both parties were proceeding to the work of death, when the seconds brought about a reconciliation. His murderous intention, however, remained. The second duel was with Humphrey Marshall, also of Kentucky, in 1808. They exchanged shots three times, and both parties were slightly wounded, when they declared themselves "satisfied." The third duel was with John Randolph, then Senator from Virginia, when Mr. Clay was Secretary of State under John Quincy Adams. At the second shot, Mr. Clay's ball passed through Mr. Randolph's dress, when both parties declared a oessation of hostilities. In these instances, indeed, he did not kill his antagonists; not, however, from want of intention, but from want of skill. But the fourth affair of murder, in which Mr. Clay has been engaged, is that which ought to stamp his name with lasting infamy; for it was he that *penned the challenge,* and arranged the terms of that fatal duel which, in February, 1838, sent Jonathan Cilley, a member of Congress from the state of Maine, to his grave. Mr. Wise, in his place in Congress, declared that Henry Clay "governed all the preliminaries" of that murderous affray; that he (Mr. Wise) "protested against the language of the challenge, which closed the door to an adjustment of the difficulty, but *was over-ruled by Mr. Clay;*" and that, "had the principals and

*As if the deed itself was not bad enough, he must add to its wickedness, the wickedness of violating the Fourth Commandment. "It was in this very chamber, Senator Holmes, of Maine, presiding in a committee of the Senate, and I in a committee of twenty four of the House of Representatives, on a SABBATH DAY, that the terms were adjusted by which the Missouri compromise was effected." Speech Feby 23, 1835 In his recent Southern tour, he has been guilty of the same sin to a most shameless extent.

the two seconds been free to act in this matter, not a shot would have been fired."* His hands, therefore, are stained with the blood of the murdered Cilley, and all the waters of the ocean cannot wash it out. Lastly, as late as 1841, he showed as much eagerness for murder as ever; for when, after that bitter war of words between himself and Mr. King, of Alabama, in the U. S. Senate, Mr. Clay pronouncing what Mr. King had said to be "unjust, false, and cowardly," intending thereby to provoke a challenge, that he might have the choice of weapons, Dr. Linn, of Missouri, handed a note to Mr. Clay, the latter said, before opening it, in tones of most embittered rage, "a challenge, I suppose; I ACCEPT IT;" thus showing that age had not cooled his ardor for the work of death.

Thus, fellow citizens, you have before you the candidate of the Whig party, for the Presidency. The law of Pennsylvania, passed March 31, 1806, reads thus: "Any person fighting a duel, challenging, or accepting a challenge, shall pay the sum of $500, and suffer one year's imprisonment at hard labor, in the same manner as convicted felons are now punished." You therefore see, that had Henry Clay been tried by our laws, he would, at three several times, have been sent to our Penitentiary.

We now ask you to listen to the warnings of some of the wisest and best men in our land. Says the distinguished Dr. Beecher, in a sermon delivered about two years after Hamilton was murdered by Aaron Burr,—

> The inconsistency of VOTING for a duellist is glaring. To profess attachment for liberty, and VOTE for a man whose principles and practice are alike hostile to liberty, is a farce too ridiculous to be acted by freemen.
>
> In our prayers, we request that God would bestow upon us good rulers; "just men, walking in the fear of God." But by voting for the duellist we demonstrate the insincerity of such prayers.
>
> But you may say, If I do not vote for the man on my side, will not this be helping his antagonist, and will not this be as bad as if I voted directly. No. It is certainly a different thing whether a vile man comes into power BY your agency, or IN SPITE of it. But suppose the duellist in all respects excepting this crime, is a better man than his opponent; of two evils may we not choose the least? Yes, of two natural evils you may; if you must lose a finger or an arm, cut off the finger; but of two sinful things you may choose neither, and therefore you may not vote for one bad man, a MURDERER, to keep out another bad man. It is "to do evil that good may come," and of all who do this, the Apostle declares "their damnation is just."
>
> And now let me ask you, in conclusion, will you any longer, either deliberately or thoughtlessly VOTE for these guilty men? Will you renounce allegiance

*See Globe and National Intelligencer of January 29, 1842, and Pennsylvanian of January 31, 1842.

> to your Maker, and cast the Bible behind your back? Will you confide in men void of the fear of God, and destitute of moral principle? Will you intrust LIFE to MURDERERS and LIBERTY to DESPOTS? Will you *bestow your suffrage,* when you know that, by withholding it, you may arrest this deadly evil—when the remedy is so easy, so entirely in your power; and when God, if you do not punish these guilty men, will most inevitably punish you?

Says Dr. Sprague, of Albany, in a sermon preached after Cilley was murdered by Graves,—

> Let every citizen, when he goes to the BALLOT-BOX, inquire whether it will be safe to put his dearest interests into the keeping of a MURDERER; and let him resolve, as he would keep a conscience void of offence, that no man who GIVES or ACCEPTS a challenge, shall EVER have his vote.

With reference to the assertion often made, that "we must choose the least of two evils," Dr. Bushnell, of Hartford, thus most solemnly exclaims:

> Merciful God! has it come to this, that in choosing rulers, we are simply to choose whether the nation shall be governed by seven devils or ten? Is this the alternative offered to our consciences and our liberties? There never was a maxim more corrupt, more totally bereft of principle, than this—that, between bad men, you are to choose the least wicked of the two.

What now, fellow citizens, shall be thought of those who, within a few weeks, have been running, in thousands, to hear the harangues of GRAVES the MURDERER, and who would elevate to the Presidency THE GREAT DUELLIST OF THE LAND?

The candidate of the Democratic party is

James K. Polk

In the first edition of this Address, fellow-citizens, you will remember that the name of Martin Van Buren was inserted in this place. He was evidently the decided favorite of the great majority of his party at the North; and no one doubted that he would receive the nomination of the Convention which was to assemble at Baltimore. Well, the Convention met. The slave-power insisted that two-thirds of the votes should be necessary to constitute a choice; northern DEMOCRATS yielded, as usual, to their masters; when lo! Mr. Van Buren, who at first had 146 out of 266 votes, is finally rejected, and James K. Polk, of Tennessee, receives the vote of the Convention.

But what had Mr. Van Buren done to displease the slave-holders? We will tell you: He had written a letter—the most creditable document he ever wrote—against the immediate annexation of Texas; that scheme of the slave-power to extend its nefarious institution. He, therefore, received but TWELVE votes from the slave states, and a slaveholder is brought forward, who is an earnest advocate of Texas annexation, with all its attendant wickedness and consequent calamities; and who has distinguished himself in nothing, but in the tyranny with which he exercised his authority for four years, while Speaker of the House, in enforcing the "gag rule," to an extent that not even its notorious author had ever contemplated.

And now we would ask, with all earnestness, how much longer, Citizens of the Free states, are ye to remain in vassalage to the slave-holding demagogues of the South? How much longer will you do the bidding of that mere handful of men, who, with the words of DEMOCRACY on their lips, are not only themselves trampling upon the dearest rights of two and a half millions of people in their own region, but have left no arts untried to make you their "allies," in support of their wicked system? Democrats of the North! ye who possess some self-respect, how much longer will you submit to these things? Answer at the ballot-box; and let the insolent "overseers" know, in a language which they will understand, that they may rule *slaves,* but shall not rule FREEMEN.

We now present to you our own candidate,

JAMES GILLESPIE BIRNEY

Of Michigan, and invite your strictest scrutiny into his character, and his qualifications for the high office for which we have nominated him. Born in Kentucky in 1792, a graduate of Princeton College, in 1810, and a Student of Law, at Philadelphia, he began the practice of his profession at Danville, his native place, and subsequently pursued it at Huntsville, Alabama. We have no space to go into the particulars of his life. His early attention to the subject of Slavery; his acceptance of the agency of the American Colonization Society, for the Southern States, as a means by which he thought he might do good to the slave; his subsequent convictions of the utter inadequacy of that bubble scheme to effect the alleged object; his long and most able letter of resignation as Agent, and as Vice President of the Society, in which he makes the just remark, "we are *living down* the foundation principles of our happy institutions;" his noble act of giving freedom to all his own slaves; his efforts, against abuse, and obloquy, and threats of personal violence, to establish a free press in Cincinnati; the great ability he displayed in conducting that press; his speeches and essays and constitutional arguments on the subject of slavery, all these incidents of his life, and many more as creditable that might be named, give abundant evidence of his ample qualifications for the highest office in our government. But his talents and attainments, however great, would be nothing in our estimation, if they were not accompanied by something higher, purer, nobler. It is his stern integrity of character; it is his high moral courage, it is his devoted and consistent piety, that make JAMES GILLESPIE BIRNEY eminently deserving the vote of every good man.

Our candidate for the Vice Presidency, THOMAS MORRIS, of Ohio, is one also, in every way worthy of your confidence. While to his moral character, no exceptions can be taken, in his public career he has shown himself to be a *true* Democrat, by his regard for the rights of *the people* and the *whole people.* After that notorious anti-abolition speech of Henry Clay, to which we have before referred, Thomas Morris, of Ohio, belonging to the so-called Democratic party, presented a preamble and a series of resolutions to the Senate, drawn up with great ability, to meet the sophistry and the declamation of the Kentucky senator. He knew that to act thus, would be to lose his position with his own party; but he took the course which duty, not self-interest pointed out, and at the next election he was left at home, to enjoy the richer rewards of an approving conscience; for

> More true joy Marcellus exiled feels,
> Than Cæsar with a Senate at his heels.

Our candidate for Governor, is

DR. FRANCIS JULIUS LEMOYNE

Of Washington county. Of him we need say but little, as he is well known throughout the State, as much for his pure and elevated character, as for his distinguished intellectual abilities. Of strict integrity himself, he would leave no honest efforts untried that our State should have, at home and abroad, the same character for integrity, *by the just payment of all her debts.* True, he has fought no battles, but those of moral principles in the cause of human rights. But the time has nearly gone by, we trust, when the fact of a man's having been engaged in one or more wars, shall be thought to make him any better qualified for filling the chair of State.

Such, fellow citizens, are the candidates which we present to you. Into their characters, and into the characters of all whom the Liberty Party, now or hereafter, may nominate for office, we invite your strictest scrutiny. If they be not found such as must meet the approbation of every good man, who desires to see the highest offices in our country, filled by "just men, ruling in the fear of God;" men who will be a "terror to evil doers, and a praise to them that do well;" do not give them your suffrage. But if they be, come and help us to put them in. As to the probabilities of our success, we have every thing to encourage us, not only in the JUSTICE, but also in the

Progress of Our Cause

The scenes of mob violence that occurred in the city of Boston, in 1835, when those who spoke publicly against slavery were threatened with every indignity, are well known. Now the Liberty Party hold their meetings in "old Faneuil Hall," the "cradle of Liberty," and that immense room is crowded with eager listeners. A daily Liberty paper, also, conducted with signal talent, is published in that city; while the vote of Massachusetts, from a few hundred in 1841, has reached to nearly 9000 in 1843. In 1836, a mob at Cincinnati tore down the press, and hunted for the life of *our candidate for the Presidency,* and assailed with personal violence others, well known as friends of the cause. Now there is published in that city, also, a daily paper, which, with consummate ability, advocates our principles. In 1837, resolutions from the state of Massachusetts, on the subject of slavery, were thrown by Congress, with contempt, upon the table; now, resolutions from the same state are referred to a large committee, of which the great champion of the right of petition is chairman. The majority in Congress against receiving all petitions of the subject of slavery, at first very large, has been growing less and less every year; until, at last, the "gag rule," as it is called, was lately carried but by barely one vote. In 1837, Dr. Crandall, of New York, was *thrown into prison,* in the District of Columbia, for having anti-slavery pamphlets in his trunk. Now, a voice breaks forth from the dark walls of a prison in that very spot; the sound penetrates the doors of the Capitol; and the petition to Congress, from a colored man, to interpose in his behalf, is referred, by a large majority, to the Committee on the Judiciary. In 1840, the first year of the organization of the Liberty party, our vote for President was hardly 7000 in all the states; while the last year, even for state officers, it amounted to upwards of 60,000: thus more than doubling itself every successive year. The returns that have been received of a few elections this Spring, show a still greater increase. New Hampshire, which last Fall, gave only 3594 votes, has this Spring given about 6000. It requires but little arithmetic to see how soon, at this rate, our cause will be triumphant. Every day we are receiving, in all the Free states, large accessions to our numbers, of true and honest hearts; while we hear from the Slave states themselves, voices all around, to encourage us in our labors. In Delaware, many of its best citizens are interested in the cause, and lately held a conference to adopt measures for the abolition of slavery in that state. In Maryland, the infamous slaveholders' convention was an eminent instance how "God makes the wrath of man to praise him," as it doubtless advanced the cause of human freedom in that state very many years; for an able weekly paper is now published in Baltimore, that takes strong anti-slavery ground. In Virginia, we receive the most cheering intelligence, that, in a number of counties, systematic efforts are making to circulate anti-slavery publications, and to spread anti-slavery principles. In Tennessee, a regular anti-slavery society has been established. In Kentucky, one gentleman writes us, "the Liberty party is destined to be the most powerful auxiliary in the hands of Providence for the overthrow of American slavery;" while that noble champion of human rights, Cassius M. Clay, by his letters and speeches, and unceasing personal efforts, is gaining for himself a name that will grow brighter and brighter as time rolls on.

Thus far at home. But if we look abroad, we find quite as much to gladden our hearts. The happy workings of emancipation in the British West Indies, have exceeded the most sanguine expectations of its warmest friends. The order and industry that there universally prevail—the wonderful improvement in morals, in education, and in every thing indicative of a nation's prosperity, are all clear manifestations of the blessing of God that attends an effort of justice and philanthropy. The Emperor of Russia has already done much, and means to do still more, for ameliorating the condition of his serfs. France and Holland will, doubtless, soon take the same steps with their colonial possessions, that Great Britain has with hers. The Bey of Tunis, even, has abolished the internal slave trade throughout his dominions, and has, himself, set to his people the noble example of giving liberty to all his own slaves, and of requiring all the officers of his court to do likewise; while Mexico and the Republics of South America are determined that their practice shall be consistent with their avowed principles of liberty. Our country, as you thus see fellow citizens, must therefore move soon in the great work, or we shall be left alone in our disgrace; with no one to sympathise with us, no one to countenance us in our course—a course as inconsistent with our professions, as it is disgraceful, and odious, and wicked in itself.

Come, then, men of Pennsylvania, citizens of the same state as Franklin, and Rush, and Wilson, and the Morrises, who thought as we think, and who, were they now living, would doubtless act as we are now acting,—come and join us in this good work. Join us, to use such moral means as to correct public sentiment throughout the region where slavery exists. Join us, to impress upon the people of the Free states a manly sense of their own rights. Join us, to place "just men" in all our public offices; men whose example a whole people may safely imitate. Join us, to free our General Government from the ignominious reproach of slavery. Join us, to restore to our country those principles which our fathers so labored to establish: join us, to hand them down afresh to successive generations. It is the cause of truth, of humanity, and of God, to which we invite your aid. It is a cause of which you never need be ashamed. Living, you may be thankful, and dying, you may be thankful, for having labored in it. We have, as co-laborers with us, the noblest allies that man can wish. Within, we have the deepest convictions of conscience; the clearest deductions of reason; and, all over the world, wherever man is found, the first, the most ardent longings of the human soul. Without, we have the happiness of nearly three millions of the human race; the honor, as well as the best interests, of our whole country; and the universal consent of all good men, whose moral vision is not obscured by the mists of a low, misguided selfishness: while we seem to hear, as it were, the voices of the great and the good, the patriot and the philanthropist, of a past generation, calling to us, and cheering us on. But, above all these, and beyond all these, we have with us the highest attributes of God, JUSTICE and MERCY. With such allies, and in such a cause, who can doubt on which side the victory will ultimately rest.

May He who guides the destinies of nations, and without whose aid "they labor in vain that build," so incline your hearts to exert your whole influence to place in all our public offices just and good men, that our country may be preserved, her best interests advanced, and her institutions, free in reality as in name, handed down to the latest posterity.

7

The Twenty-Ninth Congress, Its Men and Measures; Its Professions and Its Principles. What It Has Done for Itself, What for the Country, and What Against the Country. Being a Review of the Proceedings of the First Session of the Twenty-Ninth Congress (Washington, 1846)

From the Democratic perspective, the Twenty-Ninth Congress (1845–1847) was one of the most productive ever. Secure party majorities in both houses and an activist Democratic president united to enact a whole range of the party's long-advocated major policies into law, in particular a lower tariff and an independent treasury. President Polk also vetoed a rivers and harbors bill, in keeping with long-standing party doctrine against such federal expenditures.

The Whigs, as revealed in this angry pamphlet, written for use in the congressional elections midway in Polk's term, were horrified at what had occurred. They offered a long litany of criticism against Democratic policies and deceptions, adding to the usual domestic agenda the Polk administration's reckless foreign policy, which had produced war with Mexico and confrontation with England. "We look in vain," the Whigs concluded, "for any act of public or private good passed by the late Congress. Cursing and not blessing has fallen to the lot of the country . . ."

"By their fruits shall ye know them."

Progressive Democracy

The proceedings of the late, long, and long to be remembered, session of Congress, are of a character so marked and important, so destructive of the best interests of the country, and in some respects so novel and unprecedented, that, as Whigs, suffering severely as citizens, and as men of business, we regard them as demanding some special notice at our hands. To reform all existing abuses is a cardinal Whig principle, but known innovations upon safe and well-established principles of Government are not reforms. One of the wisest remarks of a distinguished statesman of England, and a friend to our own independence, was, that "it could not too often be repeated, line upon line and precept upon precept, until it passed into the currency of a proverb, that, *to innovate is not to reform.*" What in this day is so often denominated "progressive Democracy," is nothing more than an invasion of the sacred rights both of men and of property. As demonstrated by the rulers of the dominant party, (for we desire to distinguish between politicians of a party and the party itself,) it has often been no more than giving full freedom to the passions and prejudices of a party. It is a principle that opposes all self-control; that rushes forward headlong in pursuit of every wish and pleasure that can gratify its selfish objects. Its written creed is the liberal maxim of Jeremy Bentham, "the greatest good of the greatest number;" but the creed it lives by and practises in, is intolerance and proscription towards every man not of its own faith and combination. Whatever is brought forward in opposition to these men is regarded as aristocratic, and whoever ventures upon opposition, is denounced as antidemocratic. Every day are these progressive Democrats becoming more ultra in their principles, more peremptory in their demands, and more disposed to become usurpers of this power. We complain of this kind of Democracy as spurious, and as having no more regard for the real interests of the country, and the true welfare of the people, than the despots of the Old World have for men who day by day groan under the oppressions of a merciless tyranny. It is, nevertheless, the Democracy of the rulers of the dominant party—of men who even, when they mean well, forget that their own good intentions is no excuse for their bad actions, but who, unfortunately for the country, make their own bad actions too often harmonize with their own bad principles.

The Whig Creed, &c

Names are not principles, and in a government of delegated powers, there can be nothing but a Democracy in name. All of us however may, if we will, be true friends of the country and its institutions. As Whigs, we hope we have a higher standard of political morality than that of professing principles we never mean to practice, and of making promises we never mean to keep. We rest our creed upon the platform of that great Christian precept which proclaims "Peace on Earth and good will to men;" and by this principle we are willing to stand or fall. If we are asked our own creed, we write it thus: That we seek to enlighten men, and not to flatter them. In the diffusion of general intelligence; in the multiplication of free schools; in the moral and conscientious free press; in a truly independent representation of the people, both in Congress and with the States; in the strictest responsibility and accountability of all persons holding offices, elected or by appointment; and, above all, in that mutual respect of the rights, privileges, and immunities of each of the States, the one towards the other—in all this, and upon all this, we can rely for the permanence of our free institutions. Political honesty in office will insure political integrity in all departments of the Government; and we rest our faith and our hopes of the existence of the Government itself upon its return to the practices of the purer and better days of the Republic. The more we leave the landmarks marked out by the Constitution and the principles of the men who framed it, though we depart never so little from these principles, the more danger there is of political shipwreck. The examples of other nations warn us to stand upon our integrity, and to rebuke the men, whoever they are, and the administration, whoever controls it, who may attempt to erect new altars for political worship, and new principles as exponents of the recognised and sanctified principles of Republican Government. A poet has said as truly as beautifully of the fall of Rome, and in language prophetic of all nations doing as Rome did—

'Twere long to tell and sad to trace
Each step from splendor to disgrace,
Enough, no foreign foe could quell
Herself, till from herself she fell:
Yes, self-abasement paved the way
To villain bonds, and despot's sway.

Thus much we deem it proper to say, before entering upon a brief review of the measures of the session of Congress so recently closed. The highest and the humblest citizen can hardly fail to feel the baneful effect of these measures, though the poor man, dependant upon his daily labor for his daily bread, is likely to be much the severest sufferer from what has been done. We look in vain for any class of persons who are to be benefited, *except the capitalists and manufacturers of Europe and the officeholders at home.*

Personal Expenditures

The TWENTY-NINTH CONGRESS commenced its session on Monday, December 1, 1845, and closed on Monday, the 10th of August, 1846, the session continuing *two hundred and fifty-three days.* The *per diem* of each of the members of the House of Representatives alone, was TWO THOUSAND AND TWENTY-FOUR DOLLARS. The total *per diem* pay awarded to the members of the House of Representatives was FOUR HUNDRED AND SIXTY-SEVEN THOUSAND five HUNDRED AND FORTY-FOUR DOLLARS. The fifty-six Senators, in like manner, received each their eight dollars a day, and the members of both Houses *five hundred and seventy thousand eight hundred and eighty-eight dollars.*

The MILEAGE is to be added to this amount, and though a very small sum for the members representing the States in the immediate neighborhood of the Capitol, the aggregate is as large almost as the per diem pay of members. EIGHT DOLLARS FOR EVERY TWENTY MILES OF TRAVEL, forty dollars for every one hundred miles, and four hundred dollars for every thousand miles, and that where the real expense is not more than one tenth of the amount allowed, the members receiving the same pay whether *from* or *to* the Capitol, has long been regarded as one of the abuses of the Government. Nobody has said so much of, or promised so much towards the correction of this abuse, as our political opponents; and yet it not only continues, but in reference to what was done at the last Congress, its continuance is the subject of a new and well-founded complaint. Pending the consideration of the Civil and Diplomatic bill, Mr. DOCKERY, a whig member from the State of North Carolina, a State pre-eminently distinguished for her sterling consistency of purpose, for her honest men and her political integrity, offered an amendment regulating the mileage by the distance travelled preserving the present liberal rates for short distances, and making a gradual reduction for all distances beyond. The amendment prevailed in the House, but failed in a Committee of Conference, consisting of FOUR Democrats and TWO Whigs, who had no control over the question, and who in this, as upon other questions, were obliged to submit to whatever the majority imposed upon them. The democratic Conferees upon this bill were, on the part of the Senate, Messrs. LEWIS, of Alabama, and BENTON, of Missouri, representing two of the extremes of the Union; and on the part of the House of Representatives, Messrs, MCKAY, of N. C., and BOYD, of Ky. With all these gentlemen, there appeared to be the most ready acquiescence in what was done, and the two Houses of Congress acquiesced without a murmur of complaint. In the House there was no time for any, the previous question being moved by the chairman of the Committee of Ways and Means, as soon as the report was submitted.

Ultra Party Spirit

We may remark here, what the journal before us will prove to be correct, that at no other session of Congress was there so little political tolerance, and none where so many inroads have been made upon the freedom of debate. Like the followers of Rhoderic Dhu, at the whistle of their chieftain, every clansman has sprung to his feet armed cap-a-pie for any service before him. The rights of the minority, embodied in the privileges of free discussion, have been trampled under foot, and gentlemen have forgotten that more than one-third of their number were like all the rest, the representatives of perhaps one-half of the people of the Union. We complain of this intolerance not only as tyrannical to the Whig members themselves, but as an outrage upon the Whig party of the Union. The dominant party have legislated as if all power and all public opinion were concentrated in themselves, forgetting that even the head of this Administration, the President himself, though constitutionally elected, did not receive the majority of the votes of the American people. We think, too, that we hazard nothing in saying that a very large majority of the people will both censure and condemn what has thus far been done by the present Congress. We shall test some of these measures in detail, and apply them in their practice, by the professions which have been made in regard to them. And first—

The Annexation of Texas

The Whigs were originally opposed to annexation, for reasons which they regarded as both patriotic and just in themselves. They believed that while there was war existing between Mexico and Texas, and while our treaty stipulations with Mexico were those of two friendly nations, that annexation would at least involve us in a war with a neighboring and friendly republic. They knew that though Texas had claimed to the Rio Grande as far back as 1836, that she had never been able to maintain possession of the country between the Nueces and the Rio Grande. The citizens of Texas, with the bravery, spirit, and determination of men resolved to be free and independent, necessarily protected from invasion the country this side the Nueces; but all her exertions to secure the country, which is now the avowed cause of war, were unavailing. We find the following congratulatory announcement of annexation in the annual message of the President of last December.

"LOOK ON THIS PICTURE"

From the President's message of December 2d, 1845:

> *The accession to our territory* (the annexation of Texas) *has been a bloodless achievement. No arm of force has been raised to produce the result. The sword has had no part in the victory. We have not sought to extend our territorial possessions by conquest, or our republican institutions over a reluctant people. It was the deliberate homage of each people to the great principle of our federative union.*
>
> If we consider the extent of the territory involved in the annexation—its protective influence on America—the means by which it has been accomplished, springing purely from the choice of the people themselves to share the blessings of our union, the history of the world may be challenged to furnish a parallel.

AND NOW ON THIS!

From the special message of the President of the United States, dated May 11, 1846:

> *As war exists, and, notwithstanding all our efforts to avoid it, exists by the act of Mexico herself,* we are called upon by every consideration of duty and patriotism to vindicate with decision the honor, the rights, and the interests of our country.
>
> *Anticipating the possibility of a crisis like that which has just arrived, instructions were given in August last,* "as a precautionary measure" against invasion, or threatened invasion, authorizing General Taylor, if the emergency required, to accept volunteers, not from Texas only, but from the States of Louisiana, Alabama, Mississippi, Tennessee, and Kentucky; and corresponding letters were addressed to the respective governors of those States. These instructions were repeated; and, in January last, soon after the incorporation of "Texas into our union of States," General Taylor was further "authorized by the President to make a requisition upon the executive of that State for such of its militia force as may be needed to repel invasion, or to secure the country against apprehended invasion." On the second day of March he was again reminded, "in the event of the approach of any considerable Mexican force, promptly and efficiently to use the authority with which he was clothed to call to him such auxiliary force as he might need." War actually existing, and our territory having been invaded, General Taylor, pursuant to authority vested in him by my

> direction, has called on the governor of Texas for four regiments of State troops—two to be mounted, and two to serve on foot; and on the governor of Louisiana for four regiments of infantry, to be sent to him as soon as practicable.
>
> In further vindication of our rights, and defence of our territory, I invoke the prompt action of Congress to recognise the existance of the war, and to place at the disposition of the Executive the means of prosecuting the war with vigor, and thus hastening the restoration of peace. To this end I recommend that authority should be given to call into the public service a large body of volunteers, to serve for not less than six or twelve months, unless sooner discharged. A volunteer force is beyond question more efficient than any other description of citizen soldiers; and it is not to be doubted that a number far beyond that required would readily rush to the field upon the call of their country. I further recommend that a liberal provision be made for sustaining our entire military force, and furnishing it with supplies and munitions of war.
>
> The most energetic and prompt measures, and the immediate appearance in arms of a large and overpowering force, are recommended to Congress as the most certain and efficient means of bringing the existing collision with Mexico to a speedy and successful termination.

Of this message, we may say in the language of another, that "nothing but itself can be its parallel." But whether we compare it with itself, with the annual message of December, or with the facts in the case, it seems to us equally full of extraordinary and contradictory statements. Mr. Polk says in his message of May 11th, that—

> The army moved from Corpus Christi on *the 11th of March, and on the 28th of that month arrived on the left bank of the Del Norte, opposite to Matamoras, where it encamped on a commanding position, which has since been strengthened by the erection of field works.* A depot has also been established at Point Isabel, near the Brazos Santiago, thirty miles in rear of the encampment. The selection of his position was necessarily confided to the judgment of the general in command.

We need only ask that the reader should compare the message of May with itself, or with the message of December, in order to find within itself an answer for the extraordinary statements which are made in both of these papers. In December we are told of a "bloodless achievement," when "a crisis like the present had been anticipated in the previous August." And again we are told, both in the message of the President and in the act of Congress, of "a war existing by the act of Mexico," when elsewhere we read and know that the order to march our troops from Corpus Christi to the Del Norte was the sole cause of the war. No man believes there would have been this collision, or any war, had not the troops been removed to the Del Norte. The Administration, therefore, is responsible for this war, and for the enormous expenditure of money necessary to give vigor to our arms. We have not seen the "bloodless achievement," nor "the victory without the sword," nor "the willing people" "acquiescing in what has been done." As Whigs, we have submitted to the annexation of Texas, because the act of annexation has been consummated by all departments of our Government; but we claim to have predicted seasonably and truly the cost of the act, and are not willing that truth should be falsified now that the deed is done.

Settlement of the Oregon Question

However satisfactorily the only remaining question of dispute with England may have been settled, we cannot, upon reviewing the manner of settlement, fail to come to the conclusion, that more might have been gained, and gained with more grace and honor, than what has been accomplished. If we contrast the treaty made by Mr. Polk and Mr. Buchanan, with the high sounding pretensions of the President's message, we are humiliated by the facts; and we do not wonder, therefore, that the British Government are well satisfied with a result which secures to them so much of that which the President, his Secretary of State, and a large body of his party, declared to be our own territory. Mr. Polk has either been the instrument of a surrender of American territory, or he has been guilty of making pretensions which he never meant to make good by his own action. A large party in the Union framed their own opinions as to what was our own territory, and what ought to be done to preserve it, from the very teachings of the President and his friends. Upon the previous declarations of the Baltimore Convention—the strong defence of the American right to "the whole of Oregon," embodied in the annual message of the President—the reiterated declarations of the Executive incorporated in almost four-score speeches from both wings of the Capitol—a strong party demonstration was made. The cabalistic characters of "54–40" were emblazoned upon half the door-posts, sign-posts, and shop-boards of the cities of the Union. They were the Shibboleth of party—were painted upon the banners—emblazoned upon the corners of the streets—carved upon seals—posted in books—engraven in maps, and became the daily theme of the Organ of the Administration, and all the Government echoes throughout the land. This, we are told, was public opinion; and in the Senate of the United States, a doom was pronounced against the man who would dare to compromise this question at all, or who would yield the ninth part of a hair's breadth of territory this side of "fifty-four forty," as terrible as the doom of him whom a power above us—

> Hurl'd headlong flaming from the ethereal sky,
> With hideous ruin and combustion, down
> To bottomless perdition, there to dwell
> In adamantine chains and penal fire.

The man who should dare to compromise this question, we were told, should be consigned "to a damnation so deep, and an infamy so profound, that the hand of resurrection could not reach him!" Well, Mr. Polk has done all this—the Administration have sanctioned all this—and under what circumstances?

Mr. Polk, in his annual message, is as unfortunate in what he says upon the Oregon question, as in his allusions to the annexation of Texas. In extenuation of his fault, as he seemed to regard it, of proposing to compromise the Oregon question at all, by his first offer to Great Britain, he says:—

> The right of any foreign power to the free navigation of any of our rivers, through the heart of our country, was one which I was unwilling to concede.

Again he says—

> The extraordinary and wholly inadmissible demands of the British government, and the rejection of the proposition made in deference alone to what had been done by my predecessors, and the implied obligation which their acts seemed to impose, afford satisfactory evidence that no compromise which the United States ought to accept can be effected. With this conviction, the proposition of compromise which had been made and rejected was, by my direction, subsequently withdrawn, and our title to the whole Oregon territory asserted, and, as is believed, maintained by irrefragable facts and arguments.

"Peace or war," we were also told by the Secretary of State, on the 29th of January last, was involved in the issue of the surrender by England of the whole of Oregon. In the same letter Mr. Buchanan said:—

> *The President will never abandon the position he has taken in his message. Clearly convinced of the right of the United States* TO THE WHOLE TERRITORY IN DISPUTE, and relieved, by the refusal of the British Government to accept this offer of compromise, from the embarrassment in which the acts of his

predecessors had placed him, *he would not authorize the conclusion of a treaty on that basis.* (The basis of 49.)

Further on the President advises the legislative action of Congress, in the following strain:—

> Beyond all question, the protection of our laws and our jurisdiction, civil and criminal, ought to be immediately extended over our citizens in Oregon. They have had just cause to complain of our long neglect in this particular, and have, in consequence, been compelled, for their own security and protection, to establish a provisional government for themselves. Strong in their allegiance and ardent in their attachment to the United States, they have been thus cast upon their own resources.

"Indian Agencies and Sub-Agencies," "a suitable number of stockades and block-house forts," "an adequate force of mounted riflemen to guard and protect emigrants on their journey," "laws, civil and criminal, to the full extent the British Parliament have proceeded in regard to British subjects," "courts of record," and the framework of an entire territorial government, were recommended. And, notwithstanding these recommendations, Congress has not passed finally upon one of the measures so urgently pressed upon the attention of its members. The President was not sincere with Congress, and Congress had not that confidence in the Executive, which warranted the granting of the powers which were asked. The emigrants to the Columbia river, amidst all the perils and privations incident to a new country—savage settlements—severe poverty, and dangerous disease—exposed to all the inclemencies of season and country, and to the neglect of the country that promised its protection, have, notwithstanding, gone forward to the land of promise before them. But no laws follow them, and none of the practical blessings of our free institutions.

> The world is all before them, where to choose
> Their place of rest, and Providence their guide;

but the Executive and the dominant party, both so full of their free-will-offerings to these pioneers, who anon are to make the wilderness blossom like the rose, have failed in all their pledges towards these men, and towards those still at home, who relied in good faith upon a strict fulfilment of pledges made in the highest places, and from the highest authority of the Government. The Administration, and Congress as a prominent part and parcel of the Administration, have made the word of promise to the ear, and have broken it to the hope. Out of their own mouths we condemn them for a surrender of our own soil, the rights of our own citizens, and the rights, honor, and interests of the country. What Whigs may have done, or would have done, holding entirely different opinions, both upon the true merits of the question, and the true question at issue, is no excuse for what our opponents have done, with the loud boasting of what they would do if they had the power, and their louder censure of the opinions of the Whigs—"British Whigs," as they were called—for holding that any compromise short of the extreme claim of fifty-four forty was just and honorable! Our "heresies," as they were called, have not only become the purest orthodoxy, but our opponents have gone a league beyond us in eagerly catching at the first proposal, and that known not to be an ultimatum, of the British Government. They have claimed "the whole of Oregon or none;" they have, in the words of the President, declared it to be ours "by irrefragable facts and arguments;" they have said that "the title was clear and incontestible," and that "there should be no compromise," in the words of General Jackson, "but at the cannon's mouth;" and yet they have surrendered all that Great Britain asked us to surrender, and accepted the first serious offer the British Government ever made. Where the navigation of the Columbia river could and should have been secured to the United States exclusively and in perpetuity, it has either been surrendered for a long term of years, or FOREVER, and we fear forever, by the terms of the treaty which has been ratified, in conjunction with the charter of the Hudson's Bay Company. The English statesmen who have spoken upon this subject, and the English editors who have written about it, claim that the only construction given to the treaty upon the other side of the Atlantic is, that the navigation of the Columbia is a joint navigation. The Senator from Ohio, (Mr. ALLEN,) spoke upon one of the last days of the session, of legislating for "the little remnant" of Oregon that was left to us after the surrender that had been made; and an Administration Senator from Indiana, (Mr. HANNEGAN,) declared that there was hereafter *forever* to be a joint occupation of *all the country south of forty-nine;* whereas previous to the late treaty there was a joint occupation of all the country up to the line of fifty-four degrees and forty minutes. General CASS also appeared to regard the surrender of the navigation of the Columbia river as forever, instead of expiring a dozen years hence, with some temporary privileges granted to the Hudson's Bay Company. It was upon the motion of the Senator from Michigan that the following resolution was introduced:—

Resolved, That the Secretary of the Senate cause to be printed for the use of the Senate the following paper:

> *Extract from the charter granted to the Hudson's Bay Company by Charles II, dated May the 2d, "in the two and-twentieth year of his reign," being* 1671.
>
> The third section provides that the persons named, "and such others as shall be admitted into the said society, as is hereafter expressed, shall be one body corporate and politique, in deed and in name, by the name of *The Governor and Company of Adventurers of England, trading into the Hudson's Bay,* and them by the name of *The Governor and Company of Adventurers of England trading into Hudson's Bay,* one body corporate and politique, in deed and in name, really and fully, FOR EVER, for us, our heirs and successors, &c."
>
> SECTION 12. *And farther,* we do by these presents for us, our heirs and successors, make, create and constitute the said Governor and Company, for the time being, and their successors, the true and absolute lords and proprietors of the same territory, limits and places aforesaid, and of all other the premises, saving always the faith, and allegiance and sovereign dominion to us, our heirs and successors, for the same, to have, hold, possess and enjoy the said territories, limits and places, and all and singular other the premises hereby granted, as aforesaid, with their, and every of their rights, members, jurisdictions, prerogatives, royalties and appurtenances whatsoever, to them the said Governor and Company and their successors FOR EVER, to be holden of us, our heirs and successors, as of our manner of East Greenwich, in the county of Kent, in free and common soccage, and not in capite, or by knight service, yielding and paying yearly to us, our heir and successor, for the same, two elks and two black beavers whensoever and as often as we, our heirs and successors shall happen to enter into the said countries, territories or regions hereby granted.

We shall not stop here, again, to contrast the surrender of territory with the claims which have been set up by those administering the Government, but if this Oregon question has been again left open to litigation, and is again to become a bone of contention, (as we fear it is,) we can award no credit to the Administration that has but postponed the day of evil. But, viewed either as a temporary or a permanent measure, what becomes of the Oregon treaty, in contrast with the declarations of the message of the President, that the American continent is not to be considered as subject for future colonization by any European power? How poorly do the President's own acts, or the action of Congress, harmonize with the declaration, that "it is due alike to our safety and our interests, that the efficient protection of our laws should be extended over our whole territorial limits, and that it should be distinctly announced to the world as our settled policy, *that no future European colony or dominion shall, with our consent, be planted or established on any part of the North American continent!"*

According to the argument elsewhere, England had no claim to the Oregon; none by discovery; none, of a permanent character, by treaty; none by the law of nations; none any way, or any where. We have said already, that the President did not deal honorably with Congress, and we have just now the confession of the Organ, that the President had made up his mind, as long ago as *last December,* to lay before the Senate any proposition which Great Britain might submit. Legislation, diplomacy, even Government itself, becomes but a miserable piece of political chaffering and haggling, when such tricks are resorted to by men calling themselves statesmen. Of a similar class of politicians in England it was well said, by Mr. Burke, that "there was nothing so base as Government in their hands." Frankness and candor are as becoming in public men, and as much respected when practised by them, as in private life—always most adored when clothed in the garb of an honest purpose, and seeking to obtain honest ends.

> He is a freeman whom the *truth* makes free,
> And all are slaves besides.

From the whole management of this Oregon question, it is evident that the original object of the Executive was to "raise the whirlwind and direct the storm." War, "inevitable war," was the threatened consequence of all this; war that was never meant, never prepared for, never hoped for; but yet, from the dishonest and bullying manner in which the negotiations were conducted, war and all its consequences would have been certain, but for the firm, wise, honest, and consistent course of Whig Senators. It was a Whig Senator who submitted the proposition for settling the question at all, and a unanimous Whig vote was given for its support.

The Mexican War

Much of the action of Congress has had reference to the war with Mexico, but we have not the space to say of the subject what we could wish; and much of it would more properly become the subject of a review of the Administration than of the proceedings of Congress. Congress, however, has given a most willing acquiescence to the recommendations of the Executive. What the President proclaimed in his message, as to the "existence of war by the act of Mexico," was reiterated in the preamble of the act of Congress appropriating ten millions of dollars for the prosecution of the war. The Whig members generally voted for the appropriation, but they did so protesting against the falsehood embodied in the preamble. The appropriation of the first ten millions of dollars, with authority to call out fifty thousand volunteers, was followed by an authorized increase of the navy to the number of twenty-five hundred men, and by an increase of the rank and file of the army from eight thousand to fifteen thousand men. Under the impetus of the same war, a bill was also passed raising a regiment of mounted riflemen, a corps of sappers, miners, and pontoniers; and two supplementary war bills, authorizing not only a large increase of officers, but accompanied by provisions doing the greatest injustice to those who had, in the most perilous days of the Republic, rendered good service to the nation. Nor did the increase of officers, or the expenditure of money end here. Almost every public act passed by Congress, from the commencement of the Mexican war, has been one largely increasing the patronage and power of the Executive, already so enormous as to fill every patriotic and reflecting mind with alarm, both at the extension of this power and the disposition to abuse it. Had the framers of the Constitution, in the utmost stretch of the imagination, dreamed that, in a Republic, despotism could have gone so far, usurpation become so bold, or even the natural increase of power incident to the growth of the country become so great, that would have bound the Executive as with bands of iron, and held him as with hooks of steel, so that he could not have made those inroads upon the true principles of a Republican Government which so seriously endanger our public liberties. It becomes the Whig party, as the true conservative party of the nation, to resist these encroachments upon the Constitution.

But we have not cited all the expenditures incident to the Mexican war, nor will the amount be known until long after those who are truly responsible for its existence shall have passed from the stage of public action. Besides the bills we have named, it became necessary before the adjournment to pass an act appropriating nearly TWELVE MILLIONS OF DOLLARS, for the support of volunteer troops engaged in the war with Mexico. It also became necessary largely to increase the appropriations for the support of the navy, and of the army. For every branch of the public service, in consequence of this war, it has become necessary to impose additional burdens upon the treasury, which must ultimately be provided for by additional taxes upon the people. The amount of the cost of the Mexican war no man knows, or can pretend to know. Vessels have been chartered by the day, and the Government, for a single voyage between New Orleans and Matamoras, has been compelled to pay more than the actual value of the vessels hired. An old brig, bought by a citizen of New Orleans for one thousand dollars, was immediately chartered by the Government at an expense of three thousand, for the purpose of a single transportation of troops to the seat of war. Nearly seventy thousand dollars will be paid, for sending out a regiment of men for the conquest of California; and in reference to the raising of this regiment, and the avowed object of raising it, we maintain that the war has not been a war to repel invasion, but a war of conquest—an ambitious war for the invasion of a foreign soil, and for the enlargement of the boundaries of the United States. The letter of the Secretary of War, (Mr. MARCY,) dated June 26, 1846, to Colonel JONATHAN D. STEVENSON, of New York, who is commissioned to command the California Regiment—both gentlemen well known in New York, and out of New York—contains this instruction, embodying the terms of enlistment:

> The condition of the acceptance, in this case, must be a tender of service during the war; and it must be explicitly understood, *that they may be discharged without a claim for returning home, wherever they may be serving at the termination of the war,* provided it is in the THEN territory of the United States, or may be taken to the nearest or most convenient territory belonging to the United States, and there discharged.
>
> The men must be apprised that their term of service is for the war; that they are to be discharged as above specified; and that they are to be employed on a distant service. *It is, however, very desirable that it should not be publicly known or proclaimed that they are to go to any particular place.* On this point, great caution is enjoined.

These are instructions emanating from the War Department; instructions by which troops are to be secretly raised in New York and New England, to be secretly sent to California, and there dismissed from their country and the service of their country at the same time. No wonder that discontent, and mutiny, and trials at the drum head, and SENTENCES OF DEATH, have already distinguished the mustering of this regiment. The men complain that they have been imposed upon—promised land, protection and encouragement, upon the soil of California. The care taken that the soldiers should not know *where they were to go, or what they were to go for,* was most industriously observed to the last moment of the entire enlistment of the regiment.

Of a piece with this has been the treatment by the Government of nearly all the volunteers who enlisted for the Mexican war. Continued bad faith has distinguished the War Department and the Executive towards our brave citizens, so ready and so eager even to rush into the thickest of the fight for the defence of the country. Notwithstanding the distant point of service, the existence of a war carried on in the enemy's country, the unfavorable season for the prosecution of the war, the poor pay, contrasted with the pay of the members of Congress themselves, or contrasted with the ordinary returns of labor in the common pursuits of life, the dominant party refused to grant any increase of monthly pay to the volunteers. They were not willing to reduce their own liberal rewards, or to enhance the pay of those who were fighting the battles of the country. We deem it, therefore, but just to all to put the names of these men upon the record, and accordingly make the following extract from the journal of House proceedings:

> On Wednesday, the 20th of May, a motion was made by Mr. Andrew Stewart, of Pa., that the rules be suspended, to enable him to offer the following resolution:
>
> *Resolved,* That the Committee on Military Affairs be instructed to report a bill increasing the pay of volunteers from seven to ten dollars per month, and granting to those who serve to the end of the war, or die in the service, one hundred and sixty acres of land.
>
> The said resolution was read. And the question being put, Shall the rules be suspended? It was decided in the negative, (two-thirds not voting in favor thereof, Yeas 70, Nays 75.)
>
> The yeas and nays being desired by one-fifth of the members present, were taken as follows:
>
> YEAS.—Abbott, J. Q. Adams, Ashmun, Barringer, Bell, Blanchard, *Bowlin,* M. Brown, *W. G. Brown,* Campbell, Carroll, *C. W. Cathcart,* J. G. Chapman, *R. Chapman, Chase,* Cocke, Collamer, Crozier, Callom, Darragh, Davis, Dixon, *Edsall,* Ewing, Foot, Gentry, *Giles,* Graham, Grider, Grinnell, Harper, Hilliard, Holmes, Houston, Hubbard, Hunt, Ingersoll, *Jones,* D. P. King, T. B. King, Lewis, *W. B. Maclay, R. McClelland,* McHenry, McIlvaine, *Martin,* Miller, *Morse,* Moseley, *Parish, Payne,* Relfe, Rockwell, Root, Rusk, Schenck, Seaman, T. Smith, A. Smith, *R. Smith,* Stephens, Stewart, Thibodeaux, Thomasson, Thompson, *Tibbatts,* Trumbo, *Wentworth,* White.
>
> NAYS.—Adams, Atkinson, Bedinger, Benton, Biggs, Black, Boyd, Brinkerhoff, Brockenbrough, Brodhead, Burt, Clarke, Collin, *Cranston,* Cunningham, Daniel, Dargan, Davis, Mott, Dobbin, *Dockery,* Dromgoole, Ellsworth, Erdman, Ficklin, Fries, Garvin, Grover, Hamlin, Holmes, Houston, Hungerford, Hunt, Hunter, Ingersoll, Jenkins, J. H. Johnson, J. Johnson, King, Lawrence, Leake, Levin, J. J. McDowell, J. McDowell, *McGaughey,* McKay, *Marsh,* Morris, Moulton, Norris, Owen, Phelps, Price, Reid, Rhett, Ritter, Roberts, Sawyer, Seddon, A. D. Sims, L. H. Sims, Simpson, Stanton, Starkweather, Sykes, James Thompson, J. Thompson, Tredway, *Vance, Vinton,* Williams, Wood, Woodward, Woodworth, Yancey.

It will be seen that there were but six Whig votes in the negative, and but seventeen of the dominant party who voted to receive the resolution. Sixty-nine Democrats voted against suspending the rules, when the votes of two-thirds of the members present were necessary to bring the resolution before the House, and *one hundred and forty-four members of the dominant party* either voted against the resolution, or dodged the question upon the motion to bring it before the House.

Earlier in the month of May, (on the 12th,) by a vote of 119 to 50, and this also a party vote, the proposition to give the privates of infantry, artillery, and riflemen ten dollars a month, was also voted down. Nor does the injustice to the citizens who so freely volunteered for the defence of the country end here. Louisiana, Alabama, Missouri, Ohio, and other States, have all complained of the bad treatment their citizens have received. The Louisiana regiments, that earliest rushed to the scene of danger for the relief of their countrymen, have been rudely dismissed from the service and called home. A legion of volunteers from Missouri, troops from Alabama, and elsewhere have been treated in a like manner, and even from the Hudson to the Rio Grande, one long, loud complaint is heard against the Administration at Washington. From the Secretary of War to the humblest political agent of the Executive, there appears to be a conspiracy against the citizen soldiery. We give the following from a New Orleans paper, (the Tropic,) as a specimen of the treatment received:

> We understand that the volunteers are charged FOR SIX MONTHS' CLOTHING, or what is worse, charged a bill which pays for two years' undress clothings, according to the United States Army regulations. The clothing they are charged for frequently did not last until the volunteers got to Point Isabel. We are further informed that the sutlers in most cases, who have supplied the volunteers with stores, will be wronged out of their pay altogether. Who is to blame for these unparalleled outrages? Let some one answer.

The mustering of men into the service, who have not been permitted to take an active part in the campaign, it is supposed will cost the Government two millions of dollars. Nor is this all; lives have been sacrificed, and diseases contracted; and to crown all there has been that just irritation of mind, which leaves a stain like a wound, with those who hold themselves to have been greatly wronged by the Government, they would have died to serve. We leave this branch of our subject, asking attention to the secret messages from the President sent to the Senate upon the last few days of the session, and proposing *to buy that peace from Mexico,* which we were before made, to believe we could and should so easily conquer. Let those who can, reconcile their own idea of propriety with the conduct of the Executive in submitting his confidential message of the 4th of August to the Senate, with the following proposition:

> Under the circumstances, and considering the other complicated questions to be settled by negotiation with the Mexican republic, it is necessary that a sum of money should be placed under the control of the Executive, to be advanced, if need be, to the government of that republic immediately after their ratification. It might be inconvenient for the Mexican government to wait for the whole sum, the payment of which may be stipulated by this treaty, until it can be ratified by our Senate, or an application to carry it into effect made by Congress. Indeed, the necessity for this delay might defeat the object altogether. I would, therefore, suggest whether it might not be well for Congress to appropriate such a sum, as they might consider adequate for this purpose, to be paid if necessary immediately upon the ratification of the Treaty by Mexico. The disbursement of this money would of course be accounted for, not as secret service money, but like other expenditures.

Either the Executive did not state the truth when he declared that he meant to make no war of conquest upon Mexico, or when he stated that the war originated in consequence of the invasion of our soil. If the Rio Grande is the boundary of the United States, are we to place two millions of dollars in the hands of the Executive for securing our own to ourselves? Or, after all, are we really engaged in a war of conquest for the acquisition of territory not our own? And if so, was not this determination to take possession of California the true cause of the unfortunate war in which we are engaged? We look in vain to the Administration for anything like honesty of purpose in the origin or prosecution of this war; and the reader, who will divest himself of all party prejudices, and sit down to the examination of all that has been done by Congress, and all that is contained in the Diplomatic and Military correspondence upon this subject, will not fail to censure the Administration for its bad faith to the People of the United States.

The Tariff and the Taxes

We have just made allusion to some of the sources of the large expenditures of Congress, and before closing our review, we shall have occasion to speak of them more in detail. It is enough to say here, that the aggregate of expenditure is between *fifty-one and fifty-two millions of dollars.* Notwithstanding, these unusual and in some respects extravagant appropriations, Congress, so far from raising revenue to meet them, has actually made provision to diminish the public revenue. Upon the one hand it has largely increased the expenditures of the General Government, and upon the other it has diminished both the amount of accruing revenue, and worse than all this, the very means whereby the people are enabled to contribute to the support of Government. Congress has done that which not only robs the people, and particularly the laboring men among the people, of their prosperity, their little wealth and means of happiness; but forgetting by whom the Government itself is supported, it has deprived the people themselves of much of the means of paying the necessary taxes for the maintenance of the General Government. Like a spendthrift it has exhausted the entire patrimonial estates bequeathed to it; and after this, partly to obtain the means of living and partly to keep up appearances, it has resorted to the immoral practice of creating a credit of its own from which to borrow money of itself! It provides for a paper issue of ten millions of dollars, and authorizes the re-issue of this amount without limit as to the millions reissued, and with the only limitation, that no more than ten millions of dollars shall be in circulation at any one time. A hundred millions of paper money may be issued in this form without one dollar of specie to represent it. It is but borrowing from one pocket to pay into the other, and the Government itself his made provision, both to borrow from itself and to lend to itself. Individuals could not do this, but the Government itself being one of those "mammoth monopolies," so often railed at with impunity, is enabled to do three things peculiar to itself, though all, as many contend, in violation of every principle of constitutional right and national justice. It can create an irredeemable paper currency; it can compel individuals to receive this currency in payment of Government dues, and it can punish by fine and imprisonment all who exercise the same unconstitutional prerogatives, which the Government claims for itself. With the Treasury note bill, with the power to reissue Treasury notes, and the Sub-treasury bill in force, the Government itself is likely to become nothing short of a great manufactory of paper money. Of all kinds of cheating which the wit of man and the wickedness of man has ever invented, that of cheating one's self is the least excusable; and yet the Government will be guilty of this folly, in the execution of almost every important law which has been passed by Congress. Pay day must come at some time, and a wise administration would pay as it went along. Suppose the stringent rule of General Jackson, that "*all men who do business on borrowed capital ought to break,*" or that heartless cry of "*perish credit, and perish commerce*" should be applied to the administration of Mr. Polk, the ghost of General Jackson, and a legion of hollow promises would rise up in judgment against the principles and practices of the dominant party. But a pay day must come, however long postponed, and this brings us to a practical idea of what

Congress has done upon the subject of Revenue. We have for the first time an entirely new system of imposing duties upon imports,—a system not only new to us, but to all the world besides. Specific duties, which are so necessary to prevent frauds, and which take away all inducements for fraud, are to give way to a system which experience has demonstrated to be unsound in principle, and unsafe in practice. We are to have valuations upon the goods imported into the United States, but they are not to be home valuations. The foreign invoice, or the foreign price current, either of which may be prepared to order, are to take the place of forms tried and proved to be honest. We think, upon the evidence that has been given in the debates in Congress, as to the danger and existence of frauds from an *ad valorem* system of collecting duties, that no mind open to conviction will doubt the ordeal through which custom-house officers and custom-house oaths are to pass. Upon the decisions and sentences of the U. S. Courts in all the large cities of the Union, upon the authority of custom-house officers themselves, and upon the evidence of honest importers, we are enabled to affirm, that these frauds will exist.

Mr. EVANS, of Maine, in his tariff speech in the Senate, cited forty-seven seizures of goods, forty-seven trials by jury, forty-seven verdicts of guilty of fraudulent importations, and forty-seven convictions, and all in the courts of but three or four of the large cities of the Union. Mr. WEBSTER not only cited the strongest mercantile business authority, but the strongest official political authority, from Mr. Crawford, and from Mr. Buchanan, who said that our own severe experience upon this subject had taught us that which we ought not soon to forget. Thanks to his own confidence in Mr. Polk, and the confidence of Pennsylvania in the false lights and false promises of the Executive, we have this odious system in prospect before us. Even twenty-nine years ago, when Mr. Crawford was at the head of the Treasury Department, in answer to a resolution of the House of Representatives, calling for information as to the best means for a more faithful execution of the revenue laws, Mr. C. announced that it was prudent to diminish, as far as practicable, the list of articles paying *ad valorem* duties. A list of seventy-one articles is then given, upon which specific duties ought at once to be imposed. In 1818, after a fuller investigation of the merits of the whole question, specific duties were still more urgently recommended to the attention of Congress. From that time to the present, the aim has been to impose these duties. The chairman of the Committee of Finance in the Senate went so far at one time as to deny his belief in the existence of any frauds from under-valuations, and it was in answer to this extraordinary conviction of mind, founded upon the most erroneous information, that the examples were cited. Brief as our space is, we cannot omit the following examples cited by Mr. Webster, and they are given by him only as "a few of hundreds of cases:"

> A merchant orders goods to be shipped from France and entered at New Orleans, for the western trade, with the understanding that he is to have them at the foreign cost, with the duties and charges added.
>
> | | |
> |---|---|
> | A shipment was made with and forwarded to the purchaser, amounting to | 6,829.93 francs. |
> | At the same time the invoice forwarded with the goods to New Orleans was | 5,258.00 francs. |
> | Difference | 1,571.93 francs. |
>
> Or, $316.94 out of $1,300.94.
>
> The goods were valued therefore, in the entry, at $316 94 less than they were to the purchaser; and the purchaser was actually charged for the duty on this $316 94 as paid to the Government, amounting to $95 10. Both the Government and purchaser were, therefore, cheated out of that sum.

Here is another:

> Boston, *July 17th*, 1846.
>
> Dear Sir: I am informed that a respectable house in this city received an invoice of European goods from a foreign house, the amount of which was about $2,000, and that, after entering the goods at the custom house by the invoices, they received another invoice valuing the same goods at about $8,000, with a letter stating that the first invoice was to levy duties by, and the second to sell by.

A third case cited was where a respectable hardware firm in Boston (Messrs. Gray & Co.,) had been in the habit of making importations for years, and found themselves constantly undersold by the dealers in New York. The reason revealed itself, for the first time during the last Spring; and here we quote Mr. Webster's statement of the case:

> They had ordered a small amount of hardware to be sent to them, and in due time the goods came, and two invoices came with them. In one invoice, the cost was stated at 958 thalers; in the *other*, at 1,402. And the letter accompanying these invoices says: "You find herewith duplicate invoices of the greatest part of your order, &c. The original I send by Havre packet. *You also find herewith an invoice made up in the manner like* [that which] the most *importers of your country require; perhaps to save some duty.*"

"Now, sir, said Mr. Webster, these original invoices, the false and the true, and the original letter, which I have read, are now in my hand; and any gentleman, who may feel disposed, may look at them. Of course, Messrs. Gray & Co. carried *both* invoices to the custom-house, because they were honorable merchants; and the duties were assessed on the higher invoice. Any by this time these gentlemen were no longer at a loss to account for the low price at which this description of merchandise had been selling in the city of New York."

The tariff of 1842 wisely discriminates upon all imported goods, and imposes specific duties wherever they can be laid. The tariff of 1846 imposes an invariable system of *ad valorem* duties, and subjects the revenue to a constant source of fraud, and the importer fraudulently disposed to a series of constant temptations. The system can hardly fail to operate most unjustly upon the honest importer, and most unfavorably for the Government.

Much has been said of imitating the free trade policy of England, but never was there a greater delusion than the idea either that England has abandoned her system of protective duties, or the idea that it would be sound policy for us to follow in her footsteps if she had done so. First in regard to these specific duties: In the British tariff of Sir Robert Peel, of 714 enumerated articles, *six hundred and eight pay specific duties,* and only 106 *ad valorem* duties. In the anti-American and more British tariff of Mr. Walker and of Congress, all duties are *ad valorem;* and these valuations are made in Europe, and not at home by our own people. In the tariff enacted into a law by the British Parliament, there is a discrimination for protection in favor of all the raw material entering into the manufacture of British goods, while in the more British tariff of a so-called American Congress, there are discriminations against the labor and manufactures of the country by the imposition of some of the highest rates of duty upon the raw material. Thus, for example, the present duty on linseed oil is 25 cents a gallon, and under the law of 1846 it will be but seven cents a gallon. England imports three and a half millions of linseed free of duty, and imposes almost, if not altogether, a prohibitive duty on linseed oil. In like manner the new tariff pays a bounty to the foreign manufacturer of hemp and cordage. Thus, too, a duty is imposed on raw copper, while copper sheathing is admitted free of duty. England sends her manufactured article to the United States free of duty, and the United States imposes a tax upon the raw article, which might otherwise become a subject of extensive manufacture. The copper imported from England is made principally from copper obtained in Chili. From this country we receive directly 6,500,000 pounds; but under the new tariff the article will go to England, there to be manufactured and sent to the United States! The articles of white lead, of tin, of Peruvian bark, of all kinds of dye stuffs, of sulphuric acid or oil of vitriol, of brimstone, of undressed furs, of ivory, of hats of wool, are all discriminated against in like manner by the new law of this Congress. But there are more important interests than these to suffer from this law, and they are interests seriously affecting both the revenue and the industrial pursuits of the people. Take for example the article of molasses. What revenue is to be derived from it, when the price of the article at Havanna is but two cents a gallon? Often it has no value abroad, and is given away; and what, under such a state of fact, will be the amount of revenue derived from the article? All articles of a corresponding value vary materially, sometimes forty per cent., at the different places of export; and the difference in revenue will vary, not according to the intrinsic worth of the article imported, but according to its foreign cost at the time it may have been exported to our shores.

The discriminations against protective duties form one of the most peculiar features of the bill. Upon manufactures of wool, no higher rate of duty is imposed than upon the raw material. Manufactures of wool are actually discriminated against, upon an average of five per cent. Silk manufactures are also made war upon, and to an extent that will hardly enable the manufacturers to continue their business. The manufacturers of *mousselaine de laine,* a new and important branch of business, are also assailed by the new law; and in both of these articles, in all that relates to wool, the manufacturers of the country have no more interest than the agriculturists. It is known that orders for half a million of dollars worth of western wool have been countermanded from New England alone, after the new tariff law passed the House of Representatives, and before it passed the Senate. In what aspect then, as has been alleged, can the farmers of this country be benefited either by the British law of an American Congress, or by the British law of Sir Robert Peel. The abolition of the British corn laws is of itself an act designed for the benefit of the British manufacturers. That act may increase the exportation of American grain, but judging from the past or any well grounded probability, it is not likely to enhance the value of American grain; nor do we believe it to be possible for the farmers of the United States successfully to compete with the farmers upon the Black sea, the Baltic, and the Mediterranean. England, by *her* system, has cheapened the food consumed by her manufacturing people, and while she has reduced the duty on cotton manufactures, she has made raw cotton and almost every other article of raw material, free of all duty. Of five hundred articles upon which the duty has been reduced or removed by the tariff of Sir Robert Peel, nearly the whole of them enter into the manufactures of the country; but in the United States the duty upon the raw material is sometimes greater, than the duty on the manufactured article. Lord John

Russell, some months before he became prime minister, in a speech at Glasgow, thought it would be a very fine thing, *if it could be done,* for the American people to feed England, and for England to clothe the American people! A charming proposition truly, and the cost of it to us would be, that we should send ten or twelve millions worth of grain to Great Britain, and receive, allowing only ten dollars a year to be the value of the clothes worn for each person, *two hundred millions worth of British manufactured goods!* Lord Ashburton took a much more honest and common sense view of the subject, when he said at Winchester, on the 19th of January last, in reference to the repeal of the Corn laws, that

> Protection had existed in England from the days of the Plantagenets, whilst the whole line of country opposite to us on the continent—France, Belgium, Holland, and Prussia, indeed, almost every country in the world—monarchical Europe as well as republican America—had its protective laws and regulations. It was clear, that, in the event of a recurrence of difficulties, her (America's) first step would be again to shut her ports against us—in which case the supply from America would undoubtedly fail us. But the supply must not be expected *from America;* and we could not have a better proof of this than the fact, *that, at this moment, American corn could come here from Canada at a duty of four shillings; and yet, if the returns were examined, it would be found that nine-tenths of the foreign corn in England was from the Baltic, though the duty on the corn from its shores was fifteen shillings a quarter.* This was entirely owing to the low price of labor in the north of Europe.

Notwithstanding the important modification of the corn laws, England will undoubtedly do all she can to raise her own grain. The nation that depends upon a foreign country for the production of its bread-stuffs, is but a step removed from barbarism. Rome suffered more severely from the decay of agriculture than from almost all other causes combined. Gibbon says, that it was "a just subject of complaint that the life of the Roman people depended upon the accidents of the winds and the waves." For want of agricultural protection, says Michelet, the French historian, "the unhappy cultivators perished or fled, and the land became deserted." England has studied all this too well to be deceived into any system of permanent abandonment of the landed interests; but in the United States, so capable of producing almost grain enough for the consumption of the world, we are about to injure the agricultural interests of the country by driving men out of mechanical and manufacturing employ into the production of the soil. "It is not," as Dr. Johnson said of the Highlands, that "eggs are many, but pence are few!" If there be no money, or but little money, who will care for cheap food?

We cannot close this part of our subject without an allusion to the effect the new tariff in connection with the Subtreasury system—the one a fitting hand-maid of the other—is to have upon the labor of the country. It is the proud boast of England that "the sun never sets upon the British Dominions;" but it is the prouder boast of America that her institutions give perfect political equality to the humblest of her citizens; but what is political equality worth without the means of personal independence. "You take away my life, when you take away the means whereby I live." The Administration and Congress could not by any possible ingenuity have puzzled out a more disastrous system of measures for the labor of the country than the prominent acts of the late session of Congress. We have had already a painful evidence, not only that the capital of the country must seek new channels of investment, but that the wages of labor are to be greatly reduced. In the coal mines, among the workers of iron at the furnaces, in every large manufactory, no matter what the fabric wrought, there is of necessity to be a great reduction of the wages of labor. The laboring man will be compelled to work harder, and will earn less. The European hard-money system of wages is to be brought home to the door of every poor man's dwelling, and to the pockets of every artizan. French boots and shoes; French hats and bonnets; French made watches, and French printed books; French paper, and French cutlery; French music, and French engravings, are to take the place of American made goods. We say French, not because wages are alone small in France, for they are much higher there than in some other parts of Europe, but because we have the facts before us, to show what the wages are in Paris. Look on this picture, mechanics of America, and answer us if you are ready to work for prices paid to the mechanics of Paris, or for the much lower prices paid for labor, in Belgium, Holland, and the north of Europe.

Wages in Paris per Day.

Hatters	3	francs,	or 56	cents.
Cap Makers	2½	"	46	"
Shoe Makers	3	"	56	"
Rope Makers	3	"	56	"
Cutlers	3	"	56	"
Pianoforte Makers	4	"	75	"
Engravers	5	"	94	"
Watchmakers	4	"	75	"
Printers	4	"	75	"
Bookbinders	3	"	56	"

Paper Makers	4	"	75	"
Plumbers	3	"	56	"
Saddlers	3½	"	65	"
Tailors	4	"	75	"
Upholsterers	3	"	56	"
Coopers	3	"	56	"
Blacksmiths	3	"	56	"
Tanners	4	"	75	"
Turners in Wood	3	"	56	"
Turners in Metal	4	"	75	"
Cabinet Makers	4	"	75	"

We add now a miscellaneous list of prices for mechanical labor, in many parts of Europe, though we have not the means at hand of giving each branch of business;

European Labor.

London	$1 per day		Glasgow	66c. per day.
Falmouth, Eng	66c.	"	Dublin	94 "
Newcastle,	84	"	Marseilles	60 "
Plymouth	75	"	Cotts	40 "
Cadiz	45	"	Catalonia	30 "
Naples	37½	"	Palermo	42 "
Genoa	30	"	Vienna	62½ "
Amsterdam	50	"	Bremen,	$3 a $4 per month!!!
Antwerp	45	"	Leipsic	45c. per day.
Frankfort,	$1 p. week and board.		Bergen	42 "
Copenhagen	50c. per day.		Elsincur	36 "

Reduction here in the price of mechanical labor will fall back with twofold severity upon agricultural labor, and while no man will be spared, the agriculturists are likely to be the most severely afflicted. If the home market is destroyed, it is of no more advantage to them that the foreign market is prosperous, than it is to the mechanic, who finds his bread taken from his mouth by the cruel and oppressive acts of his own Government. A Democratic Senator (Mr. NILES, of Connecticut,) might well compare an act like this to the revocation of the edict of Nantes, a measure about as hostile to the laboring men of France, who were then among the most skilful in the world. Our Government by its new tariff is about to commit a virtual act of expulsion, not upon fifty thousand Protestants, but upon nearly nine hundred thousand persons employed in our manufactories, and upon thrice as many persons, wives, children, and servants, dependant in turn upon the labor of others for their own labor and support. It is not one man who dies when he becomes the victim of oppression; there are hearts that ache, and tears that fall, and sorrows that burn like a consuming fire, for losses that may never be known beyond the family or social circle.

Congress in its wisdom has reduced the duties on foreign imports, upon the ground that they were onerous to the people; but who among the consumers have seriously complained of the present rates of duty as burdensome? Who ever heard of the oppressive burdens under the tariff of 1842, until a class of politicians went about, like so many roaring lions, telling the people of the grievous load they carried upon their backs. But supposing it to be all that its enemies have represented it to be. Is the tariff of 1846 to be any less oppressive? Whence is to come the revenue necessary to support the General Government, but by imposing additional taxes upon the people. We imported last year $145,000,000, and received under existing rates the duty $26,346,732. To produce the same amount of revenue under the tariff of 1846, it will be necessary to add millions and millions to the importations, and to the foreign indebtedness of the country. The Secretary of the Treasury relies upon these increased importations to meet the deficiencies arising from the reduced rates of duty, but he is not kind enough, or wise enough, to point out the means of paying for what we thus import. According to some estimates we have seen, it will be necessary to increase the importations fifty millions of dollars, in order to produce as much revenue from the tariff of 1846 as has been received in a single year from the tariff of 1842. We have seen the baneful effect of these large importations already, and ought not to require any additional experience to teach us the wisdom of that common sense principle, which prohibits a man from buying more than he can pay for. If we had the space we should feel bound, before passing this subject, to recall to the mind of the reader the gross imposition practised upon the people of the Tariff States, both in regard to the opinions of Mr. Polk, and Mr. Dallas. The Kane letter is as familiar as a thrice told tale, but the speech or address of Mr. Dallas in the Senate chamber on the 28th of July, 1846, we shall answer by his declarations made in 1844.

A speech containing the following extract was delivered by George M. Dallas, at the door of his house in Philadelphia, to a Democratic procession, on the evening after the Presidential election:—

> Gentlemen—The Tariff of '42 is a Democratic measure: it was passed by the Democrats, and it will be safe in the hands of James K. Polk.

And the following verse was quite a popular one, in Pennsylvania, during the same campaign.

AIR.—"*Lucy Neal,*"
Oh poor Cooney Whigs,
What makes you look so blue!
We will have Polk and Dallas,
And the TARIFF of '42.

SUB-TREASURY LAW

This measure, once tried by the people and condemned by the people, the offspring, of a Democratic Congress, originating with politicians, and not with statesmen, or men of business, presented nine years ago as "a new expedient" and "an untried experiment," is again the law of the land. The Administration have carried it out, not as a great measure of public good, but as a strong party measure. Some of the most intelligent and distinguished men of the party would have preferred a postponement of the law to another session or another Congress, if not an entire abandonment of the law; but no such counsels prevailed. The measure was persevered in, until it finally received the sanction of the two Houses of Congress, and the approval of the President. The moral effect of a measure like this, so unlike all the established usages of the Government, so opposite to the entire practices of the State Governments, and so hostile to the spirit of our free institutions, cannot fail to be most injurious to the welfare of the country. It is a scheme borrowed from the dark ages and the despotisms of Europe, and its whole letter and spirit are in violation of the beautiful prayer taught by our Lord,—"LEAD US NOT INTO TEMPTATION, BUT DELIVER US FROM EVIL." The law creates two classes of institutions—the one for the States and the other for the General Government. It creates two currencies—the one for the Government and the other for the people; giving the better to the office-holders and the servants of the people, and depreciating the poorer, which, of necessity, becomes the currency in all the business transactions between man and man. It presupposes that there is specie enough in the country for the entire business of the country, when, at most, there is not more than eighty or one hundred millions for a business which requires five times this amount. It creates an additional arm of Executive power by the multiplication of Executive offices, and by leaving the purse strings of the nation under the more direct and immediate control of the Executive. It hoards up the precious metals, instead of scattering them abroad among the people, and their own and most necessary institutions. It is like sowing dragon's teeth to spring forth armed men who shall, by the strength of the money power of the country, make in time a successful war upon the rights, interests, and liberties of the people. It embodies the two great powers of banking—the power of issue and the power of deposite—with a mammoth Executive monopoly at the seat of Government, and branches from Boston to New Orleans, wherever there is a mint, a branch mint, or a Sub-treasury established. It widens more and more the breach between the people and the Government, and more and more removes public officers from that accountability and responsibility so necessary for a safe and honest administration of public business. This unnatural and inhuman system reminds us more of some invention hatched from the brains of counsellors, like the apostates who fell from Heaven, and who proclaimed, that—

> To do aught good never will be our task,
> But ever to do ill our sole delight—

than of a measure conceived in a spirit of personal good will, or required for the public good.

In that assembly where were found makers and worshippers of the golden calf, (the great originals of all Sub-treasurers,) the poet has painted the vaults, and mines, and minds of men who have attached this foul scheme to the laws of the land. Here is the picture:

> There stood a hill not far, whose grizzly top
> Belch'd fire and rolling smoke; the rest entire
> Shone with a glossy scurf—undoubted sign
> That in his womb was hid metallic ore,
> The work of sulphur. Thither, wing'd with speed,
> A numerous brigade hasten'd. Mammon led them on;
> Mammon, the least erected spirit that fell
> From heaven; for e'en in heaven his looks and thoughts
> Were always downward bent, admiring more
> The riches of heaven's pavement, trodden gold,
> Than aught divine or holy else enjoy'd
> In vision beatific. **** Soon had his crew
> Open'd into the hill a spacious wound
> And digg'd out ribs of gold. Let none admire
> That riches grow in hell: that soil may best
> Deserve the precious bane.

But we must pause in our review, and with much unsaid that we could wish to say, and which a searching review of the proceedings of Congress would require at our hands. There are one thousand claimants at least who have petitioned this Congress, not for charity, but for justice—justice mingled with mercy. Their petitions were received and disposed of, either with cold contempt or with rude neglect. Never, we believe, in the history of the Government, were this unfortunate and meritorious class of men treated so badly as at the late session of Congress, and ether the common jail or an indignant public opinion would await any citizen of the Union who should treat his creditors in like manner.

With few exceptions—exceptions that come

> Like angel's visits, few and far between,

we look in vain for any act of public or private good passed by the late Congress. Cursing and not blessing has fallen to the lot of the country; and nothing now remains but for the people to rebuke and punish those who have brought this evil upon the land. We appeal from Congress to the people.

8

What's the Difference? Cass and Taylor on the Slavery Question (Boston, 1848)

THE PRESIDENTIAL ELECTION of 1848 featured a significant third-party movement, made up of anti–slavery extension Whigs and Northern Democrats, who challenged the unwillingness, or failure, of the two established parties to prevent the spread of slavery into new territories. Like the members of the two major parties, the Free Soilers were quite negative in their 1848 campaign rhetoric, and they based their case on the lessons—and examples—of history. The old issues that divided Whigs and Democrats were, they claimed, no longer relevant; they had become obsolete or had been settled or overtaken by events. Only one question was now paramount: preventing the further extension of slavery. Here, unfortunately for the nation, the two major-party candidates did not differ from each other. Going over the long public record of the Whig and Democratic candidates, Zachary Taylor and Lewis Cass, the Free Soilers asked, "what reliable difference, on this great question, is there between the two? None whatever!" Both opposed restricting slavery to where it now existed. "If one [Cass] is a Northern man with Southern principles, the other [Taylor] is a Southern man with Southern principles." This was unacceptable. There was only one thing, therefore, for antislavery Whigs and Democrats to do: come together and vote for the new party. Interestingly, the pamphlet never mentions the Free Soil candidate, Martin Van Buren, by name, preferring to focus attention on the failures of Cass and Taylor.

The establishment of a National Bank is an "obsolete idea," by the confession of its friends. The questions of the Tariff and the Distribution of the Proceeds of the Public Lands, are at rest for many years, for until the vast debt incurred in the Mexican war (amounting, by the President's confession, to eighty millions of dollars) is paid, we must have a tariff, and shall not be able to divert from the National Treasury any of the proceeds of the public lands. Prominent Democrats—as the late Silas Wright—agree with prominent Whigs, that our western rivers and harbors are to be improved at the national expense. But these are *all* the questions which have divided the two great parties—the Whigs and Democrats—for several years.* Is there, then, really no great question before the country upon which opinions are divided? There is one—one in comparison with which all the others are utterly insignificant—but it is wholly discarded by the two great parties as a test of party allegiance. It is the question whether the territory now free—covering in extent five hundred and twenty-six thousand square miles, shall remain free, or shall be converted into slave territory. It is the question whether a great moral curse shall be immensely extended—whether an institution which degrades free labor, by making the laborer a vendible commodity, shall be extended to the Pacific, over territory made free by semi-barbarous Mexico—whether the slave power which has ruled this country for so many years, and which has been so solemnly denounced by our Legislature,† shall be still further strengthened. These are great questions, solemn questions, which we should put to ourselves and seriously and resolutely answer.

On this great question there is no difference between the two great parties. Retaining their party names, which in years past have indicated a clear line of difference, the whigs and democrats now stand before the country without claiming as peculiar to themselves a single great measure of the slightest practical consequence! They propose to keep up the fight when nothing remains of their principles worth fighting for or against. They propose to go into the contest upon issues which have either become obsolete, or which are practically at rest for a dozen years to come! at the same time both parties have set aside this great—this all-absorbing question of the extension of slavery.

*The veto power is sometimes spoken of as *the* great question in the ensuing election. We all admit that an *unconstitutional* act of Congress should be vetoed. But it is urged by the Whigs that a President ought not to use the Veto power in any *other* case, except only where there is "manifest haste and want of consideration by Congress." (Gen. Taylor's letter to Capt. Allison). In other words, even if a law is considered by the President to be clearly injurious to the public interest, still, if it is not clearly unconstitutional—or if there has been no "*manifest* haste, and want of consideration by Congress" in passing it, the President ought not to veto it! That is, the Whigs say that the President ought to cease to be the *adviser* of Congress. But the constitution *requires* the President from time to time, to recommend to the consideration of Congress "Such measures as he shall judge necessary and *expedient,*" that is, it requires him to *advise* Congress.

†THE LEGISLATURE OF MASSACHUSETTS, IN 1847, declared its "UNALTERABLE CONVICTION that a regard for the *fair fame of our country,* for the *principles of morals,* and for that *righteousness which exalteth a nation,* SANCTIONS AND REQUIRES ALL CONSTITUTIONAL EFFORTS FOR THE DESTRUCTION OF THE UNJUST INFLUENCE of the slave power, and for the abolition of slavery within the limits of the United States."

The democratic party have nominated

Lewis Cass

Gen. Cass was born and educated at the north. In 1846, when the Two Million Bill, as it is called, came before the Senate, with the Wilmot Proviso in it, and Senator Davis, of this State, talked against time, thereby preventing a vote in the Senate on its passage, Gen. Cass expressed his regret that the course pursued by Mr. Davis had prevented him from recording his vote in *favor* of the Proviso. At the next session of Congress, (March 1, 1847), the Three Million Bill came before the Senate, but without the Proviso in it. Mr. Upham, the Senator from Vermont, moved to amend the bill by inserting the Proviso. Gen. Cass rose, and in a speech of some length, *opposed the amendment,* on the ground that it was not the proper bill to connect the Proviso with, it being the object of the bill to enable the President to procure a peace with Mexico. In 1846, and perhaps in the early part of 1847, Gen. Cass therefore openly avowed himself in favor of the Wilmot Proviso, or the restriction by Congress of the further extension of slavery. But the subject of the Presidency coming up, Gen. Cass wrote to Mr. Nicholson, of Tennessee, a letter from which the following extracts are taken.

Washington, Dec. 24, 1847.

DEAR SIR:—I have received your letter, and shall answer it as frankly as it is written.

You ask me whether I am in favor of the acquisition of Mexican territory, and what are my sentiments in regard to the Wilmot Proviso. * *

The Wilmot Proviso has been before the country some time. It has been repeatedly discussed in Congress, and by the public Press. *I am strongly impressed with the opinion that a CHANGE has been going on in the public mind upon this subject—in MY OWN as well as others;* and that doubts are revolving themselves into conviction, that *THE PRINCIPLE IT INVOLVES SHOULD BE KEPT OUT OF THE NATIONAL LEGISLATURE,* and left to the people of the confederacy in their respective local governments.

Briefly, then, *I am opposed to the exercise of any jurisdiction by Congress over this matter;* and I am in favor of leaving to the people of any territory which may be hereafter acquired; the right to regulate it for themselves under the general principles of the Constitution. Because—

1. *I do not see in the Constitution any grant of the requisite power to Congress;* and I am not disposed to extend a doubtful precedent beyond its necessity—the establishment of territorial governments when needed—leaving to the in-

habitants all the rights compatible with the relations they bear to the Confederation.

2. Because I believe this measure, if adopted, would weaken, if not impair the Union of the States; and would sow the seeds of future discord, which would grow up and ripen into an abundant harvest of calamity.

* * * * * * *

The Wilmot proviso seeks to take from its legitimate tribunal a question of domestic policy, having no relation to the Union as such, and to transfer it to another, created by the people for a special purpose, and foreign to the subject matter involved in this issue. By going back to our true principles, we go back to the road of peace and safety. Leave to the people who will be affected by this question, to adjust it upon their own responsibility, and in their own manner, and we shall render another tribute to the principles of our government, and furnish another guaranty for its permanence and prosperity.

I am, dear sir, respectfully,
Your obedient servant,
LEWIS CASS.

A. O. P. NICHOLSON, Esq., Nashville, Tenn.

It is clear from these extracts that Gen. Cass now considers the Wilmot Proviso as *unconstitutional*—and, as every President is bound by his oath to "preserve, protect and defend the Constitution," he would accordingly *veto* the Proviso if passed by Congress. The Washington Union (of Aug. 1, 1848)—his own ardent supporter, upon this point says,

> We are happy to understand by private letters that Gen. Cass firmly stands to the ground which he has taken. Being applied to formally by a man or two of the Wilmot stamp, he declared unhesitatingly that he adhered to his Nicholson letter, and to the Baltimore Platform, and that if elected President HE WOULD VETO THE WILMOT PROVISO."

Notwithstanding Congress has, on nine different occasions, passed laws forbidding the extension of slavery into various portions of the national territory—notwithstanding these laws have been approved by Washington, John Adams, Jefferson, Madison, Monroe and Jackson, (not to mention President Polk), under the sanction of their presidential oaths, it is now said that it is contrary to the Constitution for Congress to prevent the extension of slavery to the Pacific! If a power which has been exercised so often, and whose exercise has received such sanction, is unconstitutional, what power *can* be said to be constitutional? The Democratic party stand before the country with a candidate thus pledged *to veto the only method there is of securing the blessings of liberty!* For no one really believes that the slaveholders who are about moving to California and New Mexico with their slaves, will themselves, in their local legislature, abolish slavery. Whether or not the population of New Mexico and California are to remain freemen, is a question which can only be definitely settled by Congress; and, according to the Democratic platform of principles, Congress is not to be allowed to prevent the extension of slavery!

The Whig party have nominated

Zachary Taylor

Gen. Taylor was born and educated at the South, and is now a Louisiana slaveholder. *He is a slaveholder in that section of the country where slavery exists in its worst forms.*

> The civil code of Louisiana provides,
>
> Art. 2500. The latent defects of *slaves* and *animals* are divided into two classes: vices of *body,* and vices of *character.*
>
> Art. 2502. The *absolute vices of slaves are leprosy, madness and epilepsy.*
>
> Art. 2503. The *absolute vices of horses and mules are short wind, glanders and founder.*

The following advertisement is taken from the New Orleans Bulletin:—

> NEGROES FOR SALE.—A negro woman 24 years of age, and has two children, one eight and the other three years. Said negroes will be sold *separately* or together, as desired. The woman is a good seamstress. She will be sold low for cash, or *exchanged for groceries.* For terms apply to
>
> Mayhew, Bliss & Co., 1 Front Levee.

The New Orleans Picayune, of October 18, 1846, contains the following:—

> *Credit Sale of Valuable Negro Mechanics, &c.*
>
> BY BEARD, CALHOUN & Co., Auctioneers,—Will be sold at auction on Tuesday, the 20th October, at 12 o'clock, at Bank's Arcade—the following valuable Slaves:
>
> EZEKIEL, 25 years, *a superior Carpenter,* fully guarantied.
>
> JACOB, 25 years, a *superior Carpenter and Wheelwright,* fully guarantied.
>
> CHARLES, 28 years, Engineer and rough Carpenter.
>
> DICK, 35 years, *a superior Carpenter and Wheelwright,* fully guarantied.

CHARLES, 22 years, Field Hand, fully guarantied, excepting slightly ruptured.

SANCHO, 26 years, *good house Carpenter,* fully guarantied.

MARIA, mulatress, 28 years, first rate Washer and Ironer, fully guarantied.

MARIA, negress, 13, Child's Nurse, fully guarantied.

Terms—Twelve months' credit for notes drawn and endorsed to the satisfaction of the vendor, with mortgage on the property, bearing interest 8 per cent per annum, from date of sale until paid. Slaves not to be delivered until the notes are approved of.

The servants can be seen on the morning of sale.

Act of sale before D. I. Ricardo, notary public, at the expense of the purchaser. Oct. 1846.

The following advertisement is taken from the Madison Journal, published (Nov. 26, 1847), at Richmond, La., only three counties removed from where Gen. Taylor lives.

Notice.

"The subscriber, living on Carroway Lake, on Hoe's Bayou, in Carroll Parish, sixteen miles on the road leading from Bayou Mason to Lake Providence, is ready with a pack of dogs to hunt runaway negroes at any time. These dogs are well trained, and are known throughout the Parish. Letters addressed to me at Providence will secure immediate attention.

My terms are five dollars per day for hunting the trails, whether the negro is caught or not. Where a twelve hours' trail is shown, and the negro not taken, no charge is made. For taking a negro, 25 dollars, and no charge made for hunting. JAMES W. HALL.

The St. Francisville, (La.) Chronicle of Feb. 1, 1839, gives the following account of a "negro hunt," in the parish next but one to that in which Gen. Taylor lives.

Two or three days since a gentleman of this parish, in hunting runaway negroes, came upon a camp of them in the swamp on Cat Island. He succeeded in arresting two of them, but the third made fight; and, upon being shot in the shoulder, fled to a sluice, where the dogs succeeded in drowning him before assistance could arrive.

He comes from a section of the country where the most ultra slavery notions prevail. Three quarters of the representatives and one of the senators of the state are Democrats. These senators voted invariably with John C. Calhoun, in the recent exciting debates on the Compromise and Oregon bills; and Jefferson Davis, the senator from Mississippi, and the son-in-law of Gen. Taylor, proposed an amendment to the first Oregon bill, depriving the people of Oregon, *contrary to their expressed wishes,* of the power to prohibit the introduction of slavery whist Oregon should continue a territory!

At the South, he was first suggested as the candidate for the Presidency, by ultra slavery men. Thus at the Convention of delegates of the Whig party of Georgia, held May 8, 1848, for the purpose of appointing delegates to the Philadelphia Convention, the following resolution was passed:—

> *Resolved,* That the nomination of Gen. Zachary Taylor for the Chief Magistracy of this Union meets the hearty concurrence of a majority of this Convention; but, in the spirit of a just and liberal concession, we stand prepared to support HENRY CLAY, or any other Whig who may be the nominee of the Whig party, *provided the views of the nominee accord with our own on the subject of the Wilmot Proviso and Southern rights.*

What their own views on the Wilmot Proviso were, they declared by a resolution approving of John C. Calhoun's course on the slavery question!

He was eminently the candidate of the slave states in the Philadelphia Convention. Those states had 110 votes. Of these he received 82 on the first ballot; whilst of the 166 votes held by the free states he received only 27!

He is now supported by ultra slavery men. In his support stand forth Ex-Governor Hammond and Isaac E. Holmes, the South Carolina *Democrats,* and Judge Berrien, the leader of the southern wing of the *Whig* party, the two last of whom took the same ground as John C. Calhoun, namely—that the people of Oregon ought to be explicitly prevented by Congress from excluding slavery! The following extracts express the opinions of those southern men who are *friendly** to the election of Gen. Taylor.

The following is taken from the Richmond Whig.

*As it is not in accordance with common sense to go to a man's *enemies* to find out what his real opinions are, so it is not in accordance with common sense to *attempt* to prove that Gen. Taylor is in favor of the Wilmot Proviso from the declarations of his enemies at the South. We should all say that the Boston Post was edited by a fool, if it quoted the following, from the Richmond (Va.) Republican (a Taylor paper), to prove that Gen. Cass was *in favor* of the Proviso:—

> Now is the time for action. Now, fellow citizens, while the genius of liberty wings its flight over your destinies. Now, while you see in the South a 'brilliant star,' in the person of Zachary Taylor—which will rule the people with moderation, *regarding the Constitution as his shield and protector*—who is identified with, and will be devoted to, your institutions. *Who, by his express declaration, says he will veto the Wilmot Proviso.* While, on the other hand, you see the Northern star of internal abolitionism, in all its frightful mien, with giant strides, following in the track of Lewis Cass, fresh from the "bed of hell."

Taylor and Fillmore in the South.

In looking over the accounts of the Whig meetings through the State, we discover that those persons who constitute them are composed, in a very great degree, of the *largest slaveholders among us.* They, it seems, are perfectly willing to trust Taylor and Fillmore—they have no fears for the safety of their property—they do not believe that the Whig candidates will, if elected, do any thing to impair their right to their property, or to weaken their grasp upon it. It is those disinterested gentlemen, who have no slaves themselves, that are principally alarmed on the subject.

"Those who really would be injured by any assault upon Southern rights or Southern property, feel themselves assured, if other assurances were wanting, by the fact that *Zachary Taylor is himself a slaveholder,* and that he can do nothing to injure them which will not also injure himself at the same time. If a man goes on board of a ship to cross the Atlantic, does he require bond and security—does he ask pledges of the captain that he will carry him safe to the end of his voyage? Certainly he does not. He knows that the danger of the one is the danger of the other also. He knows that if the ship go to the bottom, the Captain and crew must go along with the passengers. COMMUNITY OF INTEREST AND OF DANGER IS THE STRONGEST PLEDGE HE COULD POSSIBLY GIVE, AND THAT HE GIVES BY THE VERY TERMS OF HIS UNDERTAKING.

So it is with Zachary Taylor. WHY ASK PLEDGES OF HIM UPON THE SUBJECT OF SLAVERY, WHEN THE FACT THAT HIS WHOLE ESTATE CONSISTS OF LAND AND NEGROES, AND THAT WHEN THEY GO HE MUST BE A BEGGAR, IS THE VERY STRONGEST PLEDGE HE COULD POSSIBLY GIVE. Has Lewis Cass given any such pledges as this? Is his interest the same with that of the slaveholder? If every slave in the Union should be liberated to-morrow, does he lose anything by it?

If it can be supposed that he will be a watchful guardian over the interests of the South, IS IT NOT FAIR TO SUPPOSE THAT ZACHARY TAYLOR WILL BE FAR MORE SO?

The Richmond Times (June 13), says, "We have, as our candidate, an honest citizen of Louisiana, *thoroughly identified with the South in feeling and interest.*"

The Nashville (Tenn.) Banner says:—

> A Louisiana planter in favor of the (Wilmot) proviso! The INTOLERABLE ABSURDITY of such a proposition scarcely permits us to treat it with any seriousness.

In July last "the *Democrats* of Charleston" (S. C.), says the National Intelligencer of July 26, "held a large and enthusiastic meeting, in which the prominent and leading Democrats of the city took part." This meeting passed a series of resolutions, one repudiating Gen. Cass because he is willing to let the people of the territories exclude slavery if they see fit! The following are extracts from these resolutions.

> The opinions of Gen. Cass, promulgated in his late letter, that the inhabitants of a territory, before they are invested with the attributes of self-government and sovereignty—tenants of the public lands at the sufferance of the States—mere squatters—have the right to appropriate the territory that may be acquired by the treasure or gallantry of all the States, and to exclude from its limits the property of fourteen of the States—has been repudiated by the Press and the people of the whole South. *It is a doctrine too monstrous to be tolerated—an ostracism too degrading to be endured.*"
>
> *Resolved,* That we regard the issue now made between the States of this Union, styling themselves the free States and the States in which the institution of domestic servitude exists, *as paramount to all questions which can be presented.* That the convention of delegates from fifteen sovereign States for the accomplishment of a purpose which is the first step towards the abolition of slavery in the States, and consequently the ruin of the people in the loss of their property, and their degradation in this lawless violation of their rights, admonishes us of a stern necessity that calls for our immediate, prompt, and decided action. That in seeking one under whose lead we shall look for the best guidance in our difficulties, we turn to him, who, in the simplicity of his habits, illustrates the equality of our privileges, and in his devotion to his country, teaches us the reverence due to the institutions developed by our revolution. That with such a leader we may hope that the dangers which surround us may be happily averted. But if this hope is disappointed, we shall be best prepared to maintain our just rights, and the integrity of our whole country under his direction, who has already announced to the enemies of his country that "GENERAL TAYLOR NEVER SURRENDERS."

In the address we have the following statement of South Carolina doctrine upon this subject:

> To us it matters not HOW this insult and wrong can be effected. If in ANY WAY it can be done, we are by its exercise degraded and sunk. If the territories are the common property of the States, and if the Southern States are equal in their sovereignty and independence with the other States, our true position is, that in the territories which belong to the United States, *neither the Congress* of the United States, *nor the local government of such territories have any power to pass any law which shall interfere with the free enjoyment of such territories by the people of any of these United States, and with such property as they may choose to*

> *take there with them.* We have the opinion of Gen. Cass that there is a mode by which this prohibition can be constitutionally exercised, and when we vote for him, we confirm his opinion, and in so doing, admit our own inferiority.

These South Carolina Democrats do not object to Gen. Cass, because he pledges himself to veto the Wilmot Proviso, but because he adopts the "monstrous" doctrine that the people of the territories should be allowed to exclude slavery if they wish to! They object to Gen. Cass on this ground alone, and adopt General Taylor as the sounder man of the two! The address thus speaks of Gen. Taylor:

> His interests are our interests. *We know* that he must feel the lawless character of any attempt to interfere with our property directly—*we know* that he must feel the senseless clamor that is raised to disturb our possession of that property, as violating the law either of God or man. WE KNOW THAT IN THIS GREAT, PARAMOUNT, AND LEADING QUESTION OF THE RIGHTS OF THE SOUTH, HE IS OF US, HE IS WITH US, AND HE IS FOR US.

Still later, "a large and enthusiastic meeting of the Taylor Democrats" has been held in the same place. These extracts are taken from the account given of the meeting by the Charleston news.

> *The preamble and resolutions throughout breathe the proper spirit. They adopt the views of Mr. Calhoun, and carry them out with decided strength. Recognizing the vital principle, that which is essential to our Union, and without which it cannot exist, that "Southern men must feel a stronger affinity to each other than to the citizens of the non-Slaveholding States, no matter to which party they may belong." These resolutions strongly urge the necessity of union at the South for the sake of the South. ON THIS GROUND DO THEY URGE THE NOMINATION OF GENERAL TAYLOR.*
>
> The North has selected its man, and with no other man will that portion of the Union be satisfied, unless he comes from the North. *We of the South, if indeed we love the South, must go for the man of the South. Let those who denounce us as Whigs, because we support Gen. Taylor, denounce Mr. Calhoun, who has fraternized with Mr. Berrien, and Mr. Butler, who has fraternized with Mr. Mangum.* We have no doubt that the preamble and resolutions, when published, will exhibit the advocates of Gen. Taylor in that light which reveals their true position. They go for the South, and for GEN. TAYLOR, BECAUSE HE IS THE MAN OF THE SOUTH.

The same paper had previously said:—

If we cannot trust him who owns Southern slaves and Western mules, raises cotton, and is devoted to agriculture, lives in the heart of the Slave section—who obtained his nomination by the Southern and Western votes almost exclusively, and will only be elected by them—and who has always shown a Roman firmness—whom can we trust? While we should pledge our support to him *as a Southern man, and upon this issue,* we should give it only in this view.

The National Intelligencer, of June 17, contains the following:—

From the Savannah (Ga.) Republican.

The heart of every Whig throughout the Union and of every true patriot of whatever party, must bound with exultation at the tidings of the nomination of ZACHARY TAYLOR for the Presidency, and the consequent certainty of his elevation to that high office.

* * * * * * *

To the South he must be far more acceptible than any other man in this broad Union, for he is a Southern man and a slaveholder—one of ourselves—and no "Northern man with Southern principles."

The following is taken

From the Columbus (Ga) Enquirer.

LOOK OUT.

A desperate attempt is making, and will be made, to impress on the public mind the belief that Gen. Taylor is not thoroughly with the South on the subject of slavery. Such an attempt will only prove to what resorts our opponents are driven, in order to injure him in the estimation of his admirers. Why, who is General Taylor? and where does he live? Everybody knows that he is a citizen of Louisiana—an extensive and successful farmer—and owns more slaves than the rest of his slanderers can ever hope honestly to obtain. Is there any fear of such a man on this subject? Born in a slave State, and still residing in one—with a large portion of his capital invested in this species of property—identified from interest, inclination, and education, with the institutions around us—will any sensible man hesitate on this subject to prefer him over his opponent? * * *

From the Augusta (Ga.) Republic.

Our Democratic friends will find that they have come upon a *mare's nest* in this matter. They might as well give it up at once, for though they may be "as brisk as a bee in a tar pot" for a while, in making the charge, they will find themselves *stuck fast* by it before they are done. The General owns too many of the "niggers" for that; and he will not go for the Proviso till somebody can make one of the blackest ones white, by washing him.

From the Marion (Ala.) Review of July 6.

GENERAL TAYLOR AND THE WILMOT PROVISO.

Democratic Editors must be possessed with a feeling something akin to desperation, when they think it necessary, in order to sustain the Democratic cause, to accuse Gen. Taylor of unsoundness on the question of slavery. The charge carries such an absurdity on its very face, as not to deserve a serious refutation. General Taylor, a Southern man, the destiny of himself and his children identified with that of the South, his immense wealth consisting in slaves, and land which has to be cultivated by slaves to render it valuable—*he an enemy to the South?—he in favor of prostrating Southern rights and interests!! The very quintessence of absurdity. They might as well say that General Taylor is a free negro.* They would be believed just about as soon, and exhibit fully as much reason and truth in making the charge.

The Aberdeen (Ala.) Whig says:—

An eventful, thrilling and highly dangerous crisis has been forced upon the country by LOCOROCO DEMAGOGUES, *regardless of the sanctity of that Union, which is so dear to every patriotic American Citizen.* THE WILMOT PROVISO, AS IT IS CALLED, HAS OPENED A FEARFUL MINE BENEATH THE FOUNDATIONS OF THE SACRED CONSTITUTION. THAT MINE MAY EXPLODE AT THE HOUR OF MIDNIGHT, AND FOREVER DESTROY THE PROUDEST FABRIC OF HUMAN GENIUS AND VIRTUE. To avert this THREATENED EVIL, to close the MIGHTY CHASM that begins to yawn between the free and slave States, is a duty we owe to ourselves, to our posterity, to the memory of the illustrious dead. How shall this be done?

We must elect a man for a President of the United States who lives in our own sunny South; who is willing to peril all for the Constitution, who LOVES THE SOUTH and HER CHERISHED INSTITUTIONS.

* * * * * * *

Such a man is General Zachary Taylor. HE LIVES IN THE SOUTH, AND MAKES 1200 BALES OF COTTON ON THE BANKS OF THE MISSISSIPPI. HIS INTERESTS, HIS FEELINGS ARE ALL WITH US."

At a Taylor ratification meeting at Tuscaloosa, June 24, the following resolution was adopted:—

> *Resolved,* That Congress has no right whatever to legislate directly or indirectly, mediately or immediately upon the question of Slavery, nor to make any condition with regard to that subject in the acquisition of territory acquired by the nation, either in peace or war; nor have the settlers upon any such territory, *while it is a territory, the authority to interfere with or prohibit the removal to it of any property, whether slaves or otherwise,* carried to it by emigrants from any State of the Union. That while we express the fullest confidence in our Northern brethern, and will not anticipate from them any governmental action violative of the principles herein declared; yet in reference to it we hereby solemnly declare that we are ONE upon it; that we will suffer no interference, submit to no concession, and make no compromise. That upon this topic we FEEL, and will ACT as Southern men; maintain at all hazards, and defend at all points, our right in the matter, and STAND OR FALL together in asserting and preserving it.

The Natchez (Miss.) Courier says:—

> * * * We have not the slightest doubt but that OLD ZACK is as much opposed to the infamous proposition of that leading Locofoco of Pennsylvania, Wilmot, who first introduced the resolution to exclude slavery from any territory that may be retained west of the Rio Grande, as any man in Mississippi.

The same paper says of the charge that he would sign a Wilmot Proviso bill:—

> This MONSTROUS assertion—so entirely at war with the character of the man *and the tenor of his whole life*—could only have been made by *political leaders* when in the LAST STAGES OF DESPERATION—when they saw that *everlasting political* ROUT *and* RUIN *were approaching them* as fast as the course of time would permit.

The New Orleans Bee—a Taylor press, and good authority, too—says:—

> Gen. Taylor is from birth, association, and conviction, identified with the South and her institutions; being one of the most extensive slaveholders in Louisiana—and supported by the slaveholding interest as *opposed to the Wilmot Proviso,* AND IN FAVOR OF SECURING THE PRIVILEGE TO THE OWNERS OF SLAVES TO REMOVE WITH THEM TO NEWLY ACQUIRED TERRITORY.

The same paper speaks of the "*contemptibly ludicrous*" accusation, "that Gen. Taylor is an advocate of the Wilmot Proviso"—whilst

> Mr. Benjamin, one of the whig electors for the state of Louisiana, affirmed, in a speech at Baton Rouge, *Gen. Taylor's own residence,* that the old general was "*all right*" upon the slavery question, adding, "I CAN ASSURE MY FELLOW CITIZENS HERE THAT TAYLOR WILL PROMPTLY VETO ANY THING LIKE THE WILMOT PROVISO. THE INTERESTS OF THE SOUTH ARE SAFE IN HIS HANDS."

Other similar extracts might be almost indefinitely adduced; and it should be constantly borne in mind, that these are the arguments of Gen. Taylor's *friends.* Is anything more needed, to prove that the most ultra-slavery propagandists support him as sound, in their views?

But we are not obliged to rely upon this *indirect* evidence (however satisfactory) of Gen. Taylor's unsoundness, for *we have direct testimony of his opposition to the Wilmot Proviso.* Shortly after Gen. Taylor's return from Mexico, the Legislature of Mississippi appointed a Committee to wait on him, and invite him to Jackson (the seat of government of Mississippi), to partake of the hospitalities of the State. This Committee had a conversation with him. At the instance of the Hon. John M. Botts, Whig member of Congress from Virginia, Mr. Jacob Thompson, member of Congress from Mississippi, wrote a letter to Mr. Boone, a member of the Committee, to ascertain precisely what was said by Gen. Taylor. Mr. Boone replied, and the letter was handed to Mr. Botts, who published the following extract from it in his Address "to the whole Whig party of the United States," p. 8:—

> In regard to the conversation had with Gen. Taylor, I have to say, we did not talk on the tariff, we did on the war. He expressed himself IN FAVOR OF THE WAR, he said he was DECIDEDLY IN FAVOR OF PROSECUTING IT VIGOROUSLY, till they should yield to an honorable peace. HE WAS FOR INDEMNITY CERTAIN, AND THAT TERRITORIAL; was not wedded to any line, particularly, but thought perhaps as a kind of compromise with the Wilmot Proviso men, we had better go up to the 32d°, making the Rio Grande the Western boundary up to that degree, and said the SOUTH SHOULD NEVER AGREE TO THE PROVISIONS OF THE WILMOT PROVISO; *although he did not believe there ever would be slavery there, yet if the country was acquired* THE CITIZENS SHOULD BE LEFT FREE ON THAT SUBJECT. HE SAYS ALL MEXICO WILL EVENTUALLY COME INTO OUR GOVERNMENT BY DEGREES; THAT IT CANNOT BE

AVOIDED. On the subject of politics he said he was no politician; had been three-fourths of his life in the army; devoted his time and mind to that service, and paid but little attention to anything else.*

In order that there might be no mistake about this conversation, the following letter was sent to Mr. Botts:—

Boston, Sept. 5, 1848.

DEAR SIR,—Will you be kind enough to inform me, whether the conversation between Gen. Taylor and the Committee of the Mississippi Legislature, of which an account is enclosed, actually occurred as stated? and whether you have ever published it in the newspapers, or in any address, as genuine?

*It is said that this conversation never took place. The following is taken from the Boston Daily Advertiser, of Oct. 11:

The Worcester True Whig, having taken some pains to examine this matter, now publishes the following letter on the subject, for which it vouches:

WASHINGTON CITY, Aug. 4, 1848.

Dear Sir:—I have seen Hon. Mr. Tompkins, of Mississippi, and have inquired of him as to the reports in the newspapers of answers given by Gen. Taylor to the committee of the Legislature of Mississippi. He says that the chairman of that committee was General Henry, a Whig and particular friend of his, from whom he has received *long and minute letters, detailing the visit of the committee to General Taylor, their reception, the speeches made on the occasion,* CONVERSATION, description of the General's house, &c., in all of which he *does not allude to or mention any conversation upon party politics.* The committee was composed of gentleman of both parties; they were authorized to invite the General to accept of the hospitalities of the State, which he declined on the ground that he could not safely leave his place of residence for one day, on account of his official correspondence with the War Department. Mr. Tompkins believes that the statements alluded to, of answers to the committee by General Taylor, published in the newspapers, *are false, and made for electioneering purposes, and not entitled to the least confidence.*

The evidence of Mr. Boone's deception, therefore, is contained in an *anonymous* letter, written by *somebody,* in Washington, last August, to *somebody* else, giving an account of a conversation the first *somebody* had with the Hon. Mr. Tompkins, of Mississippi over two months ago, and which letter has been *kept entirely secret* until it is TOO LATE to get a contradiction or explanation from Mr. Boone. *What reliance can be placed on such evidence?* In a matter of the slightest consequence, *none whatever!*

But, suppose, these two somebodies to be well known, respectable men; how then does the case stand? "Long and minute letters" have been received from General Henry, "detailing the visit of the committee to Gen. Taylor, their reception, the speeches made on the occasion, conversation, description of the General's house, &c., in all of which *he does not allude to or mention any conversation upon party politics.*" Suppose he don't make any such allusion to Gen. Taylor's remarks on the Wilmot Proviso, is that the *slightest* evidence that no such remarks were made? If half a dozen honest men listen to a conversation, and one states that a certain remark was made, whilst another states something else that was said, *without alluding at all* to the other remark, whether it was or was not made, is the *mere silence* of the second witness to be taken as any evidence whatever that the first witness has deceived? Most certainly not. And yet General Henry stands precisely in the position of this second witness. It is not even pretended that Gen. Henry says that Mr. Boone was mistaken, or has deceived. Indeed there is not the least intimation that Mr. Boone's report was

So many stories are in circulation, that one hardly knows what to believe. Pardon me for troubling you, but if you will answer the above questions, it will serve to remove some difficulties in the path of many persons who do not know whether, or not, Gen. T. ever said the South ought not to consent to the provisions of the Wilmot Proviso.

Respectfully Yours,
WILLIAM I. BOWDITCH.

In answer, Mr. Bowditch received through the Post Office a pamphlet copy of the address to the Whig party, above referred to, franked by John M. Botts; and on the first page was written the following:—

---

suggested to Gen. Henry, or that his opinion of its correctness was asked. All that is or can be said, is that Gen. Henry preserves entire silence concerning the conversation reported by Mr. Boone. *He don't say whether or not he believes it—whether or not he heard it—whether or not it took place!* It is folly to argue that such mere silence is to outweigh or affect in the slightest degree the *positive* evidence of an honest witness.

Mr. Tompkins "believes" Mr Boone's report false. Perhaps he does. But what does he personally know about it? *Nothing at all!* All his information comes from Gen. Henry's *silence.* Where *are* these significantly silent letters of Gen. Henry? They have been known to exist for two months. During all this time, the report of Mr. Boone has been constantly the theme of the Free Soil papers. *Produce them all,* without garbling, if any argument is to be based merely on their silence.

But, says the Advertiser, the 'Whig' is not contented with giving this testimony. It adds:

> And now, once more, we state to these presses which are spreading forged lies, that as to this reported conversation between the Mississippi committee and Gen. Taylor about the Wilmot Proviso, GEN. TAYLOR HAS CONTRADICTED IT UNDER HIS OWN SIGN MANUAL. THIS WE KNOW. WE HAVE SEEN AND READ THAT CONTRADICTION WITH THE NAME OF ZACHARY TAYLOR AFFIXED TO IT.

If this authoritative contradiction really exists, and has been seen and read by the writer in the Whig, and the Whig thinks it of sufficient consequence to state the existence of such contradiction—WHY IS NOT THE CONTRADICTION ITSELF PUBLISHED? Who now has it in his custody? Nobody knows! To whom was it sent by Gen. Taylor? Nobody knows! When it was reported that Gen. Taylor had bought slaves in Washington, Gen. Taylor contradicted the report, and his friends with the utmost haste published, far and wide, his contradiction. The comparatively unimportant rumor is contradicted under the General's own signature. But upon this infinitely more important point of the General's views on the Wilmot Proviso—when his supporters have, as they say, a document from him, which, if true, will strike the Free Soil party with a deadly blow—they are so very confident of its truth that they dare not publish it, *we must beg leave to doubt even its existence.* Of what weight as evidence is a letter or document, the holders of which, whoever they are, do not give their names—who do not venture to say to whom it was sent by Gen. Taylor, or even to give extracts from it? Are we to believe the assertions of a *nameless* writer, who does not pretend or venture to give Gen. Taylor's words? Common sense forbids it! On the very eve of the election, some *pretended* letter from Gen. Taylor may appear, too late for the fraud to be exposed. We warn our fellow citizens against being thus deceived. It is now more than *six months* since Hon. J. M. BOTTS, of Va., who supports Gen. Taylor, as a choice of evils, published in his letter to the people of the U. S. this testimony of Col. Boone. If the statement could have been *fairly refuted,* would it not, long ago, have been done?

> The passage marked on pp. 7, 8, contains all that I know on this subject. *The original letter of Mr. Boone, the writer, is in my possession—the conversation related, has never been denied that I am aware of.*
>
> J. M. B.

The passage on p. 8 is the extract from Mr. Boone's letter, just given. Speaking of this letter, Hon. J. R. Giddings, in his speech at the Buffalo convention, said:—

> I will tell you about another letter, written by Col. Boone to the Hon. Jacob Thompson, member of Congress from Mississippi. I have the word of Mr. Thompson for saying, that Col. Boone's integrity was never doubted and never will be denied. He said to me that I was at full liberty to say that he, Mr. Thompson, fully endorsed him as a man of truth and unsullied honor. It will be remembered that Col. Boone was one of a committee of five deputed by the legislature of Mississippi to invite Gen. Taylor to visit that body, The conversation detailed in the letter was had in the presence of that committee, two of whom were whigs. These whigs having seen the letter in print, have suffered it to pass as true and correct.

There can be no doubt about the *authenticity* or *truthfulness* of the report of this conversation. *It is no anonymous production.* It is reported by Mr. Boone, a member of the Committee, and his original letter is now in the possession of Hon. John M. Botts, a *supporter* of Gen. Taylor, "though not an ultra one." The extract given above was published last March by Mr. Botts, in his pamphlet address above spoken of, and very widely circulated in that form. It has also been *very extensively* published in the newspapers, since that time; and the truthfulness of the report has never yet been denied by Gen. Taylor—by any other member of the Committee—by any one who heard the conversation—or by the authority of Gen. Taylor, or any one who heard it. Gen. Taylor has, by writing three times under his own hand, *contradicted* the interpretation given to the Signal letter, (so called), which interpretation made him out as expressing the opinion that he would not veto the Wilmot Proviso. He has also, in writing, *contradicted* the report that he had bought slaves in Washington; *but he has never yet thus contradicted the truth of Mr. Boone's report of his conversation, or authorized its contradiction.* His friends can, at any moment, get such a contradiction from him, if it is not truly stated. But they have not, as yet, dared to call upon him to speak out.

We have, then, an undoubtedly authentic letter from a man, described to be a man "of truth, and unsullied honor," detailing a conversation had in his presence, in which conversation Gen. Taylor openly avowed his opposition to the Wilmot Proviso, and his opinion that the question of slavery in the territories should be left to the citizens there, to decide as they pleased. With the exception that he does not specify the *grounds* of his opposition to the Proviso, the opinions of Gen. Cass and Gen. Taylor are identical. There is no difference in their opinions on the Wilmot Proviso.

The Mobile (Ala.) Herald publishes a communication, dated East Pascagoula, Aug. 19, 1848, from one of its correspondents. Of itself alone, it is of little value. It is of some weight as a confirmation. The following extracts are taken from this communication. Speaking of Gen. Taylor, the correspondent says:—

> The old man seems to be frank and without craft. He shuns no topic, and as far as I could discover, is accustomed to utter his opinions without regard to politicians or newspaper editors. Last evening, a group of some dozen or more of us was gathered round him, eagerly listening to an animated conversation, in which his *näive* simplicity of manner was quite charming. He ran through various topics, which he illustrated with excellent sense and varied information. *Speaking of the "free soil" movement in the North, he expressed fears that it would be the absorbing question in the present canvass, and engross all other questions. HE SAID THAT HE CONSIDERED THE "MISSOURI COMPROMISE" A FAIR AND LIBERAL LINE FOR SETTLING THE SLAVE QUESTION, AND HE WAS WILLING TO SEE IT ADOPTED.*
>
> * * * * * * *
>
> My object was to see "Old Zack;" and I gathered enough of what I saw of him to believe that he is an honest man—not politic—not afraid—resolute—moderate—steering between the ultras, and *Southern enough in his nature to be quite worthy of as much honor as we can lay on his shoulders.*

The Whig party, therefore, stands before the country with a Presidential candidate who has avowed himself to be opposed to the Wilmot Proviso—who thinks, with General Cass, that the people in the territories should be left free to admit slavery if they please—one who, by birth, education, and interest, is identified with slavery—who is himself a large slaveholder in that section of the country where slavery exists in its most revolting forms—who lives in a section where the most ultra slavery notions prevail—who at the South was first suggested as a candidate, by the most ultra slavery propagandists—who was eminently the candidate of the slave States, in the national convention—and who is now supported by men who consider slavery almost, if not quite, the corner-stone of the Republic? Only last autumn, the Whigs of Norfolk County resolved that it was their "duty" not to vote for any men, for President and Vice President, "*who are not known* by their acts, or declared opinions, to be *opposed to the extension of slavery.*" What has become of their high resolve, when they now call upon us to vote for a man who says, that the South should never agree to any restriction by Congress upon such extension? and who thinks that the people of California and New Mexico should be left free to establish slavery if they wish to?

But it is said that he is a Whig, and that opposition to the extension of slavery is Whig doctrine. True it is that he styles himself a Whig, and has accepted the nomination of the Whig convention. But in his letter published in the Charleston (S. C.) News, (Aug. 16,) he has not only said, that he "would have accepted the nomination of the Baltimore convention, had it been tendered on the same terms" as that of the Whigs, but he has actually "thankfully accepted" the nomination of the Charleston Democrats who repudiated Gen. Cass because he was only pledged to veto the Proviso. We do not now lay any stress on these circumstances. We will suppose that Gen. Taylor, if elected, will carry out the true Whig doctrine on this question. What is the true doctrine of the great Whig party? Not surely Massachusetts doctrine, or Louisiana doctrine, but that which is the doctrine of the Whigs in *all* the States. Where can we find an exposition of the doctrine of the whole Whig party, if not in the doings of the convention of the whole Whig party? The following extracts are taken from the National Intelligencer's account of the doings of the Philadelphia convention. We have, then, the highest exponent of Whig doctrine, as published in the leading Whig journal:—

> Mr. TILDEN, of Ohio. Will the gentleman give way for one moment? I have a resolution to offer, which was drawn up by all the delegation from Ohio; and the vote of Ohio will depend considerably upon the consideration which the Convention may give to this resolution.
>
> The resolution was as follows:
>
> *Resolved,* That while all power is denied to Congress under the constitution to control or in any manner interfere with the institution of slavery within the several States of this Union, it nevertheless has the power *and it is the duty of Congress to prohibit the introduction or existence of slavery in any territory now possessed, or which may hereafter be acquired by the United States.*
>
> * * * * * * *
>
> Mr. TILDEN said he did not desire to make a speech, but he wished to say what the feelings of the Whigs of Ohio were. They were embodied in the resolution which he had read. They had been proclaimed at all their primary meetings; they had been set forth in their State Convention; and the delegation from Ohio therefore felt constrained to put forth this resolution, and to ask for its adoption by this Convention, for it was a part of their political faith.
>
> Mr. BROWN, of Pennsylvania, was surprised to see such a resolution offered

to this Convention, and that gentlemen should come here with an evident determination to distract their counsel. They had listened to the language which had been uttered by gentlemen with patience, but things might go so far that patience might cease to be a virtue. *They were assembled there to carry out the glorious Whig principles, and were they to be diverted from their purpose by a set of factionists?* [Applause and hisses.] He moved that the resolution be laid on the table.

The motion to lay on the table was agreed to.

In the opinion of the Philadelphia convention, the principle of "no more slave territory," is *not* one of "the glorious Whig principles." The convention was not to be diverted from their purpose "by a set of factionists," whose object was to arrest the further extension of slavery! The following extracts will suffice to show how this action of the convention is looked upon by the *anti-slavery* slave-holding Whigs at the South:—

"GLORIOUS NEWS.—THE UNION PRESERVED.—THE REPUDIATION OF THE WILMOT PROVISO BY THE WHIG CONVENTION." Under the above head the Montgomery (Alabama) Journal, a Whig paper, announces with inexpressible satisfaction, that the Whig Convention promptly met the question of the Wilmot proviso, and repudiated a resolution adopting that doctrine at once, by an overwhelming majority. It would not touch the unclean thing.

From the Macon (Ala.) Republican.

WILMOT PROVISO REPUDIATED BY THE WHIG CONVENTION.

What will the Locofocos say now—they who have all along contended, against light and knowledge, and in utter contempt of truth, that Provisoism was chiefly confined to the Whig party? Who are now the friends of the South? Alas for Democracy! The Whigs of the Union have met and decided this momentous question—they have repudiated it like men, like patriots, like Whigs! They have indignantly refused to give it countenance! They have rejected it by a decided and overwhelming majority!

A resolution was introduced into the Whig National Convention, recognising and adopting the Wilmot Proviso; but it was rejected almost unanimously, without discussion. It was treated as a stranger—as a thing entirely out of place. The only wonder is, how it came there—being, as it is, a bantling of Locofoco paternity. The thing was generated and warmed into life by the Democracy, nurtured and sustained by its natural parent, and of course possessed no affinity with Whiggery—and, consequently, it was hooted out of the Convention.

The same paper of July 6, says:—

A resolution was offered by a delegate from Ohio, affirming the principles of the Wilmot Proviso. Mr. Brown, of Pennsylvania, denounced it as fanatical, and indignantly moved to lay it on the table. The cry was raised, to make this a test vote. Agreed, was shouted on all sides; and it was laid there; *not ten votes being in its favor!*

But besides this action of the Convention, we have the best of evidence that the Wilmot Proviso is not a party question. Judge Berrien, the Whig, opposes the proviso, side by side with John C. Calhoun, the Democrat; and John M. Clayton, already more than once spoken of as Whig candidate for the presidency, on July 5 last, in the Senate, said:—

We repudiate the question altogether as a political question: and I say, that whenever the members of the great Taylor republican party, which I hold at this moment to be the great majority of the country, shall descend so low as to make a geographical party out of this Wilmot Proviso, with a view to President-making or getting offices and power in the country, they will lose my respect, and I think that of every honest man. An attempt is now being made, to force this upon us as a party question by the extreme partisans of the North and the South. *But neither the one side nor the other of the question forms any part of our platform;* and I hope there will be patriotism enough among the American people to keep the question apart from party politics forever.

And who was pronounced by Mr. Winthrop, recently, at Worcester, to be a *sounder* and *better* Whig than Judge Berrien?* Let no one, therefore, say, that because Gen. Taylor says he is a Whig, therefore he is in favor of the Wilmot

*The following extract from a letter written by Judge Berrien to a Taylor meeting in Georgia, is taken from the "Southern Whig" published at Athens, Georgia.

We take the liberty of publishing an extract from the letter of our distinguished Senator, Judge Berrien, in answer to the invitation tendered by the Committee through the writer of this. It will show our distant readers what degree of confidence can be placed in the ridiculous slander, that this faithful, able, and eloquent guardian of Southern rights would not support Gen. Taylor in the approaching contest. After stating that he is prevented from attending the meeting by sickness in his family, he adds:

"I ask you to make known to our fellow-citizens who will be assembled on the 30th inst., the reason why I am not with them, not so much to explain my absence, for that is comparitively unimportant, as to enable me through the proper organs of the meeting to say to them how deeply important I feel it to be, that we should work with "might and main" in the present canvass—that *I consider it as the most important Presidential election, especially to* SOUTHERN MEN, *which has occurred since the foundation of the Government.*

"*We have great and important interests at stake—if we fail to sustain them now, we may be forced too*

Proviso; for the Whig Convention has repudiated the proviso with contumely, and leading Whigs declare it not to be part of the Whig platform.

It is also said that Gen. Taylor is pledged not to veto the proviso, if passed by Congress. The Whigs do not say that he is opposed to the extension of slavery, or that he is in favor of the proviso; but only that he is pledged not to veto it if passed. This pledge has been said to be contained in the following letter from Gen. Taylor to the editor of the Cincinnati "Morning Signal":—

Headquarters, Army of Occupation,
Camp near Monterey, May 18, 1847.

SIR,—I have the honor to acknowledge the receipt of your letter *with the enclosure of your editorial, extracted from the Signal of the 13th April.*

At this time my public duties command so fully my attention, that it is impossible to answer your letter in the terms demanded by its courtesy, and the importance of the sentiments to which it alludes; neither, indeed, have I the time, should I feel myself at liberty, to enter into the few and most general subjects of public policy suggested by the article in question. *My own personal views were better withheld till the end of the war,* when my usefulness as a military chief, serving in the field against the common enemy, shall no longer be compromised by their expression or discussion in any manner.

From many sources I have been addressed on the subject of the Presidency; and I do violence neither to myself, nor to my position as an officer of the army, by acknowledging to you, as I have done to all who have alluded to the use of my name in this exalted connection, that my services are ever at the will and call of the country, and that I am not prepared to say that I shall refuse if the

---

soon to decide whether we will remain in the Union at the mercy of a band of fanatics or political jugglers—or reluctantly retire from it for the preservation of our domestic institutions, and all our rights as freemen. If we are united we can sustain them—if we divide on the old party issues, we must be victims.

"WITH A HEART DEVOTED TO THEIR INTERESTS ON THIS GREAT QUESTION, AND WITHOUT RESPECT TO PARTY, *I implore my fellow-citizens of Georgia, Whig and Democratic, to* FORGET FOR THE TIME THEIR PARTY DIVISIONS—TO KNOW EACH OTHER ONLY AS SOUTHERN MEN—*to act upon the truism uttered by Mr. Calhoun,* that on this VITAL QUESTION—*the preservation of our domestic institutions,* the *Southern* man who is *farthest* from us, is *nearer* to us than any *Northern* man can be—that Gen. Taylor is identified with us in feeling and interest—was born in a slaveholding State—educated in a slaveholding State—is himself a slaveholder—that his slave property constitutes the means of support to himself and family—that he cannot desert us, without sacrificing his interest, his principles, the habits and feelings of his life—and that with him, therefore, our institutions are safe. I beseech them, therefore, from the love which they bear to our noble State, to rally under the banner of Zachary Taylor, and with one united voice to send him by acclamation to the Executive chair."

Respectfully, your fellow-citizen,
J. McPHERSON BERRIEN.

MR. J. H. CHRISTY.

country calls me to the Presidential office, but that I can and shall yield to no call that does not come from the spontaneous action and free will of the nation at large, and void of the slightest agency of my own.

For the high honor and responsibility of such an office, I take occasion to say, I have not the slightest aspiration. A much more tranquil and satisfactory life, after the termination of my present duties, awaits me, I trust, in the society of my family and particular friends, and in the occupations most congenial to my wishes. In no case can I permit myself to be the candidate of any party, or yield myself to party schemes.

With these remarks, I trust you will pardon me for thus briefly replying to you, which I do with a high opinion and *approval of the sentiments and views embraced in your editorial.*

With many wishes for your prosperity in life, and great usefulness in the sphere in which your talents and exertions are embarked, I beg to acknowledge myself,

Most truly and respectfully,
Your obedient servant,
Z. TAYLOR, Maj. Gen. U. S. Army.

James W. Taylor, Esq. Cincinnatti, O."

The following is an extract from the long editorial which was sent to Gen. Taylor. It appeared in the Signal of April 13, 1847:—

> The American people are about to assume the responsibility of framing the institutions of the Pacific states. We have no fears for the issue, if the arena of the high debate is the assemblies of the people and their representative halls. *The extension over the continent beyond the Rio Grande of the ordinance of* 1787, *is an object too high and permanent to be baffled by presidential vetoes. All that we ask of the incumbent of the highest office under the constitution, is to hold his hand, to bow to the will of the people as promulgated in legislative forms, and restrain the executive action in its appropriate channels!* Give us an honest administration of the government, and an end to all cabals of a cabinet—all interference from the White House—designed to sway or thwart the action of the American people. If such simplicity and integrity should guide the administration of Gen. Taylor, the North and West would yield to it a warm support and hearty approval.

Notwithstanding Gen Taylor says, in the first part of his letter, "My own personal views were better withheld till the end of the war,"—thus leaving it to be inferred that he did not mean then to express his views,—still he expresses his *approval* of the sentiments and views embraced in the editorial. Among these views is this: that the veto power ought not to be used, to prevent the extension of the ordinance of 1787 over the territories west of the Rio Grande. Hence it would be fairly enough argued, that Gen. Taylor will not veto the Wilmot Proviso if passed by Congress, if he had not written the following letter to the editor of the Tuscaloosa (Ala.) Monitor, who has published it with Gen. Taylor's leave:—

Headquarters, Army of Occupation,
Camp near Monterey, Nov. 1847.

SIR,—Your letter of the 4th ult. has been received. In reply to your remarks concerning a letter which I addressed some time since to the editor of the Cincinnati Signal, *I have no hesitation in stating that it was not my intention in that communication to express an opinion either in concurrence with or in opposition to any of the views embraced in the editorial to which it refers.*

The letter itself, like most other letters of mine on unofficial matters which have found their way into the newspapers, was not intended for publication, but simply written as a matter of courtesy in answer to one which I had received from the gentleman in question. For this object, it was entirely sufficient; though, under the belief that it would never go beyond this point, it is quite probable that it may not have been prepared with that care and critical accuracy which appears to be so much required by politicians. *It was simply my desire, on that occasion, as has been my custom uniformly through life, to express my respect for opinions which I believed to be honestly entertained, and, as long as thus held, my approval of his maintaining them.*

Should it ever become my official duty to give my opinions on any or all of the political questions referred to in the article above mentioned, I shall discharge the duty to the best of my judgment. Until then, my opinions on such matters are neither necessary nor important.

I need hardly add, in conclusion, that this communication is not intended for the public prints.

I am, Sir, very respectfully,
your obedient servant,
Z. TAYLOR.
Major General U. S. A."

A similar letter was written to Mr. James R. Doolittle, of Wyoming, N. Y., but it is unnecessary to cite it; as this alone is sufficient to show that the Northern interpretation of the Signal letter is wrong. Mr. B. M. McConkey, of Cincinnati, published in the Cincinnati Atlas, of July 21, 1848, the following communication and letter:—

MR. EDITOR,—Last February, I addressed a letter to General Taylor, propounding three interrogatories. Two of them are immaterial at the present time; the third was as follows:—

"Should you become President of the United States, would you veto an act of Congress which should prohibit slavery or involuntary servitude forever, except for crime, in all the territories of the United States, where it does not now exist?"

As General Taylor's reply may assist the interpreter of the Allison letter, I offer it for publication. It is as follows:—

Baton Rouge, La., Feb. 15, 1848.

SIR.—I have the honor to acknowledge the receipt of your communication of the 3d inst.

In reply to your enquiries, I have to inform you that *I have laid it down as a principle, not to give my opinions upon, or prejudge in any way the various questions of policy now at issue between the political parties of the country, nor to promise what I would or would not do were I elected to the Presidency of the United States; and that in the cases presented in your letter, I regret to add, I see no reason for departing from this principle.*

With my profound acknowledgments for the friendly sentiments towards me which you have been pleased to express,

I remain, Sir, with great respect,
Your obd't serv't,
Z. TAYLOR.

Mr. B. M. McConkey, Cincinnati.

This letter is clear and explicit. Gen. Taylor is asked, directly, whether or not he would veto the Wilmot Proviso; and he answers, equally directly, that he has laid it down as a principle not to promise what he would, or would not do, if elected; or to prejudge, in any way, the various questions of policy at issue between the political parties. *But if, in February,* 1848, *he had laid it down as a principle not to promise whether he would or would not veto the Wilmot Proviso, it cannot be believed that in May,* 1847, *he had pledged himself not to veto it.*

Still, however, he is said to have pledged himself in the letter to Capt. Allison, from which the following extracts are taken. It matters not whether this pledge or committal is *expressly* made, or whether it is only a just *inference,* from any general rule or principle laid down in this letter. *In either case,* he stands pledged or committed. *In either case, Gen. Taylor fully knew, when he was writing the letter, that, as an honest man, he was pledging himself not to veto the proviso.*

Baton Route, April 22, 1848

Dear Sir,—My opinions have so often been misconceived and misrepresented, that I deem it due to myself, if not to my friends, to make a brief exposition of them upon the topics to which you have called my attention."

* * * * * * *

I confess, whilst I have great cardinal principles which will regulate my political life, *I am not sufficiently familiar with all the minute details of politicallegislation, to give solemn pledges to exert myself to carry out this or defeat that measure. I have no concealments. I hold no opinion which I would not readily proclaim to my assembled countrymen;* but crude impressions upon matters of policy, which may be right to day and wrong to-morrow, are, perhaps, not the best tests of fitness for office. One who cannot be trusted *without pledges,* cannot be confided in merely on account of them.

I will proceed, however, now to respond to your inquiries."

* * * * * * *

Second—The veto power. The power given by the constitution to the executive to interpose its veto, is a high conservative power; but in my opinion should never be exercised, *except in cases of clear violation of the constitution, or manifest haste and want of consideration by Congress.* Indeed I have thought that for many years past, the known opinions and wishes of the executive have exercised undue and injurious influence upon the legislative department of the government; and for this cause I have thought our system was in danger of undergoing a great change from its true theory. The personal opinions of the individual who may happen to occupy the executive chair, ought not to control the action of Congress upon questions of domestic policy; nor ought his objections to be interposed where questions of constitutional power have been settled by the various departments of government, *and acquiesced in by the people.*

Third—Upon the subject of the tariff, the currency, the improvement of our great highways, rivers, lakes, and harbors, the will of the people, as expressed through their representatives in Congress, ought to be respected and carried out by the executive.

He says the veto power "should never be exercised except in cases of clear violation of the Constitution, or manifest haste or want of consideration by Congress." But he has never said that the Wilmot Proviso is constitutional. How then can he be said to have pledged himself not to veto it? Southern

Whigs are united to a man in holding the opinion that the proviso is *not constitutional.*

Thus the Richmond (Va.) Republican says:

> Now for General Taylor, what does he say?—Why, *he says he will stand by the Constitution in the administration of affairs.* Well, *This* WILMOT PROVISO IS MOST UNQUESTIONABLY UNCONSTITUTIONAL IN EVERY SENSE OF THE TERM, consequently HE IS COMPELLED TO VETO IT, *because it would come under that class of measures which he would denominate unconstitutional.*

What evidence is there that Gen. Taylor does not agree with the writer in the Richmond Republican and the rest of his Southern *Whig* brethren? *None whatever!* But without such evidence, there can be no pledge extorted from the Allison letter.

But, say the friends of Gen. Taylor at the *North,* he will not veto the Proviso, because the questions of the constitutional power to pass it, "have been settled by the various departments of government, *and acquiesced in by the people.*" *This is not really true!* It is not true that slavery has ever yet been excluded from ALL the national territory. It was not done by the ordinance of 1787—because then there evidently was an understanding that the territory *South* of the Ohio was to be *slave,* whilst all *North* of it was to be *free.* South Carolina had authorized her delegates to cede her lands, south of the Ohio, months *before* the ordinance was passed—but the cession was not actually made until one month after; still, however, her lands *really* belonged to the Union at the time the ordinance was passed. North Carolina ceded her Western lands on the express condition that Congress should not "emancipate slaves." Nor was slavery excluded from *all* the territory acquired from France. Another compromise between slavery and freedom was made, and all south of the Missouri compromise line, and the State of Missouri north of it, were allowed to be slave territory. The constitutional power to exclude slavery from really *all* the national territories has, therefore, never yet been settled by the various departments of government, and acquiesced in by the people. The South has always claimed and got for slavery nearly, if not quite, one half of the national territory. But the very thing which it is proposed now to do, in passing the proviso, is *wholly to exclude slavery from all the national domain;* and Gen. Taylor may with perfect truth say,—as the people have never acquiesed in such an exercise of power, and as the various departments of government have never acted on such a proposition, "I am not committed by anything in this letter not to veto it."

Gen. Taylor has been described as plain, blunt, and honest. Would he, with studied language, *covertly* give an opinion upon the most important question of the day? In the next sentence to that we have referred to, he says, that upon the tariff, &c., the will of Congress ought to be respected and carried out by the executive; but he does *not* say that the will of Congress, on the Proviso, ought to be thus respected; and yet in the same breath he says that he holds no opinion which he would not readily proclaim. If, when he comes to enumerate those subjects upon which he thinks the action of Congress ought to be respected by the President, he omits all mention of the Wilmot Proviso—the greatest of all questions—what is the fair inference? Is it that he thinks the action of Congress on this matter, also, should be respected? No!

But what does he say on the subject of pledges? *Only nine weeks* before he wrote the Allison letter, he stated, as we have just seen, in the McConkey letter, that he had laid it down as a principle, not to promise whether he would or would not veto the Wilmot Proviso, and he then acted on the principle. Is it to be supposed that after this deliberate announcement of his principle, he would in the short interval of only two months abandon it wholly, and pledge himself not to veto the Proviso? We cannot believe it possible. And yet this entire abandonment of principle must be believed by all those who think that he is thus pledged.

We have just seen the resolution and address adopted at the meeting of the Charleston (S. C.) democrats. It will be remembered, that opposition alike to the Wilmot Proviso, and the "*monstrous*" doctrine that the people of the territories should be allowed to exclude slavery if they wished—that is, *deadly hostility to every method there is of preventing slavery extending to the Pacific,*—formed both the corner-stone and superstructure of these resolutions. A newspaper containing these resolutions was forwarded to Gen. Taylor by Mr. Pringle, the chairman of the meeting. In his letter, Mr. Pringle says, "the preamble and resolutions so fully explain the views of my fellow-citizens, as to need no comment from me." There can, therefore, be no doubt that Gen. Taylor read the resolutions, and consequently that he was fully aware that the nomination came from men so thoroughly in favor of the extension of slavery that not even Gen. Cass was acceptable to them. *Gen. Taylor was fully aware that he had been nominated* SOLELY *because he was believed to be* MORE *favorable to the extension of slavery than Gen. Cass.* Under these circumstances he wrote the following letter:—

Baton Rouge, La., Aug. 9, 1848.

SIR,—I have the honor to acknowledge the receipt of your communication of the 26th ultimo, officially announcing to me my nomination for the presidency by a large meeting of the Democratic citizens of Charlestown, S. C., held at that city on the 26th ult., and over which you were the presiding officer.

This deliberate expression of the friendly feeling existing towards me among a large and respectable portion of the citizens of your distinguished State, has been received by me with *emotions of profound gratitude;* and though it be but a poor return for such high and unmerited honor, I beg them *to accept my heartfelt thanks.*

Concluding that this nomination, like all others which I have had the honor of receiving from assemblages of my fellow-citizens in various parts of the Union, has been generously offered me, *without pledges or conditions, it is thankfully accepted;* and I beg you to assure my friends, in whose behalf you are acting, that should it be my lot to fill the office for which I have been nominated, it shall be my unceasing effort, in the discharge of its responsible duties, to give satisfaction to my countrymen.

With the assurances of my high esteem,
I have the honor to be your ob't servant,
Z. TAYLOR.

To W. B. Pringle, Esq.

How, we ask, could Gen. Taylor, simply as an honest man, "thankfully" accept this nomination *if*—less than four months before—he had solemnly pledged or committed himself not to go even as far as Gen. Cass,—if he considered himself pledged or committed *not* to do the *only* thing which made Gen. Cass *at all* acceptable to the South, viz. veto the Wilmot Proviso? Would not Gen. Taylor, or any other honest man, IF he had been committed in behalf of freedom, have said to Mr. Pringle, I cannot consent even to *appear* to be the *favored* candidate of *slavery extensionists.* The sincerity of the candidate for freedom must not even be suspected. Your friends have greatly mistaken my position. I ought to be even more objectionable than Gen. Cass, because my sentiments are not nearly so favorable to your views as his. You made the nomination under a clear mistake as to my opinion. Considering myself committed in behalf of freedom, by the general principles in regard to the veto power, which I have laid down in my letter to Captain Allison, I cannot with any self-respect consent to stand as the candidate of ultra slavery propagandists, and, therefore, decline the nomination. *Your friends would have cut off their right hands sooner than have voted for me, if they had known my real sentiments.* How can I accept the nomination and conceal my sentiments, thereby deliberately deceiving honest men? WE SAY, THEREFORE, THAT GEN. TAYLOR, OR ANY OTHER HONEST MAN, WOULD HAVE MADE HASTE TO REFUSE THE NOMINATION OF THE

CHARLESTON SLAVEHOLDERS, IF HE HAD PLEDGED OR COMMITTED HIMSELF NOT TO VETO THE WILMOT PROVISO; OR IF HE HAD LAID DOWN A GENERAL RULE OF ACTION, AN ADHERENCE TO WHICH IN HIS OPINION WOULD OBLIGE HIM TO REFRAIN FROM VETOING THE PROVISO. Inasmuch as he is honest, and has accepted the nomination, we say he cannot consider himself thus pledged or committed.

We know of no other evidence of Gen. Taylor's sentiments besides that which we have examined. Anonymous letters, and the reputed existence of unpublished letters cannot be relied on in a matter of this great moment. No tariff man would for an instant rely upon such evidence as we have considered, in order to prove another to be a protectionist. No Washingtonian would rely upon such evidence to prove another to be a Temperance man. Nor can men who are opposed to the extension of slavery, rely upon such evidence to prove a Louisiana slaveholder to be pledged not to veto a restriction upon such extension.

What, then, is the difference on this great question between the two candidates? Gen. Cass avows his opposition to the Proviso. So does Gen. Taylor. Gen. Cass says that the question of slavery in the territories should be left to be settled by the people of those territories. Gen. Taylor says the people of the territories should be left free to admit slavery if they please. Gen. Cass would *not on any terms* have accepted the nomination of the Buffalo Convention. Gen. Taylor *thankfully* accepts the nomination of men who avow their deadly hostility to everything which can possibly prevent the extension of slavery to the Pacific! What reliable difference, on this great question, is there between the two? None whatever! If one is a Northern man with Southern principles, the other is a Southern man with Southern principles. Both candidates are utterly unworthy the suffrages of a free people.

9

Speech of Hon. Stephen A. Douglas, of Illinois, Delivered in Richmond, Virginia, July 9, 1852 (Richmond, 1852)

Senator Stephen A. Douglas (1813–1861), a rising star of his party and an active seeker of the Democratic presidential nomination in 1852 traveled to Richmond that year to remind a rally of the party faithful all of the familiar reasons why they had to turn out on election day. He stressed the continuing relevance of the traditional policy differences between Democrats and Whigs and the dangers posed to the nation by Whig policies and their candidate, Winfield Scott. Interestingly (in light of earlier Whig focus on the same issue), Douglas assailed the Whig candidate for being a professional army officer, a career Douglas contended that was particularly unsuited for a man who aspired to the presidency of a free republic. In his review of party differences, Douglas also mentioned the restrictive, nativist positions of the Whigs, prefiguring an issue that took on much power in the next few years. Although his tone was much less strident in this widely distributed speech than many similar endeavors over these years, Douglas clearly and directly covered the ground and rang all the bells that Democrats had long called their own.

Mr. Douglas visited Richmond on the invitation of the Central Democratic Association, tendered him through its president and committee. He addressed the Association in the African Church—the most capacious building of the place—on Friday night. A vast audience collected to hear him—filling to overflow the entire hall and galleries, and blocking up the doors, windows, and aisles. He was listened to throughout with profound attention and respect; and his clear statement of facts, and cogent applications of them, have made a deep impression upon the people of Richmond.—*Richmond Examiner.*

Mr. D. was greeted with rapturous and continued applause, and proceeded to address the meeting substantially as follows:

Mr. President: I am not insensible to the compliment conferred upon me by your kind invitation to address the democracy of the "Old Dominion"—a State which, more than any other, has the honor of having imbodied and proclaimed to the world that genuine creed of democracy which has been our text-book in all political contests. I am the more gratified at it, because I have the honor to reside in and represent a State which was once "THE COUNTY OF ILLINOIS, IN THE STATE OF VIRGINIA." Since that county has become one of the sovereign States of the Union, like her illustrious mother, she has never departed from the faith, nor failed to sustain the democratic nominees at any presidential election. [Applause.] Always true to the rights of the States and to the bond of the federal Union—never departing from those great landmarks laid down by Kentucky and Virginia in the resolutions of '98–'99—I trust that, like the Old Dominion, Illinois will always be found faithful not only to the principles but to the candidates of the Democratic party. [Cheers.]

In the present contest we have not only a "platform," but standard-bearers which unite and harmonize the sentiments of our entire party through out this broad land. I have heard of no democrat who repudiates the platform. [Applause.] I know of no section of the party which thinks that it ought to be "defied" or "spit upon." [Renewed applause.]

The platform is an embodiment of the principles of the party upon all questions to which it extends, and is in perfect harmony with the whole system of principles which it is our purpose to carry into effect.

We have not only been fortunate in our platform, but equally so in our candidates. [Great applause.] It is not said of the democratic convention that one section sold out their principles in order to get their man, [great applause;] for democrats hold that it is not only essential to have sound principles, but to have honest and patriotic men to carry those principles into effect. No matter how pure your principles may be, if you have not men of intelligence, of honesty, of patriotism, and who understand your creed, your principles are not safe in their hands. Hence, as democrats, we invite the most rigid and strict scrutiny into the public and private character of Franklin Pierce and William R. King. [Great applause.] We lay their whole history, private and public, before the world, and challenge investigation.

Take Franklin Pierce from his boyhood up. So far as his personal honor and character are concerned, even the breath of slander has never dared to speak against them above a whisper, and then not without looking to see what honorable man might be present to repel the accusation. [Applause.] Take his public career in the legislature of his own State, in the halls of Congress, or wherever else fortune may have taken him in the discharge of duty, and we defy our political opponents to point to one act of infidelity to his duty [Great cheering.] He is not an obscure and unknown man. He has served several periods in the Congress of the United States, and voted upon all important questions which came before him. He has served several years in the Senate of the United States in times that required the nerve and the patriotism of every man to be called into active requisition There is his record and we invite you to examine it. Try him by his votes, by his speeches, by his acts, and let any democrat find aught of which he can complain. Upon all of the party questions that were agitated during the administration of the immortal Jackson, or of Mr. Van Buren, covering the period in which he was a member either of one or the other house of Congress, Franklin Pierce was found to be true to the constitution, true to the rights of the States—a national man upon all occasions, and sectional upon no question. [Great applause.]

During his nine years' service in the two houses of Congress, he acquired an enviable reputation as a debater and a statesman. He retired from the Senate in 1842 in consequence of domestic afflictions and obligations, which a man of his sensibilities was not at liberty to disregard.

During the administration of President Polk he invited Mr. Pierce to accept a seat in his cabinet. They had been associated in the House of Representatives, and knew each other well. They had stood by OLD HICKORY during the war with the bank and the moneyed power; and it was natural that Mr. Polk should desire to avail himself of the services of a man whose ability, fidelity, and patriotism he had witnessed and seen tested on so many and such trying occasions.

Mr. Pierce felt constrained to decline it from the same causes which induced him to resign his seat in the Senate.

Soon afterwards the United States found themselves engaged in a foreign war; and a call was made upon the citizen soldiery to repair to the scene of action and repel the insolent foe who had dared to invade their native land.

Then it was that Mr. Pierce did not feel himself at liberty to decline the call. He volunteered as a private; but was not allowed to remain long in the ranks—being appointed colonel of his regiment, and subsequently a brigadier general in the army. The records of the department and the history of the war furnish satisfactory evidence that he displayed ability, skill, and gallantry of a high order in the performance of his military duties. I am aware that the whigs have been in the habit, lately, of assailing the military conduct of General Pierce. Instead of any direct charge, they deal in that cowardly mode of insinuation which is worse than direct and open calumny; because it does not take the responsibility of bold and specific accusation. They nickname him "The Fainting General," and talk about his having fallen from his horse on the field of battle. While they do not dare openly to say that these acts are evidence of cowardice on his part, yet there is no other motive for the insinuation except to instil into the minds of the American people the impression that he was a coward. If that be true, why not have the manliness to come up openly and charge the fact? I do not know how it is in the Old Dominion, but I have reason to believe that the same rule applies here as in the great Northwest. There we hold that man comparatively honorable who utters a calumny openly, and boldly meets the responsibility, when contrasted with the slanderer who will sneakingly insinuate that which he dares not openly avow. [Great cheering.]

Now, fellow-citizens, I have but one answer to make to all these insinuations in reference to General Pierce's military character; and that answer is simply this: General Winfield Scott, in his official reports, under the sanction of an oath, has given the lie direct to every base slanderer who dares intimate or insinuate such an imputation. [Applause.] I wish every whig to remember that, if he ever utters or repeats this charge, his candidate for the presidency has pronounced and proven him a calumniator; and that by making the charge he also accuses General Scott of falsehood in his official reports to the government. Do our whig friends expect to commend their candidate to the favorable consideration of the American people by branding him with official falsehood, whilst at the head of that gallant army in which he gained all of his laurels? Either General Scott is unworthy of public confidence, or Franklin Pierce was a brave, gallant, and skilful general. [Great applause.]

I have no charges to make against the military conduct, the gallantry and heroism of the illustrious general whom the whigs have presented to the people of the United States as their candidate for the presidency. I will not depreciate his merits as a soldier, because truth and honor forbid it. [Applause.] I will refrain, because as an American, I have too much pride of country to cast the slightest shade of dishonor upon those glorious deeds which form a part of American history. The laurels of Scott, achieved while fighting the battles of his country upon the Canadian frontier, or in the various Indian wars, or in the more recent Mexican campaigns, are common property; and I am as proud of them as any of our whig friends, who, after having opposed each of these wars, are now striving to elevate a military chieftain to the presidency solely upon the ground that he was a gallant hero, in what they believed to be an unjust cause. [Great applause.]

But, fellow-citizens, we are to deal with Gen. Scott, during this campaign, not as the general-in-chief of the American army—not in the performance of his professional duties; but in a new character which he has lately assumed—that of a partisan candidate, seeking political honors. It is of the politician that I am now to speak, and not of the general. I propose to submit to you, and to the American people, the question, whether, when General Scott departs from the line of his profession, and from that course of duty in which he has acquired all his honors and his glory, it is wise and patriotic to convert A GOOD GENERAL INTO A BAD PRESIDENT. [Cheers.]

General Scott is presented to the American people by the Whig National Convention as a candidate for the presidency. That convention, before proceeding to this nomination, formed and proclaimed to the world a platform. Of that platform I have but little to say; for in all things, except upon the slavery question, it is a genuine whig concern, to which every democrat is presumed to be utterly and irreconcilably opposed So far as it relates to the slavery question, it is a plank stolen from the democratic platform for which they now attempt to claim credit before the American people. [Applause.] After the convention had thus proclaimed the platform, it proceeded to nominate a candidate for the presidency who had partinaciously refused on any public occasion ever to endorse the platform, or to give any assurance of his approval of its principles. True, he wrote a letter to a member of the convention, in which he said, substantially, that "if you will nominate me I will write a letter in which I will express sentiments as strong in favor of the Compromise as I did to you in private." I will not write a letter for *publication* now, because that would look like bidding for the presidency." [Laughter.] "But you are at liberty to show this to Jones, and Botts, and other friends." [Great laughter.] Now, gentlemen, what do you think of the frankness of the old soldier? He writes no letters for publication, lest he might be suspected of electioneering; but sends private notes to members of the convention pledging himself to make a publication in favor of certain principles in the event of his nomination. Is this manœuvre sanctioned by "*Scott's Infantry Tactics*" as adopted in the army, or has the old soldier been taking lessons in political tactics from Gen. Seward? [Renewed laughter.]

Well, General Scott received the nomination "unanimously," according to the official proceedings of the convention. [Laughter.]

Fellow-citizens, did you ever hear of a unanimous nomination which was made in defiance of the fifty-times repeated protest and remonstrance of the delegations from one half of the States of the Union represented in the convention? Every southern delegation voted against him more than fifty times, day after day, and night after night; and yet the nomination was "unanimous." [Great laughter.] "The nomination of General Scott, therefore, presents to the American people this extraordinary anomaly: for the first time in the history of our party contests has a sectional nomination ever been forced upon either of the two great parties. You may talk of the dangers to the American Union growing out of partisan strife and political contests—you may tremble at the scenes through which we have all recently passed, connected with the slavery agitation; but yet there was nothing in all that so perilous to the safety of the Union as a sectional nomination for the presidency, where the North demanded the nomination of a particular man upon a sectional issue, and the delegations from every southern State, without exception, resisting the nomination as dangerous to their rights and institutions. A nomination forced upon the South by the abolition wing of the whig party north is now presented to the American people as a "unanimous nomination." It matters not whether the North forced the nomination upon the South, or the South upon the North, the danger consists in the fact that a territorial line divided men's opinions; that northern men were one way, and southern men the other. But, after the nomination is made, we are told that it was a fair compromise, because the South received the platform, and the North obtained the candidate, under the direction of men who "defy" and "spit upon" the platform. Thus we have Winfield Scott before us as a candidate for the presidency. After mature deliberation, he proceeds to accept the nomination, and to write the letter which he had promised Mr. Archer in the private note that was found in Botts's breeches-pocket. [Laughter.] Let us see whether that letter is as strong as the one which he promised to write. He says:

"Not having written a word to procure this distinction," [laughter,] "I lost not a moment, after it had been conferred, in addressing a letter to one of your members to signify what would be, at the proper time, the substance of my reply to the convention; and I now have the honor to repeat, in a more formal manner, as the occasion justly demands, that I ACCEPT THE NOMINATION WITH THE RESOLUTIONS ANNEXED."

Now, gentlemen, I desire to know what is the meaning of the words "with the resolutions annexed." Does he mean that he approves the resolutions? If so, why did he not say so, as the candidate for the vice presidency (Mr. Graham) did, in his letter of acceptance? Or, why did he not do as that gallant and honest man (Franklin Pierce) did, and say, "I accept the nomination upon the platform adopted by the convention, not because this is expected of me as a candidate, but because the principles it embraces command the approbation of my judgment?" There you have an honest man speaking from an honest heart, without any equivocation, dissimulation, or mental reservation. Here you find that General Scott "accepted the nomination, with the resolutions annexed"—that is to say, using language susceptible of two constructions—one at the North, and another at the South. In the North, it will be said that he accepts the nomination, *notwithstanding* the platform; that he accepts it, although he "defies" the platform; that he accepts it, although he "spits upon" the platform. At the South, he accepts it, with an approval of the platform. I submit the question to you, whether that language was not framed studiously for the purpose of enabling men, north and south, to read it one way or the other, as the public pulse should beat in their particular localities. Again: I submit to you, was it the general-in-chief of the army who fought the battles in Mexico that conceived this part of the letter, or was it his commander-in-chief, General Seward, who dictated it? [Great applause.]

But I have heard it said that there is another part of this letter which helps the matter out. Here it is. Towards the conclusion of the letter, he says: "Finally, for my strict adherence to the principles of the Whig party, as expressed in the resolutions of the convention and herein suggested, with a sincere and earnest purpose to advance the greatness and happiness of the republic, and so on, "I can offer no other pledge or guarantee that the known incidents of a long public life, now undergoing the severest criticism." He can give no other pledge "than the known incidents of a long public life, now undergoing the severest criticism." What "incidents" are there referred to as the "pledge" for his future conduct? Certainly not his military career for forty years; for that was not an incident of his life. It constitutes his principal, nay, his whole public career; and beside, that military life is not "now undergoing the severest criticism," or any criticism. It was not, then, his military career to which he referred when he spoke of the known incidents of his life, which would afford a guarantee of his political principles and conduct. To what, then, did he refer? His series of political letters did constitute "incidents" in his long life—well known incidents; and those incidents are now undergoing the severest criticism. Hence to those letters he must have referred as the only pledges he was willing to give for his political fidelity. I repeat, what are those incidents as contained in the political letters to which allusion is so pointedly made? First, a pledge to support the annexation of Canada to the American Union; second, a pledge to the creed of the native-American party; third, a pledge for the gradual emancipation of slavery; fourth, a pledge for the support of the bankrupt law; fifth, a pledge for a national bank; and so on through the whole series of federal measures, stretching out like MacBeth's procession of ghosts, some in existance, and others supposed to have become "obsolete ideas." To these incidents—to the pledges contained in these political letters—he must be understood as referring as the only guarantees he will give to carry out the principles laid down by the whig party, and suggested in his letter of acceptance. We here find the principles and issues upon which this campaign is to be fought. It is true that there are yet one or two other planks to be added to the platform; for General Scott was not willing to "annex" the whig resolutions, and stop there. He wished to convey the idea distinctly that that was not the ground upon which he stood exclusively, if he stood upon it at all. Hence we find him going further and saying that "the political principles and measures laid down in those resolutions are so broad that but *little is left for me to* ADD." [Laughter.] A modest man! He accepts the nomination "with the resolutions annexed," and then adds a little. [Renewed laughter.] Let us see what he adds. He says: "I therefore barely suggest, in this place, that should I, by the partiality of my countrymen, be elevated to the chief magistracy of the Union, I shall be ready, in my connexion with Congress, to recommend or to approve of measures in regard to the management of the public domain so as to secure an early settlement of the same favorable to actual settlers, but consistent, nevertheless, with a due regard to the equal rights of the whole American people in that vast national inheritance.

A GENTLEMAN in the meeting. "What does he mean?"

MR. DOUGLAS. I hear a gentleman behind me asking what does General Scott mean by this? That is precisely what I was going to ask you, gentlemen. What does he mean? I will tell you what I suppose he means. He means that, inasmuch as there are two bills now pending before Congress in relation to the public domain radically antagonistic to each other, to wit: the homestead bill and the bill to divide and distribute the public lands among the States, and inasmuch as the new States are for one of those bills and violently against the other, and inasmuch as the old States are for the other bill and opposed to the homestead bill, he says, "I am for the one favorable to actual settlers—that is, the homestead bill—*so as to secure the rights of the old States in this vast national inheritance.*" [Great laughter.] In other words, "I am for the homestead bill, so as to defeat it, and pass the distribution bill." That is the argument to be used in the old States. Or, "I am for the distribution bill, so as to defeat it, and pass the homestead bill;" and this will be the argument in the new States. Now, I defy any living man to tell what is the real meaning of the paragraph which I have just read, or on which side of either of these two antagonistic questions is General Scott committed by this letter. Is he for the homestead bill, or for the distribution bill? In my State, when I go home and visit the actual settlers upon the broad prairies, I expect to hear General Scott's friends claim that he is the best advocate in America of the homestead bill; and in Old Virginia, in New England, in New York, in all the old States, they will say "he is publicly committed against that 'vile and infamous' measure, and in favor of distributing the lands among the old States." They will attempt to prove each proposition in turn by the language used in his letter of acceptance. I again submit the question, was this part of the letter the production of the general-in-chief of the American army, or did it originate with the commander-in-chief of his political fortunes? Does it bear the marks of a frank, honest, straightforward old soldier, or of the tricky politician?

Again, General Scott, in this letter of acceptance, incorporates another plank into the platform which was adopted at Baltimore and "annexed" at Washington. He proposes "also to recommend or to approve of a single alteration in our naturalization laws, suggested by my military experience, viz: Giving to all foreigners the right of citizenship who shall faithfully serve in time of war one year on board of our public ships, or in our land forces, regular or volunteer, on their receiving an honorable discharge from the service."

This is the suggestion of his military experience. Recollect, that in 1841 General Scott was only hesitating between an alteration in our naturalization laws, requiring a residence of twenty-one years in this country as a necessary apprenticeship for naturalization, and a total repeal of all laws on the subject—in other words, for incapacitating foreigners from ever becoming citizens of this country at all—and that his "*mind then inclined to the latter alternative.*" Recollect, that in 1841 he claimed to be the *originator* of the great native-American party—pledged himself to its support—was *fired with indignation* against those foreigners who claimed to be citizens, and to vote, and enjoy the privileges of our laws. Since 1841 the only military experience of General Scott has been in Mexico, thousands of miles from the sight, hearing, and influence of American institutions. He means, therefore, that *this* military experience teaches him that a year's service in a foreign land, beyond the reach of our laws, beyond the hearing of our language, where an American newspaper never comes, where an election is an unknown and inconceivable event, where the name of the constitution is never heard, and under the martial rule which nullifies both law and constitution—he says that a twelve-months' service under these circumstances fits a man for citizenship as well as a whole life spent here in the pursuits of a citizen's life, and in the daily observation of the practical working of our institutions. Such is the result of his experience in the Mexican war.

But it is a subject of doubt whether General Scott proposes this "single alteration" as a substitute for our existing naturalization law, or whether he proposes it as an additional law, so that we shall have two distinct laws of naturalization. I am compelled to believe that he intends the former proposition; for I need not tell this audience that the constitution of the United States gives Congress the power to pass "a *uniform* rule of naturalization," and power to pass no other. If, therefore, General Scott means that we shall have two modes of naturalization—one being the existing form, and the other a year's service in the army—his proposition is unconstitutional, and impossible, and an absolute absurdity. Is it possible that this candidate for the presidency never read the constitution? I am unwilling to assume the fact, and do not like to put upon his words such a construction. There is a difficulty indeed in construing them—they are equivocal, like all the rest of his letter. But there is this well-known rule of construction—that when a document admits of two meanings, one impossible and absurd, the other consistent, intelligible, and significant, we are bound to take the latter. Now, if this clause in the letter means that General Scott desires an *addition* to our naturalization laws which would destroy their uniformity by giving unequal advantages, and offering different modes of naturalization to different persons, he proposes an "alteration" which is impossible under the constitution. But if he means that this single alteration shall be a substitute for all our laws—in other words, if he means that a year of military or naval service shall be the sole means of naturalization—then his proposition, however inexpedient, is a proposition for a uniform law; is consistent with the constitution; is consistent with his former declarations, and consistent with itself. Such, then, we are bound to believe his meaning to be—namely, that by an enlistment into our naval or land forces, and one year's service only, shall an emigrant to this country become a citizen of the United States. What a plank for a platform! Is this a principle of the whig party? If it is, the country ought to know it: Or is it only the utterance of a forked tongue—another gull-trap—constructed to catch Native votes under one construction, and the votes of our adopted citizens under a different construction. Charity even requires this construction, for should General Scott, by any strange accident, by any marvelous hallucination of this people, become the President of the United States—should he in good faith strive to make the alteration he proposes, and should he succeed in doing so—what results would come of that event! We have now an army of 10,000 men, all told. But 250,000 foreigners come every year to these shores. If an enlistment becomes necessary to make these people citizens, our standing army will soon contain a million of men. Are all these emigrants to be turned into the army and navy for naturalization? Or is it proposed that they shall remain in a land of freedom, disfranchised, deprived of all political rights, of all participation in the civil affairs of the country, and reduced to a system of political bondage more intolerable than that from which they fled in their native land?

The democratic party has ever been just and liberal to all foreigners that come here. That party has made this country a home for the exile, an asylum for the oppressed of all the world. We make no distinctions among our fellow-citizens. Uniform naturalization and equality under the law has been our principle from the beginning, and will be through the coming time. [Applause.] It is this wise, just, and honest policy that has attached the foreign vote to the democratic party. And we are willing to let them judge now between ourselves and a candidate who sets up this transparent blind between his present position and his real principles, as expressed in his memorable letter of '41. If General Scott has changed his opinion since that day—if all the indignation which "fired" him then has melted down to love and admiration under the operations of "his military experience"—why does he not say so like a man? I am unwilling to believe that a gallant soldier would have done thus, had he written a letter himself; but I will not undertake to say what his political file-leader would not do while he held the pen.

Gentlemen, this letter of General Scott accepting the nomination is a fertile theme for a speech. It has manifold charms and attractions. I thought it would take me but a few moments to get through with it; but it contains so many novel and rare features, that you will bear with me for calling your attention to other portions of it.

It will be remembered that the whig party, from time immemorial, have been in the habit, in every election, of charging the democracy with proscription—with proscribing honest men for opinion's sake—turning them out of office merely for a difference of political sentiment, and putting democratic partisans in their places. "Proscribe proscription," has been the whig motto. It was so when Henry Clay was the gallant standard-bearer of the whig party. Every whig in America was horror-stricken at the odious doctrine, that "to the victors belong the spoils." Every whig then denounced the idea of removing a man from office merely because of a difference of opinion on the subject of partisan politics. When General Taylor was the whig candidate four years ago, you were told upon every stump, in the public press, and through every vehicle of communicating intelligence to the people, that no man was to be removed in consequences of his political sentiments; that it made no difference whether he was a whig or a democrat; if he was honest and capable, he was to be protected in the station he held. What do we find now? General Scott, in his letter of acceptance, in cunning and adroit language, solemnly pledges himself that no democrat shall ever hold office under his administration, but that abolition whigs may do so without the slightest hindrance; this is my translation of that part of his letter. Now let us recur to his own words.

He says: "In regard to the general policy of the administration, if elected, I should, of course, look among those who may approve that policy for the agents to carry it into execution; and I should seek to cultivate harmony and fraternal sentiments throughout the whig party, without attempting to reduce its members by proscription to exact conformity to my own views.". He would seek agents from among those who approved the policy of his administration. As democrats *do* NOT approve, and *cannot* approve, of the policy of such an administration as his would be, they are excluded from ever holding office under an administration at the head of which General Scott may be placed. Can language be more clear and explicit, that a man differing from him in politics cannot participate in the honors and emoluments which his country may have to award to merit and patriotism? Proscription of all political opponents is boldly proclaimed in advance. He says, in substance, "Democrats, take notice: you do not approve of my policy; you cannot be selected as my agents; you cannot enjoy any of the patronage of the government; it is to be distributed only to those who do approve the policy of the administration." But then, looking around and seeing Mr. Seward and his abolition followers, he adds, "but I will cultivate harmony and fraternal sentiments throughout the whig party, without attempting to reduce its members by proscription to exact conformity to my own views." No fraternal feeling is to be cultivated between him and the democracy; no friendly sentiments are to prevail between him and us. This brotherhood and fraternal feeling are only to be among the members of the whig party; and they are not required to conform to his views, if they belong to any branch of the universal whig party, and are numbered among his supporters.

This language is broad enough to let in Mr. Seward and the whole of his abolition followers, at the same time that their appetite for the spoils is whetted by the assurance that no honest democrat should ever hold office under his administration, and therefore they may enjoy a monopoly of all the honors and patronage of the government.

Gentlemen, I ask you to bear in mind that this is the first time that any candidate for the presidency, from the days of Washington to this moment, of any political party or creed, has avowed that the entire patronage of the government should be confined exclusively to the men who sustained and supported the policy of an administration.

This humiliating declaration is now made for the first time. There never has been a democratic administration in this Union that did not retain at least one-third of their political opponents in office. This was emphatically the case under the administrations of General Jackson, Mr. Van Buren, and

Mr. Polk, and yet the whigs have been in the habit of pointing to those as the most proscriptive of all the administrations during the history of our republic.

True the most important and responsible of the offices were held by the friends of the administration, yet a large portion, from one-third to one-half, of all the offices were invariably enjoyed by our political opponents. But General Scott, as the candidate of this anti-proscriptive party, pledges himself that no office, high or low, shall ever be held by a democrat, no matter how honest, capable, and useful he may have been in the public service. Whatever his services and character, he must walk the plank. Can you believe that the man of the last war, the hero of Lundy's Lane, the victor at Chapultepec, could entertain such sentiments if he had not become the tame instrument of a heartless demagogue? Proscription such as he avows has never yet been heard of in this country. An old companion in arms—one, perhaps, who had stood by him in those very battles to which I have referred, where he may have left an eye, a leg, an arm; who may have a family dependent for bread upon his continuance in office—must make room for a sleek whig or some selfish abolitionist. Such is the doctrine of this letter. I cannot believe that it is the sentiment of a soldier's heart. I had rather believe that he wrote it as a king writes, *through the premier who is to manage his administration.* [Great applause.] But if such is to be the morality, the theory and the practice of his administration, why not elect its real chief to bear the responsibility? [Cheers.] Why blot out the refulgent glory that now encircles the name of Scott, and wither the laurels which his profession has won him? Why repeat the story of Taylor? *His* honor, too, knew not a stain, until you made him a President, with Clayton for his premier.

Why has the whig party forgotten with an oblivion so complete all that it once said about military politicians? Time was when they preferred "war, pestilence, and famine," to the election of a military chieftain, referring to General Jackson, who did not at the time of his nomination hold any commission in the army, who *never was* a soldier by profession, and who had entered the army only in the hour of danger, as Pierce did—and, like him, sheathed his sword when the war was over. [Great applause.]

We have yet to see a professional soldier succeed as a statesman. Washington was no military man by profession, following the army for a living. He was a civilian in the fullest sense of the word. He was reared for civil pursuits. He held civil offices both before and after the Revolution. He was a member of the Continental Congress that founded the Union, and a member of that convention which framed our constitution. *He* knew whether naturalization laws ought to be uniform or not. The period during which Washington held a commission in the army constituted indeed but a very few years of his long life. He was the first of our citizen-soldiers. [Cheers and applause.] Andrew Jackson, too—

[Here Mr. Douglas was interrupted by long and hearty cheers. He continued—]

Gentlemen, it does my heart good to hear democrats applaud the name of Andrew Jackson. [Renewed applause.] Andrew Jackson started in life as a poor attorney; was United States Attorney under Washington, a senator of the United States from Tennessee, and a judge of the supreme court of his State, before he ever drew a sword. When his country was involved in war, only, did he, like Washington, leave the pursuits of a citizen for the duties of a soldier; and like Washington, when war was at an end, he threw up his commission and went to a farm. Like Washington, also, he left that farm again only to become the President of the United States. He was not a member of the military profession; like Washington, he was never more than a citizen-soldier. Of forty years of public service not more than five or six were spent in the army, and the rest in civil life. [Cheers.] So with Harrison. He commenced his career as a young physician—he held many civil offices before he went into the army; he went to the army at last only as Mr. Pierce did, because there was war in the land; and when he was nominated for the presidency, he had long since ceased to hold the commission of a military officer.

But next we come to the name of Taylor. He was the first, the very first professional soldier who ever became the Chief Magistrate of this country. My friends, *was there anything in the result of that experiment which invites you to repeat it?* If he had lived for one year more than he did with that Cabinet about him, would this Union be extant at the present time? I believe General Taylor to have been an honest and a sincere man; but at the time of his death he was simply *taking a military view of a civil question;* and neither whig nor democrat, who is at all informed upon the history of that period, will be disposed to deny that he had already committed himself to steps which would have led inevitably to a civil war between the federal government and several sovereign States in our Union, and thereby have rent in fragments the entire confederation.

Why is it that the South American republics do not thrive—why do they have no peace—why do they live in a perpetual revolution? They have adopted our laws; they have copied our constitutions; yet they do not succeed, while we do. Why do not like causes produce like effects? Because, while between their institutions and ours there is a good parallel, in their *administration* of them they make a grand difference. In those republics the commanders of their armies are invariably candidates for the presidency, while with us, such has never been the case until the present time. In those republics, when a civilian is the candidate of one side and the commander-in-chief is set up by the opposite party, the civilian is generally elected by the people; *but the soldier invariably takes possession of the office by the sword.* Hence their civil wars, resulting in anarchy and despotism, and destroying every vestige of liberty. Now, *we* are importing this unhappy policy, this *Mexican* policy, into the United States. We are copying misfortune—borrowing a fatal fault. This practice of settling on the commanders of the army for the highest civil offices, I repeat, is an innovation on our theory and our practice, and the history of those miserable sister States ought to settle the question of its expediency.

It was the hand of Providence that saved us from our first and only *military administration.* Taylor was gathered to his fathers; Fillmore reigned in his stead—a man who previous to that time, had never furnished such proofs of superiority of statesmanship as to cause him to be looked to as a candidate for the first office—a man of respectable talents, respectable character, and of gentlemanly deportment, who has performed no great and striking act to signal his administration in history. Yet, regarding his official term in contrast with the military administration that preceded him, we feel—ay, all one can say is Fillmore was a real *godsend!* It was the calming of the waters when the ship was sinking in the tempest. All, therefore, look kindly on Mr. Fillmore, and we like to give him all the consolation we can after the bad treatment he received at Baltimore, *because he was a whig, and yet did no harm to the country!*

Yet, for the simple reason that he did no harm to his country—ay, because he has been a national President, and because he has kept within the bounds of his official oath—Mr. Fillmore has been repudiated by his party. Is not this so? Was not Mr. Fillmore defeated by the abolition sentiment and abolition party of the North, and by that alone? Did not every southern State stick to him to the death? Could all the whigs in the Union, except Seward and the abolition whigs, have defeated him at Baltimore? And would Seward or any abolition whig have raised a cry upon Millard Fillmore if he had acted in office upon the principles of his Buffalo letter, instead of on the principles of the Compromise of 1850?

But though we cannot be otherwise than grateful for a FILLMORE administration in the place of a TAYLOR regency—and though we must admit that on the subject of slavery Mr. FILLMORE has done tolerably well *for a whig;* yet there is another view to be taken of the present administration's career. It is a view of certain features in it for which the *whig party* is responsible, even more than Mr. Fillmore himself. If my time were not already exhausted, into many transactions of the present administration I should like to inquire. I should like, for instance, to ask why it was that when Spain broke the stipulations of her treaty with us and butchered fifty of our citizens without a trial, *we* had to make apologies instead of *Spain.* It matters not whether the participators in the Cuban affair were right or wrong. Admit that they were wrong. Still, under the liberal stipulations of the treaty they were entitled to a fair and open trial, with forms distinctly designated. But they were butchered without a chance of law; murdered in cold blood; and then we apologized because an irresponsible mob, coming no one knows whence, going no one knows where, tore down a house in New Orleans. The blood of our countrymen cried from the ground, and there was no ear for the cry at Washington. But for the Spanish consul's house we made an humble apology; we put our forehead in the dust before offended royalty; and the flag of stars was trailed in the dust before the banner of Castile.

I should like to inquire, too, into the policy adopted by the whig party relative to the South American republics and the rights of Great Britain over Central America. I should like to know why it is that the United States cannot make treaties with independent powers on our own continent without consulting the British cabinet, and without the interference of English agents. Would the Nicaragua business have stained the page of our diplomatic history, if a democratic administration had occupied the departments of our government during the last four years? Could any others than whig politicians have truckled, as Clayton and his associates have done throughout that translations, to British power?

I should like to have compared the expenditure of the late whig administration with that of former democratic governments. I should like to get some explanation why it is that the expenses of this government have suddenly increased from about thirty to near sixty millions of dollars. I should like to know why a whig administration cost more in profound peace than a democratic administration does during a great war.

I should like to hear some explanation of the way in which the whig party reconciles its professions about proscription during the last canvass with the practice of its administration since the commencement of its official term. They promised that none but the incapable and the dishonest should be proscribed, and then they proscribed nearly every democrat in office. Now, are we to understand that every democrat is incapable and dishonest? Does the whig party give this explanation of its conduct? Scarcely so. Yet such is the inference they would have others to make. Not content with depriving men of their bread, they turn them away with a tarnished name. I would not complain of the late proscription if the true reason was alleged for it. But what language is too strong for the iniquity, the heartless cruelty and selfishness of the insinuated slander behind which they seek shelter?

However, there will be no complaint on this score relative to their present candidate. He brandishes the sword in advance. He proclaims war without quarter beforehand, and comes at you in feather and epaulet. Well, my friends, if you are deluded by this man as you were by Taylor, all that I can say is, that you deserve your fate. But I do not fear that you will or can be. We are now coming to a fair trial of the relative strength and numbers of the parties; and in such a contest when did we fail? Let us then go to work boldly. Let us throw false delicacy aside, and, disregarding whig friends, let us expose the political conduct of our adversaries without fear, yet without imitating their assaults upon private character. If, in so doing, we shall be true to ourselves, neither abolitionism nor federalism will prevail against us, and the success of our principles, with the election of those who represent them, is already a foregone conclusion. [Tremendous and long-continued applause.]

It was eleven o'clock when Mr. Douglas concluded. A vote of thanks to him for his able discourse was then proposed by the president of the association, and unanimously passed by the meeting; and after nine rousing cheers for the "Young Giant of the West," the assemblage dispersed.